THE CAMBRIDGE COMPANION TO

DARWIN

Each volume in this series of companions to major philosophers contains specially commissioned essays by an international team of scholars, together with a substantial bibliography, and will serve as a reference work for students and non-specialists. One aim of the series is to dispel the intimidation such readers often feel when faced with the work of a difficult and challenging thinker.

The naturalist and geologist Charles Darwin (1809–82) ranks as one of the most influential scientific thinkers of all time. In the nineteenth century his ideas about the history and diversity of life – including the evolutionary origin of humankind – contributed to major changes in the sciences, philosophy, social thought and religious belief. This volume provides the reader with clear, lively and balanced introductions to the most recent scholarship on Darwin and his intellectual legacies. A distinguished team of contributors examines Darwin's main scientific ideas and their development; Darwin's science in the context of its times; the influence of Darwinian thought in recent philosophical, social and religious debate; and the importance of Darwinian thought for the future of naturalist philosophy.

New readers will find this the most convenient and accessible guide to Darwin currently available. Advanced students and specialists will find a conspectus of recent developments in the interpretation of Darwin.

Jonathan Hodge is Senior Lecturer in History and Philosophy of Science at the University of Leeds.

Gregory Radick is Lecturer in History and Philosophy of Science at the University of Leeds.

OTHER VOLUMES IN THE SERIES OF CAMBRIDGE COMPANIONS

AQUINAS *Edited by* NORMAN KRETZMANN *and* ELEONORE STUMP
HANNAH ARENDT *Edited by* DANA VILLA
ARISTOTLE *Edited by* JONATHAN BARNES
AUGUSTINE *Edited by* ELEONORE STUMP *and* NORMAN KRETZMANN
BACON *Edited by* MARKKU PELTONEN
SIMONE DE BEAUVOIR *Edited by* CLAUDIA CARD
DARWIN *Edited by* JONATHAN HODGE *and* GREGORY RADICK
DESCARTES *Edited by* JOHN COTTINGHAM
DUNS SCOTUS *Edited by* THOMAS WILLIAMS
EARLY GREEK PHILOSOPHY *Edited by* A. A. LONG
FEMINISM IN PHILOSOPHY *Edited by* MIRANDA FRICKER *and* JENNIFER HORNSBY
FOUCAULT *Edited by* GARY GUTTING
FREUD *Edited by* JEROME NEU
GALILEO *Edited by* PETER MACHAMER
GERMAN IDEALISM *Edited by* KARL AMERIKS
HABERMAS *Edited by* STEPHEN K. WHITE
HEGEL *Edited by* FREDERICK BEISER
HEIDEGGER *Edited by* CHARLES GUIGNON
HOBBES *Edited by* TOM SORELL
HUME *Edited by* DAVID FATE NORTON
HUSSERL *Edited by* BARRY SMITH *and* DAVID WOODRUFF SMITH
WILLIAM JAMES *Edited by* RUTH ANNA PUTNAM
KANT *Edited by* PAUL GUYER
KIERKEGAARD *Edited by* ALASTAIR HANNAY *and* GORDON MARINO
LEIBNIZ *Edited by* NICHOLAS JOLLEY
LEVINAS *Edited by* SIMON CRITCHLEY *and* ROBERT BERNASCONI
LOCKE *Edited by* VERE CHAPPELL
MALEBRANCHE *Edited by* STEVEN NADLER
MARX *Edited by* TERRELL CARVER
MILL *Edited by* JOHN SKORUPSKI

NEWTON *Edited by* I. BERNARD COHEN
and GEORGE E. SMITH
NIETZSCHE *Edited by* BERND MAGNUS
and KATHLEEN HIGGINS
OCKHAM *Edited by* PAUL VINCENT SPADE
PLATO *Edited by* RICHARD KRAUT
PLOTINUS *Edited by* LLOYD P. GERSON
RAWLS *Edited by* SAMUEL FREEMAN
ROUSSEAU *Edited by* PATRICK RILEY
SARTRE *Edited by* CHRISTINA HOWELLS
SCHOPENHAUER *Edited by* CHRISTOPHER JANAWAY
THE SCOTTISH ENLIGHTENMENT *Edited by*
ALEXANDER BROADIE
SPINOZA *Edited by* DON GARRETT
WITTGENSTEIN *Edited by* HANS SLUGA
and DAVID STERN

The Cambridge Companion to DARWIN

Edited by

Jonathan Hodge
University of Leeds
and
Gregory Radick
University of Leeds

CAMBRIDGE
UNIVERSITY PRESS

CAMBRIDGE UNIVERSITY PRESS
Cambridge, New York, Melbourne, Madrid, Cape Town, Singapore, São Paulo

Cambridge University Press
The Edinburgh Building, Cambridge CB2 2RU, UK

Published in the United States of America by Cambridge University Press, New York

www.cambridge.org
Information on this title: www.cambridge.org/9780521771979

First published 2003

A catalogue record for this publication is available from the British Library

ISBN-13 978-0-521-77197-9 hardback
ISBN-10 0-521-77197-8 hardback

ISBN-13 978-0-521-77730-8 paperback
ISBN-10 0-521-77730-5 paperback

Transferred to digital printing 2006

CONTENTS

CONTRIBUTORS

JOHN HEDLEY BROOKE is Andreas Idreos Professor of Science and Religion at the University of Oxford, where he is Director of the Ian Ramsey Centre and a Fellow of Harris Manchester College. His books include *Science and Religion* (1991), *Thinking about Matter* (1995) and, with Geoffrey Cantor, *Reconstructing Nature: The Engagement of Science and Religion* (1998).

DANIEL C. DENNETT is University Professor and Director of the Center for Cognitive Studies at Tufts University. His books include *The Intentional Stance* (1987), *Consciousness Explained* (1991), *Darwin's Dangerous Idea* (1995), *Kinds of Minds* (1996) and *Brainchildren: Essays on Designing Minds* (1998).

JIM ENDERSBY is Adrian Research Fellow at Darwin College, University of Cambridge. He has published on the history of the life sciences, in particular on botany and its imperial context in the nineteenth century. He is currently writing a book on the Victorian botanist Joseph Hooker.

OWEN FLANAGAN is James B. Duke Professor of Philosophy and Chairman of the Philosophy Department at Duke University, where he also holds professorial appointments in psychology, neurobiology and literature. His books include *Self-Expression* (1996), *Dreaming Souls* (1999) and *The Problem of the Soul: Two Visions of Mind and How to Reconcile Them* (2002).

JEAN GAYON is Professor of Philosophy and History of Life Sciences at the University of Paris 1–Panthéon Sorbonne. His books include

Darwinism's Struggle for Survival: Heredity and the Hypothesis of Natural Selection (1998) and, as editor, *Buffon 88* (1992).

JONATHAN HODGE is Senior Lecturer in History and Philosophy of Science at the University of Leeds. His books include *Origins and Species* (1991) and, as co-editor, the *Companion to the History of Modern Science* (1990). He is currently completing a book on Darwin's theorising in the notebook years.

DAVID L. HULL is Professor Emeritus in the Department of Philosophy at Northwestern University. His books include *Darwin and His Critics* (1973), *Philosophy of Biological Science* (1974), *Science as a Process* (1988) and *Science and Selection: Essays on Biological Evolution and the Philosophy of Science* (2001).

PHILIP KITCHER is Professor in the Department of Philosophy at Columbia University. His books include *Vaulting Ambition: Sociobiology and the Quest for Human Nature* (1985), *The Lives to Come: The Genetic Revolution and Human Possibilities* (1996), *Science, Truth and Democracy* (2001) and *In Mendel's Mirror: Philosophical Reflections on Biology* (2003).

DIANE B. PAUL is Professor of Political Science and Director of the Program in Science, Technology, and Values at the University of Massachusetts at Boston. Her books include *Controlling Human Heredity: 1865 to the Present* (1995) and *The Politics of Heredity: Essays on Eugenics, Biomedicine, and the Nature–Nurture Debate* (1998).

GREGORY RADICK is Lecturer in History and Philosophy of Science at the University of Leeds. He has published on the history and philosophy of the life sciences, in particular on Darwinism and the sciences of animal minds. He is currently writing a book on the experimental study of the evolutionary origins of language.

ROBERT J. RICHARDS is Professor in the Departments of History, Philosophy and Psychology at the University of Chicago, where he is a member of the Committee on Conceptual and Historical Studies of

Science and Director of the Fishbein Center for the History of Science and Medicine. His most recent book is *The Romantic Conception of Life: Poetic Understanding of Science and Philosophy in the Age of Goethe* (2002).

ALEX ROSENBERG is Professor in the Philosophy Department at Duke University, where he is a member of the Center for Philosophy of Biology. His books include *Philosophy of Social Science*, second edition (1995), *Philosophy of Science: A Contemporary Approach* (2000) and *Darwinism in Philosophy, Social Science and Policy* (2000).

MICHAEL RUSE is Lucyle T. Werkmeister Professor of Philosophy at Florida State University. His books include *Monad to Man: The Concept of Progress in Evolutionary Biology* (1996), *Mystery of Mysteries: Is Evolution a Social Construction?* (1999), *Can a Darwinian Be a Christian? The Relationship Between Science and Religion* (2000) and *The Evolution Wars: A Guide to the Debates* (2001).

PHILLIP R. SLOAN is Professor in the Program of Liberal Studies and the Program in History and Philosophy of Science at the University of Notre Dame, where he directs the Program in Science, Technology and Values. His most recent book is the edited volume *Controlling Our Destinies: Historical, Philosophical, Ethical and Theological Perspectives on the Human Genome Project* (2000).

ELLIOTT SOBER is Hans Reichenbach Professor at the University of Wisconsin, Madison. He is the author of *The Nature of Selection* (1984), *Reconstructing the Past* (1988), *Philosophy of Biology* (1993) and, with David S. Wilson, *Unto Others: The Evolution and Psychology of Unselfish Behavior* (1998).

KIM STERELNY has appointments in philosophy at the Australian National University and Victoria University of Wellington. His books include *The Evolution of Agency and Other Essays* (2001), *Dawkins vs. Gould: Survival of the Fittest* (2001) and, with Paul Griffiths, *Sex and Death: An Introduction to Philosophy of Biology* (1999). His *Thought in a Hostile World* will shortly be published.

C. KENNETH WATERS is Associate Professor in the Philosophy Department at the University of Minnesota, where he directs the Minnesota Center for Philosophy of Science. He has published on the philosophy of evolutionary biology and genetics. He is currently engaged in a study of the gene-centred approach of molecular biology.

PREFACE

This volume is about the life, work and intellectual legacies of Charles Darwin. The aim is to provide an accessible and up-to-date guide to Darwin and his influence. As we explain more fully in the Introduction, we have tried to meet the needs and interests of a wide range of readers. In keeping with the *Cambridge Companion* series, however, the emphasis is on Darwin as a thinker and on Darwinian themes within philosophy.

It gives us great pleasure now to express our warmest thanks to our own editor at Cambridge University Press, Hilary Gaskin. We have been indebted throughout to her guidance and encouragement. Our gratitude is likewise profound to the contributing authors who have joined in the project and seen it through to completion. We appreciate especially their congenial, expert participation and their willingness to adapt their presentations to the distinctive demands of a collaborative volume. Our thanks go also to James Sumner for providing an exemplary index.

Jonathan Hodge and Gregory Radick
Division of History and Philosophy of Science
School of Philosophy
University of Leeds

JONATHAN HODGE AND GREGORY RADICK

Introduction

1 DARWIN AND PHILOSOPHY

Some scientific thinkers, while not themselves philosophers, make philosophers necessary. Charles Darwin is an obvious case. His conclusions about the history and diversity of life – including the evolutionary origin of humans – have seemed to bear on fundamental questions about being, knowledge, virtue and justice. Are we different in kind from other animals? Do our apparently unique capacities for language, reason and morality point to a divine spark within us, or to ancestral animal legacies still in evidence in our simian relatives? What forms of social life are we naturally disposed towards – competitive and selfish forms, or cooperative and altruistic ones? Once we adopt a Darwinian perspective, moreover, how should we respond to such venerable doctrines of the Western tradition as Aristotle's essentialism, Descartes' dualism of body and mind and Kant's rejection of the very possibility of a natural science of the mind?

The Cambridge Companion to Darwin aims to facilitate understanding of such issues. It provides an introduction to Darwin's thinking and to the various and often contentious uses made of his legacies today. To serve these ends, the volume departs somewhat from the precedents of earlier volumes in this series. The chapters come in four clusters, two broadly historical and two broadly philosophical. The first cluster concerns Darwin's theorising. The second looks at his setting, and the reception and influence Darwin had in his own time. The third examines Darwinian themes in such branches of current philosophy as ethics, social philosophy, philosophy of mind and philosophy of biology. The fourth offers examples of philosophers making up their minds – and not always agreeing with each other – over Darwinian alignments for philosophical enquiries in the future.

This array of chapters does, we hope, provide a balance between the more enduring and the more ephemeral themes in Darwinian discussions through the decades. It provides, too, for mutual illumination between older and newer versions of the enduring themes. So, for example, the reader will find Robert Richards on how Darwin dealt with emotions and ethics, together with Owen Flanagan on how recent Darwinian studies of the emotions clarify the meaning of ethical statements. John Brooke tells of Darwinism and theism in the Victorian context, and Michael Ruse of Darwinism and theism today. Diane Paul looks at the relations between Darwinism and the old eugenics, while Philip Kitcher asks whether Darwinism can help us find a moral path through the new eugenics.

This companion aspires, then, to be introductory and synoptic, suited to any reader, whether philosopher or not, who is interested in Darwin. Nevertheless, the volume is specially adapted to the distinctive concerns of philosophers. The emphasis throughout is on concepts, contexts and controversies. As such, the volume cannot pretend to omniscience. Nor does it present authoritative consensus. On the historical side, there are divergences between those who see Darwin as a Romantic, and those who see him, at least as much, as a child of the Enlightenment. On the philosophical side, there are some who see limits to what philosophy can gain from Darwinian resources, and others who see no limits whatsoever.

II DARWIN, THE TREE OF LIFE AND NATURAL SELECTION

As an introduction to the first two clusters of chapters, it will be appropriate here to sketch the shape of Darwin's life and work. Born in England in 1809, Darwin had a privileged, private, local schooling. His father was an exceptionally wealthy and unusually free-thinking doctor, a prominent figure in the town of Shrewsbury, county seat of Shropshire, some hundred and fifty miles north and west of London. Darwin's schooling was followed by five years at university: two years' training in medicine at Edinburgh University; then, after a change of ambition, three years at Cambridge University, studying that mix of subjects, mainly geometry, theology and classical literature, which then prepared one for a career in the Anglican church. Next came five years going round the world as a naturalist on HMS *Beagle.* Returning in 1836, Darwin – no longer wanting to be a clergyman and in any case too well off to need to work – lived for five years in London, where, in a series of notebooks, he developed almost all the theoretical insights he would later publish over the rest of his life. Finally, from 1842 until his death in 1882, Darwin lived in a Kentish village some sixteen miles south and east of London. For many years he did not go into print with what would be his most famous, even notorious theory, the theory of the origin of species by means of natural selection. In 1858, the biogeographer and specimen collector Alfred Russel Wallace sent Darwin an unpublished sketch of a very similar theory. Darwin then prepared an abstract of the big book he was still in the process of writing. The abstract appeared as *On the Origin of Species*, published in November 1859, while Darwin was hiding from the public in Ilkley, a spa town in the West Riding of Yorkshire.

The *Origin* expounds Darwin's general account of what would soon be called organic or biological evolution. Almost all of his subsequent, more specialised studies, such as *The Variation of Animals and Plants under Domestication* (1868) and *The Descent of Man, and Selection in Relation to Sex* (1871), can be read as amplifications or applications of the *Origin*'s two main proposals. The first was that all the species that have ever lived on earth may form a single tree of life. Any group of similar species – the gull species, say – is descended, in irregularly branching divergences, from a single, common ancestral species; and, further, all the bird species likewise are descended from a more remote single ancestral stock. Indeed, all animal and plant species may share a common ancestry when traced back sufficiently far in time. The second proposal was that natural selection has been the main cause or agency responsible for all this divergent, adaptive and progressive change from ancestral to descendent species: divergent in that many very different species often descend from a single ancestral one; adaptive in that, in the course of divergence, the ducks, say, have been fitted to diving and the hawks to swooping for their food; progressive in that adaptation has generally entailed specialisation, so that higher animals have more specialised parts – mouth parts and locomotive limbs where their oldest ancestors absorbed nutrients and moved themselves with their whole bodies.

Darwin called natural selection by that name to indicate an analogy with the selective breeding by humans of domesticated animals and plants, or artificial selection. This analogy, built up over the first four chapters of the *Origin*, deserves special attention, as the rest of the book amounts to a series of defences and applications of it. Roughly speaking, the first chapter, on 'variation under domestication', has two halves. (Page references in what follows are to the first edition of the *Origin*.) In the first half (7–29), Darwin argues that, when humans domesticate a species, new conditions of life are imposed upon that species, causing much new inheritable variation. In the second half (29–43), Darwin shows how human breeders have taken advantage of this inheritable variation, selecting for breeding, over successive generations, those organisms that happen to vary in desirable directions. Though the individual variations are slight – colouring slightly deeper, racing speed slightly faster, and so on – their gradual accumulation eventually results in new varieties, more closely matched to human needs and desires.

The next chapters shift the argument from domesticated plant and animal breeding to nature. The topics of inheritable variation and its selective accumulation are now dealt with separately. In the second chapter, on 'variation under nature', Darwin argues that, in nature too, there are changing conditions and hence variation, but the variations are much less plentiful than on the farm. In the third chapter, on the 'struggle for existence', he argues that, due to competitive struggle, inheritable variation accumulates selectively in nature too, but with the result that, over long stretches of time, much greater changes can be achieved than on the farm.

For the modern reader, one of these farm-to-nature moves is easier to assimilate than the other. Textbook versions of Darwinian theory still often include something about the small selectional achievements of the stockbreeder in comparison with the larger outcomes of fitness differences in nature. Much harder to understand nowadays is why Darwin fusses over the effects of domestication on variation versus the effects of natural environmental changes on variation. Even less comprehensible, from the point of view of the present, is why Darwin assumes variation under domestication to be more extensive than variation under nature.

Here we need to take account of some bygone biology. Unlike biologists today, and indeed unlike some biological thinkers at the time, Darwin believed that variation was the exception, not the rule (43). Other things being equal, offspring resemble their parents. In Darwin's view, when offspring do not resemble their parents, it is because the parents' reproductive systems have suffered some sort of disturbance, due to changes in the conditions of life. How changed conditions disturb reproductive functioning Darwin does not claim to know – though he is prepared to conjecture that it has something to do with nutrition (7). But, he argues, once reproductive functioning has been thus disturbed, then, if viable offspring can be produced at all, they will vary. If conditions remain unstable (as under domestication), this variability will continue for generations to come. At least some of the variations will be, or will become, hereditary. As to why an organism varies in one way rather than another – a topic treated at length in the fifth chapter – Darwin argues that a number of causes come into play, including inheritance, reversion to ancestral characters, the effects of use and disuse, and the direct action of the environment.

From Darwin's perspective, domestication is an extreme and sustained change in a species' conditions of life. The challenge he feels is thus to show that in nature too, albeit on a smaller scale, changed conditions have caused variation. The second chapter takes up this challenge. Here Darwin attempts to show that, while variation is less extensive in nature than on the farm, nevertheless it is more extensive than many naturalists at the time suspected. He attributes the underestimate of variation in nature in part to the fact that taxonomists, devoted to describing the essential features of species, 'are far from pleased at finding variability in important characters' (45). Especially significant, in his view, is that such natural variation is most abundant in groups containing large numbers of species, exposed to the greatest range of conditions of life. Variability persists where it has prevailed in the past. Hence species belonging to larger genera tend to have more varieties than species belonging to smaller genera – a pattern utterly mysterious on the view that species are the products of isolated acts of creation. For Darwin, varieties are but 'incipient species' (52), while species are but 'strongly-marked and well-defined varieties' (55). Furthermore, as Darwin argues later, since 'geology plainly proclaims that each land has undergone great physical changes', organisms in the past must indeed have experienced changed conditions of life, and as a result 'varied under nature, in the same way as they generally have varied under the changed conditions of domestication' (468).

In the third chapter, Darwin identifies the struggle for existence as what ensures that inheritable variation in nature accumulates selectively and so adaptively. According to Darwin, citing the precedent of the political economist Thomas Robert Malthus, there is a natural tendency for each species to increase in number geometrically. But there are also many checks on this tendency, such as food scarcity, predation, unfavourable changes in climate, disease and competition with other species. As a result, there is a struggle, more and less metaphorical, to survive and reproduce. Darwin emphasises how dense is the economy of nature, with each species tending to expand to the utmost, at the expense of other species. He compares the 'face of Nature' to 'a yielding surface, with ten thousand sharp wedges packed close together' (67) – that is, each organism and species competes to drive itself as fully as possible into the environment, exploiting resources and so increasing in numbers. Among the intense, complex and interlocking relationships relating organisms to one another and their environmental conditions, it is the organism-to-organism relationships that matter most. Competition between individuals that are most alike will be strongest.

At the beginning of the third chapter, Darwin indicates briefly how inheritable variation and the struggle for existence combine to adapt species to their environments:

> Owing to this struggle for life, any variation, however slight and from whatever cause proceeding, if it be in any degree profitable to an individual of any species, in its infinitely complex relations to other organic beings and to external nature, will tend to the preservation of that individual, and will generally be inherited by its offspring.... I have called this principle, by which each slight variation, if useful, is preserved, by the term of Natural Selection, in order to mark its relation to man's power of selection. (61)

Darwin discusses the principle more fully in the fourth chapter, on 'natural selection'. The main contributions of this chapter are twofold. First, Darwin systematically compares artificial with natural selection, arguing for the greater power of the latter to modify species. Over centuries, human breeders have diversified and adapted distinctive breeds of domesticated species. Nature has millions of years to work, and is more precise and more comprehensive as a selector, discriminating between the smallest differences.

Second, he relates natural selection to the branching tree of life, via extinction and what he calls the principle of 'divergence of character' (111). For Darwin, extinction is an inevitable consequence of ever better adapted varieties or species arising through natural selection. Since nature is at all times fully inhabited, new kinds of organisms can emerge only by displacing pre-existing ones. And since competitive struggle is often most intense between similar kinds of organisms, an emerging variety or species will often drive to rarity and then extinction those varieties or species nearest to it in structure, constitution and habits. At the same time, the more the descendants of a common ancestral species diverge from one another in these respects, 'by so much will they be better enabled to seize on many and widely diversified places in the polity of nature, and so be enabled to increase in numbers' (112). Darwin goes on to compare the diversification of species in a region to the specialisation of organs in a body. Just as a greater 'physiological division of labour' (115) brings more efficient functioning, so, Darwin argues, a greater diversification of species enables a region to support larger numbers of organisms.

In later editions of the *Origin*, Darwin added a section to this chapter entitled 'On the Degree to which Organisation Tends to Advance'. Here he deals with an apparent difficulty for the claim that natural selection produces progressive change. If the claim is true, why are there still so many unspecialised organisms around? Darwin's answer, in effect, is that natural selection produces greater specialisation other things being equal – and other things are not always equal. To increase specialisation or, in Darwin's terms, advance organisation, natural selection requires both suitable variation and propitious conditions of life. But sometimes more highly organised variants simply do not arise in a particular lineage. Even when they do arise, low organisation is sometimes more adaptive than high organisation.

There is of course more to Darwin's arguments in these chapters. In Kenneth Waters' analysis of the reasoning in the *Origin*, he explores in detail how the analogy between artificial and natural selection works, and how it relates, or does not, to the rest of the book. But even this sketch will suffice to explain why Darwin's theorising was controversial and consequential – especially when extended to the case of our own species.

III HISTORICAL REVISIONS

Much entrenched wisdom about Darwin has recently been corrected. Two examples may serve here. First, it now seems certain that, contrary to what many older histories imply, Darwin became a committed and active believer in the 'transmutation of species' – new species arising in descent with modification from earlier ones – only some months after his return from the *Beagle* voyage. Second, again contrary to older and even some newer accounts, Darwin did not arrive at his theory of natural selection in an instant, after reading Malthus' treatise on population in September 1838. Rather, Darwin constructed the theory in several steps spread over many weeks. Nor, it seems, did he reckon it his first truly satisfactory theory of the origin of species, but merely an even more satisfactory version of the theory that he already had.

Historians have been learning to track the subtleties in Darwin's thinking. They have also been learning to think in more critical ways about Darwin's science in its wider context. Old choices no longer appeal – between, for example, insisting that Darwin had debts only to natural-scientific sources in his notebook theorising, and insisting on the contrary that Darwin drew deeply on the writings of the theorist of capitalism Adam Smith. These two views do not exhaust all the possibilities. One could well conclude that Darwin's theorising drew on all kinds of resources within and beyond the natural sciences of the day, including political economy, without accepting that there is compelling evidence for direct debts to readings in Smith.

Large, even ideological, divisions of opinion among historians can be associated with differences in the interpretation of Darwin. The results of specialist scholarship alone do not determine how the accompanying controversies proceed. This volume does not pretend to rise above those controversies or their motivations. On one point, especially, it takes sides. In popular if not in academic representations of Darwin, he is often portrayed as a naïve, innocent, schoolboyish, outdoor, nature-loving traveller and collector, whose theories emerged out of a conjunction of genius, luck and exceptional observational opportunity. This Darwin was a naturalist, a man of science, but not a man of ideas, not a man fully joining in the larger collective life of the mind of the age. Darwin himself undoubtedly contributed to this portrayal in many ways; and his immediate family, in their many writings about him, have often perpetuated it. More generally, it fits with a Wordsworthian strain in the English national preference for certain kinds of cultural heroes.

For all their disagreements on other matters, Darwin scholars now concur in emphasising that the older portrayals could hardly be more wide of the mark. Darwin was indeed a man of ideas, a thinker, even at times, yes, a philosopher in our sense and not just in the former sense of a man of science. So – and this is immediately apposite to this volume – there is no paradox to address, no wondering how someone so at odds with our standard notions of a philosopher could nevertheless leave writings behind that have intrigued many philosophers. To lose this paradox is to lose an iconic stereotype of Darwin, long cherished in older scientific and literary circles. It may be appropriate to insist, then, that the stereotype was never a fact about Darwin but rather an interpretation, with no claim to be forever preserved from revision.

Darwinian enthusiasts in science and philosophy sometimes appear defensive and evasive about certain aspects of the larger Darwin story, most obviously the historical connections between Darwin's writings and various political and social doctrines – Nazism is the paradigm, of course – that invoked Darwinism in the name of their absurdities and atrocities. For the purposes of the present volume, it has seemed appropriate to include rather than exclude these connections. What is more, wherever this volume does make exclusions, these should not be taken as signs of denial or dismissal. We regret, for instance, that we were unable to include a discussion of the philosophical tradition – pragmatism – that, in its lineage from Peirce, James and Dewey in the nineteenth century to Quine, Davidson, Putnam, Habermas and Rorty in our own time, has drawn most fully and decisively upon Darwinian science.

Dewey in particular holds an important place not just in the history of philosophical uses of Darwinism, but in the historiography of such uses. He was among the first in a long line of thinkers to argue that Darwinian science challenges one of the central themes in the Western intellectual tradition: essentialism. This comprehensive thesis about the historical significance of Darwin goes roughly as follows. From the ancient Hebraic and Hellenic writings to the syntheses of those sources in the Middle Ages and on to the discussions in Darwin's day, the forms – the essences – of natural species, including mineral, plant and animal species, were held to constitute the very order of nature, given to the creation by God. By contrast, the thesis continues, for Darwinian science, plant and animal species are not ultimate constitutive elements of the order of nature, but contingent products of an orderly course of nature. The order in Darwinian nature does not arise from conformity to forms, but from general, causal laws. Furthermore, these very laws entail variation over time and space in all species; and this variation implies – quite inconsistently with the essentialism of Plato or Aristotle, say – that no species, human or plant or animal, has any essential nature. Darwinism, in brief, made essentialism untenable.

The time may have come to question this comprehensive thesis, for several reasons. Most obviously, it presupposes a great deal of uniformity in the pre-Darwinian tradition. Opposing Darwin to Plato and Aristotle risks conflating the two philosophers' very different doctrines; indeed, Aristotle was arguably not at all an essentialist about natural kinds and natural order. Moreover, it may be that Darwinian science does not preclude essentialism about species, nor then about humankind. If Darwinian essentialism is a coherent position, then today's neo-Aristotelian ethical theories or 'virtue ethics', along with many current versions of evolutionary psychology, can uphold the assumptions they seem to require about human nature. There are very large historiographical and philosophical issues at stake here. In this volume, Elliott Sober, Daniel Dennett and Philip Kitcher explicitly endorse much, if not all, of the comprehensive thesis; while Owen Flanagan is apparently one of those for whom human nature lives on after Darwin. We would emphasise our hope that their disagreements will prompt readers to pose new questions about this old issue.

IV FROM PHILOSOPHICAL NATURAL HISTORY TO PHILOSOPHICAL NATURALISM

Darwin thought of himself as a 'philosophical naturalist'; as, that is, a scientific student of natural history – of geology, botany and zoology – where being scientific meant being concerned with general causal and explanatory theories, and not merely with observing, collecting, describing and classifying. In our day, many philosophers are engaged in agreeing and disagreeing with a position known as 'philosophical naturalism'. This volume concludes with a trialogue between Daniel Dennett, Owen Flanagan and Philip Kitcher that is in large measure a debate over the importance of Darwinian thought for the future of naturalist philosophy.

The links between philosophical natural history in Darwin's generation and philosophical naturalism in ours are sometimes straightforward, sometimes not. Some scientific theories proposed in Darwin's generation made reference to a supernatural realm – for example, those theories interpreting the unity of structure in the body plans of vertebrates as grounded in a formal archetype that was itself an idea in God's mind. Darwin's theories, most obviously his theory of descent with modification by means of natural selection, made no such overt references to the supernatural. In that sense, his theories, like others of the day, were naturalistic rather than supernaturalistic. Today's philosophical naturalism continues and extends such subsumings of phenomena within nature – for example, by attempting to trace human ethical values, not to a Divine Will, but to human evolution.

The new philosophical naturalists have other aims that do not map at all straightforwardly on to Darwin's aims, however. Philosophers of a generation or two back, especially in the Anglophone world, often contrasted the natural sciences with, on one side, the formal sciences of logic and mathematics, and, on the other side, ethics. It was said that, where the natural sciences were descriptive and explanatory, the formal sciences and ethics were prescriptive and normative (although it was usual to distinguish sharply between the normative principles of logic and the norms inherent in ethical values). Philosophy itself was often located with the formal sciences, rather than with the natural sciences. Moreover, impassable barriers were held to exist between the natural-scientific and the formal, and between the natural-scientific and the ethical.

Philosophical naturalism often defines itself as doing away with such barriers. It is committed to the continuity, if not the outright merging, of the natural sciences with all other kinds of judgements and themes, including the theories of philosophy itself. On the modern philosophical-naturalist view, there are no reasons for supposing in advance that the findings of the natural sciences will prove useless to other areas of enquiry. The natural sciences are, therefore, allowed to serve as sources of insight on any topic the philosopher may be investigating, and as resources for philosophy itself.

So far as these recent issues were none of Darwin's concern, his philosophical natural history was distinct from the new philosophical naturalism. Moreover, the attempt to subsume the human mind within nature is now carried out on distinctly post-Victorian terms. According to one popular view, the mind is to the body as computer software is to computer hardware. To have a mind is thus to be running a programme. Of course, comparing people to machinery is an old strategy for naturalising the mind, for, although machines are artefacts, they are not mysterious or miraculous. Once it was clocks or telephone exchanges that provided the leading comparisons. Now it is computers. We can call this general sort of naturalism about the mind 'machinism', and the newer variety 'computationist machinism'.

Machinism is distinct from a second strategy for naturalising the mind, exemplified in Darwin's work: to insist that people are animals, and that the study of human minds rightly falls within the biological sciences. We can call this 'biologism', and the Darwinian variety 'Darwinian biologism'. For modern philosophical naturalists, some integration of these two latter-day varieties of naturalism about the mind, computationist machinism and Darwinian biologism, has often seemed irresistible. In several of the later chapters in this volume, and most explicitly in Daniel Dennett's chapter, the success of that integration is taken for granted. The legacy of Alan Turing, the mid-twentieth-century founder of modern computational theory, has, it seems, combined with the legacy of Charles Darwin to naturalise the mind wholly.

Can this be right? Should philosophical naturalists accept that it is really Turing and Darwin all the way up and all the way down in matters mental? Two observations in particular suggest caution. First of all, computationist machinism – known in its more unqualified versions as 'strong AI' (for 'Artificial Intelligence') – is a controversial, minority view in psychology; while Darwinian theory enjoys a secure consensus in biology. Second, computationist machinism is itself a blend of two doctrines, computationism and machinism, which, from a historical vantage point, appear ill at ease not only with each other, but, in fundamental ways, with Darwinian biologism.

Although computers are a twentieth-century invention, computationism is much older, descending from Newton's contemporary Leibniz (and, arguably, more remotely from the Pythagoreans). It holds that everything is rationally intelligible only in so far as it instantiates mathematical rules and ratios. As understood by Leibniz and his followers, computationism was explicitly hostile to all versions of materialism. By contrast, machinism was constructed in the eighteenth century, by La Mettrie and others, as a new materialism, opposed to anything like the computationist heritage. For the machinists, cogitating humans were but more complex versions of the automata then delighting French savants. Seen against this background, computationist machinism is an unpromising hybrid of divergent doctrines.

Historical awareness likewise casts doubt on the attempt to unite either of these doctrines with Darwinian biologism. As is well known, Darwin was a materialist about the mind, believing that the organisation of the brain caused mental functioning. If we grant that Darwinian biologism follows Darwin in his materialism, then computationism, with its anti-materialist commitments, looks an unlikely partner. Machinism, although materialist, appears no more readily integrated, for Darwin's materialism was, again, biologistic – originating not with the machinists such as La Mettrie, but with medical writers such as Cabanis, who compared the brain to other living organs rather than non-living machines. More generally, in Darwin's view, and on most Darwinian views past and present, evolution by natural selection is in no obvious sense computational or algorithmic.

What such considerations suggest, in sum, is that Darwinian biologism may fit at best uneasily with both sides of a residual dualism in computationist machinism, a dualism of algorithmic software and mechanical hardware. Harnessing Turing and Darwin together may, then, raise as many challenges as it resolves. The unresolved challenges include taking seriously consciousness and the emotions. Like Darwin himself, the first psychologists who drew on his work – most notably William James – never segregated cognition from either conscious awareness or emotive feelings. By contrast, in strong AI, as in the cognitive psychology of the 1960s and 1970s as a whole, there was hardly more engagement with these two topics than there had been among the behaviourists. Recently, however, consciousness and the emotions have returned as central concerns for philosophers and psychologists. In the light of these developments, Darwinian agendas for naturalising the mind look newly appropriate, even as Darwin-Turing integrations become more difficult.

We offer these reflections in the spirit of one of the main messages of this volume: that Darwinism is a protean phenomenon. There has never been a single best interpretation of Darwin's ideas or their implications. All new orthodoxies should be examined with scepticism fortified by a sense of history. This companion to Darwin does not therefore ally itself with a cliché that has carried over from the twentieth into the present century: that, with Marxism and Freudianism dead, but Darwinism alive and well, biological views of humankind remain the sole surviving options. Among other defects, any such view begs too many questions – after all, there are plenty of prominent authors, the French philosopher-historian Michel Foucault for one, who have responded to the rumoured deaths of Marxism and Freudianism by turning to Nietzsche rather than Darwin as a nineteenth-century ancestor. Little is to be gained from attempts to secure privileged dominion for Darwinian perspectives. In offering a sample of historical and philosophical interpretations of Darwin and Darwinism, this volume seeks rather to promote better informed debate about Darwin and his influence – what it has been, and what, in a future full of other philosophical options, it should be.

Part I
Darwin's theorising

PHILLIP R. SLOAN

1 The making of a philosophical naturalist

> The law of the succession of types, although subject to some remarkable exceptions, must possess the highest interest to every philosophical naturalist.[1]

When Charles Darwin penned these lines in 1837, he was twenty-eight years old, fresh from the *Beagle* voyage, and a self-described 'philosophical naturalist.' As such, he was engaged neither in natural history nor in natural philosophy. Natural history, in the tradition of the Swedish botanist Linné (Linnaeus), concerned the systematic ordering of animals and plants and the discovery of new species. Natural philosophy, in the tradition of Descartes and Newton, concerned the search for general physical laws. Darwin was aligning himself with investigators whose work fell outside these traditions. Some were interested in a comparative anatomy based on ideal forms – the so-called 'transcendental' anatomists, such as the French zoologist Etienne Geoffroy Saint-Hilaire and his Scottish disciple Robert Knox. Others, such as the geologist Charles Lyell, were interested in building comprehensive theories about the earth and its inhabitants.[2]

Philosophical naturalists spoke of various 'laws of life'. They debated the existence of laws, for example, said to relate taxonomic groupings in regular circular arrangements, as in the so-called quinarian system, or to govern organic functions such as the development of the embryo. Another law under discussion was the law of the succession of types. In different areas around the world, it seemed, living species had replaced extinct species of the same kind or type. Living armadillos in South America, for instance, had apparently replaced the armadillo-like creatures fossilised in the rocks of that continent. In the 1830s, patterns like this one, at once biological and geological, were attracting attention from leading geologists and palaeontologists.

The young Darwin aspired to discover and explain such patterns. Combining the interests of the comparative anatomists and the theoretical geologists, he sought to integrate geology, the study of the distribution of plants and animals (biogeography), and the causal analysis of the processes of biological change. This 'philosophical' perspective was in place before he formulated his evolutionary theory, and provided crucial preconditions for its later development. Indeed, when he wrote in the late 1830s about the succession of types, he had already found the causal explanation he would set out, more than twenty years later, in the *Origin of Species* (1859): that living and extinct species often belong to the same type because they share a common ancestry.[3]

I EARLY SCIENTIFIC INTERESTS

The outline of Darwin's early life, sketched many times, including twice by himself,[4] begins with his birth in Shrewsbury in February 1809, the fifth of six children born to Robert Waring and Susannah Wedgwood Darwin. The Darwins' world was one of wealth and privilege, filled with visits to family, country-house balls and matchmaking. The wealth came from both sides of the family, as did the intellectual ambience in which Darwin grew up. From his father, a physician trained at both Leiden and Edinburgh, Charles absorbed something of the ethos of the Scottish medical tradition, in particular its philosophical materialism about life and matter. Equally unorthodox religious and scientific doctrines, including the transmutation of species, had been publicly manifest in the writings of his famous – even notorious – grandfather, the natural philosopher and minor poet Erasmus Darwin. Counterbalancing these tendencies were Charles' mother and his three older sisters Marianne, Caroline and Susan. From them Darwin acquired a Unitarian sensibility that acknowledged a Creator, though not the divinity of Jesus Christ. These different influences from the male and female sides of his family helped define the complex relation he had to conventional religion to the end of his life.

At the age of eight, Charles was enrolled in the school of the local Unitarian minister, the Reverend George Case. Following the death of his mother in 1817, Charles boarded nearby at the prestigious Shrewsbury School, then under the direction of Samuel Butler. In later life, Darwin recalled the seven years he spent at the school with disgust, characterising its classical education as the nadir of his intellectual development.[5] Nonetheless, it was there that the boy's precocity and interest in scientific subjects first came to light. Always a passionate collector, he was introduced to more systematic scientific enquiry by his brother Erasmus Alvey. Five years older than Charles, Erasmus had preceded him at Shrewsbury School. After graduation, Erasmus pursued the family medical profession through a new elite route that began with admission to Christ's College, Cambridge, and to the new medical curriculum instituted by John Haviland. As part of this curriculum, Erasmus attended the chemical lectures of James Cumming, who taught the new chemistry of Antoine de Lavoisier and Humphry Davy. Erasmus also attended the mineralogy course of the Reverend John Stevens Henslow, later to become Charles' mentor. Well before Charles himself arrived at Cambridge, he thus acquired from its teachers, through Erasmus, a taste for 'philosophical' pursuits. Together, Charles and Erasmus created their own makeshift chemistry laboratory at Shrewsbury, in which they carried out an array of chemical experiments during school holidays, replicating those enacted in Cumming's lectures. Nearly all of the very earliest surviving letters to Charles are instructions sent from Cambridge by Erasmus, detailing glassware and chemicals to be purchased in preparation for their joint chemical enquiries.

II STUDIES IN EDINBURGH

Following his own graduation from Shrewsbury School, in autumn 1825, at the age of sixteen, Charles travelled with Erasmus to Edinburgh to begin the study of medicine at Edinburgh University medical school. Whereas Erasmus was attending Edinburgh to complete the external degree requirements for the MD in the new Cambridge medical curriculum, their father had decided, in Charles' case, to omit the Cambridge preparation, and enrol him directly in medical school. Rooming together during this first academic year, the brothers read widely in the literature of medicine and natural philosophy, and were soon collecting and studying the marine invertebrates abundant along the shores of the nearby Firth of Forth.

The standard view of these years, drawn largely from Darwin's *Autobiography*, has emphasised Charles' disaffection with his medical studies. But letters and other documents from the time reveal a much more complex picture. Edinburgh was, after all, still known as the 'Athens of the North', and was a place of active controversy over the latest medical and scientific developments, including those that were flooding in from the Continent. Although Charles (and many others) were bored with the famously dreadful lectures of some of his professors, there were several features of the university environment that engaged a young man with precocious scientific interests.

There were opportunities, for example, to advance in chemistry; and in the first term, Charles enrolled in the demonstrative lecture course in chemistry given by Thomas Hope, successor to the chair of chemistry formerly held by the great Joseph Black. Charles enjoyed Hope's lectures very much.[6] In Hope's lectures he was also exposed to the controversial geological theories of Edinburgh's James Hutton.[7] Hutton had opposed the so-called 'Neptunist' geological theories of the German mineralogist Abraham Werner. For Hutton, it was not the action of water, but the effects of heat, that formed the geological strata. Such was his enthusiasm for Hope's lectures that Charles remained in Edinburgh after Erasmus' graduation in spring 1826, in order to complete Hope's second series of 'very good Lectures on Electricity', reviewing, among other things, the electrical theories of Charles Dufay and Benjamin Franklin, and the results of recent galvanic experiments on organisms.[8]

In his second year at Edinburgh, Charles' interests shifted decisively away from medical study to more theoretical interests in natural history. In autumn 1826 he enrolled in the intensive, five-day-a-week natural history lectures given by the chairholder in natural history, Robert Jameson. From these lectures, Charles learned about such matters as classification, fossils and the local geology. Around this time he also met the comparative anatomist Robert Edmond Grant, then working as an assistant to Jameson on excursions with students along the beaches and the nearby hills – the most probable context for the meeting of Grant and the young Darwin. It was Grant who had introduced the controversial theories of the French zoologists Geoffroy and Jean Baptiste de Lamarck into Edinburgh discussions. Geoffroy, one of the main architects of the 'Idealist' morphology, had claimed to find structural affinities, or 'unity of type', between kinds of animals previously classified as belonging to wholly separate taxonomic groups. According to Lamarck, the plants and animals presently existing had arisen through a natural process of transformation, owing to the complexifying properties of the fluids running through their tissues, and the adaptive changes brought about when habits changed in response to altered environments.[9]

Beyond Jameson's lectures and Grant's conversations, there was also the company of like-minded students. In November 1826, Charles was elected to the student Plinian Natural History Society. Sponsored by Jameson, this group consisted mostly of students of medicine, some to become lifelong friends. The regular meetings immersed him in discussions of scientific topics generally, and sometimes of controversial theoretical issues in the life sciences, such as the relations of life and instinct to mental powers, and the relations between asexual propagation and sexual generation.[10] Here Charles presented his first scientific paper, in March 1827. Reporting on the mode of generation in a small colonial marine invertebrate, the bryozoan *Flustra*, Darwin described in detail his microscopic studies of these lowly forms, in which he had found that the ova had the properties of self-motion.[11]

Darwin's time in Edinburgh proved crucial in several respects. It was there that he first encountered the scientific debates that would engage him as a budding philosophical naturalist. He also developed specific interests in animal physiology, bioelectricity and reproduction. But the most immediate effect of Edinburgh upon Darwin was to deflect him from a career in medicine. When Darwin entered Christ's College, Cambridge, in January 1828, he was en route for a career in the Anglican clergy – a respectable profession for a long line of Cambridge graduates with a passion for natural history and science.

III STUDIES IN CAMBRIDGE

Darwin's student years at Cambridge (January 1828–June 1831) immersed him in a very different intellectual world from the hurly-burly medical environment he had left in Edinburgh. The life of the university was defined by the collection of nearly independent separate colleges, some founded as early as the thirteenth century, governed by boards of celibate Fellows in Anglican orders, with college life still retaining some of the monastic character of its medieval origins. All persons admitted had to subscribe to the Thirty-Nine Articles of the Anglican communion. Instruction, primarily by tutorials supplemented by occasional lectures by appointed professors, was generally aimed at preparing students for a series of examinations, leading to graduation either in an honours curriculum (Tripos), or, as in Darwin's case, a lower 'pass' curriculum, resulting in a BA degree. For completion of his course of study, Darwin was required to show competence in one of the four Gospels or the Acts of the Apostles in the Greek; in the works of the Anglican theologian William Paley, especially his *Evidences of Christianity*; in Locke's *Essay Concerning Human Understanding*; and in certain writings of Adam Smith, most likely his *Theory of Moral Sentiments*. Mathematical requirements were in the *Elements* of Euclid.[12]

The tradition of the *Autobiography* has characterised Cambridge college life in these years as a leisurely world with little academic rigour. Against that image of Cambridge must be balanced the numerous signs of a vigorous intellectual life, such as the reformed medical curriculum in which Charles' brother Erasmus had enrolled, and the founding in 1819 of the Cambridge Philosophical Society. This society was transforming the scientific culture of Cambridge, sponsoring meetings of Cambridge faculty and graduates to discuss contemporary issues in chemistry, geology, botany, electrical theory, mathematics, optical theory, plant physiology and animal and plant classification. Many of the Fellows and Professors of the university had affiliated with this society by the time Darwin arrived as a student, including the mineralogist and botanist Henslow, the geologist Adam Sedgwick, and the polymath William Whewell, all important as his mentors during these years. Among the other regulars were the chemist Cumming, the anatomist William Clark and the architect of the new medical curriculum, John Haviland. By 1836, the Society had 490 Fellows, with another 58 eminent British and foreign honorary Fellows.[13]

Records from Charles' first year at Cambridge are sparse, and do not give a clear picture of his scientific contacts and interests, though an incipient network of scientific associations was already in place thanks to Erasmus. Their first cousin W. D. Fox was the most important of Charles' early intellectual and social connections. A lifelong correspondence commenced after Fox's graduation in summer 1828.

The early letters reveal that Charles' Edinburgh interests in marine invertebrates were giving way to a passionate study of the local beetles, with Charles making contacts with such leading entomologists as London's F. W. Hope, who would go on to establish the Entomological Society of London in 1833, of which Charles was a founding member *in absentia*.[14]

In 1828 Darwin began attending Friday evening meetings at Henslow's apartments. At these meetings, scientifically inclined students met for discussions with senior tutors associated with the Cambridge Philosophical Society (from which students were excluded).[15] Henslow had only recently vacated the chair of mineralogy to take up the Regius chair of botany, and commenced his first course of botanical lectures that spring. In form and content, Henslow's botany course was highly sophisticated for its day, and imported into Cambridge the latest Continental and British botanical theories.[16] The course was particularly modelled on the writings of the Genevan botanist Augustin Pyrame de Candolle, which emphasised both physiological and classificatory botany. Many faculty and students, including Darwin, would attend Henslow's course more than once.

IV THE TRANSFORMATIONS OF 1831

Following the completion of his BA examinations in late January 1831 – he was ranked tenth of 178 candidates[17] – Darwin spent a further two terms in Cambridge to fulfil a residence requirement needed to receive the degree. In this period of leisure, he again attended Henslow's botany course, and a particularly close association developed with Henslow. Plans began to emerge for a post-graduation summer expedition to the volcanic island of Tenerife, in the Canaries, with Henslow and three other students. Most likely under Henslow's tutelage, Darwin now began to read two works by two prominent men of science who would profoundly influence his subsequent thinking: the astronomer John Herschel, son of William, and author of the newly published *Preliminary Discourse on the Study of Natural Philosophy* (1830); and the biogeographer, explorer and interpreter of nature, Alexander von Humboldt, whose *Personal Narrative of Travels to the Equinoctial Regions of the New Continent* recorded the 1799–1804 expedition of Humboldt and his companion Aimé Bonpland to the interior of South America, with a stop on the way at Tenerife.

Herschel's new book, on the aims, structure, achievements and procedures of science, presented Darwin for the first time with a systematic account of scientific methodology. In the crucial second part of this work, Herschel set forth a theory of how the human mind works in relation to the senses. Secure natural knowledge arises through a process of induction, but this is not passive induction, and Herschel appealed to Francis Bacon's distinction between 'active' and 'passive' observation to make this distinction. Facts are classified under empirical laws, and higher theories, as Herschel wrote, 'result from a consideration of these laws, and of the proximate causes brought into view in the previous process, regarded all together as constituting a new set of phenomena'.[18] Herschel argued that the aim of science was to ascribe certain phenomena to 'true causes' (*verae causae*), 'causes recognized as having a real existence in nature, and not being mere hypotheses or figments of the mind'.[19] From this time forward, the language of Herschel appears in Darwin's writings, and the search for 'true causes' also became Darwin's goal.[20]

The nature and significance of Humboldt's influence is more elusive, but arguably even more far-reaching, and, in the interpretation of this chapter, decisive in forming Darwin's peculiar understanding of a 'philosophical' naturalist. He likely first learned of Humboldt's theories in detail through Henslow's botany lectures in spring 1831, and the effect was transformative. He speaks of how he worked all morning 'till Henslow's lecture', all the while in his 'head... running about the Tropics: in the morning I go and gaze at Palm trees in the hot-house and come home and read Humboldt: my enthusiasm is so great that I cannot hardly sit still on my chair.... I never will be easy till I see the peak of Teneriffe [*sic*] and the great Dragon tree; sandy, dazzling, plains, and gloomy silent forest are alternately uppermost in my mind.'[21] From Humboldt, more than any other author, Darwin acquired the vision of a comprehensive and holistic science of the natural world, a science concerned above all with *interrelated* phenomena – biological, geological and atmospheric. Humboldtian science sought to determine from 'the arrangement of brute matter organized in rocks, in the distribution and mutual relations of plants and animals' the 'laws of their relations with each other, and the eternal ties which link the phaenomena of life, and those of inanimate nature'.[22] Plant forms were to be related to geography and geology, and the distribution of vegetation was related to the physical parameters of the atmosphere and the physical topography of the land. Humboldt's vision was unlike anything Darwin had previously encountered. It thereafter supplied him with a paradigm of scientific synthesis that connected specific enquiries into detailed phenomena with general theorising on the grandest scale. Just as important, it altered Darwin's sensibility, priming him to experience nature at once conceptually and aesthetically.

The lessons Darwin drew from Herschel and Humboldt applied to science in general. Darwin also acquired a new practical skill in this period. To prepare himself more deeply in geology for the anticipated Canaries expedition, in the spring Darwin accompanied the Regius professor of geology and current president of the Geological Society of London, the Reverend Adam Sedgwick, in a survey of the geology around the Cambridge area. In July, Darwin made his own private geological survey of the region around Shrewsbury. In August he joined Sedgwick in a survey of the geology of north Wales along the Clwyd valley and surrounding areas. He would later recall that this excursion gave him the skills he needed for the geological work of the *Beagle* years.[23] Although the death of a co-organiser put an end to the Tenerife expedition, he did not have long to wait for another opportunity to put those new skills to use. His teachers had recommended him to the Naval Admiralty Office as the ideal person to join HMS *Beagle* on a surveying voyage to the tip of South America. The vessel's young commander, Captain Robert FitzRoy, had requested a gentleman civilian companion, responsible for his own expenses, and knowledgeable in geology, with whom to dine and share interests. When Darwin returned from Wales, a letter of invitation awaited. With the reluctant approval of his father, he accepted the position.

It was in the months of preparation before departure, in the autumn of 1831, that he encountered the work of his third great 'philosophical' mentor, the former barrister and geologist Charles Lyell, through the presentation of the first volume of Lyell's recently published *Principles of Geology* by Captain FitzRoy as the *Beagle* was preparing for its extensive sea voyage. In this first volume Darwin read Lyell's lengthy historical review of the science of geology in which Lyell interpreted the reasons for the failure of the earlier schools of geology to supply a satisfactory account of the geological history of the earth. Singled out for criticism was the French naturalist George Cuvier, whose synthesis of geological history and palaeontology had deeply influenced Darwin's previous mentors in geology – Jameson, Sedgwick and Humboldt. Later dubbed 'catastrophism', Cuvier's doctrine held that the sudden action of volcanoes, floods, rapid climatic cooling and earthquakes in the past had produced drastic changes in the surface of the earth, resulting in periodic and sudden extinctions of fauna and flora. Against Cuvier, Lyell posed his own 'philosophical' view, which emphasised the 'undeviating uniformity of secondary causes'. After all, quite generally, one is 'guided by his faith in this principle', in judging 'the probability of accounts [...] of former occurrences', and in often rejecting 'the fabulous tales of former ages, on the ground of their being irreconcilable with the experience of more enlightened ages'.[24] On the basis of this principle, dubbed 'uniformitarianism' by subsequent commentators, Lyell claimed that the causes of geological changes operating in the past must be assumed to be identical with the causes observed acting at the present, and at the *same intensity*.[25] This principle forms the framework within which he analysed the geological and fossil record. Alongside the non-historical and geographical approach he encountered in Humboldt, Darwin now had an authority who had introduced the issue of historical process and temporal causation in a new and exciting way.

Darwin's encounter within one calendar year with three major synthetic scientific thinkers gave him models for a lay scientific career, one tied neither to clerical duties nor to teaching. These three authorities were bold theorists, as well as meticulous describers of natural phenomena, and their theorising received respect rather than disdain from his mentors like Henslow. All of them had been or currently were travellers to exotic places: Herschel was then at the Cape of Good Hope, mapping the southern heavens; Humboldt was a famous explorer of the tropics; Lyell had travelled extensively on the Continent learning its geology. A new vocation was opening before Darwin as he prepared for the *Beagle*'s departure.

V UNDER SAIL

After several months of preparation and delays, the *Beagle*, a small man o'war converted into a coastal surveying ship, left Devonport,

England, in late December 1831. It would not return until early October 1836. Although originally intended to be a surveying trip to the southern tip of South America, the expedition eventually turned into a circumnavigation of the globe. The voyage made Darwin into one of the great sea-going naturalists of his era, an explorer in the tradition of Johann and Georg Forster, the father-and-son team who had accompanied the later voyages of Captain James Cook to the South Pacific in the eighteenth century. For fifty-eight months the small ship would be Darwin's primary home and workplace. In its ten-by-eleven-foot poop cabin, housing the library of the *Beagle* – there were around 245 volumes – Darwin carried out shipboard studies of marine organisms obtained by dredging and net hauls, and analysed the geological specimens acquired in his land explorations.[26] It was here, too, that he drew up his synthetic reflections in the later months of the voyage.

It is difficult to appreciate in our age of instant communication the degree of isolation this kind of adventure entailed, or the sense of cultural disconnectedness that Darwin experienced on the return home after five years at sea. A letter to Darwin from home and its return response might take as long as eighteen months to complete the circuit. Requests for books and supplies, and their eventual arrival, had to follow the same slow route. The second volume of Lyell's *Principles* (1832), dealing with Lamarckism, biogeography, the birth and death of species and the formation and distribution of coral reefs, reached Darwin remarkably quickly in Monte Video, Uruguay, in late 1832. The third volume (1833), treating in detail the classification of main geological periods, the use of fossil shells to characterise sedimentary rocks, and offering further reflections on the causes of geological change, was received at the Falklands in spring 1834. Other works took much longer to catch up with the ship. Some requested works apparently never reached the *Beagle* at all.

During this period, Darwin's thought developed in ways that are not easy to characterise. As we have seen, he left England well prepared in several areas of science, with a general intellectual formation indebted to several mentors – principally Grant, Henslow and Sedgwick (in person), and Humboldt, Herschel and Lyell (on the page). Naturally enough, Darwin had taken up a number of their beliefs about the world and its proper study. In the course of the voyage, however, he found himself applying, testing and modifying these beliefs against a set of personal experiences that far transcended those of his teachers and intellectual heroes.

Darwin's development in this period was illustrated in empirical researches and theoretical reflections. His extensive empirical investigations in the *Beagle* years – in zoology, geology and natural history – are recorded in the four bound Zoological Diaries, the three bound Geological Diaries and the ten volumes of 'Notes on Geology of the Places Visited during the Voyage'. More reflective and synthetic observations of places and peoples can be found in the so-called *Beagle Diary*, which formed the basis for the work that made Darwin a public figure, the *Journal of Researches* (1839). In addition to these sources there are the eighteen pocket field notebooks that served as the original records for the *Beagle Diary*; ample correspondence (now published); and the catalogues of specimens. There are also several documents, drawn up on the return leg of the voyage, containing important synthetic reflections on coral reefs, geological formations and the interrelations of geological and biological issues.

During the first leg of the journey, from England to the Cape Verde Islands, off equatorial Africa, Darwin commenced his first 'Zoological Diary', filling it with descriptions of unusual invertebrates collected with a net trawl. He illustrated some of these descriptions with ink drawings of the creatures as viewed under a microscope.[27] At the island of St Jago (now Sao Tiago) in the Cape Verdes, where the *Beagle* was stationed from mid-January to early February 1832, Darwin's zoological discussions shifted to studies of land and intertidal invertebrates. It was here that he began his geological notebooks, commencing with a study of the tiny Quail Island in the harbour of Porto Playa on St Jago.

From this date we can follow a developing research agenda into biological and geological issues that was maintained throughout the voyage. His earliest zoological and geological entries at St Jago both employ a similar narrative style of description strongly reminiscent of Humboldt's *Personal Narrative*. His geological records very quickly demonstrate his new practical skills in field geology, and his explanations display his early conversion to Lyellianism. His notes on both zoological and geological issues interweave detailed description and experimental enquiry. There are descriptions of strata, analyses of the superposition of layers of rock, and details of experiments using a blow-pipe and chemical reagents to determine the precise mineral composition of rock specimens. There are careful descriptions of organisms in a living state and also under experimental conditions. There are discussions of the complex geological layering of formations on Quail Island and St Jago. There are estimates of the probable antiquity of mineral deposits based on the shells of various molluscs – a method worked out in detail in the latter sections of the first volume of Lyell's *Principles*. We find Darwin seeking naturalistic explanations for the layering of geological formations, and appealing to a gradualist, rather than catastrophic, subsidence and elevation of the land.[28] There is a discussion of superficial or 'diluvial' layers in which no mention is made of a sudden flood as the cause, a popular belief in British geological circles at the time.

Two general features of Darwin's writings from this time stand out. One is the interweaving of description, causal explanation and reports of occasional experimental enquiries. The other is the roughly parallel treatment of biological and geological topics. Both the interweaving and the parallelism would remain constant through the five years of the voyage. The vastly larger amount of geological writings (1,383 folios) compared to zoological writings (368 folios) reflects in part the different amounts of working time Darwin actually spent on land and sea. His geological descriptions and explanatory analysis were the results of often extended overland journeys, eight of these in South America alone, with one of nine weeks' duration (Valparaiso to Copiaco, Chile). In these investigations Darwin sought to characterise entire regions and their general stratigraphy. In his marine zoological work, by contrast, Darwin was often hampered by poor conditions. Much of the time aboard ship was spent in the rough waters of South America, where cramped working conditions and Darwin's continued sea-sickness prevented sustained concentration. Nonetheless, Darwin's zoological interests were sustained through these years, deeply focused on a few select problems presented by specific groups of organisms, primarily the colonial invertebrates and other 'plant-animals', the same group he had studied as a student in Edinburgh.[29]

VI SYNTHETIC THEORISING ON THE *BEAGLE*

As we have seen, Darwin had encountered examples of grand, synthetic theorising prior to the *Beagle* voyage. In four examples between 1834 and 1836, we find Darwin's own efforts to realise similar syntheses. The first of these projects relates to the detailed zoological enquiries. One issue that had attracted Darwin to the study of the 'plant-animals' – the groups forming the colonial marine forms (coelenterates, bryozoans, corals and also the coralline algae) – was the extent to which these creatures truly linked the animal and plant kingdoms together. Several of the works in the *Beagle*'s library dealt with the issue, including the zoological works of Lamarck.[30] Most authors he read on the topic denied a genuine link between plants and animals. But Darwin's investigations on the *Beagle* led him to the opposite conclusion. In Darwin's view, what unified plants and animals was a common mode of reproduction, centring on the action of 'dynamic' granules found in the protoplasm of colonial animals and plants. In a series of writings between 1834 and 1836, he came to the conclusion that a similar 'granular' matter was found in both the lowest plants and animals and involved in their reproduction, justifying the claim there was 'much analogy between Zoophites & Plants'.[31] This theory of a unifying vital matter, often designated 'gemmules' in the *Beagle* documents, would reappear in altered form in 1868 in the hypothesis of pangenesis.

A second example of Darwin's synthetic ambition in the *Beagle* years is his attempt, while he was still in South America, to relate his extensive geological work to biological questions. In a ten-page manuscript written in early 1834 and entitled 'Reflections on Reading my Geological Notes', Darwin summarised his examination of the geology of the eastern side of the South American continent in order to reveal it 'as one grand formation'.[32] Appealing to gradual uplift as the primary cause of geological change, but still allowing for the suddenness of its action, Darwin related this elevation of the sea floor to the appearance of life:

> May we conjecture that these [repeated elevations] [....] began with greater strides, that rocks from seas too deep for life [....] were rapidly elevated & that immediately when within a proper depth. life commenced [....] The elevations ≪rapidly≫ continued; land was produced on which great quadrupeds lived: the former inhabitants of the sea vanished (perhaps an effect of these changes) the present ones appeared ≪on the new beaches≫. – The present quadrupeds roamed about [....][33]

In this document, Darwin also queried the origin of the continent's inhabitants – 'from whence came its organized being [*sic*]' – and speculated on how the quadrupeds from south of the La Plata river 'may easily have traveled from their Northern original homes'.[34] Rapid elevation also supplied Darwin with an explanation of how species became extinct, or nearly extinct, in Patagonia. The elevation of the land, he wrote, '*seems* to have destroyed them suddenly: though in the South allowing partial re-appearances: if not destroyed highly injurious'.[35]

A third example of his efforts at integration is the so-called 'Geology Note', composed either on the island of Chiloe or at the port of Valdivia in western South America in February of 1835.[36] While on Chiloe in June and July of 1834, Darwin had been deeply impressed with the power of vegetative reproduction in the local apple trees. His interest in the general question of reproductive power and its endurance dated at least from Henslow's botanical lectures.[37] With this long-standing interest now re-awakened, Darwin began to explore the extent to which reproductive power was related to issues of geological dynamics, in particular the problem of explaining the extinction of the large 'mastodon' (*Macrauchenia patachonica*, later reclassified as a relative of the camel), whose fossilised remains he had unearthed at Port St Julian in Patagonia in January 1834.

Commenting on Lyell's discussion of the birth and death of species in the *Principles*,[38] Darwin struggled with two alternative explanations. The first, attributed by Lyell to the Italian historical geologist Giovanni Brocchi, explained the extinction of species as due to the exhaustion of a finite quantity of life force. On the Brocchian view, species extinction was thus dependent on internal causes, on analogy with the eventual extinction of a vegetative lineage propagated from an apple tree. The other view, favoured by Lyell, related the extinction of species to slow external changes in the physical conditions of existence. In the 'Geological Note', Darwin seems torn between these two explanations. He was now convinced there had been a *gradual* birth and death of species; but he recognised that this fact was consistent with both explanations of extinction. He puzzled generally over the whole notion of some species dying out and other species being born to replace them. As a 'false analogy', he thinks it plausible that there might be a limited duration of life-force in a species similar to that in apple trees, 'A ~~fact~~ ≪supposition≫ in contradiction to the fitness ~~wit~~ which the Author of Nature has now established. – '[39] The Brocchian alternative seems to have won Darwin's allegiance by the end of the voyage.

The fourth, and best known, example of Darwin's synthetic theorising is his theory of coral reef formation. His reflections along these lines began while the *Beagle* was still on the South American coast, before the ship had encountered any great reef-building corals, and were probably stimulated by his reading of Lyell's (second-hand) account of the structure and formation of the Pacific coral reefs.[40] Darwin had been instructed by his mentors before the *Beagle*'s departure to learn more about coral reefs. The corals also formed a crucial link between his functional biological investigations on the colonial invertebrates and the geological enquiries.

As Lyell made clear, a satisfactory theory of reef formation required the solution to three issues. First, it needed to explain how coral polyps grow and communicate within a reef. Darwin had been thinking about the general question of growth and communication among colonial organisms for some time, in the course of his studies of the colonial sea fans and bryozoans. In the case of these organisms, the connections between the separate colonies were contemporaneous, while the connections between the components of great coral reefs were largely historical. The second issue to be faced was the need to explain why corals grow where they do, and in particular to explain the relation of reef formation to available light. The third explanatory issue was a problem in geological dynamics: what explains the differences between fringing, barrier and atoll reefs? Lyell, for his part, had proposed that atolls, for example, were formed on the tops of rising submarine volcanoes. More generally, he emphasised the gradual elevation of the sea floor in the formation of reefs.

Except for minor encounters with coral reefs at St Jago in 1832, the east coast of South America and the Galapagos, Darwin's personal acquaintance with the great reef-forming varieties awaited contact with Tahiti on 15 November 1835.[41] Some time following the visit to these islands, he first sketched out his new theory of coral reef formation.[42] Prior to these reflections, Darwin had adopted Lyell's conclusion on the importance of elevation in bringing coral reefs into being. Now Darwin struck out on his own, producing a theory that accepted gradual Lyellian mechanisms, but which emphasised the importance of gradual subsidence in the formation of all three forms of reefs.

VII 'LIKE ANOTHER SUN [HUMBOLDT] ILLUMINES EVERYTHING I BEHOLD.'[43]

These syntheses provide much insight into Darwin's theoretical preoccupations and prowess in the *Beagle* years. Just as important are the 'general conclusions' he developed, particularly in the *Beagle Diary*, but also in the Zoological Diaries. These reflections develop the rudiments of a general philosophy of nature in which Darwin sought to integrate the land, sea, forest and landscape, encountered in a holistic experience of nature reminiscent of Humboldt's own reflections.[44] This personal experience of 'Nature' was an experience that, as Darwin later recalled, was 'intimately connected with a belief in God, [and] did not essentially differ from that which is often called the sense of sublimity'.[45] Consider his notes to himself on crossing the Andes between Valparaiso and Mendoza Chile in March of 1835:

> When we reached the crest & looked backwards, a glorious view was presented. The atmosphere so resplendently clear, the sky an intense blue, the profound valleys, the wild broken forms, the heaps of ruins piled up during the lapse of ages, the bright colored rocks, contrasted with the quiet mountains of Snow, together produced a scene I never could have imagined. Neither plant or bird, excepting a few condors wheeling around the higher pinnacles, distracted the attention from the inanimate mass. I felt glad I was by myself, it was like watching a thunderstorm, or hearing in the full orchestra a chorus of the Messiah.[46]

These emotive responses to the natural world did not shape Darwin's scientific research in a straightforward way. Rather, they reveal the general, holistic tenor of Darwin's reflections in this period, and so throw light on why it is we cannot draw sharp distinctions between 'geography', 'geology', 'zoology' and 'botany' in characterising Darwin's work at this time. Attention to the Humboldtian, integrative dimensions of Darwin's thought likewise makes sense of numerous *Diary* passages on the relations of thought and matter, the animal and the human, the civilised and the savage. As for thought and matter, in such works as the *Ansichten der Natur* of 1807, and in considerable detail in the later *Kosmos*, Humboldt rejected a sharp distinction between the living and the dead, the conscious and the unconscious, the animate and the inanimate. On animals and humans, in the *Personal Narrative*, the work of Humboldt that Darwin studied most closely in these years, Humboldt wrote of the 'intellectual powers' of monkeys, and of similarities between humans and apes.[47] And as for the civilised and the savage, Humboldt was also concerned with the relations of endemic and European peoples, and the explanation of the differences between them.[48]

Darwin's remarks on aboriginals deserve close attention in this connection, particularly those generated by his encounter with the native peoples of Tierra del Fuego in January 1833 and March 1834. Darwin did not theorise systematically about the Fuegians or other aboriginals during these years, and we have no general synthetic document of his views. His *Diary* discussions nonetheless read almost as a kind of dialogue with Humboldt. As Humboldt had concluded after his own encounter with the original peoples, Darwin was impressed with the artistic skills of the Fuegians, which he likened to 'the instinct of animals'. Again with Humboldt, Darwin believed that the Fuegians were 'essentially the same creature' as himself, and yet utterly and profoundly different – 'how little must the mind of one of these beings resemble that of an educated man. What a scale of improvement is comprehended between the faculties of a Fuegian savage & a Sir Isaac Newton! Whence have these people come? Have they remained in the same state since the creation of the world?'[49] Again like Humboldt, Darwin attributed the diversity of human beings within the one stock to the action of a creative 'Nature', rather than to the traditional Creator of.the Bible. 'Nature', Darwin wrote, 'by making habit omnipotent, has fitted the Fuegian to the climate & productions of his country.'[50] At the other end of the scale, Darwin detected a Humboldtian dynamism and energy, even attributing primitive awareness to extremely low forms of life, as when he writes of how the colonial invertebrate *Crisia* displays a 'co-sensation & a co-will over whole Coralline'.[51] Taken as a whole, the *Diary* entries and stray comments in other materials reflect an abiding, Humboldtian concern with the place of human beings in nature, and more generally with the relation of consciousness to the panoramic world his *Beagle* adventures were revealing to him.

When the *Beagle* landed at the Galapagos Archipelago in October 1835 for six weeks of sailing between the islands, interspersed with inland geological exploration and specimen collecting, Darwin had already developed considerably as a 'philosophical' naturalist. A long literature, drawing on Darwin's own later autobiographical remarks, has helped sustain a legend that the Galapagos period was crucial for the development of his later theories. In fact, the Galapagos experience was only one, if perhaps the most prominent, example among several encounters with the phenomena of island biogeography. His studies on the Falklands and the Chonos Archipelago had preceded this. The Galapagos experience in itself was neither necessary nor sufficient for the genesis of his later transmutationist views. Indeed, his time in the Galapagos appears to have had little immediate impact on his thinking. It was only after returning to England that Darwin came to emphasise the Galapagos as the site of a major epiphany.[52]

Notwithstanding the important reflections in February 1835 on species birth and death, there is nothing in the documentary archive of the *Beagle* voyage that maps directly on to the issue of the transmutation of species, not at least as Darwin engaged this issue in his post-voyage notebooks during the spring and summer of 1837. Nonetheless, we can see in the integrative efforts described in the last section, and in the holistic vision of nature outlined in this section, that Darwin the voyager was seeking to synthesise his observations along several lines of enquiry. All of this activity would form the background of his research on his return to England.

VIII 'MY HEAD IS QUITE CONFUSED WITH SO MUCH DELIGHT'[53]

Following short stops at New Zealand, Australia, the Keeling (now Cocos) Islands, Mauritius, the Cape of Good Hope (where Darwin conversed with Herschel himself), the central Atlantic Islands, Bahia (again), Brazil and the Azores, the *Beagle* reached Falmouth on

2 October 1836. The England he found on disembarking had changed much in his five years of absence. People were travelling widely on railroads; new authorities, many of them German, had entered scientific discourse; new scientific societies had been formed, and others were now flourishing, such as the British Association for the Advancement of Science, founded in the year the *Beagle* sailed. After the isolation of the long voyage, Darwin was understandably eager to share his experiences with others, and to catch up on what he had missed. Not least, there were great piles of journals and books to be read if he was to participate in debates and conversations within the scientific community. His priority was to integrate and connect his detailed investigations cautiously together. Although once planning to become a parson-naturalist, he had now decided on the career of a metropolitan gentleman of science.

It was evident to those who knew him that Darwin had returned as a highly skilled and creative investigator. A public identity as a geologist had been prepared in advance by Henslow's unauthorised publication of geological reflections from some of Darwin's letters of 1834, and by the prior reception of his shipments of South American minerals and fossils. But Darwin's geologising was only one facet of his complex intellectual make-up and rising scientific reputation. His extensive collections of birds, fish, insects and plants won admiration within the Zoological Society of London.[54] Soon associating with Lyell and with Richard Owen, London's foremost comparative anatomist, Darwin was soon engaged in the analysis of his fossil materials and their relation to geological dynamics.

By early 1837, Darwin was positioned to make the great synthesis of issues for which he is now best known. In the background stood the totality of his experiences and reflections. As he analysed his *Beagle* specimens and notebooks, he was able to draw upon the range of scientific competencies, reflections and inspirations that had filled the past five years. The training of the Edinburgh and Cambridge years; his manifold encounters with strange places and peoples; the revelations of the tropical rainforests that created an experience that Darwin wanted to 'fix for ever in my mind'[55]: all were drawn into the investigations that would occupy him for the next twenty years and beyond. When he wrote, shortly after his return, of a law governing the succession of species in time that would interest 'every philosophical naturalist', he was writing as one who had indeed become one himself.

NOTES

1. C. Darwin [1839] 1986, 164.
2. On the meaning of the term 'philosophical naturalists', see Rehbock 1983, 'Introduction' and the Introduction to this volume.
3. C. Darwin [1859] 1964, ch. 10.
4. C. Darwin 1958. For his earlier autobiographical sketch of August 1838, see F. Burkhardt *et al.* 1985–2001, *Correspondence* II, 438–41 (hereafter *CCD*). See also Browne 1995; Desmond and Moore 1991; Bowlby 1990; Bowler 1990; Brent 1981.
5. C. Darwin 1958, 9. See also Browne 1995, 23–7.
6. C. Darwin Papers, University Library, Cambridge, DAR 5, Series 1: 'Notes on Dr. Hope's Chymistry'.
7. Secord 1991.
8. Darwin to Caroline Darwin, 8 April 1826, in *CCD* I, 39.
9. On Lamarck, see R. W. Burkhardt 1977. On Geoffroy, see Rehbock 1983, ch. 1 and Appel 1987, esp. ch. 4.
10. Browne 1995, 72–82.
11. C. Darwin, 'Notebook of Observations Edinburgh, 1827', in Barrett 1977, II, 285–91. For further discussion, see Endersby, this volume.
12. Darwin to W. D. Fox, 25–29 January 1829, in *CCD* I, 74, 75 n.7.
13. Hall 1969. For membership list see Anon. 1836.
14. F. W. Hope to Darwin, 15 January 1834, *CCD* I, 363.
15. C. Darwin 1958, 22.
16. Henslow 1828, 1833.
17. *CCD* I, 112 n.3.
18. Herschel [1830] 1987, 190.
19. Herschel [1830] 1987, 144.
20. For further discussion see Hull, this volume.
21. Darwin to Caroline Darwin, 28 April 1831, in *CCD* I, 122.
22. Humboldt [1814–29] 1966, I, viii. On Humboldt's project of a 'physics of the earth' see Dettelbach 1996, 258–92. See also Nicolson 1987, 1990. For further discussion of Humboldt's relation to Darwin see Sloan 2001, R. J. Richards 1999 and Richards, this volume.
23. Darwin to Henslow, 18 May 1832, in *CCD* I, 238. See also Browne 1995, 141–3.

24. Lyell [1830–3] 1990, I, 76.
25. Lyell [1830–3] 1990, I, 163–6.
26. See list in 'The Books on Board the *Beagle*', Appendix IV in *CCD* I, 553–66.
27. Keynes 2000.
28. Darwin Papers, Cambridge, DAR 32.1, fol. 18r.
29. See Sloan 1985 for a quantitative discussion of these interests.
30. Sloan 1985, esp. 105 ff.
31. Darwin Papers, Cambridge, DAR 5, fol. 99. See full transcription of this document in Sloan 1985, 106–7.
32. Darwin Papers, Cambridge, DAR 42, fol. 7, as in Herbert 1995, 31.
33. Darwin Papers, Cambridge, DAR 42, fol. 7. Slight revisions of the transcription in Herbert 1995, 31–2.
34. Darwin Papers, Cambridge, DAR 42, fol. 10, as in Herbert 1995, 33.
35. Darwin Papers, Cambridge, DAR 42, fol. 10v, as in Herbert 1995, 33.
36. Darwin Papers, Cambridge, DAR 42, ser. 3. See full transcription in Hodge 1983, 19–20.
37. See Sloan 1986, esp. 373–87.
38. Lyell [1830–3] 1990, II, 128–31.
39. Darwin Papers, Cambridge, DAR 42, fol. 2v; Hodge 1983, 20.
40. Lyell [1830–3] 1990, II, ch. 18.
41. *Diary*, entry for 21 November 1835, in Barrett and Freeman 1986 (hereafter *Works*), I, 324.
42. Darwin Papers, Cambridge, DAR 41. See complete transcription in Stoddart 1962.
43. *Diary*, entry for 28 February 1832, *Works* I, 38.
44. See *Diary* entries for 28 February, 26 May and 19 December 1832; 9 June and 17 August 1834; 21–22 March 1835; and 1 May 1836 for examples (*Works* I).
45. C. Darwin 1958, 65. See Kohn 1996; J. Campbell 1974; Sloan 2001. On Darwin's emulation of Humboldt, see letter of Caroline Darwin to Darwin, 28 October 1833, *CCD* I, 345.
46. *Diary*, *Works* I, 266–7.
47. See Humboldt [1814–29] 1966, III, 106, 172.
48. Humboldt [1814–29] 1966, III, 240.
49. *Diary*, *Works* I, 194.
50. *Diary*, *Works* I, 195.
51. Keynes 2000, 228.
52. Sulloway 1982a, 1982b.
53. Darwin to Josiah Wedgewood, 5 October 1836, *CCD* I, 504.
54. Darwin had reserved for himself the invertebrate volume of the *Beagle* zoology. See letter of Darwin to Henslow, 14 October 1837, *CCD* II, 51.

This volume never appeared, unless one considers the various minor papers on marine invertebrates, and even the great work on the barnacles, as aspects of this original plan for an invertebrate volume. I am indebted to the valuable paper by Love (2002) for clarifying my understanding of this intended invertebrate volume of the *Zoology*.

55. *Diary*, entry for 1–6 August 1836, *Works* 1, 379.

JONATHAN HODGE

2 The notebook programmes and projects of Darwin's London years

I FROM THE *BEAGLE* YEARS TO THE LAWS OF LIFE

In March 1837, five months after returning from the *Beagle* voyage, Darwin settled in London. He was to live in the capital for five years. They were by far his most productive years intellectually. During them, he formulated almost all the main theories later published in the 1850s, 1860s and 1870s: his theory of the origin of species – natural selection; his theory of generation or reproduction and heredity – pangenesis; his theory of the origin of the moral sense in man from ancestral animal social instincts; and his interpretation of the expression of the emotions in man and animals. Of his prominent intellectual productions only two – the theory of sexual selection and the principle of divergence of varieties and species – came later, and they were conceived as elaborations of the theory of natural selection.

In these five London years, two periods were quite exceptionally consequential: the spring and early summer of 1837, immediately after his move to London, and the summer and early autumn of the following year, 1838. At each of these times Darwin made vast escalating moves in his thinking and his theoretical ambitions. By mid-September 1838, indeed, his ambitions had reached a peak never later to be surpassed. One can therefore read the rest of his life as so many sequels to the brainwork of these months.

The work was mostly done in a series of small leatherbound notebooks. In or about July 1837, Darwin opened two notebooks. One, 'A' as he labelled it, was devoted to geology; the other, 'B', was headed '*Zoonomia*' and devoted to the laws of life.[1] It is the first two dozen pages (B1–24) of entries in B that show us what comprehensive and subversive conceptions Darwin had been developing over the four months since March. For in these pages, in a single, sustained spell of writing, Darwin outlines an entire system of argumentation structured to conform to the precedent set by 'the Lamarckian system' – with its 'transmutation of species' – as presented and rejected by Charles Lyell in 1832, in the second volume of his *Principles of Geology*. B was eventually followed by C, which was filled by July 1838. It was then that Darwin opened both D, a successor to C, and M; with M devoted to 'metaphysics', meaning not, as it had of old, the theory of being, but, as it had come to mean more and more over the previous century, the theory of mind including morality and sociality. Darwin filled D and M at a much faster rate than before. Successors, E and N, were begun at the beginning of October, 1838 and continued until the next summer, 1839.

Since the 1960s, study of these notebooks and associated manuscripts has been transforming the understanding of Darwin's entire life and work, and for three reasons especially.[2] First, Darwin kept his notebook theorising secret from even his closest friends; so his voluminous correspondence throws little direct light on the life of his mind. Second, whereas older biographies followed Darwin's often seriously misleading autobiography in looking at the young man as a precursor of the later, published author, this practice is now rejected. For the arrows of causation, explanation and narration obviously require that the London Darwin should be read as a postcursor of the Edinburgh, Cambridge and *Beagle* Darwin, and the Darwin of the publishing years as the postcursor of the covert notebook theorist. Third, studied as products of their time and place – London in the 1830s – Darwin's most influential thoughts can be set in their original contexts. No legend of the London Darwin as an isolated, secretive recluse is remotely sustainable. Secretive, yes, but isolated recluse, no. He read voraciously, on all kinds of subjects within and beyond the sciences; but he also met and talked with many kinds of people. He moved in several circles, some formal such as the Geological Society, some informal such as the coterie of his brother's friends, who included prominent literary and political figures.[3] Far from fostering only narrow concerns with textual minutiae, studying Darwin's early unpublished writings can prompt reappraisals of the widest and most challenging historiographical issues, as in other cases – Marx and Freud most conspicuously.

This chapter seeks to bring out the scope and character of Darwin's zoonomical theorising in the notebook years, 1837–9; to show how the theory of natural selection was constructed over the autumn, winter and spring months of 1838–9; to indicate how Darwin's published writing developed from the work of the notebook years; and to suggest a reinterpretation of the social and economic alignment of Darwin's science.

II SPRING 1837: MEETING A SYSTEMIC CHALLENGE

Darwin's voyage around the world ended with several months mostly at sea rather than on land, and, even more than before, spent reading, writing and reflecting rather than exploring, observing and collecting. In geology his theoretical speculations had become global, as he concluded that the earth at any one time had large areas undergoing subsidence of the surface while other areas are elevated, all by roving, untiring agencies acting, à la Lyell, with uniform intensity on average through a vast past and on to an indefinite future. Darwin's theory of coral islands took its place in this comprehensive scheme; coral islands being formed, not as Lyell had said in elevations, but in slow subsidences. The theory lay, then, at the intersection of the two main clusters of Darwin's preoccupations as a scientific theorist: his Lyellian preoccupations with the stably balanced causes of terrestrial change in the physical and organic worlds; and his Grantian preoccupations with lower animal growth and reproduction ('generation') and with individual versus associated or colonial life, preoccupations going back to his apprenticeship to Robert Grant in invertebrate zoology at Edinburgh. Although countering Lyell's specific views on coral islands, Darwin was conforming himself to the master's ideals for theorising in geological science. Likewise, at the same intersection, Darwin's generational theory of species extinctions – through expiry of a limited vital duration for each species – held since early 1835, countered Lyell's view of extinctions as caused by upsets to local competitive, geographical balances, upsets initiated by climate changes, invasive immigrations and the like. Darwin's theory was, however, explicitly conformed by him to Lyell's controversial insistence that the births and deaths of species, the exchanges of new species for old, were going on continually throughout all times past, present, and so too future; while barriers and avenues to species migrations, such as mountain ranges or land bridges, were no less continually formed and destroyed by the constant, gradual action of igneous and aqueous agencies.[4] For Darwin, as for Lyell, the geologist studies the geography – of life, land and sea – in those modifications wrought over time by uniformly acting causes that have made the history recorded in the rocks.

In his geologist's historical geography for plant and animal species, Lyell had offered no account of what one might see if the birth or creation of a species came within one's experience. However, he hypothesised that each species originated in one place, not many, and as a single first pair or lone hermaphrodite, and that the place of origin was determined, providentially, by adaptational considerations alone; each species being introduced, then, at the most suitable place at that time, in its soil, climate and in the animal and plant life already there. So, conversely, any region has received those endemic species, and hence too those genera, families and orders of species that could best flourish in the conditions there. Once originated, any species multiplies in numbers, extends its range and varies in adapting to new circumstances; but the variation is limited so as never to lead to a new species arising by the modification of an old one, *pace* Lamarck and other 'transmutationists' who had urged the unlimited modifiability of species in changing circumstances. For Lyell, new species arise independently of any others, as special independent creations.[5]

Just when and why Darwin began to disagree with this Lyellian account of the origin of species has proved difficult to discern. On one reconstruction, he may well have first favoured the transmutation of species a few months before landing back in England, when pondering the distribution of certain bird species living on the mainland of South America and studied closely earlier in the voyage. However, any favouring of transmutation before his return was probably tentative and limited, for no explicit elaboration of such a commitment survives. By contrast, in March, he recorded transmutationist reflections that are far from tentative. He had now received Richard Owen's authoritative judgements on his South American mammal fossil specimens and even more decisively John Gould's on his bird specimens, especially those specimens from the Galapagos Islands.

The primary issue was for Darwin raised by the close resemblance between many bird species that Gould said were peculiar to the Galapagos and species on the mainland – species often of genera confined to South America or at least to the New World. As Darwin now thought, these resemblances defied any explanatory appeal, such as Lyell would make, to a principle of adaptation to conditions at the place of origin; because the conditions on the rainy, forested mainland were so different from those on the arid, barren islands. Why, despite this difference in conditions, had the new species – originating on the new island land raised from beneath the ocean seas – resembled closely species already living on the nearest, older, continental land? The resemblances were explicable by heredity with migration and transmutation; as, likewise, with the resemblance between the extinct and extant mainland mammal species. Ancestral heredity and adaptive modification can explain what adaptation alone cannot.[6]

Darwin saw a parallel between this disagreement with Lyell and his earlier one over extinction. Species deaths from the expiry of limited species vital durations were his alternative to the Lyellian failures of species to adapt to new conditions. Likewise, a genus or family may be unrepresented on a continent today not because its species are ill adapted to conditions there, but because no descendants of the single species ancestral to the group have yet migrated there. Species are adapted to their locations, but the original absences of supra-specific groups from these regions are not explicable, any more than are extinctions, by exclusive reference to adaptive considerations. Generally, then, ancestry and so transmutation as well as adaptation has determined the timing and placing of the coming in and going out of species on the Lyellian earth's surface. For extinctions, Darwin – drawing yet further on his Grantian preoccupations with generation – now defends limited vital durations for species, as for plant graft successions, by insisting that all generation, sexual or otherwise, has a common feature in proceeding by division. He does not, however, go on to integrate his new commitment to species originations by transmutation with his views on generation.[7]

These March 1837 reflections are highly theoretical, abstract and general, but they are limited in what they engage. Confined to common ancestry and descent with adaptive diversification within genera, families and orders, they do not consider how change might go over an unlimitedly long run, nor therefore how change and progress have gone from the earliest life of all up to the arrival in recent times of man himself.

It is in the next four months that Darwin does make the momentous move to treating all these most comprehensive and controversial issues in an explicit, systemic way. Surprisingly, there is no biographical tradition of confronting the full force of the inevitable query: Why did he, how could he, do this? A documentary difficulty may make the query harder to answer but it does not absolve biography from the attempt; for almost no documents survive from these four months that record how the transition was motivated and made; and it may be that Darwin committed few such reflections to paper, desperately busy as he was with preparing for publication his *Journal of Researches into the Geology and Natural History of the Various Countries Visited by H.M.S. Beagle* (1839). It is then to the July 1837 opening of *Notebook* B itself that one has to turn, expounding as it does the outcome of this transition. This exposition shows that one has, more than anything else, to look to Darwin's relations at this time with four sources of precedental instruction and inspiration: Lyell, Lamarck, Grant and his own grandfather, Erasmus Darwin.

Lyell had insisted that anyone favouring the transmutation of species had to consider all the further issues, about spontaneous generations, life's progress from monads to mammals and an ape ancestry for man, raised by Lamarck's entire system. Lyell's insistence was meant as a warning; but Darwin took it as a challenge defining his systemic agenda. But why should he be moved to meet this challenge? A decade before, Grant had not only given Darwin preoccupations with generation to last him a lifetime, he had surprised him with explicit admiration for Lamarck's views. While Grant had had no new direct roles in Darwin's thinking since then, he had evidently encouraged his protégé when at Edinburgh to study the writings, especially the *Zoonomia* (1794–6), of another whom Grant admired much: Darwin's grandfather, an author often associated with Lamarck's views since he also had upheld a natural, prolonged production of the highest from the lowest life and an ape ancestry for man. The young student grandson had read, too, a biography of Erasmus Darwin, so beginning half a century of fascination – even identification – with his forebear marked eventually by the writing of a new biographical memoir.[8] In the summer of 1837, he not only took *Zoonomia* as his own title and henceforth habitually compared his thoughts with that book's teachings on life and mind, he was also soon theorising that the very purpose of sexual generation, itself the *sine qua non* for all adaptive and progressive change in life, was to enable animals to transmit their constitutional characters not merely to their children but also their grandchildren.

Seeing how the grandpaternal precedent moved Darwin to take up Lyell's challenge indicates where Darwin's agenda was located for him socially. Although notorious in conservative and orthodox circles for his sympathies with the French Revolution and his threats to biblical religion, Erasmus Darwin had never been seen as a skeleton in the family closet. On the contrary, his name was celebrated and his books cherished, most decisively by his son, Charles Darwin's revered father, a man his children knew to be religiously no believer. The grandfather's views, far from being dissociated from the family's high social rank and exceptional wealth, were then, for the grandson, fully concordant with their gentlemanly status and continuing assimilation – through marriages, friendships and more tangible investments in extensive town and country property – to those ranks of the landed gentry standing in the hierarchy of national society just below the aristocracy proper and distinctly above those mercantile burghers and others known to the French as the bourgeoisie. For Darwin to be inspired by the family's precedent in meeting the challenge in the response made to Lamarck by Lyell – himself a prominent practitioner of landed, gentry science – was to affirm a concordance between this intellectual life and this economic livelihood.

III THE OPENING OF *NOTEBOOK* B, JULY 1837: AN INAUGURAL SKETCH OF A SYSTEM AND ITS FIRST REVISIONS

Lamarck's own articulation of his system made primary the action of fluids within all living bodies, actions constituting life itself and producing a recurrent escalation of organisation up a series of classes and large families from monads to mammals. Adaptive responses to changing external circumstances accounted for ramifying departures, within classes, from this serial progression. The indefinite mutability of species was, then, making possible both linear progress and arboriform diversification. By contrast Lyell's exposition of the system opens with the unlimited mutability of species adapting to changing conditions allowing a ramifying common descent, not merely for families or orders of species but, ultimately, for all life from a single, common ancestral origin. The second part of Lyell's exposition then presents the progress from monads to mammals, its internal causes, and eventual outcome in the ascent of man. Darwin's systemic sketch opening *Notebook* B likewise only introduces progress from monads to mammals and man in its second, final, part. For the first part takes up two prior tasks: explaining how the powers peculiar to all sexual generation make possible adaptive changes in altering circumstances and so the formation of new species from old; and explaining how divergent reiterations of such species formations entail over aeons a common descent for families and classes, so providing explanations for those geographical and palaeontological generalisations about species that remain inexplicable if species are supposed to have arisen in independent creations whose timing and placing have been determined by adaptational considerations alone. After this first part, corresponding to the first part of Lyell on Lamarck, Darwin goes to his second part, again matching Lyell on Lamarck, to consider the progressive tendencies raising life from monadic, infusorial beginnings up to mammalian perfection. However, he invokes no additional internal causes making for progress, assuming rather that these progressive tendencies arise from adaptive changes and so from the same powers of sexual generation invoked in his sketch's very first sentences.[9]

Those powers, Darwin argued there, arise from the two features distinguishing all sexual from any asexual generation: maturation in the offspring produced and the mating, crossing, of two parents. The first is innovative in enabling new adaptive variations to be acquired in altered circumstances; the second is counterinnovative when offspring are in character intermediate between their two parents. Migration and isolation of a few individuals and consequent inbreeding in new circumstances can circumvent this counterinnovative action of crossing, and so allow a new variety to form, and then diverge sufficiently from the parent stock as to become eventually intersterile with that parent stock and so no mere variety but a new species. It is the ramifying reiterations of such species formations that make possible the adaptive diversification of a family or class from its common ancestral species. However, this argumentation, in Darwin's first part, does not resolve all the issues engaged in his second part. Here all change is not only adaptive but also progressive. Some lowly species living in constant conditions may not change at all; while other species do so only slowly. There is no necessitation of an invariable rate of change nor then of progress. Within any group, high extinct species produced by fast-changing lines of descent can, then, be succeeded by lower species branching out from old, slow, low lines. If ramified and varied in rate according to circumstances, a tendency for progress in all adaptive species formations can accommodate any regressions in the palaeontological successions of supraspecific groups. Darwin follows Lamarck in having progress initiated by monads produced all the time in spontaneous generations; but, unlike Lamarck, he supposes that the lifetime of any monad's entire issue, although vast, is limited. So those lines of life that have changed and therefore progressed most must have changed most quickly; hence mammal species have, as Lyell had noted, shorter species lifetimes than molluscs do; hence too among species of higher animals there are more gaps of character from more extinctions. Species deaths by extinctions are compensated for by splittings and branchings, so that the total number of species is, as in Lyell, constant on a long run average. Although the buddings of the tree of life are dependent on contingent geographical circumstances and so irregular, there is a tendency towards threefold diversifications into aquatic, aerial and terrestrial ways of life; if a dominant one of these, the terrestrial say, has further aquatic and aerial issue then a tendency for groups to have five sub-groups – as the so-called quinarian taxonomists taught – is explained.

Such is Darwin's inaugural sketch of a zoonomical system (B1–24). Strikingly, he soon revises consequentially not the first part (from sexual generation to species formation and biogeography) but the second part on monads, progress and the tree of life. For he quickly rejects the limited monad lifetime as entailing falsely the eventual simultaneous extinctions of all the species within one family or order. He then has to find another account of the correlation between greater character gaps, more branched affinities, shorter species lifetimes and higher grades of organisation. Reinterpreting the correlation, he concludes that gaps within and between groups correlate not with the organisational perfection of the groups but with their taxonomic width. For, in the buddings and splittings in the tree of species branchings, when one ancestral species has a dozen descendent species, there must be a dozen lines ending without splitting in extinctions, given that the total species number is not increasing. In the greater multiplying of species in the diversifying descent of a large group, a class, say, rather than a mere genus, there will be vastly more extinctions and so more gaps in character, within and between such groups.

With this new version of the tree of life, any special properties the monads had are explanatorily redundant and they are henceforth no longer invoked. For what remains, for all times since the earliest life on earth, is the multiplicative and diversifying splitting and branching of some species and the extinctions of others. In this arboriform process, any species as a quasi-individual is born, lives and dies but once; and so likewise any supraspecific group issuing from its single, ancestral species. Moreover, only one species in an ancestral group has had descendants in any particular offspring group, so there is no general tendency for fish species, say, to have mammalian descendants. One fish species did so once, due presumably to exceptional circumstances, as all the rest have not. Darwin's new tree of life with its treatment, at once Lyellian and Grantian in its resources, of species as generating, dividing and multiplying quasi-individuals, has now departed fundamentally from any scheme, such as Lamarck's, of recurrent escalations of life through a given array of particular taxonomic types each distinguished by its own peculiar organisational structure (B25–44). And so, indeed, will Darwin understand his tree for the rest of his own life. For he has now reached, in the summer of 1837, an abstract, referentially anonymous scheme like the one familiar from the sole illustration in the *Origin*, labelled, as is that diagram, not with the names of particular groups – fish or finches or whatever – but only with letters and numbers representing its schematic themes about the cumulative arboriform outcome from the births, lives and deaths of species in the indefinitely long run of times past and present.

IV FROM SUMMER 1837 TO SPRING 1838: DEVELOPING THE THEORY OF ADAPTIVE SPECIES FORMATIONS

As Darwin continued his systemic zoonomical theorising over the coming months, he formulated a further project: a promissory prospect to be made possible by what he was doing, but not to be actually pursued, only contemplated as a future agenda. The structure of this prospective project was taken directly from the precedent set by the customary interpretation of the most prestigious physical science of the day: Newtonian celestial mechanics. This science was seen to have a threefold pyramidal structure. At the base were particular astronomical observations, such as Tycho Brahe had supplied, of planetary motions. In the next level up were lawful generalisations about those motions, most prominently the laws Kepler had found – that the planets move in ellipses, for instance. These were descriptive not causal laws. Finally, at the top level there are causes: the lawful causes, the lawful forces of gravitation and inertia, which enabled Newton to subsume and explain what Kepler and Tycho had contributed. Darwin's promissory project was to have such a threefold structuring. At the bottom would be assembled cases of geographical series of congeneric species – cases of two or more very similar species that are geographical neighbours. On the assumption that new species arise from the transmutation of earlier ones, such a geographical series could be interpreted as a record of a temporal succession whereby one species has given rise to others. So interpreted, such instances of change between species allow and support generalisations about these changes: laws of change in Darwin's phrase, just as Tycho's instances of planetary motion enabled Kepler to discern his laws. Finally, then, Darwin's project would proceed to the third, consummating achievement: finding lawful causes of change that explain the causeless laws below. These lawful causes of change would, indeed, invoke the very laws of life, the lawful causation that constitutes life itself.[10] On this prospect, then, the theory of adaptive species formation is facilitative and prolegomenal; it makes possible the interpretation of accessible geographical facts as records of changes over time that would not otherwise be knowable. In this strategy, Darwin was following Lyellian precedents. Lyell had investigated how species are observably limited in space today, so as to infer generalisations about what limits their duration in time and causes their eventual extinctions.

Because Darwin only discussed this prospective project briefly and never worked at completing it, only its outline character can be discerned from his notebooks. What he did work at from July 1837 was improving the species formation theorising by explaining two permanent changes: adaptive divergence in structures and instincts and loss of fertility in crossings with the parent stock. Cases of nonblending of parental characters, especially in human interracial crosses, Darwin took as signs of incipient constitutional incompatibility between the races. An instinctive aversion to interracial pairing suggested, moreover, that greater constitutional divergence would be accompanied by a consistent disinclination to interbreeding, which would then allow constitutional divergence to proceed to a further stage when intersterility would arise. At this stage racial divergence would have become species divergence, for all the usual criteria for specific distinction would have been met (B33–4; B120). This line of thought got heavy support, in Darwin's view, when the amateur ornithologist William Yarrell told him that when two breeds of domestic animals are crossed – two breeds of dogs, say – the offspring have the characters of the older breed. Darwin was to elaborate many corollaries from this generalisation, which he would dignify as Yarrell's law. He soon took it to show that over successive generations any hereditarily perpetuated characters became more and more firmly and powerfully embedded in the hereditary constitution, so that a blending constitutional compromise between two very old breeds is impossible, and that, through a natural coordination of mind and body, they would be instinctively averse to interbreeding.[11]

This reflection gave him a new way of comparing and contrasting species formation in the wild and race formation in domesticated species; and so a new way to counter Lyell's extensive invocations of domestic breed formation in discrediting any transmutations of species. Some breeds of dog, for example, that are markedly different in size, build and habits, interbreed readily and successfully, Darwin reflected; whereas wild species differing to that extent do not. He took it that domestication itself, this unnatural condition, vitiated the instinctive aversion to interbreeding that naturally in the wild would accompany such a degree of divergence in structural and habitual characters. On this reasoning, as Darwin saw it, conspecific domestic races were providing analogical support for his theory of species formation in the wild. For dog, sheep and cattle breeds, say, showed how character divergence between varieties could arise over a long succession of generations, a divergence wider than many wild congeneric species showed; and, on the vitiation of instincts under domestication premise, they confirmed that in the wild such varieties would not interbreed and so would not be counted by naturalists as varieties but as good species. So, the very absence of very distinct varieties in wild species is evidence that varieties in the wild, unlike races under domestication, do become species by ceasing to interbreed and then going on to become incapable of interbreeding.

From the early months of 1838, Darwin persistently drew a contrast between two sorts of domestic races: natural races or varieties and artificial ones. The natural varieties are due to natural causes rather than to human artifice. Such natural varieties are local varieties, isolated regionally so as not to be interbreeding with others, and distinguished by characters that arose as they adapted slowly over many generations to local conditions and circumstances. By contrast artificial varieties are often monstrous, distinguished by variations that have arisen as rare, maturational accidents; and these variations have only persisted thanks to the human art of picking, selective breeding, that has made races, often in a few generations, which could never be formed and flourish without benefit of that human art. As Darwin read about the art of selective breeding, he became more convinced at this time that species formation in the wild was to be compared with natural variety formation in domesticated species and contrasted with the making of artificial varieties.

Darwin's view of species formation was always that it was an adaptive achievement. Rather than becoming extinct, dying without issue, a species may succeed in adapting sufficiently to new circumstances to give rise to one or more offspring species. Darwin came to contrast adaptive variations in individuals with monstrous variations. When a puppy moves to a cold climate and grows thicker fur than its parents, that is an adaptation. The variation is induced by the surrounding conditions and is advantageous. By contrast, a puppy born with thick fur in a warmer country is a monstrous variation: it is a response, in a sense an adaptive response, to rare, unhealthy conditions within the womb. Both adaptive and monstrous variations are made possible by sexual generation; but only the adaptive variations contribute to species formation; rare, monstrous variations are blended out in crossing and are less able to survive and procreate anyway. More and more, Darwin came to see adaptive structural variations as initiated by changes in habits and so in the use of organs. If jaguars, in his example, take up swimming for fish prey when their country becomes flooded, then a new variety distinguished by webbed feet could arise through the inheritance of this acquired character. This webbed-foot exemplar instantiated for Darwin his long-standing view of threefold diversifications into aerial, aquatic and terrestrial ways of life. Such webbed foot exemplars were prominent in Lamarck and in Lyell's epitome of him, too. For Darwin, the initiation of structural change by habit change complemented his view of instinctive aversions to interbreeding as initiating eventual species formation (C62–6 and 82–5).

V FROM SUMMER 1837 TO SUMMER 1838: THE TREE OF LIFE, PROGRESS AND SPECIES PROPAGATION

The modifications Darwin was making to his theory of species formation or species propagation did not in themselves call for further revisions to the tree of life as the representation of how these propagations proliferated over long aeons. From as early as the summer of 1837, the tree was conceived as asexually growing, in that a group of offspring species issued from a single parental species not from a pairing of two. However, species propagations were in a sense quasi-sexual, in that a species changing in response to altered circumstances was, as Darwin saw it, quasi-mating with those fresh circumstances. Without the influence of fresh circumstances, the species would die childless, with no successor offspring species, when its limited vital duration expired, like an asexual tree grafting succession. Conversely, just as such an asexual succession can avoid childless death through a fresh sexual union, so a species is saved from extinction, death without issue, by its quasi-sexual interaction with those circumstances (B61–72).

These analogies of Darwin's do not make the growth of the tree of life analogous to the maturation of a single organism, for in no sense has the tree grown up maturationally since the Carboniferous age or indeed any earlier time in the past; grown yes, but not grown up. Nor then is this unending growth seen as fulfilling any original maturational destiny or completing any prior plan finally consummated, say, with man's arrival. The construction of the tree as a representation of the history facilitated no such interpretations of it. And, indeed, Darwin never revised it so as to make it do so. However, he remains throughout the notebook years and beyond seriously committed to progress in the history of life if not to any completion, maturational or otherwise. Here he had, as he was very aware, to worry about challenging Lyell, who had opposed all claims that the fossils evidenced a progression in the creation of the main types of life. One way Darwin could avoid a direct challenge was to take his tree growth as a representation only of those changes since the time – whenever that might have been – when the earth was first stocked with all those main types. However, in accepting that individual embryonic maturations ('ontogenies' in the later jargon) recapitulate all past ancestral changes ('phylogenies'), he had to contemplate an earth when the reptile ancestors of today's mammals had not yet had any mammal descendants, an earth which was, moreover, *pace* Lyell, not fit perhaps for mammals, from too little cooling from an original molten state. Again, although reluctant to assume that the eventual formation of man with his distinctive moral life was the sole purpose of all the prior, prehuman progress of life, he was drawn to assume that it was one purpose of the institution by God of those laws of generation that made that progress not just possible but inevitable if not invariable (B49; E48–9).

A decision Darwin was making in the summer of 1838 served to segregate these commitments concerning progress from the formulation of his theory of species propagation itself. He accepted the view that ideally a theory offered to explain certain kinds of facts should be supported in two ways. It should be supported both independently of those facts it is being used to explain and by showing how well it does explain them.[12] In conformity with this ideal and so too with structural precedents in his July 1837 sketch and in Lyell's version of Lamarck, Darwin resolved to argue for his species propagation theory in two ways. First, he would argue for it by citing the peculiar powers of sexual generation, including Yarellian constitutional embedding, and by citing the diversification of domesticated species into natural varieties. Here then he would be establishing the existence in nature of these causes and their adequacy, their competence, to bring about adaptive species formations in any long run of time, so as to yield such species propagations and diversifications as the tree of life represented. Then, in a second body of argumentation he would show how this theory could explain, could connect and make intelligible, many different kinds of facts about species: biogeographical facts, palaeontological facts, comparative embryological facts and so on. This twofold structure and strategy of argumentation is very much what he would adopt in arguing for his theory of natural selection in the *Origin*.[13] And Darwin's commitment to it was in place many months before he had first formulated that theory. One consequence, in the summer of 1838, of designing his argumentational case in this way, was that those issues – concerning the first forms of life, the subsequent progress in life's ascent and any correlation that ascent may have had with any cooling and calming of an earth originally nebular and molten – would appear not in the presentation of the species propagation theory itself, nor in presenting its evidential credentials independently of its explanatory virtues; but later on in the exposition, when those virtues were elaborated for biogeography, palaeontology, embryology and so on. In the summer of 1838, Darwin was only resolving to write in this way on his theory's behalf; his notebooks contain no sustained acting upon that resolution. What they do show, however, is that he was, much more than before, seeing his various conclusions on diverse topics as being, eventually, potentially publishable, public science.

VI SUMMER 1838: EARTH, LIFE AND MIND

The summer of 1838 was a remarkable period in Darwin's life and work. He contemplated marriage for the first time, it seems, even drawing up the pros and cons in a written note. He began to date some of the entries in his notebooks. He wrote an autobiographical memoir of his youngest years. He began keeping a record of his health and the anxieties it gave him. A new, heightened awareness of his own vitality, mortality and sexuality shows itself in and between the lines of much that he writes from now on.

His notebook work becomes more concerned with taking stock and assessing where he stands. He is explicit in encapsulating his views on this or that subject by summarising what his 'theory' says, his theory of sexual differentiation, say, or of geographical distribution. In July, opening his new *Notebook* M, on 'metaphysics', he records several dozen pages of anecdotes, generalisations and abstract reflections arising from discussions with his father on the mind in health and disease, on reasoning, memory and madness. In September, he opens a new section of his *Notebook* D at the back of that notebook, a section devoted to generation, an enquiry now emerging as a distinct endeavour in its own right. He ranges into religion and ethics as never before, and indeed as never again, in so far as the scope, ambition and intensity of his intellectual and emotional questionings will not exceed this peak hereafter. The earth, life and mind are now all encompassed by the divisions of his notebook labour.

On the earth, indeed, he had already earned a reputation as a published authority on grand theoretical issues, having in May gone public with his most comprehensive claims about the earth's crust and its up and down movements upon a fluid interior. In his *Notebook* A he now, covertly, considers what no disciple of Lyell should: the possible beginnings of the earth and even its end; violating as he does Lyell's echoes of Hutton's insistence that the earth as known from our observations shows no vestige of a beginning and no prospect of an end (A104–21). Darwin will, however, never violate this Huttonian proscription in any public text.

Darwin had two reasons for taking up mind as a special subject. First, his general account of adaptive changes in all species, plant or animal, had their changes initiated by habits, a faculty of mind broadly construed to include even lowly plant life. Second, committed as always to comprehend mankind in his theory of species propagation, Darwin now took up the challenge of finding natural, gradual causes for that consciousness and conscientiousness commonly deemed distinctive of our species. This challenge led him to engage some long-standing doctrines and traditions. The inheritance of thought from parents to offspring denies any equation of thought with conscious mentation, Darwin argued. Again, one should look to our animal ancestors, not, as Plato would have us, to some previous existence of the soul in heaven, for the source of our innate ideas. Studying the baboon, Darwin muses, can tell us more about the mind than reading Locke can. Human morality could have arisen, must have indeed, once the social instincts we share with animals were interacting with the intellect – the reasoning and memory – possessed by early humans. The elaboration of this theory required in 1838 the inheritance of acquired effects of mental habits, and all Darwin's later versions of the theory will do so too. In bringing mind within his science, Darwin declared himself a materialist and a necessitarian ('determinist' in later jargon); for mental actions, as the functions of the brain, are caused by material organisation. And, just as chance in the physical world is not a lack of causation but only a lack of known causation, so – Darwin is explicit – the illusion of free will is likewise only an illusion that there is no causal necessitation of the feeling, belief or decision enacted by the mind. Having subsumed mind materially and causally within his science at this time, Darwin never later had to construct new ways to secure the continuity between man and animals or between man and the lawful order of nature.[14]

His thoughts about generation now followed two new lines.[15] First, he concluded that in ontogeny, and hence in phylogeny, hermaphroditic sex precedes the separation in sexes found in higher animals. Second, he considers whether the egg or ovule in a female that is fertilised by the male's insemination may be, prior to that fertilisation, like an asexual bud that is therefore incapable of maturing and through maturation of acquiring novel variations from the influence on it of prenatal and postnatal conditions. These two lines of thought, once integrated, led to new extensions to the longstanding view that all adaptive change is ultimately made possible by the maturations and matings distinctive of sexual generation. They led, too, to a fresh examination of how the variations occurring in maturing individuals now are related to those past, long past, progressive changes made by their ancestors and recapitulated in their own ontogenies. The need to integrate the understanding of adaptation and of progress becomes more acute. Darwin's integration insists that new variations will have to be in harmony with the older changes now being recapitulated; but he does not conclude from this that progress in the scale of organisation is due to any inherent tendency that counters the tendency to change adaptively in changing circumstances, and he insists that while the acquisition of heritable variation by maturing offspring is the very purpose of sexual generation, that purpose is sometimes fulfilled by variations that may bring neither rises in the scale of organisation nor advantageous new characters. These novel reflections on sexual generation did not, then, call for any revisions in the species propagation theory, as Darwin had already formulated it earlier in the year.

VII SUMMER 1838: GOD, MAN, SCIENCE AND NATURE

When Darwin reflects at this time on God and man, one theme dominates: the greatness of God and by contrast the lowliness of man. God is, especially, too great to be properly presumed to intervene in nature in special, miraculous creations of particular species with their distinctive detailed structures and habits. God's greatness is manifest in his institution of very general causal laws that bring about such productions naturally and lawfully, just as physical science has shown planetary motions to be subject to lawful government and not miraculous interference. Man's lowliness makes it proper for him to see himself not as an angelic species, but as an animal without any supernatural spark of divinity that might put him beyond scientific, lawful causal explanation. There is a God and men truthfully believe there is, but this belief like any other is the result of the brain's material organisation which is itself the outcome of a long, gradual improvement of our animal ancestry. God designed the laws of nature so as to ensure this and all the other outcomes of life's changes and progress. Human humility about human lowliness entails, then, that science discloses the designed providence of the lawful order of nature; but entails, too, that the naturalist can never expect to discern the Divine intention fulfilled by particular structures or relations among individuals or species. To attempt to read the Divine Mind is to forget how far above the humble human it is, and to forget how far below Divine knowledge is human knowledge. This humility is consistent with cognitive optimism about nature, however. Human brains and minds are fitted, ultimately through their improvement in lawfully ordained changes, to infer from observation and experience what are the laws of nature, including the laws of life.

In taking these stances, Darwin found encouragement and enlightenment in Auguste Comte's views and also in William Whewell's very different views. Comte's thesis, that human thought about nature and man moves from theological through metaphysical (*sensu* theory of being) and finally to scientific phases, delights Darwin, who sees himself taking zoology from theology to science. But Darwin, unlike Comte, did not think that causal theories give way to acausal lawful generalisations as science goes from the metaphysical to the scientific phase. On Darwin's ideal of science the very object of the enquiry is to find real, true, known causes: lawful causes, of course. Darwin welcomed Whewell's Kantian insistence that *a priori* principles, such as the principle that every event has a cause, have to be brought presuppositionally to the interpretation of experience and not inferred as conclusions from experience if there is to be scientific knowledge. Whewell, drawing on Plato, took these principles to be Divine Ideas implanted in man's soul at creation. Darwin, invoking his doctrine of instincts as habits become hereditary over long successions of past generations, took these principles, *a priori* as they are now known, to have originated as *a posteriori* generalisations learned from earlier, ancestral experiences. This learning depended ultimately on designed laws, but not in any way that made man's capacity to do science depend on any spark of supernatural divinity making his thinking deeply discontinuous with animal mentality. Indeed, many animals seem to think in accord with these same *a priori* principles.[16]

No exclusively biblical belief has any authority in Darwin's science; his notebooks make no appeals to Old Testament events or chronologies; and the New Testament is cited for barely more than its morality of treating one's neighbour as oneself. More surprisingly, Darwin consistently shows no concern for a life after death made possible by any immortality of an immaterial soul – an intense preoccupation of Lyell when contemplating Lamarck's and later Darwin's own theories. Nor is it easy to discern the ground for Darwin's, lack of concern for a person's, even his own, fate after death. Perhaps he counted on the Unitarian Joseph Priestley having been right in thinking that people are resurrected bodily, in a life after this one that is consistent with a materialist denial of any soul ever existing as a separable immaterial substance. At the end of the next decade, Darwin will be deeply disconcerted by the old Christian teaching that disbelievers such as his father suffer endless punishment after death; but the Darwin of the notebook years, although full of anxieties about his bodily ills and about the risk from inbreeding – he was engaged in the autumn of 1838 to his cousin – seems content to leave unexplicated the possible import of his science, including his 'metaphysics', for the prospect of life after death, an issue he knew formed the very rationale for so much religious doctrine and sentiment.[17]

VIII FROM AUTUMN 1838 TO SPRING 1839: THE CONSTRUCTION OF THE THEORY OF NATURAL SELECTION

From the middle of September 1838 Darwin's pace slows strikingly. The theory of natural selection emerges gradually, from late September 1838 to mid-March 1839, in languid, intermittent notebook theorising work; so discrediting any stereotypes – fostered by Darwin's later reminiscences and much scholarship in the same vein – of a single moment of decisive insight during intense activity.[18] Nor is this the making of a theory where there was none before. Rather, Darwin is making successive modifications to the earlier theory of adaptive species formation, 'my theory' as it had long been called and will continue to be so. Despite innovations on other topics, the busy summer of 1838 had seen no direct modifications to that earlier theory; and, conversely, over the months of the emergence of natural selection, in changing his mind about adaptive species formations Darwin keeps constant his views on those other topics, concerning the earth, life and mind. The new theory's development involves no general rethinking of the widest agendas.

A first modification adds to the earlier theory while replacing none of it. On 28 September, Darwin reflects on his reading of Thomas Robert Malthus on population (D134–5).[19] He dwells initially on the implications of Malthusian superfecundity for the liability of species to become extinct in changing conditions. Then in just one final sentence he considers its implications for the species surviving such changes. Reading in Malthus of some human populations doubling in quarter of a century and of Malthus' general analysis of the checks to population, Darwin concludes that all species are pressing so hard on others that there is everywhere a fragile competitive balance that even very slightly changing conditions can upset, so bringing to some species total population loss. For Darwin this insight allowed a wholehearted return to Lyell's view of extinctions, and so an abandonment – never to be reversed – of his own view, going back to 1835, that some extinctions at least came from an expiry of limited vital duration rather than from external contingencies. A generational theory was thus replaced with an ecological one (to use an anachronism for Darwin's and Lyell's thinking about the 'economy of nature').

So much for the losing species then, but what of the winners? In his closing sentence Darwin looks to them in considering what is 'the final cause' (his phrase) of all this populational pressing. It is, he argues, to sort out proper, or fitting, structure and so to adapt structure to these changes in conditions. Structure is then adaptively improved in animals and plants, just as, he reflects, Malthus shows how the energy of ancient peoples was providentially enhanced by life and death struggles as excessive fertility forced their tribal migrations and imperial invasions onto common contested ground. Thus does Darwin respond to Malthus as one theist extending another's teleology and theodicy for superfecundity and empire.

This Malthusian sorting is proceeding both within and among species; but no analogy, even implicit, is drawn with the picking or selecting practised by human breeders. Nor is there any shift here away from Darwin's views on how sexual generation ensures adaptive change in changing conditions. Indeed, what Darwin dwells on over the next two months is how this sorting bears on the acquiring of advantageous variations in individual maturations, and so bears also on his sustained geological preoccupation at this time with relations between the exchanges of species and the changes of conditions over vast periods of time. Only a structural variation that is adaptive for the whole lifetime of an individual will, he emphasises, be retained and not eliminated in the Malthusian crush of population over many generations; variations adaptive to foetal circumstances alone will not do so. Retained variations will eventually become, by Yarrellian embedding, strongly heritable and so, not being replaced by later modifications, can be accumulated in progressive changes over long periods of time. The new Malthusian insights are thus integrated with earlier views on both adaptation and progress.

On 27 November, in his *Notebook* N (the sequel, recall, to M on subjects metaphysical), Darwin pursues a topic distinct from long-run adaptation and progress but bearing directly upon it (N42). For he here makes for the first time an explicit contrast between two principles both capable of explaining how adaptive change in structures and habits could proceed in the short run. One 'principle' is familiar enough, indeed: an adult blacksmith, thanks to the inherited effects of his habits, has children – sons at least – with strong arms. The other principle has no precise precedent in any earlier reflections: any children whom chance has produced with strong arms outlive others. The contrast is direct. Chance production means here, as it has all along for Darwin, production by small, hidden and rare causes effective prenatally, so that the opposite of chance is postnatal habits. What is new, then, is the conviction that those products of chance with the same benefits as the effects of habits can contribute to adaptive change; because, although rare, individuals with such beneficial variant structures will survive over future generations at others' expense. However, Darwin acknowledges a difficulty in deciding which adaptive structures – and instincts, because these principles apply, he notes, to brain changes – have been due to which of the two principles. By the Sunday after Tuesday the 27th, he is, in E, again considering principles. This time there are 'three principles' and they can, he says, 'account for all' (E58). Strikingly, none of the three is new to him: that grandchildren resemble grandfathers; that there is variation in changing circumstances; and that fertility exceeds what food can support. These three principles are consistent with the earlier two; and Darwin may well have constructed their conjunction so as to subsume those earlier two while circumventing the unresolved difficulty of deciding which adaptive changes should be credited to which one of those two. Such a reading certainly fits what Darwin will say in the weeks, indeed decades, to come.

A further innovation is made within a few days perhaps, and within a fortnight at most. It arises, it seems, from Darwin's comparing of wild predatory canine species with sporting breeds among domesticated dogs. Strikingly reversing what he has been saying for months, Darwin now decides that there is at work in nature among wild species a process of 'picking' or selective breeding just as in man's making of varieties of domestic species (E63). Nature's Malthusian sorting is now reinterpreted as nature's picking. He is soon arguing that because nature's selective breeding is so vastly more prolonged, more discriminating and more comprehensive than man's, a causal analogy can be conformed to the traditional form of proportionality: the greater cause, selection by nature, is adequate to proportionally greater effects than the intraspecific adaptive divergence produced by the much lesser cause, man's selection; these greater effects could include, then, the unlimited interspecific adaptive divergences in the tree of life (E71). Species formations henceforth are to be compared, by Darwin, not as before with local, natural varieties in domestic species, but with varieties made by the human art that has its natural analogue in the selective breeding entailed by the struggle for existence. By March 1839, Darwin is resolving to argue publicly that 'my theory' ascribes species formations to a natural process of selection 'analogous' to man's (E118). The transformations of 'my theory' making this analogy essential to its very formulation have now given it the structure and content it will have twenty years later in the *Origin*. What these transformations have not done is to resolve the indecision over the two principles of 27 November. Man's selective breeding, Darwin will always accept, works sometimes with chance variations, sometimes with the heritable effects of habits. This selective breeding analogy, like the three principles, will always, then, subsume both of those two.

Man's and nature's selective breeding depend equally for their efficacy on the special powers of sexual as opposed to asexual generation. Comparing and contrasting the two kinds of selective breeding does not replace the comparing and contrasting of the two kinds of generation. But the theory of natural selection, as an ecological – economy of nature – theory now constituted by the breeding analogy, can and will have its argumentation developed separately from any theorising about all generation. As a theory of the main cause of the growth, the generation, of the tree of life, natural selection, with its Lyellian and Malthusian struggles among and within species, can then be detached from any theory of generation that pursues Darwin's even older Grantian preoccupations. But both enterprises will continue to draw inspiration from the grandpaternal precedent set by Erasmus Darwin.

IX FROM THE NOTEBOOKS TO THE BOOKS

One can map Darwin's notebook projects on to his books. *Notebook* A contributes to the geological volumes on South America and on coral and volcanic islands. M and N, on metaphysics, are consummated mostly in *The Descent of Man* (1871) and *The Expression of the Emotions in Man and Animals* (1872). The zoonomical enquiries divide in their legacies. The generation of individuals has its final synthesis in the hypothesis of pangenesis, apparently first formulated in 1841, but only published in 1868 in *The Variation of Animals and Plants under Domestication*. The generation of the tree of life by means of natural selection has the *Origin* (1859) all to itself.[20]

Such mappings show that much zoonomical and metaphysical thinking from the months before the emergence of natural selection was never set aside but was, rather, actively carried through by Darwin into the published works, sometimes seeming to fit uneasily with later views. What does not survive, however, is an explicit quest for the laws of life; this quest being barely mentioned once natural selection is fully formulated in the winter and spring of 1838–9. Two reasons for this eclipse suggest themselves. First, the promissory project aiming at these laws depended decisively on using geographical successions over time. But with natural selection a quite different strategy is adopted, as the accessible changes wrought by man in the short run provide the inferential avenue to nature's workings over inaccessible aeons. The study of domesticated species displaces biogeography here, although biogeography will later take other evidential roles, especially in supporting the principle of divergence. Second, natural selection, although arising from the lawful tendencies of heredity, variation and superfecundity, themselves outcomes from the most general generative powers of life in nutrition and growth, was never seen by Darwin to have a law of its own. There was then no law that is to natural selection as the inverse square of the distance law – with proportionality to mass products – is to the force of gravitational attraction. In that sense natural selection is lawless. So, further, where Newton's science invoked a notoriously mysterious cause – the attractive force itself – but a clear and distinct law, with Darwin it is the other way round: heredity, variation and superfecundity, and hence natural selection, are obvious, manifest, even familiar, features of animal and plant life; however, their myriad interactive outcomes in myriad circumstances – the endless resultant natural selections – are not subsumable within any one generalisation, any single statement of law. Such considerations may have ended Darwin's aim of emulating the Newtonian consummation of Kepler's nomic legacy.

If Darwin's promissory Newtonian ambition was not fulfilled, was he not nevertheless the Adam Smith of the living world? In articulating a tendency to adaptive divergence, the *Origin* does after all invoke the cardinal Smithian doctrine of progress through the division of labour; and Darwin in the 1850s had indeed studied the economists' treatment of such themes. However, the notebook theorising of the 1837–9 period is not so readily assimilated to any such precedents. Contrary to recent legend, the notebooks and other documents from the time include no sure signs of direct debts to readings in political economy in the months before Darwin read Malthus.[21] What is more, those characteristics of Darwin's theorising – most obviously his individualism – that seem to show traces of such sources, do not always fit well with them. For it was Darwin's preoccupation with individual sexual generations, as initiating new individual lives in the offspring produced, that led him to refer the production of species to the powers and actions of individual organisms; and his pursuit of this premise was at odds with what political economists assumed, as Darwin took these powers and actions not to be answering only to individual self-interest, but to be lawful provisions not for the good of those individuals themselves but for the good of species faced with changing circumstances, and so for the goods eventuating from the progress made in the larger proliferation of the tree of life.

These issues about progress and interests, individual and otherwise, require a historiography for the ideology of Darwin's science. For they require, at a minimum, the locating of that science in relation to the Enlightenment, the French Revolution and the 'Industrial Revolution' (an anachronistic category dating from late in the nineteenth century and now subject to revisionist criticism calling for quotation marks); a locating, too, therefore, in relation to liberalism, socialism and conservatism, and in relation to aristocratic, bourgeois and proletarian class interests and conflicts. As for the Enlightenment, the programmes and outcomes of Darwin's notebook science are unequivocally continuous with the projects definitive of the first, the mid eighteenth-century, phase of the Enlightenment and are anathema to all late eighteenth- and early nineteenth-century counterings (including romantic counterings) of it.[22] Equally, in its commitment to gradual, adaptive progress Darwin's version of nature allied itself with reformist liberal alternatives to both socialist revolution and conservative reaction as political philosophies. So, if one accepts that conjunctions of liberalism and the Enlightenment were also naturally conjoined with bourgeois interests, is there not here, then, a presumption that Darwinian science was bourgeois in its ideology?

To see how deeply such a presumption can mislead requires appreciating new emphases in the historiography of English social and economic life, new histories of the English capitalisms in their *longues durées*.[23] For the English capitalisms of the 1830s were much more like the capitalisms of the England of the 1730s than was formerly recognised. In the 1730s the national economy was capitalist, triumphantly so with the seeing off of the main, Dutch rival; but was not predominantly bourgeois or industrial – in so far as that means principally making goods in factories with machines.

Likewise, then, in the 1830s the dominant capitalisms of agriculture, banking, colonies, trading, commerce and property, domestic and imperial, already dominant a century earlier, continue their hegemony, with the political and social corollary that the landed aristocratic and gentlemanly, rather than the urban, middle-class or bourgeois interests, are still the ruling class interests.

That Darwin and his family fit exactly into this peculiarly English pattern of ascendant aristocratic and gentlemanly capitalisms is manifest, once one learns to avoid the older, discredited stereotypes of the 'Industrial Revolution'. The *Beagle* voyage, with its aristocratic captain and its Admiralty mission to advance the informal imperial opportunities opening up in South America, fits this pattern no less exactly.[24] Again, so do Darwin's preoccupations with land, food and population, lying at the intersection of his Lyellian concerns with the historical geography of species' migrations, invasions and extinctions and his Malthusian concerns with superfecundity, tribal and imperial expansions, struggles, defeats and conquests. Any thought that such preoccupations were by this time fading residues of an *ancien régime* fast becoming *passé* can be answered by reading, for instance, in books of the 1830s by the man later picked out by Marx in *Capital* as the most instructive analyst of the capitalism of the age: Edward Gibbon Wakefield. Putting Malthus together with Smith, to counter Ricardo's economic views, Wakefield and his many influential followers reasserted, as Malthus himself had, the older privileging of land, population and food in economic theory and practice. They did so on behalf of a new argument, widely acted upon in coming decades: that English capitalism, like any other eventually, can only go forward by going sideways; for it must export not only excess population but capital and labour that has become underdeployed in the mother country; and it must do so by extending its entire social and economic structure to new colonial settlements. There, in Australia, New Zealand and Canada, say, with colonial land values kept high by government intervention – the decisive policy proposal of the Wakefield school – the dominant aristocratic and gentlemanly interests will be, as in England itself, properly and profitably pursued together with other interests distinctive of the middling and working classes.[25] Alerted by such ideological analyses and projections in the England of the 1830s, one can recognise in Darwin's account of nature not the urban sites of machinofacturing capitalism in Manchester, Leeds and elsewhere, still often marginal as they were to the social, political, economic and cultural life of the nation. Rather, one can recognise in the selective breedings, stock and crop improvements, dominant species and horizontal territorial competitions of life the agrarian, financial and imperial ways and means of those aristocratic and gentlemanly capitalisms which had first become nationally hegemonic early in the previous century, were now burgeoning even more in power and prestige, following the defeat of the French, and so moving on to their later, Victorian pre-eminence at the apogee of the British Empire.[26]

NOTES

I am grateful to James Moore and Gregory Radick for discussions of this chapter, and to the Arts and Humanities Research Board for grant support.

1. For Darwin's notebooks, see Barrett *et al.* 1987, *Charles Darwin's Notebooks* (hereafter *Notebooks*). As in this superb edition, references in this chapter will be to the manuscript page numbers.
2. The recent biographies by Desmond and Moore (1991) and Browne (1995) have extensive references to this literature.
3. In addition to the biographies listed above, see Manier 1978 and Rudwick 1982.
4. For further discussion, see Sloan, this volume.
5. For a more detailed analysis of these views of Lyell, see Hodge 1982.
6. See *Red Notebook* 127–32 in the *Notebooks*. For a more detailed discussion see Hodge 1990 and the articles by Sulloway cited therein.
7. *Red Notebook* 132 in the *Notebooks*. See also Endersby, this volume.
8. Browne 1995, 83–5.
9. For a more detailed discussion of Darwin's sketch and Lyell's exposition of Lamarck, see Hodge 1982.
10. This explication of Darwin's promissory project is founded on numerous passages in B and C; comparing B224–7 with E51–5 is especially instructive.
11. See the index entry for Yarrell's law in the *Notebooks*, and Endersby, this volume.
12. On various aspects of Darwin's allegiance to this epistemic and methodological *vera causa* ideal, see Waters, Hull and Radick, this volume.
13. For a more detailed discussion, see Hodge 2000.

14. For further discussion, see Richards, this volume, and esp. R. J. Richards 1987.
15. For further discussion, see Endersby, this volume, and Hodge 1985.
16. On Darwin and Comte see Schweber 1977. On Darwin and Whewell, see Curtis 1987. These studies markedly overestimate the influence of Comte and Whewell on Darwin.
17. See Brooke, this volume.
18. For a much more detailed analysis, see Hodge and Kohn 1985.
19. See Radick, this volume.
20. See Richards, Endersby and Waters, this volume.
21. For Darwin and the political economists, see, e.g., Schweber 1980 and Gordon 1989. Note that for Adam Smith the principle of the division of labour covered traditional forms of manufacturing – literally making by hand – even more obviously than machinofacturing, and that Darwin's appeal to the principle in his account of divergence among varieties and species depended on his extension of it to subsume the greater yield of plant growth from a patch of land when there is a greater diversity of species. For Darwin on divergence, see the Introduction to this volume.
22. For alternative, Romantic readings, see, e.g., Sloan and Richards, this volume.
23. See, e.g., Price 1999, J. C. D. Clark 2000, Anderson 1992, Wood 1991 and Hudson 1992 for introductions.
24. On gentlemanly capitalism and informal imperialism, see Cain and Hopkins 1993.
25. See, e.g., Semmel 1970.
26. On other aspects of the cultural conditioning of Darwin's theorising, see Radick, this volume.

JIM ENDERSBY

3 Darwin on generation, pangenesis and sexual selection

I GENTLEMANLY GENERATION

In the summer of 1838, Charles Darwin considered marriage. The disadvantages included losing the 'freedom to go where one liked', while staying single would mean avoiding 'the expense & anxiety of children'. But then, he reflected, 'only picture to yourself a nice soft wife on a sofa with good fire, & books & music perhaps'. Not to mention an 'object *to be* beloved and played with. better than a dog anyhow'. Wedlock won; within months he was engaged and then married to his cousin, Emma Wedgwood. The pairing brought anxieties, however, especially over whether marriage between such close relatives would issue in unhealthy children.[1]

As a philosophical naturalist, Darwin had long been interested in reproduction or 'generation', to use the term of the day.[2] Generational issues would eventually lead him to study subjects as diverse as barnacles, flowers, pigeons and domestic animal and plant breeding. His hypothesis of pangenesis, probably first formulated in 1841 but only published in 1868, was an attempt to give a unified account of all kinds of generation, from the healing of wounds in trees, to propagation by buds and grafting, to sexual pairings and fertilisation. Moreover, in Darwin's view, since sexual pairings – whether decided by male combat or female choice – were selective, they enabled a selectional evolutionary process separate from, and sometimes in tension with, natural selection. His theory of sexual selection argued that something like a peacock's tail, while lowering the peacock's chances of survival, might give him a reproductive advantage as long as peahens choose the males with the finest tails. Whether writing of birds or humans, Darwin always described females as 'coy' and modest, while the males fought aggressively over them; he saw the patterns of his society repeated throughout the natural world.

This chapter looks at Darwin's beliefs about generation in the context of his wider theorising and its social setting. The discussion takes in the theoretical legacies from the eighteenth century; the development of Darwin's views on generation from his student days at Edinburgh onward; and the politics of gender, marriage and gentlemanly life in the Darwin family and in Victorian Britain at large. The aim is to see the world of generation as Darwin did, putting ourselves in his place. For the later Darwin in particular, this will mean putting ourselves in his garden, because botany rather than zoology was often central to his thinking about generation. As he moved among his flowers, pollinating and observing, his children helped monitor his experiments, while his wife Emma patiently ran the house and protected him from the intrusions of the outside world. Darwin the Victorian paterfamilias is as important as Darwin the last great gentlemanly naturalist in understanding his views on sex, marriage and generation in plants and animals alike.

II A LEGACY OF GENERATIONAL ISSUES

From ancient times, and following Aristotle's precedent most prominently, natural history and natural philosophy had dwelled on plant and animal generation – the making and remaking of living matter – in all its diversity: with parents and without ('spontaneous' generation); with and without sex. The Swedish botanist Carl Linné (Linnaeus) gave the topic new vitality in the eighteenth century by classifying higher plants according to the numbers of female carpels and male stamens – on the assumption that sexuality was as widespread among plants as among animals.[3] Darwin's grandfather, the physician Erasmus Darwin, exploited the poetic potential in Linnaeus' images, making the poet's garden, in his *Loves of the Plants* (1789), a scene of vegetal orgies – to the shocked dismay of more prudish naturalists.[4] Not everyone was convinced that sex was so ubiquitous, however; in the early decades of the new century, the issue was still far from settled.[5]

As a young naturalist in the making at Edinburgh University, Darwin read his own grandfather's treatise *Zoonomia*, possibly at the suggestion of his mentor, the anatomist Robert Grant.[6] Grant was a specialist on the 'zoophytes' ('animal-plants' or plant-like animals) and a supporter of Jean Lamarck's theories about the transmutation of species. Under Grant's tutelage, Darwin compared and contrasted plant and animal reproduction by examining the zoophyte genus *Flustra*, presenting his first scientific paper on the 'eggs' that swam forth from the parent polyp before settling in rocks to continue the sedentary life of their species.[7] Darwin's *Flustra* investigations connected with issues about colonial and individual life in animals and plants. Were corals associations or individuals? Was a tree a colony of buds?[8] Later, at Cambridge, botanical studies with John Henslow deepened these interests.[9] Controversially, Henslow argued that asexual reproduction in plants – by 'subdivision', as he called it – was rare but natural, occurring in such species as elm trees; whereas most horticulturalists by that time thought it unnatural, yielding only short-lived plants.[10]

Darwin's early influences – Erasmus Darwin, Grant and Henslow – shaped much of his thinking about a wide range of generational issues, in particular about the sexual and the asexual, the individual and the colonial, and the natural and the unnatural.[11] Throughout the *Beagle* years, and especially in association with the extensive microscopical studies he carried out on invertebrate animals, these issues would continue to fascinate Darwin and direct his enquiries.

III THE *BEAGLE* AND BEYOND

Darwin's theorising on the *Beagle* was shot through with generational preoccupations. His studies of invertebrates convinced him that, at the most minute level, tiny granules of living matter were involved in all plant and animal reproduction.[12] On the island of Chiloe (near Chile), he found apple trees being propagated asexually in ways fitting Henslow's views.[13] A new interest in corals and their propagation enabled Darwin to integrate his Grantian heritage with Lyell's writings in geology. By early 1835, Darwin – here breaking with Lyell – was ascribing the extinction of some mammal species to an inherent limitation on species lifetimes; in Darwin's view, this limitation was analogous to the limitation on the total lifetime of the descendants of an asexual graft in apple-tree propagation.[14]

After returning from the voyage, Darwin looked for evidence that species, like both individuals and grafted descendants, have a limited lifetime. He began to argue that species died for the same reasons grafted trees did: in both cases the generational process was the same because generation proceeded by division, and division transmitted only the limited vitality present at the beginning of a species' life. From this hypothesis, Darwin initially concluded that sexual and asexual generation were substantially similar.[15] However, by July 1837, when he commenced his notebook theorising on the formation of new species from earlier ones – transmutation of species – he had decided that although all generation was indeed divisional, there were two crucial differences between sexual and asexual generation. First, sexual generation involved the mating of two parents, or more precisely, the fertilisation of the female element by the male element. Second, sexual generation involved maturation in the offspring thus produced. Mating and maturation would preoccupy him intently from now on.

As Darwin saw these distinctively sexual processes, mating was evolutionarily conservative, and maturation evolutionarily innovative, in ways that had no analogue among asexual species. In species where males and females mated, individual differences between the parents were blended out, producing offspring intermediate in character. Generally, then, mating ensured the uniformity of a species-character across its geographical range, despite local variations of conditions. But in those same species, the fact that the offspring matured left some scope for the emergence of adaptive variation to changing conditions of life, and therefore for innovation to balance the conservatism. In Darwin's view, only immature, maturing organisms were impressionable by environmental influences; and this was the only means by which adaptive and heritable variations could be acquired.[16]

Normally, mating and maturation remained balanced, so for transmutation to occur that balance needed to be upset in favour of maturational innovations. According to Darwin, the migration of some individuals to fresh conditions, with isolation from the parent stock, could lead to a new local variety being formed – one that could eventually diverge sufficiently to become a new species, especially if divergence later produced sterility between the new and old stocks.[17]

From the start of this notebook theorising, Darwin accepted that individual maturation repeated, and recapitulated (in the later term), the changes in form gone through by the species' entire ancestry since life began.[18] So, maturation, in recapitulating former changes, somehow made possible new ones allowing further adaptation and progress. In Darwin's thinking, the role of maturation was complemented by that of mating and fertilisation. Sexual reproduction introduced crossing and blending that allowed adaptations to immediate circumstances to be conserved and passed on, producing cumulative, progressive change which could eventually allow higher forms of life to arise. Sexual generation served, then, not the good of individuals, but the good of species that have to change or become extinct; eventually, sex allowed the formation of human from lower animal life.

Within a year, Darwin was speculating on how species with separate sexes might have arisen from hermaphroditic ancestors. He concluded that the hermaphroditic condition comes first and gives way later to the separation of sexes through the loss – the 'abortion', as he put it – of one or other sexual structure and activity. He also speculated, especially in the summer of 1838, on how fertilisation works; tentatively concluding that a female egg, in a higher animal, is like a plant bud: vegetative, passive and exactly like its parental source in inner constitution; while male semen is animate and active in impressing on the egg some influence, making it mature in ways different from the parental maturation. Darwin (in keeping with a long-standing, male-dominated tradition) assumed that adaptation and progress in life were largely initiated by males, with females ensuring that the changes initiated were enduring and cumulative.[19]

In the late 1830s, Darwin had developed several components of the theory he later referred to as 'descent with modification'. Sexual reproduction was the key to 'modification': it created variations but blended them, so that new forms didn't diverge so quickly; and of course sex was also central to 'descent', as it provided the means by which the modifications were passed on. However, Darwin still had no mechanism to explain either variation or inheritance; and as he began to look for one, he accumulated new mysteries to solve.

IV BUDS, BARNACLES AND BIRDS

In September 1838, Darwin took a break from his notebooks on species to visit Loddiges, the celebrated London nursery garden. He noted afterwards that he had seen '1279 varieties of roses!!!'. This profusion intrigued him; if there was enough variation in nature to produce 1,279 varieties of roses, why did not *Rosa* fragment into 1,279 species? He observed that Loddiges' gardeners propagated their new cultivars by taking cuttings, precisely because asexual reproduction was conservative; allowing the roses to set seed would have blended out the desired varieties. In the same notebook entry, Darwin reminded himself that some animals were like plants, in that taking 'cuttings' from them could propagate the species; grafting rose cuttings was 'like cutting off tail of Planaria' (a genus of flatworm), which resulted in both parts of the worm re-growing into complete worms. The worms reminded Darwin that some lizards grew new tails if they lost their old one; asexual reproduction thus seemed to be akin to 'healing of wound' – presumably each part of an organism 'must have the knowledge how to grow, & therefore to repair wounds'. From this sequence of associations, he concluded that if roses (like the Chiloe apple trees) could be grown from cuttings – and worms could be grown in the same way – then 'in the separated part every element of the living body is present'.[20] Perhaps there was nothing unique about sperm, pollen and eggs – they were merely the specialised forms of some ability which was diffused throughout an organism.

When Darwin visited Loddiges, he was once again thinking about plant fertilisation. Although most flowers possess both male and female parts, plant breeders believed that self-fertilised flowers were not as vigorous as cross-fertilised ones. Even hermaphroditic flowers seemed to avoid regular self-fertilisation, with the wind or insects acting to transfer pollen between different plants. Darwin set out to find out what the effects of self- and cross-fertilisation were. His curiosity was prompted partly by concerns about his own inbreeding with Emma.[21] Indeed, it was shortly after their wedding that he began the observations on flower-breeding that formed the basis for the full-blown experiments of the 1860s.[22]

While the flower researches were getting underway, Darwin began a lengthy study of living and fossil barnacles (*Cirripedia*); from 1846 until 1854 he worked away at his barnacles, eventually producing two large books on them.[23] The most intriguing aspect of these creatures was, once again, their sexual characteristics. Most barnacle species were hermaphroditic, but others had distinct sexes. Most surprising was the *Beagle* specimen that had first led him to study barnacles, a tiny species he named *Arthrobalanus*, in which the males were so tiny that they lived inside the females' shells, almost like parasites. Such species seemed to Darwin to be intermediates between the common hermaphroditic barnacles and the ones with separate sexes.[24]

Darwin was also fascinated by the variability of barnacle species – further proof of nature's ability to generate variation. Barnacles, like flowers, were often hermaphrodites, and yet, just as in the plant kingdom, constant self-fertilisation was avoided. Barnacles helped to confirm Darwin's earlier suspicions about the common nature of animal and plant reproduction; and as he studied the dizzying diversity of barnacle reproductive strategies, he decided that all organisms must originally have reproduced asexually, then hermaphroditically and finally sexually.[25]

Further evidence that nature abhorred prolonged self-fertilisation came in the first of Darwin's botanical books, *On the Various Contrivances by which British and Foreign Orchids are Fertilised by Insects* (1862).[26] As the book's subtitle – 'on the good effects of intercrossing' – indicated, *Orchids* was mainly concerned with the extraordinary array of complex mechanisms that these plants possessed to ensure that they were cross-fertilised by insects, rather than self-fertilised. A secondary concern was the 'design argument', from the intricate complexity of plants to the existence of an intelligent, designing God. By showing that these mechanisms were the product of natural laws, Darwin mounted what he privately referred to as 'a "flank movement" on the enemy'.[27]

Darwin had found intriguing connections between the reproduction of plants and animals, but so far he had found these connections with very simple animals. Would they hold with the higher animals, even with humans? Would the problems associated with interbred orchids reappear in the offspring of two breeds as closely related as the Darwins and the Wedgwoods? Darwin had grown up in the country, surrounded by friends and relatives who bred horses and dogs, so the farmyard seemed a natural place to turn for answers about animal breeding.[28]

Darwin had earlier sent professional animal breeders a questionnaire, but got very little response. So, starting in 1855, he started breeding pigeons for himself.[29] Among his aims was to determine the truth of Yarrell's law: that, when two varieties were crossed, it was the older breed whose characters tended to dominate in the offspring. What this showed, it seemed to Darwin, was that characters become more firmly and more strongly embedded in the hereditary constitution with the passing of time and generations, with consequences in the short run for species formation, and in the long run for structural progress.[30] Unfortunately, the pigeon experiments provided a great deal of counter-evidence to Yarrell's law, and Darwin became convinced of the need for alternative explanations. However, it is characteristic of his approach that he did not dismiss such older 'laws' entirely, but merely decided they were only partial explanations.[31]

V A TREATISE ON BREEDING

In 1868, Darwin published *The Variation of Animals and Plants under Domestication*, which – among other things – attempted to explain the often perplexing phenomena of inheritance.[32] Darwin drew particular attention to four puzzles: the tendency of offspring to show the characters of their remote ancestors rather than their parents ('reversion'); the tendency of fruit produced from the splicing together of two different kinds of tree to have a hybrid, intermediate character (graft hybrids); the ability of some animals and plants to regrow damaged or severed parts (regeneration); and lastly, the curious case of Lord Morton's mare.

Darwin's examples of reversion were the characteristically homely ones of domestic pigeons reverting to their wild-type colouring, or horned sheep and cattle re-appearing in polled breeds. Such reappearances were problems for breeders, who could not be sure how many generations were needed before 'the breed may be considered as pure, and free from all dangers of reversion'.[33] Knowing why and how ancient characters could reappear promised to throw light on the mechanism of inheritance and also the emergence, despite blending, of new species from varieties. Darwin also recognised the need to understand what prevented new varieties from reverting to their ancestral condition; otherwise reversion could provide, not supporting evidence for the gradual transmutation of species, but fatal evidence against it. His pigeon-breeding experiments had suggested that reversion was too rare to be a problem; but knowing the mechanism would help him explain why that was the case.[34]

The other aspect of reversion that concerned Darwin was so common that it had rarely struck anyone as needing explanation, but he wondered how a man could transmit characters to his grandson, via his daughter – 'characters which she does not, or cannot, possess'.[35] How was it possible, for example, for a boy to grow up with a beard like the one that his mother's father had borne, given that his mother had no beard? From questions like these, Darwin concluded that the ovules and spermatozoa of higher animals must be 'crowded with invisible characters, proper to both sexes... and to a long line of male and female ancestors separated by hundreds or even thousands of generations from the present time'. Yet, these characters, 'like those written on paper with invisible ink', were not visible, but 'lie ready to be evolved whenever the organisation is disturbed by certain known or unknown conditions'.[36]

Graft hybrids were another of Darwin's enigmas. He discussed cases where grafting had produced a plant 'resembling in every important respect a hybrid formed in the ordinary way by seminal reproduction.'[37] These cases reinforced the suspicion, first aroused by the Chiloe apple trees, that the ability to create a new individual was indeed diffused throughout the plant. Another old question that he returned to in *Variation* was regeneration, the power of some organisms to re-grow parts. He noted that salamanders could regenerate their limbs, which seemed to suggest that whatever controlled the growth of the limb must be present throughout the organism. The similarities between graft-hybrids and regeneration led Darwin to speculate that these abilities might be related.[38]

Finally, there was the singular case of Lord Morton's mare. The mare had been mated with a male quagga (a now-extinct, South African species of striped horse) and, as expected, produced quagga-like foals with some stripes. However, Darwin records, 'she was subsequently sent to Sir Gore Ouseley, and produced two colts by a black Arabian horse'. Much to Sir Gore's astonishment, these foals also had a few quagga-like stripes. This case appeared to show that what Darwin called 'the direct action of the male element on the female form' could be permanently impressed on a female and persist over several generations, even though other matings subsequently occurred.[39] Darwin believed that the same prepotency occurred in plants, in that pollen from another species might have a permanent effect on a plant's 'ovarium', so that the influence of the foreign species would be apparent in subsequent generations.[40] He developed this idea with one of his characteristic analogies between the level of the species and that of the individual, by comparing the influence of the male on a specific offspring with that of changed environmental conditions on a lineage.[41]

Variation is in many ways the culmination of Darwin's generation theorising: from his earliest experiments with *Flustra* and the zoophytes he had been persuaded of the continuity between animals and plants; his time with Henslow and his experiences aboard the *Beagle* contributed to his belief that sexual and asexual reproduction were points on a continuum; worms and salamanders had suggested a link between healing and reproduction; blending inheritance in pigeons and roses had shown him just how much variation sex could generate, while at the same time acting as a regulator, to stop species fragmenting into extinction; and maturation and Lamarckian inheritance showed the continuous impressionability of the embryo and the adult, respectively. With this background in view, it becomes clear why the *Variation*'s 800 pages of detailed cases culminate in the 'Provisional Hypothesis of Pangenesis' – far from being a hasty afterthought, it was a systematic attempt to connect some of Darwin's longest-held ideas.

VI THE HYPOTHESIS OF PANGENESIS

Darwin introduced his hypothesis by summarising his problems, and then offered a rather brief description of his self-confessedly 'imperfect' solution, pangenesis. He proposed that every part of an organism can 'throw off minute granules which are dispersed throughout the whole system', and that these 'multiply by self-division, and are ultimately developed into units like those from which they were originally derived'. He named these granules 'gemmules', and argued that 'they are collected from all parts of the system to constitute the sexual elements'.[42]

Although Darwin coined the term, pangenesis was not a new idea. Its origins went back to the ancient world and many eighteenth-century naturalists had propounded various versions of it. By Darwin's day, however, the idea was much out of favour.[43] To see why he revived and developed the pangenesis hypothesis, we need to understand how, in his view, the hypothesis resolved his various puzzles. In the case of reversion, he argued, for example, that a boy could inherit his grandfather's beard from his mother because 'the secondary characters, which appertain to one sex, lie dormant in the other sex; that is, gemmules capable of development into the secondary male characters are included within the female; and conversely female characters in the male'. The same process could explain all the other enigmatic atavisms that Darwin had described.[44] And because gemmules were supposedly dispersed throughout the organism, they could explain both graft hybrids (since the elements needed for reproduction were not restricted to the reproductive organs) and the regeneration of missing limbs (since the gemmules that made them were circulating elsewhere in the body).

Pangenesis made connections between many of Darwin's ideas: the relationships between embryos, adults and species; the link between sexual and asexual reproduction; the concomitant view that there is no deep difference between gametes and asexual buds; and his confidence that reproduction is continuous with growth and healing.[45] It is also important to remember that Darwin's gemmules were conceived as self-propelled, largely autonomous creatures (not unlike the 'eggs' of the zoophytes, which Grant had also called gemmules) which multiplied themselves and then combined to determine the character of the new organism. In his discussion of reversion in hybrids, Darwin argued that 'unmodified and undeteriorated gemmules', present in two hybrids, 'would be especially apt to combine'.[46] Such phrases seem to imply a form of competition among the gemmules: the 'pure' un-hybridised gemmules are described as 'undeteriorated' (and thus 'fitter'); their superiority allowed them to dominate and thus re-assert the organism's original characteristics. The more gemmules there were from one parent, the more that parent's specific characters would predominate – and that, it seemed, explained the dominance associated with Yarrell's law. The gemmules of the older species were more stable and vigorous, and this was what allowed them to compete successfully against those of the younger species.[47] Darwin also presumed that in such a competition, the male elements would predominate. He thereby explained the apparent prepotency of the male in such cases as Morton's mare.[48] In Darwin's view, the persistence of male influence was due to gemmules being 'capable of transmission in a dormant state to future generations', when they might be re-awakened.[49]

As already noted, Darwin thought that there was good evidence that acquired characteristics could be inherited, but he recognised that such inheritance raised the question of 'how can the use or disuse of a particular limb or the brain affect a small aggregate of reproductive cells, seated in a distant part of the body?' Pangenesis was intended to explain this too: since gemmules were produced throughout an organism's life, a changed organ would produce changed gemmules.[50]

As Darwin tried to explain everything from reversion to graft-hybrids he brought together many of the themes that were his life-long preoccupations. 'Inheritance', he wrote, 'must be looked at as merely a form of growth, like the self-division of the lowly-organised unicellular organism.' Darwin stated the general point succinctly:

> Each animal and plant may be compared with a bed of soil full of seeds, some of which will soon germinate, some lie dormant for a period, whilst others perish. When we hear it said that a man carries in his constitution the seeds of an inherited disease, there is much truth in the expression. No other attempt, as far as I am aware, has been made, imperfect as this confessedly is, to connect under one point of view these several grand classes of facts. An organic being is a microcosm – a little universe, formed of a host of self-propagating organisms, inconceivably minute and numerous as the stars in heaven.[51]

VII METHOD, ARGUMENT AND THE PANGENESIS HYPOTHESIS

The hypothesis of pangenesis was clearly not an aberration on Darwin's part. It had a long tradition behind it, and he saw it as the logical culmination of his generation thinking.[52] Jonathan Hodge has argued that Darwin's thinking can be divided into three stages. From 1835 on, his theory of species extinction from an inherent limitation on lifetime prompted him to hold that all generation – sexual and asexual – was essentially the same, being a process of division. From 1837 on, without repudiating that division thesis, Darwin concentrated on the interaction of two parents and on maturation in their offspring as two features marking off all sexual reproduction from any asexual reproduction, thus making adaptive variation and descent with modification possible. Third, from 1841, he became convinced, mainly perhaps on reflecting on such phenomena as graft hybrids, that all generation, from healing to breeding, was ultimately sexual, in that it was due to micro-ovules, or gemmules, that were engaged in acts of quasi-fertilisation.[53]

After *Variation* had been published, Darwin wrote to his friend Joseph Hooker, the botanist:

> Have you ever met with any tangible & clear view of what takes place in generation, whether by seeds or birds. – Or how a long-lost character can possibly reappear – or how the male element can possibly affect the mother-plant – or the mother animal so that her future progeny are affected. Now all these points & many others are connected together, – whether truly or falsely is another question – by Pangenesis.[54]

Hooker, like many of his contemporaries, was not persuaded, however. He wrote to George Grey, the New Zealand governor, that *Variation* was 'a wonderful book' and had produced 'a *profound sensation*' but that 'pangenesis is a stumbling block to me, I grant all its premises & all its results, but I do not see how my understanding is helped by the hypothesis of multiplying germs or gemmules or atoms'.[55] Although Darwin had made intriguing links, Hooker felt that, in the absence of direct evidence for gemmules, Darwin's hypothesis explained nothing. Hooker's scepticism about the pangenesis hypothesis thus contrasted sharply with his support for the theory of natural selection; and a comparison of Darwin's argumentative strategies in the *Origin* and the *Variation* holds clues to a possible explanation for this difference in response.[56]

Darwin had used the final chapters of the *Origin* to show how his theory could explain a diverse range of phenomena.[57] This accumulation of evidence was much more than merely corroborative detail; he hoped to demonstrate that a single theory – natural selection – could explain a diversity of apparently unconnected evidence. Doing so was central to his philosophical approach to scientific enquiry; Darwin was trying to establish a consilience of inductions. The British philosopher William Whewell had proposed 'consilience' (literally 'jumping together') as a solution to the long-standing problem of evaluating hypotheses.[58] According to this doctrine, a hypothesis gained especially strong empirical support when it turned out to explain phenomena of kinds not contemplated when the theory was first formulated.[59] More generally, if a hypothesis could explain numerous and diverse kinds of facts, it was much more likely to be true than if supported by facts of just one kind. The more a theory could successfully explain, the more likely it was to be true.[60]

A large part of what made the pangenesis hypothesis plausible to Darwin was that – just like natural selection – it seemed to explain so much.[61] But the theory of natural selection had more than explanatory success in its favour. Darwin had presented the theory as following inductively from independently evidenced phenomena; even his critics agreed that plants and animals varied, that selective breeding could create new varieties, and that there was a struggle for existence. The theory of natural selection linked these phenomena without positing any unobserved new entities. The pangenesis hypothesis was quite different. No one had detected a gemmule; yet Darwin was convinced that they must exist, because, if they did exist, the diverse and often puzzling phenomena of inheritance 'jumped together' into a single explanatory scheme. He clearly hoped to repeat the strategy of the *Origin* with pangenesis, even quoting Whewell in his support.[62] But perhaps Darwin was led astray by his own skills of rhetoric. After all, the structure of the *Origin*'s argument bore no relation to the process by which he had arrived at his theory; the consilience of inductions merely boosted his theory.[63] Yet, emboldened by the *Origin*'s success, Darwin seems to have regarded consilience as his starting point for the pangenesis hypothesis. The gemmules could almost be described as 'consilience particles'; they made apparent connections between Darwin's problems, but were provided with no additional evidence.

Hooker's letter to Grey about pangenesis also mentioned that 'Darwin is at work on a book on Man! Which will I expect, turn the scientific & theological worlds upside down.'[64] It certainly did; but when the *Descent of Man* appeared in 1871, the bulk of Darwin's long-delayed discussion of human origins turned, not on natural selection or pangenesis, but on sexual selection.

VIII THE THEORY OF SEXUAL SELECTION

In 1860, Darwin wrote to Asa Gray, the American botanist, that 'The sight of a feather in a peacock's tail, whenever I gaze at it, makes me sick!'[65] Darwin's nausea was prompted by the apparent inability of natural selection to explain such an extravagant but apparently useless feature; as he noted: 'the long train of the peacock ... must render them a more easy prey to any prowling tiger-cat than would otherwise be the case'.[66] How to explain features that did nothing to aid birds in the struggle for existence – and might even hinder them?

Darwin's proposed solution to this puzzle arose from the fact that peacocks, as he wrote, 'display their attractions with elaborate care in the presence of the females', almost always 'during the season of love'.[67] He concluded that the peacock's tail must be a sexual ornament. It had evolved because the most vigorous and healthy of the peacock's ancestors grew the biggest tails and used them to attract the most vigorous and healthy of the proto-peahen females. The vigorous thus mated earliest and most often, producing a large number of offspring, who would inherit either their father's large tail or their mother's preference for large tails. Over many generations, peacocks' tails would continue to get bigger and bigger, eventually resulting in the extravagant structure of the modern peacock.[68] Sexual selection was especially plausible to Darwin because he believed in the inheritance of acquired characteristics (which pangenesis supposedly explained). In Darwin's view, merely being strong and healthy would allow a peacock to grow a bigger tail, and this acquired character would be inherited by his offspring.[69]

Darwin argued that natural selection alone could not have produced male ornaments because they were not essential for survival. After all, 'the females, which are unarmed and unornamented, are able to survive and procreate their kind'.[70] Just as he had done in the *Origin*, Darwin drew on evidence from the farmyard, noting how breeders had improved the secondary sexual characteristics – plumage and so on – of gamecocks and pigeons.[71] According to Darwin, sexual selection had two distinct aspects: male combat and female choice.[72] He allowed that the females of the lower animals played a substantial role in sexual selection; but, in humans, the evidence of Victorian society seemed to him to demonstrate that men had largely seized the power of choice. This seizure in turn explained an otherwise awkward anomaly – that it was human females, rather than males, who ornamented themselves to attract a mate. As Darwin saw it, just as men selected pigeons to fit their ideals of beauty, they tended to reject potential brides who failed the aesthetic test. Just as the theory of natural selection came out of the animal breeders' gazettes and the pigeon-fanciers' clubs, the theory of sexual selection was partly produced by Darwin's social and domestic situation.[73]

For Darwin, sexual selection explained a set of facts that natural selection could not: the apparently useless differences between males and females. It is no accident that sexual selection appeared in the *Descent of Man*; the two topics were always closely linked in Darwin's thinking.[74] He believed sexual selection might explain how different human races arose: a beautiful European woman may repel an African man, while an African woman's ideal man would be rejected by an Asian woman.[75] Beauty, for Darwin, was very much in the eye of the beholder and as such offered no more survival benefit than the peacock's tail did. Darwin speculated that such variations were the key to understanding the emergence of different human races. He argued that in 'savage' cultures the 'strongest and most vigorous men' will become chiefs and have the pick of the most attractive women (according to their local standard of beauty). The chiefs will often have several wives and – being wealthy – will have the food and other resources to raise the most offspring, so that 'after the lapse of many generations' the chiefs' arbitrary tastes will 'modify to a certain extent the character of the tribe'.[76] The same mechanism explained how humanity had diversified from a single ancestral species into numerous races with distinct moral codes and, Darwin assumed, widely varying intellectual abilities. He believed moral and intellectual traits were acquired and passed on in 'Lamarckian' fashion and that sexual selection would thus allow variations in moral or intellectual standards to become part of the make-up of a particular human race; people could have local tastes in morality, just as they had local tastes in beauty.[77]

However, it was not just races who varied in their mental prowess. Darwin also believed that men were as intellectually superior to women as white people were to black ones. Darwin argued that these differences resulted from natural and sexual selection over many generations. Male ancestors of humans would have had to compete successfully with rival males and would also have had 'to defend their females, as well as their young, from enemies of all kinds, and to hunt for their joint subsistence'. As a result, men had inevitably become both more intelligent and stronger than women, although Darwin did admit that 'women have become more beautiful'.[78]

For Darwin, 'man has ultimately become superior to woman'. Nevertheless, he believed that, because pangenesis entailed the equal transmission of characters to both sexes, the difference between men and women was not as great as it might have been. Indeed, without the distributive equity that pangenesis enforced, 'man would have become as superior in mental endowment to woman, as the peacock is in ornamental plumage to the peahen'.[79] On the pangenesis hypothesis, just as male characteristics such as the colour of a beard were present but dormant in women, so too might be the gemmules for male intellectual superiority. Darwin speculated that, if they were given equal access to education, women might eventually match men in intellect.[80] But he viewed the education of women as a waste of time and resources – an unsurprising conclusion, perhaps, for a man who had pictured his marriage as involving a 'nice soft wife', not a self-confident intellectual equal, and who clearly thought the decision to marry was entirely his, not Emma's.[81] Darwin's assumptions about women's status were common among educated Victorian men. Somewhat ironically, several of his contemporaries – such as Alfred Russel Wallace and St George Mivart – rejected Darwin's proposal that female choice could have played any role in evolution because females were so notoriously fickle. Wallace and Mivart thought female tastes changed too often for them ever to be considered a 'force' akin to natural selection.[82]

Darwin's theory of sexual selection was published, and largely dismissed, at a time when Victorian feminists were demanding the vote – the National Society for Women's Suffrage had been founded in 1869 – as well as access to higher education and the learned professions. Educated women were even discreetly discussing the attractions of contraception. For Darwin and his male contemporaries, such developments fuelled fear that the uneducated, inferior lower classes would soon outbreed their educated betters.[83] Another, older anxiety of Darwin's reappeared in the *Descent*, when he argued that the government should use the census to discover once and for all 'whether or not consanguineous marriages are injurious to man' – and outlaw them if necessary.[84]

Darwin's consanguineous marriage to Emma was still very much on his mind in the 1870s. The flower-breeding experiments he had begun just after he married eventually resulted in *The Effects of Cross and Self Fertilisation in the Vegetable Kingdom* (1876), another book largely concerned with the harmful effects of in-breeding. The same preoccupation was central to *The Different Forms of Flowers on Plants of the Same Species* (1877), which showed why hermaphroditic flowers, such as primulas, often had two different flower forms (a phenomenon now known as heterostyly). Once again, Darwin showed that nature had evolved a mechanism to avoid self-fertilisation. As he tabulated his flower results, his thoughts must surely have turned to his own children. Several appeared sickly and were frequently ill. Two had died in infancy.[85] Throughout his life, the marriages of animals and flowers were thus entangled with the implications for and consequences of his own marriage.

Poignant as they were for Darwin personally, his botanical discoveries had theoretical consequences as well. His experimental results related directly to his earlier reflections on barnacles, especially on the transition from hermaphroditic states to those in which the sexes are fully separate. Gradually he began to place greater emphasis on sterility, rather than geographic isolation, as a major mechanism of species formation. Heterostyly seemed the first evolutionary step on the road to the sterility barrier between species.[86] In his view, his plant experiments showed that crossed plants were more vigorous than self-fertilised ones, and that developing sterility between populations helped produce new species.

IX GENERATION MATTERS

Darwin's engagement with issues of generation extended over fifty years, from his early observations on sea-mats to his late experiments on flowers. This engagement stimulated a great deal of private theorising about transmutation, and also two of Darwin's most important public doctrines: the hypothesis of pangenesis, and the theory of sexual selection. The latter theory, after a long spell in the scientific wilderness, is now widely celebrated. By contrast, pangenesis is still seen in many quarters either as a piece of inexplicable folly, or as a visionary but flawed attempt to anticipate modern genetics.[87] It makes more historical sense, however, to see the hypothesis as an attempt to draw together the strands of Darwin's generation theorising, using some of the same argumentative strategies that had worked so well in the argument of the *Origin*. Darwin surveyed his mass of evidence and tried to devise a single theory that would allow all his facts to 'jump together' into a single explanation. He was well aware that he was speculating, and knew that at least some aspects of his theory would turn out to be wrong. But when men such as his cousin Francis Galton tried to test it experimentally, pangenesis proved even more 'imperfect' than Darwin had feared.[88]

Darwin lived at a crucial transitional period in the history of the life sciences, when the gentlemanly traditions of natural history, which made no real distinctions between 'amateurs' and 'professionals,' were gradually being transformed into the laboratory-based science that we now recognise as biology.[89] This change has contributed to the unease that modern readers sometimes feel with the generational strand in Darwin's theorising. Although discriminating in his choice of correspondents, Darwin nevertheless tended to assume that the eye-witness reports of his fellow gentlemen could be trusted as scientific evidence.[90] Moreover, his informants were very often other men, who generally shared his assumption that nature had allotted very different roles to males and females. In cases like Lord Morton's mare, for example, Darwin assumed that the 'male principle' was more powerful and potent than the female.[91] His supposition deflected him from the possibility that the striped offspring of the unstriped father and mother were simple cases of reversion; rather than showing the enduring influence of the mother's previous, striped mate, the stripes reveal that domestic horses had striped ancestors. (Long after the quagga's extinction, striped foals continue to be born today.) Darwin's prejudices were also explicit when he wrote about sexual selection. In every species, he argued, 'it is the males that fight together and sedulously display their charms before the females; and those which are victorious transmit their superiority to their male offspring'. The most the females could do is choose. The female, in Darwin's view, is by nature 'coy, and may often be seen endeavouring for a long time to escape from the male. Every one who has attended to the habits of animals will be able to call to mind instances of this kind.'[92]

The historian Evelleen Richards has pointed out that there is a high degree of circularity in Darwin's arguments here. He described animals in terms of Victorian sexual morality (thus 'coy' females), and then 'naturalised' human actions by analogy with animals interpreted in the Victorian way (thus Darwin compared 'young rustics' at a fair to courting birds).[93] It is worth remembering, however, that feminists were still very much the minority in Darwin's day, and most Victorian women, like Darwin himself, viewed existing gender roles as entirely natural.[94] Endorsing or condemning Darwin's opinions on women – or on race – is as futile as trying to re-invent him as a pioneer of genetics. It is more illuminating to place him back in the context of his times – a theorist, not of genetics, but of generation, pondering the reproduction of flowers, animals and the gentlemen who bred them.

NOTES

I am grateful to Nick Hopwood, James Moore, Evelleen Richards, James Secord, Rebecca Stott, Pamela Thurschwell and Paul White for reading and commenting on various drafts of this chapter, and to Jon Hodge and Greg Radick for their extensive guidance and feedback.

1. C. Darwin 1958, 231–4, italics in original. See also Browne 1995, 379; Desmond and Moore 1991, 256, 269; E. Richards 1983, 57.
2. Hodge 1985, 207; Bartley 1992, 310.
3. Farley 1982, 7–8; Bartley 1992, 307–8; Allen 1994, 35–7, 46–7; Koerner 1996, 154–5; Koerner 1999, 15–16; Schiebinger 1996, 163, 171–2, 174–5.
4. Browne 1989, 595–7; Farley 1982, 28–9; Schiebinger 1996, 173–4.
5. Farley 1982, 28–9.
6. Browne 1995, 61–2.
7. The 'ova' of *Flustra* (a genus now classified as a Bryozoan) were in fact its embryos. Hodge 1985, 210; Browne 1995, 75, 80–2; Jordanova 1984; Sloan 1985, 77–9.
8. Sloan 1986, 384–5, 388, 393.
9. Sloan 1986, 373–7. On Henslow, see Walters and Stow 2001.
10. Sloan 1985, 101–2.
11. Hodge 1985, 208–11; Farley 1982, 53.
12. Sloan 1986, 388–93; Hodge 1985, 211.
13. C. Darwin [1839] 1986, ch. 14, entry for 4 February; Sloan 1985, 101–2; Hodge 1985, 211.
14. Sloan, this volume.
15. Barrett *et al.* 1987, *Charles Darwin's Notebooks, Red Notebook*, MS p. 132. See also E. Richards 1994, 394, 407–8.
16. Hodge 1985, 214–15, 218–19.
17. Hodge 1985, 220; *Charles Darwin's Notebooks, Notebook* B, MS pp. 5–10 (hereafter B5–10); Farley 1982, 107–9; E. Richards 1994, 407–8; Depew and Weber 1995, 114–15, 130–1; Bartley 1992, 312.
18. Hodge 1985, 219. On the connection between embryological and evolutionary theories, see R. J. Richards 1992; [Chambers] [1844] 1994; and Secord 2000.
19. D 162–79.

20. Allan 1977, 122–3; D128–31.
21. Hodge 1985, 223; Desmond and Moore 1991, 280, 290, 447, 619–20.
22. Allan 1977, 127–8; Hodge 1985, 223.
23. Browne 1995, 471–2, 510.
24. Browne 1995, 471, 477–80, 513.
25. Browne 1995, 479–80, 482, 513–14, 527–8; Ghiselin 1969, 134.
26. C. Darwin 1862.
27. Darwin to Asa Gray, 23–24 July 1862, quoted in Ghiselin 1969, 136. See also F. Burkhardt *et al.* 1985–2001, *Correspondence* x, 331 (hereafter *CCD*).
28. Secord 1981, 164.
29. Bartley 1992, 309, 329.
30. Hodge, this volume; also Bartley 1992, 310–11; C. Darwin [1875] 1998, II, 59–60; Hodge 1985, 220–1; Browne 1995, 157, 354–5.
31. Bartley 1992, 323.
32. Bartley 1992, 313–14.
33. C. Darwin [1875] 1998, II, 2–5, 9.
34. Bartley 1992, 323–7.
35. C. Darwin [1875] 1998, II, 393.
36. C. Darwin [1875] 1998, II, 35–6.
37. C. Darwin [1875] 1998, I, 417.
38. C. Darwin [1875] 1998, II, 349, 380; cf. Olby 1966, 100 and Geison 1969, 384–5.
39. R. W. Burkhardt 1979, 3; Hodge 1985, 224; C. Darwin [1875] 1998, I, 435.
40. C. Darwin [1875] 1998, I, 435; R. W. Burkhardt 1979, 6.
41. Hodge 1985, 220–1.
42. C. Darwin [1875] 1998, II, 370.
43. Farley 1982, 27–31; Zirkle 1946, 119–22, 140–4.
44. C. Darwin [1875] 1998, II, 393.
45. Hodge 1985, 228–9; Geison 1969, 375.
46. C. Darwin [1875] 1998, II, 394–5.
47. C. Darwin [1875] 1998, II, 59–60; Hodge 1985, 220–1; Browne 1995, 157, 354–5; Geison 1969, 377–8.
48. Hodge 1985, 211, 230.
49. C. Darwin [1875] 1998, II, 370.
50. C. Darwin [1875] 1998, II, 367.
51. C. Darwin [1875] 1998, II, 398–9.
52. Hodge 1985, 227–9.
53. Hodge 1985, 209.
54. C. Darwin to J. D. Hooker, 23 February 1868, in F. Darwin [1888] 1969, III, 78.

55. J. D. Hooker to George Grey, 31 May 1868. Italics in original. Grey Papers, vol. 22, Auckland Central City Library, Auckland, New Zealand.
56. Desmond and Moore 1991, 550–1; Ruse 1993b, 28–30.
57. C. Darwin [1859] 1964, chs. 7, 8, 10, 11, 12 and 13.
58. For background, see Hull, this volume.
59. Ruse 1993b,13–14.
60. Oldroyd 1986, 142–64.
61. Bartley 1992, 330–1.
62. Whewell, quoted in C. Darwin [1875] 1998, II, 350.
63. See Hodge and Waters, this volume.
64. J. D. Hooker to George Grey, 31 May 1868.
65. Darwin to Asa Gray, 3 April 1860, *CCD* VII, 140; Cronin 1991, 113.
66. C. Darwin [1871] 1981, II, 97. *Descent* was originally published in two volumes, but the modern facsimile referred to combines these into a single volume; I have indicated the original volume to which I am referring as I or II.
67. C. Darwin [1871] 1981, II, 399.
68. Of course, Darwin also recognised that the mechanisms of sexual selection varied from species to species according to their mating patterns.
69. Obviously, modern biologists reject this hereditary mechanism; nevertheless what Darwin christened sexual selection is still regarded as an essential part of an organism's overall 'Darwinian fitness'. See Cronin 1991; G. Miller 2000.
70. C. Darwin [1871] 1981, I, 258.
71. C. Darwin [1871] 1981, I, 259.
72. C. Darwin [1871] 1981, I, 259–60.
73. E. Richards 1983, 60–1, 64–5, 78. Evelleen Richards argues (p. 78) that Darwin 'put into men's hands the modifying and shaping power of the breeder, and that he did so for the purely cultural reason that it was inconceivable to this proper Victorian that human evolution could have been modified and shaped by female caprice or by female sexuality and passion'.
74. E. Richards 1983, 66–7.
75. C. Darwin [1871] 1981, II, 343–54.
76. C. Darwin 1871, II, 369.
77. E. Richards 1983, 68–9. For further complementary discussion, see R. J. Richards, this volume.
78. C. Darwin [1871] 1981, II, 326–7, 372; E. Richards 1983, 73–6.
79. C. Darwin [1871] 1981, II, 328–9.
80. C. Darwin [1871] 1981, II, 329.
81. E. Richards 1983, 87; cf. McCord 1991, 454.
82. Cronin 1991, 172; more generally, see Erskine 1995.

83. See Paul, this volume; E. Richards 1983, 72–3, 94; McCord 1991, 453.
84. C. Darwin [1871] 1981, II, 403.
85. Desmond and Moore 1991, 280, 290, 447; Hodge 1985, 218; Allan 1977, 127–8.
86. C. Darwin 1877; Ghiselin 1969, 143–5.
87. One of the founders of the Mendelian theory, the Dutch botanist Hugo de Vries, did see himself as vindicating parts of Darwin's pangenesis hypothesis. For general background, see Olby 1979.
88. Geison 1969, 378–9; Oldroyd 1980, 141.
89. See Nyhart 1996; Allen 1994; Morrell and Thackray 1981; Desmond 2001; and Morrell 1990. On professionalisation, Darwinism and the spontaneous generation debates, see Strick 2000.
90. Secord 1981, 175–6.
91. C. Darwin [1875] 1998, II, 361; E. Richards 1997, 119–20; Jann 1994.
92. C. Darwin [1871] 1981, I, 271–3.
93. C. Darwin [1871] 1981, II, 122; E. Richards 1983, 77–9.
94. E. Richards 1983, 87.

ROBERT J. RICHARDS

4 Darwin on mind, morals and emotions

I HUMAN EVOLUTION THROUGH HUMBOLDTIAN EYES

From the beginning of his theorising about species, Darwin had human beings in view. In the initial pages of his first transmutation notebook (*Notebook* B), he observed that 'even mind & instinct become influenced' as the result of adaptation to new circumstances.[1] Considering matters as a Lyellian geologist, he supposed that such adaptations would require many generations of young, pliable minds being exposed to a changing environment. After all, Captain FitzRoy had attempted to 'civilise' the Fuegian Jemmy Button by bringing him to London and instructing him in the Christian religion; but back in South America, Button reverted to his old habits, demonstrating, in Darwin's words, that the 'child of savage not civilized man' – transmutation of mind was not the work of a day.[2] Darwin had nonetheless quickly become convinced that over long periods of time human mind, morals and emotions had progressively developed out of animal origins. As he bluntly expressed it in his first transmutation notebook: 'If all men were dead, monkeys make men. – Men make angels.'[3] Presumably the transmutation of human beings into those higher creatures remained far in the future.

From July 1837, when he jotted these remarks in the first few pages of his *Notebook* B, to the early 1870s, with the publication of his *Descent of Man* and *Expression of the Emotions in Man and Animals*, Darwin gradually worked out theories of the evolution of human mentality that, in the main, we still accept. In the case of moral behaviour, he produced a theory of its evolution that stands as a most plausible empirical account, and displays the range and subtlety of his thought. These theories merit close examination in their own right. But a better understanding of them can also lead to a better understanding of Darwin himself. As we shall see, this Victorian gentleman's conception of human mind had roots traversing a large swath of native ground, with some, though, penetrating to quite foreign soil, namely, German romanticism.

Darwin's conception of nature, as well as his estimate of that smaller nature found in human beings, took definite shape during his five-year voyage on the *Beagle*. His experiences during the journey occurred within a framework already prepared by his enthusiastic reading of Alexander von Humboldt's *Personal Narrative of Travels to the Equinoctial Regions of the New Continent, 1799–1804*, a multi-volume work that originally sparked his desire to sail to exotic lands.[4] Indeed, while a student at Cambridge he took to copying out long passages from the *Personal Narrative* and reading them to his rather patient friends. When he got the opportunity to embark on the *Beagle*, he brought along Humboldt's volumes as his vade mecum. Humboldt, a protégé of Goethe and friend of Schelling, represented nature not as a stuttering, passionless machine that ground out products in a rough-hewn manner but as a cosmos of interacting organisms, a complex whose heart beat with law-like regularity, while yet expressing aesthetic and moral values. Darwin did not plunge far below the surface of Humboldt's thought; but he nonetheless felt the power of the German's representations. He even remarked in his diary during the voyage back to England: 'As the force of impression frequently depends on preconceived ideas, I may add that all mine were taken from the vivid descriptions in the Personal Narrative which far exceed in merit anything I have ever read on the subject.'[5]

Humboldt's name litters Darwin's diary and the book he made out of it, his *Journal of Researches* (1839). That adventurer's romantic conception of nature would lie at the foundation of all the Englishman's later work on species and especially on the human species.[6] The creative force of nature would often, in Darwin's estimate, work through that most mundane yet transcendent faculty – instinct.

II THEORIES OF INSTINCT, EMOTION AND REASON PRIOR TO THE *ORIGIN*

The phenomenon of animal instinct would serve Darwin as the ground for understanding its outgrowth in human reason and moral behaviour. He initially employed the conception of instinct, however, more generally in his explanation of species change. Prior to having read Malthus, he had formulated several theories to account for heritable modifications. The most prominent theory depended on the inherited effects of the use of organs, so-called 'use-inheritance'. Darwin assumed that in a changed environment, an animal might adopt habits that would accommodate it to the new conditions. Over many generations, these habits would, he believed, become instinctive, that is, expressed as innately determined behaviours. Such instincts, in time, would slowly alter anatomy, producing adaptive alterations, or so he supposed.

This 'view of particular instinct being memory transmitted without consciousness' had the advantage, he thought, of distinguishing his explanation of adaptive species change from Lamarck's, which he interpreted as appealing to a *conscious willing* – 'Lamarck's willing absurd', he told himself.[7] Even after Darwin adopted natural selection as the principal means for producing species change, he still retained use-inheritance in his explanatory repertoire: it would become one of those sources for variation on which natural selection might work; and in some instances, he would simply credit use-inheritance as the cause of an attribute that could not easily be explained by natural selection.

After he had returned from his voyage, Darwin often visited the Zoological Society, where he had deposited for analysis and classification many of the animal specimens he had brought back on the *Beagle*; he thus had frequent occasion to visit the Society's menageries. During April 1838, he spent some time watching the apes and monkeys at the gardens; and he reflected on their emotional outbursts, which seemed to him quite humanlike. He was especially interested in an orang-utan that 'kicked & cried, precisely like a naughty child' when teased by its keeper.[8] In his notebooks, he placed such typical reactions within the framework of his theory of instinct: 'Expression, is an hereditary habitual movement consequent on some action, which the progenitor did, when excited or disturbed by the same cause, which ≪now≫ excites the expression.'[9] So, for example, Darwin speculated that the emotional response of surprise – raised eyebrows, retracted eyelids and so on – had arisen by association with our ancestors' efforts to see objects in dim light; now when the analogously unexpected object or event confronted us, we would react in an instinctual way, even though the light was perfectly adequate.[10] In this construction, the expression of emotion thus had no particular usefulness; it was understood, rather, as a kind of accidental holdover from the customary behaviour of ancestors. Darwin would retain this basic notion about emotional display for the account he would later develop in the *Expression of the Emotions in Man and Animals* (1872). Emotional expression had its roots in instinct, and, in Darwin's view, reason did as well.

In August 1838, Darwin began reading David Hume's *Inquiry Concerning Human Understanding*.[11] Hume's representation of ideas as less vivid copies of sensations perfectly accorded with Darwin's intuitions about the continuity of animal and human mentality: for if ideas were but copies of sensuous impressions, then animals would be perfectly capable of thought. Darwin developed this sensationalist epistemology in his *Notebook* N, where he proposed that simple reasoning consisted in the comparison of sensory images and that the recollection of several such images producing a pleasant state was of the very nature of complex thought.[12] And just as Hume understood reason to be a kind of 'wonderful and unintelligible instinct in our souls',[13] so Darwin thought intellectual activity to be a 'modification of instinct – an unfolding & generalizing of the means by which an instinct is transmitted.'[14] Human intelligence was, then, not opposed to animal instinct but grew out of it in the course of ages.

In finding the antecedents of human rationality in animal sources, Darwin really opened no new epistemological ground. Carl Gustav Carus, Goethe's disciple and an author whom Darwin read in early 1838, asserted the decidedly romantic thesis that mind and matter ran together throughout nature. Adopting Carus' language, Darwin contemplated a nature alive with mind. He reflected that 'there is one living spirit, prevalent over this world... which assumes a multitude of forms according to subordinate laws'. And like Carus, he concluded that 'there is one thinking... principle intimately allied to one kind of matter – brain' and that this thinking principle 'is modified into endless forms, bearing a close relation in degree and kind to the endless forms of the living beings'.[15] Darwin's assumption of cognitive continuity between men and animals would not even have offended the religiously minded among his own countrymen. Several natural theologians whom he read during the late 1830s and early 1840s – John Fleming, Algernon Wells and Henry Lord Brougham, for instance – did not blanch at finding some glimmer of reason exhibited even among the lower animals.[16] But no animal, in the estimation of these British writers, gave evidence of any hint of what was truly distinctive of human mind – namely, moral judgement. If Darwin were to solidify his case for the descent of man from lower animals, he would have to discover the roots of moral behaviour even among those creatures. And so he did.

III MORAL THEORY PRIOR TO THE *ORIGIN*

Darwin's own moral sensitivities received considerable assault during his South American travels, especially from the Brazilian slave trade. His family cultivated strong abolitionist sentiments, which originated with both of his grandfathers; and his sisters kept him informed about the efforts in Parliament to emancipate the slaves in the British colonies.[17] Darwin had his convictions reinforced by the many observations Humboldt himself had made about the loathsome trade in human beings.[18]

Darwin's own fury could be barely suppressed when he witnessed African families being separated at slave auctions and slaves being beaten and degraded. When finally the *Beagle* left Brazil, he rejoiced that 'I shall never again visit a slave-country.' He perceived immediately that utilitarian motives would do little to restrain this kind of evil: 'It is argued that self-interest will prevent excessive cruelty; as if self-interest protected our domestic animals, which are far less likely than degraded slaves, to stir up the rage of their savage masters. It is an argument long since protested against with noble feeling, and strikingly exemplified, by the ever illustrious Humboldt.'[19] This last remark about the deficiencies of utilitarian considerations to adjudicate moral responsibility came in the revised edition (1845) of Darwin's *Journal of Researches*. Prior to this time, he did make an effort to found an initial hypothesis about the evolution of morals on utilitarian grounds.

Darwin knew quite well William Paley's *Moral and Political Philosophy* (1785) from his undergraduate days at Cambridge. Now, while exploring the various branches of his developing theory in early September 1838, he momentarily adopted Paley's central rule of 'expediency'.[20] This rule grounded moral approbation in what, in the long run, would be useful, that is, beneficial either to an individual or a group and, as a consequence, would supply the pleasure God intended for mankind.[21] Darwin gave this rule a biological interpretation:

> Sept 8th. I am tempted to say that those actions which have been found necessary for long generation, (as friendship to fellow animals in social animals) are those which are good & consequently give pleasure, & not as Paley's rule is those that on long run *will* do good. – alter *will* in all such cases to *have* & *origin* as well as rule will be given.[22]

Darwin here suggested that those habits that preserved animals – such as friendship and nurture of young – must have been practised over many generations and so became instinctive. What we call 'good', then, are those long-term, beneficial instincts that have proved necessary for social cohesion and development. Hence, Darwin supposed that what Paley took to be a forward-looking rule – act to achieve general utility in the *future* – might be transformed into one describing instincts that arose from social behaviours which had been beneficial over long periods in the *past*. But this biologised Paleyan ethics receded from Darwin's purview after he examined a volume containing a more penetrating analysis of morals – the Scottish philosopher James Mackintosh's *Dissertation on Progress of Ethical Philosophy* (1836).

In his *Dissertation*, Mackintosh – an admired relative of Darwin's – objected to Paley's notion that selfish pleasure ultimately motivated right action. Mackintosh rather sided with those who believed instead that human nature came outfitted with a deep sense of moral propriety. Human beings, he believed, acted spontaneously for the welfare of their fellows and immediately approved of such actions when displayed by others. Yet he did not deny the utility of moral conduct. In a cool hour we could assess moral behaviour and rationally calculate its advantages; but such calculation was not, he thought, the immediate spring of action, which lay coiled in the human soul. Mackintosh thus distinguished the *criterion* for right conduct – utility – from the *motive* for such conduct – an innate disposition.

This analysis fitted rather smoothly into Darwin's developing conception of moral behaviour, a conception that both appreciated the utility of ethical behaviour and recognised its deep biological roots as well. Darwin's notes on Mackintosh's *Dissertation* reveal, however, that he discovered a jarring patch in the original theory, but one which he believed his own biological approach could pave over. The difficulty was this: What explained the harmony of the criterion for moral conduct and the motive for such behaviour? Why were we moved to act spontaneously in a way that we might later, in a moment of reflection, recognise to have social utility? Not impressed with Mackintosh's faint appeal to a divine harmoniser, Darwin suggested that the innate moral knowledge we harboured was really an instinct acquired by our ancestors. The instinct did, indeed, have social utility; but, like all instincts, it had an urgency not connected with any rational calculation of pleasures and pains. Such instincts, Darwin thought, would be sufficiently different from our other more abrupt and momentary instincts in that they would be persistent and firm and thus evoke a more reverential feeling.

Darwin moved with alacrity along this line of thought because in this instance, as in many others, he found that his theory of biological development solved a problem that remained loose and frayed in the humanistic literature. On 3 October 1838, a few days after Malthus furnished a key insight about adaptation of structure to changing conditions, the young naturalist reformulated his theory of moral conscience along the lines suggested by Mackintosh. Darwin assumed that habits of parental nurture, group cooperation, community defence, and so on, would be sustained over many generations, driving such habits into the heritable legacy of a species, so that they would be manifested in succeeding generations as instincts for moral conduct. These instincts would be distinguished from fleeting inclinations and less persistent impulses, which might occur in one generation and depart with the next. When an individual with sufficient intelligence recalled, well after the heat of the moment, a behaviour elicited by these deeply ingrained dispositions, he or she would feel renewed satisfaction and also would be able to perceive on reflection the social utility of the behaviour. Darwin thus solved the problem of the coincidence of the moral motive and the moral criterion.

Darwin worked out the basic framework of his moral conception without the aid of the theory of natural selection. Moreover, when he later began to apply that theory to explain instincts, he stumbled at the brink of a yawning conceptual abyss, which threatened to swallow his entire theory of evolution by natural selection. The crucial difficulty was this: the social instincts most frequently gave advantage to the recipients of moral actions, not to their agents; but natural selection preserved individuals because of traits advantageous to themselves, not to others. Darwin first met this difficulty when studying the social insects in the 1840s, when the problem became even more complicated.

Soldier bees and ants displayed anatomical traits and instinctive behaviours that served the welfare of their colonies, not directly themselves. Indeed, a soldier bee might defend the hive at the cost of its own life. Moreover, these insects were neuters; consequently they could not in the first instance pass beneficial adaptations to succeeding generations. How then could their other-regarding traits be explained, and, more generally, how did the attributes of neuters arise? Darwin worried about this problem for some time, fearing it would allow the Creator a return to those provinces from which he had lately been banished.[23] Only during the first months of 1858, while labouring on the manuscript that would become, in its abridged form, the *Origin of Species*, did Darwin discover the solution to his problem. He concluded that 'natural selection might act on the parents & continually preserve those which produced more & more aberrant offspring, having any structures or instincts advantageous to the community'.[24] Thus the soldier bee which sacrificed its life for the hive would have had its instincts honed over generations, not by individual selection but by natural selection preserving those hives that had individuals with traits that profited the entire community. With this account, which he reiterated in the *Origin of Species*, Darwin had the key to the puzzle of human moral action: as he would argue in the *Descent of Man*, altruistic impulses would give tribal clans advantages over other clans, and thus such instincts would become characteristic of evolving human communities.

IV THE MORAL CHARACTER OF NATURE IN THE *ORIGIN*

Darwin is usually taken to have introduced into biology a thoroughgoing mechanism. In the words of one set of scholars: 'Natural-selection theory and physiological reductionism were explosive and powerful enough statements of a research program to occasion the replacement of one ideology – of God – by another: a mechanical, materialistic science.'[25] This sort of cold-blooded Darwinism, it appears, left man morally naked to the world, since nature, bereft of the divine stamp, became 'morally meaningless' – or so it is commonly believed.[26] But did Darwin believe it?

A straightforward reading of the *Origin of Species* indicates that Darwin hardly had a machine in mind as the model for nature. Rather, he articulated nature so as to display its moral spine. This should not be surprising if one recalls that Darwin had looked upon wild nature during the *Beagle* voyage through Humboldtian eyes – eyes that had a romantic glint. Even the surface of the *Origin*'s conceptions ripples with moral suggestion. Consider Darwin's presentation of the very idea of natural selection. He compares it with man's selection, to the moral advantage of the former. Where man 'selects only for his own good', nature selects 'only for that of the being which she tends'. Nature is a model not only of selflessness, but of care and industry. Natural selection 'is daily and hourly scrutinizing, throughout the world, every variation, even the slightest, rejecting that which is bad, preserving and adding up all that is good; silently and insensibly working, whenever and wherever opportunity offers, at the improvement of each organic being in relation to its organic and inorganic conditions of life'.[27] Can it be any wonder, then, that the productions of nature are 'far "truer" in character than man's productions'? They plainly manifest, in Darwin's resonant phrase, 'the stamp of far higher workmanship'.[28]

The lilting poetry of these phrases might be taken as merely decorative metaphor, not harbouring argumentative substance. But a look back at the predecessors to these phrases in Darwin's earlier manuscripts suggests otherwise. In a passage from his essay of 1844, Darwin strove to make clear to himself, through images and metaphors, the conception of a selecting nature towards which he was groping. Suppose, he wrote, that a being with powers of perception far superior to man, and with 'forethought extending over future centuries', were, with 'unerring care', to do the selecting. Then there would be 'no conceivable reason why he should not form a new race', adapted 'to new ends'. Furthermore, his superior art and 'steadiness of object' would produce organisms far more different from the original stock, with far greater 'beauty and complications' in their adaptations, than comparable organisms 'produced by man's agency'.[29]

The being that Darwin here imagines has those qualities characteristic of the recently departed Deity. Acting with preternatural intelligence, it sees into the future, cares for the welfare of its creatures and selects them for their beauty and progressive adaptations. This being, in more muted colours, continues to operate in the *Origin of Species*, where the guarantee is issued that since 'natural selection works solely by and for the good of each being, all corporeal and mental endowments will tend to progress towards perfection'.[30] Despite having become a more reserved individual, Darwin yet portrayed nature in the *Origin of Species* in the manner that he had absorbed from his Humboldtian experiences during his youthful voyage of adventure, namely, nature as having a moral and aesthetic intelligence. It is, then, not surprising that when he turned specifically to consider the distinctive character of human beings, he did not leave them bereft of those traits he accorded nature.

V THE DEBATES OVER HUMAN EVOLUTION, 1859–71

In the late 1860s, Darwin initially approached the problem of human evolution quite modestly. He had originally intended to consider human beings only from the point of view of sexual selection, which he thought could explain the different attributes of males and females of the many races of mankind. He engorged the second part of *The Descent of Man, and Selection in Relation to Sex* (1871) with detailed discussions of sexual selection throughout the animal kingdom, with only the last two substantive chapters devoted to human sexual dimorphism and racial differences. He argued that male combat for females among our ancestors would have contributed to the male's larger size, pugnacity, strength and intelligence. In his view, the particular features of female beauty in the different races – generally hairless bodies, cast of skin, shape of nose, form of buttocks and so on – arose from male choice. Women generally displayed the tender virtues; but their intellectual attainments were largely due, Darwin thought, to inheritance from the male parent. In a letter to a young American female college student, he did venture that if women went to university and were schooled over generations as the sons of the gentry were, then they would, via use-inheritance, become as intelligent as men. But were this to happen, 'we may suspect that the early education of our children, not to mention the happiness of our homes, would in this case greatly suffer'.[31]

Several events occurred during the 1860s that caused Darwin to alter the limited intentions he had for his book on human descent. Early in the decade, his great friend Charles Lyell waded into the undulating opinions forming about human evolution in the wake of the *Origin*. But the hedging argument of his *Antiquity of Man* (1863), which displayed a style familiar at the Old Bailey, drove Darwin to distraction. Though Lyell admitted the physical similarity of human beings to other primates, he yet argued that the mental and moral constitution of humans placed them far above any other animals in the scale of being. Linguistic ability in particular demonstrated the wide gulf separating the mind of man from that of animals. This was no chasm that could be bridged in 'the usual course of nature'. The move from animals to man, Lyell intimated, had to be carried on the wings of a divine spirit.[32]

Alfred Russel Wallace initially stood ready to combat Lyell's theological construction of human mind and morals. In a lecture delivered to the Anthropological Society of London in 1864, he produced an ingenious defence of the naturalistic position. He argued that natural selection, operating on our animal forebears, produced the various races of men, though not yet their distinctive mental and moral characters. Only after these races appeared would natural selection operate on the various clans and tribes, preserving those groups in which individuals displayed sympathy, cooperation and 'the sense of right which checks depredation upon our fellows'.[33]

Three features of Wallace's account of the evolution of human mind and morals stand out. First, he conceived the selective environment to be other proto-human groups – which would have an accelerating effect on the evolutionary process, since social environments would rapidly change through responsive competition.

Second, he proposed that selection worked on the group, rather than the individual – which allowed him to explain the rise of altruistic behaviour, that is, behaviour perhaps harmful to the individual but beneficial to the group. In his original essay on the transmutation of species (1858), Wallace conceived of the struggle for existence as occurring among *varieties* instead of individuals.[34] He continued to think in such group terms when considering the evolution of moral behaviour. Finally, in a note to the published version of his talk to the Anthropological Society, he mentioned that he was inspired to develop his thesis by reading Herbert Spencer's *Social Statics*.[35] Spencer's own early brand of socialism had pulled Wallace to his side. In *Social Statics* (1851), Spencer had envisioned a gradual and continual adjustment of human beings to the requirements of civil society, with individuals accommodating themselves to the needs of their fellows, so that eventually a classless society would emerge in which the greatest happiness for the greatest number would be realised.[36] Spencer assumed that the inheritance of useful habits would be the means by which such evolutionary progress would occur, while Wallace believed natural selection to be the agent of that progress.

Darwin welcomed Wallace's solution to the evolution of human morality, since he himself had developed certain views about community selection in social insects congenial to his friend's position. Darwin would emphasise, however, that the members of small tribes, of the sort Wallace envisioned, would probably be related; and so a disadvantage to a given individual practising altruism would yet be outweighed by the advantage of the practice to recipient relatives. Ultimately, however, Darwin would drop this qualification, and simply embrace group selection as operative in human (and animal) societies.[37]

Wallace's faith in a naturalistic account of human evolutionary progress nevertheless succumbed to the evidence of higher powers at work in the land. Though raised as a materialist and agnostic, Wallace had chanced to attend a séance, which piqued his empiricist inclinations. Shortly thereafter, in 1866, he hired a medium in order to investigate the phenomena usually attendant on the invocation of the spirit world. Wallace, gentle soul that he was, became a true believer (unlike Darwin, who regarded spiritualism as rubbish). Wallace's new conviction focused his attention on certain human traits – naked skin, language, mathematical ability, ideas of justice and abstract reasoning generally – which would confer no biological advantage on individuals in a low state of civilisation. Indeed, Wallace believed that, for sheer survival, human beings need a brain no larger than that of an orang-utan, or perhaps one comparable to that of the average member of a London gentleman's club. Such traits as abstract reasoning and moral sensitivity, therefore, could not be explained by natural selection. Yet in both aboriginal and advanced societies, individuals displayed these qualities. While his friend Herbert Spencer regarded such properties as explicable only through use-inheritance,[38] Wallace found a unique explanatory mode of selection that his new faith could provide.[39] In his estimation, distinctively human traits had been artificially selected for us: 'a superior intelligence', he proposed, 'has guided the development of man in a definite direction, and for a special purpose, just as man guides the development of many animal and vegetable forms'.[40] Humans were thus like domestic animals in the hands of higher spiritual powers. Their superintendence of the selection process had ensured that distinctively human traits, for human advantage, had won out in the long struggle for existence.

When Darwin learned of Wallace's turnabout, he was dumbfounded: 'But I groan over Man – you write like a metamorphosed (in the retrograde direction) naturalist, and you the author of the best paper that ever appeared in the *Anthropological Review*!'[41] Though Wallace's flight to other powers than nature was fuelled by his new faith, the crux of his argument had force: since natural selection operated only on traits that provided some immediate biological advantage, how might one explain human traits that seemed not particularly useful at all?

Another writer, though friendly to the Darwinian cause, yet spied a comparable problem in the assumption of human evolutionary progress. William Ratherbone Greg, Scots moralist and political writer, discovered that a keen moral sense might spread seeds of wicked growth. A highly civilised society, he remarked, would be inclined to protect not only the physically weak from the winnowing hand of natural selection but the intellectually and morally degenerate as well. So protected, the inferior types would have the opportunity to outbreed their betters. Greg, a Scots gentleman of refined sensibility, regarded the case of the Irish as cautionary. While the 'careless, squalid, unaspiring Irishman' sired offspring early and often, the 'frugal, foreseeing, self-respecting, ambitious Scot' delayed marriage and had few children. The profligate and degenerate Irish yet seemed to be winning the evolutionary race in the trait that counted – reproduction. 'In the eternal "struggle for existence"', Greg concluded, 'it would be the inferior and less favoured race that had prevailed – and prevailed by virtue not of its good qualities but of its faults.'[42] The considerations of Lyell, Wallace and Greg spurred Darwin to expand his intended volume on sexual selection to tackle these apparent barriers to a naturalistic understanding of human evolution.

In the face of Greg's argument, Darwin collected in the *Descent* considerable evidence about the fortunes of the reprobate. On the basis of this evidence, he maintained that many natural checks to the less fit would ultimately forestall their advance: the debauched would suffer higher mortality, criminals would sire fewer offspring, and the bad would likely die young.[43] Yet it could be that the likes of the Irish, though decidedly less able, would simply crowd out the British. After all, though evolutionary progress was general, it was 'no invariable rule'.[44]

VI MIND IN THE *DESCENT*

Lyell's and Wallace's objections to the application of natural selection in the case of man proved more difficult to counter than Greg's, but they brought Darwin to several ingenious solutions to the problems posed. Linguistic ability stood chief among the features of intelligence that had to be considered. In dealing with this problem, Darwin reverted to a theory he had initially entertained in his *Notebook* N, which he kept in 1838 and 1839. There he sought to develop a naturalistic account of the origin of language. He supposed that our aboriginal ancestors began imitating sounds of nature (e.g., 'crack', 'roar', 'crash') and that language developed from these simple beginnings.[45] In the late 1860s, while working on the *Descent*, Darwin made frequent enquiries of his cousin, the linguist Hensleigh Wedgwood, about the origin of languages. Wedgwood had allowed that it was part of God's plan to have man instructed, as it were, by the natural development of speech. He argued that language began from an instinct for imitation of sounds of animals and natural events, which under 'pressure of social wants' developed into a system of signs.[46] Darwin embraced this confirmation of his original ideas, though, of course, dispensing with the theological interpretation.

Darwin also relied on another book in formulating his thesis about the function of language in human evolution. This was by a German linguist, August Schleicher, a friend and colleague of the morphologist Ernst Haeckel and a new convert to Darwinian theory. In his *Die Darwinsche Theorie und die Sprachwissenschaft* (*Darwinian theory and the science of language*, 1863), Schleicher maintained that contemporary languages had gone through a process in which simpler *Ursprachen* had given rise to descendent languages that obeyed natural laws of development.[47] He argued that Darwin's theory was thus perfectly applicable to languages and, indeed, that evolutionary theory itself was confirmed by the facts of language descent. In a subsequent pamphlet, Schleicher himself constructed the kind of argument that Darwin would employ in the *Descent*, that is: 'the formation of language is for us comparable to the evolution of the brain and the organs of speech'.[48] Schleicher maintained that the several languages of mankind produced the various types of mind displayed by the different races. Ernst Haeckel took up this argument in his *Naturliche Schöpfungsgeschichte* (*The Natural History of Creation*, 1868), which Darwin read while composing the *Descent*. Darwin wrote to a friend after reading Haeckel's work that it was 'one of the most remarkable books of our time'.[49] Darwin's notes and underlining in the book are quite extensive. He was particularly interested, as shown by his scorings and marginalia, in Haeckel's account of Schleicher's thesis that the evolution of language was the material side of the evolution of mind.[50] Here then Darwin had a counter-argument to Wallace's, one by which he could solidify an evolutionary naturalism.

Darwin conceded that Wallace had been correct: for sheer survival, our animal ancestors had sufficient brain power. But he could now blunt the further implication of his friend's argument. Citing Schleicher, he argued in the *Descent* that developing language would rebound on the brain, producing more complex trains of ideas; and constant exercise of intricate thought would gradually alter brain structures, causing a hereditary transformation and, consequently, a progressive enlargement of human intellect beyond that necessary for mere survival.[51]

Darwin's general theory of the rise of human intellect thus depended on the inheritance of acquired characteristics, or at least that is one of the strands of argument he employed. Yet it was not the only strand. Darwin's explanations in the *Origin* and the *Descent* were rhetorically robust – if the reader did not like one line of consideration, the author was ready with another line. His second strand of argument relied on community selection. In the *Descent*, Darwin contended that if a tribe of our aboriginal ancestors contained among its members some mute, inglorious Newton, an individual who through inventiveness and intellectual prowess benefited his tribe in competition with other tribes, then he and his relatives would survive and reproduce.[52] Darwin enunciated here an idea that bears strong affinities to what is now known as 'inclusive fitness'. A heritable trait that confers little or no benefit on an individual but sufficiently advances the cause of relatives will be preserved and spread along with the group. Darwin first developed this theory of community selection to solve the problem of the evolution of the social insects; it now became the key to understanding the evolution of social human beings.

VII MORALS IN THE *DESCENT*

In the first volume of the *Descent*, the question of human moral judgement occupied the greatest measure of Darwin's attention. Moral sense was by common consent that attribute most distinctive of human beings. Both Lyell and Wallace could not conceive that a refined moral sense might have arisen naturally from animal stock. After all, moral behaviour did not prove particularly beneficial to those exercising it – hence natural selection could not account for it. In explaining the rise of moral behaviour, Darwin again moved from the individual as the object of selection to the community. While 'a high standard of morality' indeed conferred small or no advantages to individuals, tribes of individuals endowed with 'patriotism, fidelity, obedience, courage, and sympathy', and the readiness 'to give aid to each other and to sacrifice themselves for the common good', would be 'victorious over most other tribes; and this would be natural selection'. Furthermore, as the victorious, moral tribes supplant the defeated, immoral ones throughout the world, 'the standard of morality and the number of well-endowed men will thus everywhere tend to rise and increase'.[53]

Community selection proved an ingenious way to understand the evolution of human altruism. It yet had its own difficulty: How do these moral traits arise *within* one tribe in the first place? After all, as Darwin noted, it is not likely that parents of an altruistic temper would raise more children than those of a selfish attitude. Moreover, those who were inclined to self-sacrifice might leave no offspring at all.[54] Darwin employed his theory of use-inheritance to explain the origin of such social behaviours within a given tribe. He proposed two related sources for such behaviours. The first is the prototype of contemporary theories of reciprocal altruism. Darwin observed that, as the reasoning powers of members of a tribe improved, each would come to learn from experience 'that if he aided his fellow-men, he would commonly receive aid in return'. From this 'low motive', as he regarded it, each might develop the habit of performing benevolent actions, which habit might be inherited and thus furnish suitable material on which community selection might operate. The second source relied on the assumption that 'praise and blame' of certain social behaviours would feed our animal need to enjoy the admiration of others and to avoid feelings of shame and reproach. This kind of social control would also lead to heritable habits.[55]

One salient objection to any theory of the biological evolution of moral conduct points to the often very different standards of acceptable behaviour in various cultures. Darwin recognised that what might be approved as moral in one age and society might be execrated at a different time and place. The Fuegians might steal from other tribes without the slightest remorse of conscience, while an English gentleman would regard such behaviour with contempt. But members of these vastly different cultures would, nonetheless, commonly endorse the obligation to deal sympathetically and benevolently with members of their own particular group. The English gentleman and lady – or, perhaps, their descendants – with more advanced intellects would have learned that tribal and national differences were superficial; and thus they would have perceived a universal humanity underlying inessential traits. Their own instinctive sympathies would thus have been trained to respond to all human beings as members of a common tribe. In Darwin's conception, then, evolution would have moulded the most primitive human beings to react altruistically to brothers and sisters; but over the ages, cultural learning, coupled with increased intelligence, would reveal just who those brothers and sisters might be.[56]

'Philosophers of the derivative school of morals' (e.g., Bentham and Mill), Darwin observed, 'formerly assumed that the foundations of morality lay in a form of Selfishness; but more recently in the "Greatest Happiness principle" '.[57] Virtually all scientists and philosophers who have considered the matter have located these utilitarian principles at the foundation of an evolutionary construction of ethics. Michael Ghiselin provides the prototypical example. He has argued that, according to Darwin's theory, since an altruistic act furthers the competitive ability of self and family, that act is 'really a form of ultimate self-interest'.[58] Richard Dawkins, a defender of Darwin, yet warned 'that if you wish, as I do, to build a society in which individuals cooperate generously and unselfishly towards a common good, you can expect little help from biological nature'.[59] These sentiments, quite obviously, do not reflect Darwin's own view. Our moral instincts, he believed, would urge us to act for the benefit of others without calculating pleasures and pains for self. And since such altruistic impulses, at least in advanced societies, would not be confined to family, tribe or nation, he confidently concluded that his theory removed 'the reproach of laying the foundation of the most noble part of our nature in the base principle of selfishness'.[60]

VIII THE EXPRESSION OF THE EMOTIONS

Though Darwin believed that human intelligence and moral responses had their roots in the animal mind, he conceded that these faculties had yet developed far beyond those of our progenitors. By contrast, he considered human emotions and their display not to have comparably progressed. The fear displayed by his little dog over a wind-blown parasol differed little, he thought, from that of the native who trembled because invisible spirits might be causing a lightning storm – or, as Darwin intimated, from the Christian's fear of the wraith of an unseen God.[61] Certainly few English sportsmen would have difficulty reading human-like emotions off the expressions displayed by their dogs The belief that humans shared comparable emotions and expressions with animals accorded with a common intellectual tradition that can easily be traced back to Aristotle. Yet

Darwin's own evolutionary analysis in his *Expression of the Emotions in Man and Animals* (1872) has a peculiar and, for us, an unexpected contour, which can only be understood in the light of an unusual theory worked out by one of his contemporaries.

Sir Charles Bell's *The Anatomy and Philosophy of Expression* (1844) displays a research physician's detailed knowledge of facial anatomy and a devoted humanist's understanding of emotional depiction in art and literature. Bell argued that the smiles and frowns, laughs and sighs, beams and grimaces of the human countenance functioned as a natural language by which one soul communicated with another. Ultimately this repertoire of signs, he asserted, referred back to its divine author, who 'has laid the foundation of emotions that point to Him, affections by which we are drawn to Him, and which rest in Him as their object'.[62] Thus according to Bell, the expression of the emotions served for communication, human and divine.

Darwin read Bell's book with considerable interest. He focused on the physician's precise descriptions of the structure and operation of facial muscles during the expression of emotions. He denied, however, the theological foundation for emotional expression that Bell divined. But in rejecting Bell's particular conception of the utility of emotional response, he rejected completely all notions of utility for the expressions. Emotional display, to be sure, had an evolutionary history. Darwin's many comparisons of facial movements in children, adults, the insane, as well as in apes, dogs and cats – done with the aid of photography and sketches – showed similarities across ages, sexes and mental capacities. This kind of comparative evidence bespoke a common origin for emotional expression. But since he could discover no social or communicative function in these emotional reactions – unlike neo-Darwinians today – his theory of natural selection did not readily apply.[63] Instead, Darwin appealed to a number of other principles, especially his notion that instinctive reactions could derive from practices that had been, by dint of exercise, scored into the heritable substance. He argued that among our ancestors, if a certain mental state was often accompanied by actions that brought relief or gratification, then those actions thereafter accompanied the mental state – for example, the turning away and the wrinkled nose of disgust, elicited originally by the sight of some repulsive object, might again be displayed due to the feeling alone. Darwin called this the 'principle of serviceable associated habits' and used it to explain variously frowning, dejection, smiling and so on.[64] He formulated two more principles to handle other kinds of expression. The 'principle of antithesis' specified that when certain actions were connected with a particular state of mind, an opposite state would tend to elicit an opposite action. For instance, a hostile dog will stand rigid with tail stiff and hair erect, while a docile, happy animal will crouch low with back bent and tail curled. Finally, there was the principle (borrowed from Herbert Spencer), according to which a violent emotion might spill over to adjacent nerve pathways and produce an outward effect – when, for example, great fear caused trembling.[65]

IX CONCLUSION

Among the many sources for Darwin's ideas about nature, German romanticism supplied one of the deeper and more powerful currents. The anatomist Richard Owen served as one especially important conduit for this tradition. His Goethean morphology and Schellingian archetype theory, suitably reconsidered, formed staples of Darwin's own intellectual repertoire. The doctrine of embryological recapitulation, a fundamental feature of German romantic biology, became a main supporting pillar of Darwin's general theory.[66] Darwin modelled his *Journal of Researches* on Humboldt's *Personal Narrative*; and Humboldt, that doyen of German science in the first half of the century, returned the compliment by singling out in his book *Kosmos* the merits of the young English adventurer.[67] Humboldt conceived nature as an organism exhibiting interacting parts; and Darwin, rejecting the clockwork universe of his English heritage, discovered many ingenious ways of tracing out those organic interactions in the *Origin*. Humboldt's nature had those aesthetic, moral and creative properties characteristic of the retired Deity; and these are exactly the features exhibited by natural selection. We usually take the measure of Darwin's ideas looking backward, from the photograph by Julia Cameron, who portrayed Darwin as a sad English prophet. But in his youth, this future fixture of the Victorian establishment sailed to exotic lands, became intoxicated with the sublimity of their environs, and tested his mettle against the forces of man and nature. Like many of the romantics, he also discovered the human core of that nature, and continually reckoned with it as he constructed his general theory of evolution.

Mind, morals and emotions occupied Darwin's attention in his early notebooks and found places even within the *Origin of Species*, which ostensibly avoided the problem of human evolution. His argumentative strategy in the *Descent* and in the *Expression of the Emotions* continued that of the *Origin*. He employed vast amounts of empirical evidence gathered from many different sources and was able to show that when properly juxtaposed, evolutionary consequences quite naturally followed. But he did not simply rely on the observations of others. He, of course, made use of his own experience on the *Beagle* voyage, especially his knowledge of tribal life among the Indians of South America and his encounters with the slave trade. Further, he stuffed these books with experiments and mathematical calculations of his own devising. The language of his arguments and experiments did not have the dry, crusty sound of many of the empirical studies from which he drew. His prose had a poetic lilt and his tropes, such as nature scrutinising the internal fabric of organisms, allowed the reader to feel the more comfortable presence of a larger power watching over all of life. The Humboldtian message was that nature was no meaningless machine, but an intelligent and moral agent, to be understood through aesthetic judgement as well as analysis.

On Darwin's account, nature had a multiply dependent structure. Darwin's arguments often mirrored that structure. He would advance several possible causes to explain the same event, holding those events in a tangled bank of organic relations. Thus, not only did he account for man's big brain by appeal to group selection, he had the inherited effects of language by which to reinforce his naturalistic theory. He secured human moral character with the interacting forces of community selection, reciprocal altruism and inculcated habit. The principal force, community selection, along with an evolving intellect, would ensure that human nature might preserve an authentic moral core. As he interpreted his own accomplishment, his theory thus escaped the reproach of grounding human moral capacity in 'the base principle of selfishness'. Darwin's subtle, artistic effects, along with his voluminous evidence and compelling arguments, have rendered his conclusions powerful even today for the supple of mind.

NOTES

1. Barrett *et al.* 1987, *Charles Darwin's Notebooks, Notebook* B, MS p. 3 (hereafter B3).
2. B4.
3. B169 and B215.
4. Humboldt [1814–29] 1966.
5. Keynes 1988, 443.
6. R. J. Richards 1999 and 2002b. For further discussion of Humboldt's contribution to Darwin's conception of nature, see Sloan, this volume.
7. C171 and C63.
8. Darwin to Susan Darwin (1 April 1838), in F. Burkhardt *et al.* 1985–2001, *Correspondence* II, 80 (hereafter *CCD*).
9. M107. Double wedge-brackets indicate a later insertion into the entry.
10. M95.
11. See M104 and *Darwin's Reading Notebooks*, in *CCD* IV, 438 (Darwin Papers, Cambridge, DAR *119: 3v).
12. N21c.
13. Hume [1739] 1888, 179. Darwin refers to this passage in N101, and remarks: 'Hume has section (IX) on Reason of Animals . . . he seems to allow it is an instinct.'
14. N48.
15. C210e. I read 'world' for the transcription 'word'. Darwin studied Carus in translation. See Carus 1837.
16. See especially Fleming 1822, I, 220–2; Wells 1834, 20; and Brougham 1839, 175. Darwin's copy of Fleming, with annotations, is held in the Manuscript Room of Cambridge University Library. His notes on Brougham and Wells are, respectively, in N62 and N68–72. He wrote: 'Lr. Brougham . . . says animals have abstraction because they understand signs.—very profound.—concludes that difference of intellect between animals & men only in Kind [*sic*, degree].'
17. See Susan Darwin to Darwin (3–6 March 1833), in *CCD* I, 299.
18. See Humboldt 1814–29, III, 3.
19. C. Darwin [1860] 1962, 497.
20. Paley [1785] 1806, I, 89–90.
21. Paley, [1785] 1806, I, 76.
22. M132e.
23. This problem and other aspects of the development of Darwin's moral theory are more extensively discussed in R. J. Richards 1987, chs. 2 and 5.
24. C. Darwin 1975, 510.
25. Lewontin *et al.* 1984, 51.

26. S. F. Cannon 1978, 275.
27. C. Darwin [1859] 1964, 83–4.
28. C. Darwin [1859] 1964, 84.
29. C. Darwin 1909, 85.
30. C. Darwin [1859] 1964, 489.
31. Darwin to Caroline Kennard (9 January 1882), Darwin Papers, Cambridge, DAR 185. For further discussion of Darwin's arguments on sexual selection, see Endersby, this volume.
32. Lyell 1863, 505.
33. Wallace [1864] 1991, clxiii.
34. Darwin and Wallace 1958, 268–79.
35. Wallace [1864] 1991, clxx.
36. Spencer [1851] 1970. Spencer's own trajectory moved from an early, youthful enthusiasm for radical socialism (with land held in common) to the laissez-faire individualism of his later years. See R. J. Richards 1987, chs. 6–7.
37. Darwin generalised his concept of community selection to include what is today called group selection – that is, selection of groups of individuals for traits that benefit the group, even if its members are not related. By the sixth edition of the *Origin* (1872), in a passage that underwent gradual change through the editions, he asserted: 'In social animals it [natural selection] will adapt the structure of each individual for the benefit of the community; if the community profits by the selected change.' For the several passages, see C. Darwin 1959, 172.
38. Spencer contended that the higher mental powers required delicate co-adaptation of elemental traits that themselves could have provided no advantage singly. Moreover, many mental powers – aesthetic preference, for instance – had no survival value at all, and could not, therefore, have arisen by natural selection. See Spencer [1864–7] 1884, 1, 454–5.
39. Wallace wrote to Darwin (18 April 1869) to say that his altered view about human evolution derived from his empirical testing of the medium's power. See Marchant 1916, 1, 244.
40. Wallace 1870, 359.
41. Darwin to Alfred Wallace (26 January 1870), in Marchant 1916, 1, 251.
42. Greg 1868, 361. Darwin quotes this passage with some relish in C. Darwin [1871] 1981, 1, 174.
43. C. Darwin, [1871] 1981, 1, 174–80.
44. C. Darwin [1871] 1981, 1, 177.
45. See N65. See also R. J. Richards 2002a.
46. See Wedgwood 1866, 13–14 and 129.
47. Schleicher 1863. See also Taub 1993 and Alter 1999, 73–9.
48. Schleicher 1865, 21.

49. Darwin to William S. Dallas (9 June 1868), Darwin Papers, Cambridge, DAR 162.
50. Darwin's copy of Haeckel 1868 is held in the Manuscript Room of Cambridge University Library. For Darwin's annotations, see Di Gregorio 1990, 359–60.
51. C. Darwin [1871] 1981, I, 57.
52. C. Darwin [1871] 1981, I, 161.
53. C. Darwin [1871] 1981, I, 166.
54. C. Darwin [1871] 1981, I, 163.
55. C. Darwin [1871] 1981, I, 163–5.
56. C. Darwin [1871] 1981, I, 100–1.
57. C. Darwin [1871] 1981, I, 97.
58. Ghiselin 1973, 967.
59. Dawkins 1976, 3.
60. C. Darwin [1871] 1981, I, 98.
61. C. Darwin [1871] 1981, I, 67–8.
62. Bell [1844] 1873, 78.
63. On the present-day discussion about Darwinism and emotional expression, see Flanagan, this volume.
64. C. Darwin [1872] 1998, ch.1.
65. C. Darwin [1872] 1998, chs. 2 and 3.
66. See R. J. Richards 1992, 91–166.
67. Humboldt 1845–62, II, 72.

C. KENNETH WATERS

5 The arguments in the *Origin of Species*

I ORIGINS AND CHARACTER OF THE *ORIGIN*

Reading *On the Origin of Species* is a rite of passage for many biologists and its reasoning continues to play a pivotal role in biological thought. It is often said, following Darwin himself, that the *Origin* is 'one long argument' (459).[1] There is something important in this remark. Readers expecting the *Origin* to be structured around a narrative account find the book perplexing. Unlike the paradigmatic early Victorian book on evolution, the Edinburgh journalist Robert Chambers' *Vestiges of the Natural History of Creation*, published anonymously in 1844, the *Origin* was not written as a history of life's evolution on earth.[2] Rather, the *Origin* was structured as an *argument*. Hence, Darwin's insistence that his book was one long argument provides an indispensable clue for reading the text.[3] But it is not clear that it should be read as *one* argument. Although Darwin may have designed his book to be read as one long argument for evolution by means of natural selection, many of his readers must have read it differently. We know this because the *Origin* persuaded many readers to accept the 'evolution' idea but not the 'by means of natural selection' part of Darwin's view.[4] These readers were not swayed by one long argument for evolution *by means of natural selection*. So, to understand the reasoning that influenced Darwin's readers, it is better to think of the *Origin* as a body of argumentation flexible enough to allow readers' views of the reasoning to differ from what Darwin might have intended. The aim of this chapter is to provide a guide to the *Origin*'s flexible and sometimes elusive body of reasoning.

Charles Darwin wrote the *Origin* as an abstract, not a scientific treatise. In Darwin's day, treatises were the typical vehicles for advancing a wide-scale revision of a scientific field. Like Charles Lyell's *Principles of Geology*, they were usually multi-volumed, carefully documented and filled with technical details.[5] Darwin originally summarised his ideas on evolution in unpublished essays completed in 1842 and 1844.[6] These informal essays were not intended to be treatises. Apart from telling a few friends, Darwin kept his evolutionary ideas to himself and prepared nothing for publication on the subject until 1857, when he began writing a full-scale treatise. This work was interrupted in the following year when he received an unpublished article from Alfred Wallace which anticipated many of Darwin's own ideas about evolution, including the idea of natural selection.[7] This prompted Darwin to set aside the massive book in progress – eventually edited and published by R. C. Stauffer in 1975 – and to write an abstract, while friends arranged to have short extracts from Darwin's earlier writings included with the publication of Wallace's article.[8] Darwin completed the abstract within nine months and called it *On the Origin of Species by Means of Natural Selection*.[9] Unlike the partially written treatise, the abstract – the *Origin* – was not in a technical style nor copiously referenced. Instead, it closely followed the tone and form of the two informal and unpublished essays that Darwin had composed on the topic nearly two decades before.

Darwin revised the *Origin* five times and wrote prolifically on evolution until his death in 1882, but he never returned to the project of the large treatise.[10] Nevertheless, despite the *Origin*'s informality, or perhaps because of it, Darwin achieved the aim of the most ambitious writers of scientific treatises: he led scientists to alter dramatically the way they investigated and explained a wide variety of phenomena. In fact, the *Origin* elicited a more dramatic shift of thought than that brought about by any scientific treatise of the Victorian or perhaps any era. This hastily written abstract pushed Darwin's contemporaries to revise their fundamental assumptions about the place of humans in nature.

II TWO CENTRAL IDEAS IN THE *ORIGIN*: THE TREE OF LIFE AND NATURAL SELECTION

The reasoning in the *Origin* involves two central ideas: the tree of life and natural selection. According to the first idea, species change over time, with some species going extinct while others continue or split into multiple descendent species. Darwin illustrated the resulting pattern as diverging branches of a tree. The second idea, natural selection, offered an account of how species could change. According to this idea, species changed through a process of selection akin to the method of artificial selection that breeders used to modify domesticated varieties of plants and animals.

In advancing the tree of life, Darwin challenged the then nearly universal view that species were immutable. This placed him in opposition to two sets of well-established beliefs. The first set concerned inheritance. Although not much was understood about inheritance, biologists generally believed that the range of variation within a given species was fixed. They thought there were definite limits to how far individuals could vary from their species type. They recognised exceptions to this rule, such as the rare appearance of two-headed turtles; but they believed that such exceptions usually perished, and that, when they survived, their monstrous traits were washed out in the process of inheritance. These ideas implied that the form of any given species could not change beyond fixed limits. The second set of beliefs that posed a challenge to the tree of life concerned the well-established phenomena of adaptation. Work in the tradition of natural history indicated that species were perfectly adapted to their environments. This raised a fundamental question that confounded early adherents to evolution: if species are always perfectly adapted to their environments, or even just extremely well-adapted, how could species change and yet remain well-adapted? Darwin answered this question with the idea of natural selection.

Natural selection plays the dominant role in Darwin's pluralistic account of the causes responsible for evolution. According to this idea, evolutionary change is brought about by the 'selection' of individuals with variations that give them an advantage for survival and hence a better chance to produce descendants. Their descendants are likely to inherit these variations and hence the descendent generations will gradually shift towards the forms of the fittest parents. Darwin illustrated the process with a hypothetical example. Wolves might appear with a slight variation that makes them fleeter and more capable of capturing prey. Such wolves would have an advantage over wolves lacking this trait, and hence the fleeter wolves would produce more offspring. Their offspring would be likely to inherit the variation for swiftness and hence the prevalence of the variation would increase in the next generation. Darwin claimed this process would repeat itself, generation after generation, until the trait eventually became established in the species. When this process of variation, selection and inheritance repeats itself over thousands and thousands of generations, the descendants of the original species will have new features which will distinguish them markedly from their distant ancestors.

The tree of life and natural selection played distinct roles in the *Origin* and it is important to distinguish between them. It is also helpful to keep in mind that the tree of life itself involves two different ideas: the idea of one species changing into another, or *transmutation*; and the idea of species splitting into two or more species, resulting in *common descent*. The claim of common descent distinguishes Darwin's theory of evolution from those of his precursors. Although Darwin didn't insist that all species are related through a single common ancestor, he held that all animals descended from at most four or five ancestral species and all plants from at most four (484). This idea is logically distinct from transmutation, because individual species might dramatically change over time without ever splitting. Each species might have its own, first ancestor from which it evolved. This is what Jean Lamarck believed. His account of evolution included as many distinct spontaneous generation events as there are species. Each spontaneous generation event gave rise to a separate lineage, with each lineage evolving along one of two or three evolutionary pathways.[11] On Lamarck's account, amphibians have fish-like ancestors, but they do not have any ancestors in common with today's fish. On Darwin's account, however, today's amphibians and today's fish do have ancestors in common. The idea of common descent is logically distinct from Darwin's idea that natural selection is the dominant mechanism of transmutation. Natural selection might occur without the splitting of one species into two and such a splitting might be brought about by a process that does not involve natural selection.

III OVERALL STRUCTURE OF THE *ORIGIN*

Darwin did not write the *Origin* as a story beginning with a lifeless Earth and culminating with the appearance of today's species.

Instead, he began with artificial selection, the method breeders used to alter domestic varieties. Why? Jonathan Hodge and others have answered that Darwin intended to construct an argument for his theory in accordance with the ideal for scientific reasoning set out by his contemporary, John Herschel. Herschel claimed that the best examples of science establish a true cause, or *vera causa*. Establishing a *vera causa*, according to Herschel, entails demonstrating three things: (1) the *existence* of the cause; (2) the *adequacy* or competence of the cause to produce the effects to be explained; and (3) the *responsibility* of the cause for the effects. Herschel insisted that demonstrations of the existence and adequacy of the cause must be independent of the reasons we have for thinking that the cause is actually responsible for certain phenomena.[12]

It is easy to understand why Darwin began the *Origin* with artificial selection if we assume that he was trying to establish natural selection as a *vera causa*. In brief, he used artificial selection as a way of introducing his argument for the existence of natural selection and then drew an analogy between artificial and natural selection in order to argue for the adequacy of natural selection. In the first chapter, he showed that artificial selection is the cause of change in domestic races and identified this cause with two components: variation and selection. He then argued that natural counterparts to these components exist in nature in the second and third chapters.

Darwin argued for the adequacy of natural selection by appealing to the analogy between artificial and natural selection. His basic argument, presented in the fourth chapter, was that components akin to those for natural selection – variation and differential fitness – are adequate for transforming varieties in the domestic situation, so the similar (but much stronger) components in nature must be adequate for transforming species. (The arguments sketched here are described in detail in the sections that follow.) This account seems to leave the third component of natural selection, inheritance, out of the picture. Darwin dealt with inheritance as a background component, one that obviously exists in nature as it does in the domestic situation. Hence, the question for Darwin was not whether inheritance exists in nature. Of course it does. The question was whether it affects the adequacy of natural selection. Darwin answered this question with the analogical argument.

Darwin commenced his case for the responsibility of natural selection in the fifth chapter by showing that his view could explain

Table 5.1 *The* Origin*'s overall argument structure*

	General description of part	Chapters	Herschelian interpretation
Part 1	Presents observations from natural history and an analogical argument from artificial selection	1–4	Demonstrates the existence and adequacy of transmutation by means of natural selection
Part 2	Deals with a miscellaneous collection of problems confronting his view	6–9	Some arguments defend the idea that transmutation by means of natural selection is adequate, others defend the idea that it is actually responsible
Part 3	Explains how his view can explain many groups of facts	5, 10–13	Demonstrates the responsibility of transmutation by means of natural selection

many groups of facts, ranging from embryology to the geographic distribution of species. Darwin's arguments for existence and adequacy, contained in chapters 1 to 4, are separate from his arguments concerning responsibility, which are contained in chapters 5 to 13. Hence, the *Origin* is structured to satisfy Herschel's demand that the adequacy and existence of a *vera causa* be established independently of its responsibility.

Chapters 5 to 13 are all aimed towards showing that Darwin's theory identifies the *vera causa* of a wide range of phenomena. However, a division is apparent. Chapters 6 to 9 address criticisms of his view. The remaining chapters (5, and 10 to 13) provide positive arguments to the effect that Darwin's theory identifies the causes responsible for the phenomena. Hence, the *Origin* is loosely organised into three parts, as represented in table 5.1.

Contemporary historians and philosophers have offered a variety of alternative interpretations of the structure and logic of the *Origin*.[13] Michael Ruse has argued that Darwin drew upon the epistemological ideals of William Whewell as much as he did upon those of Herschel. Both Whewell and Herschel based their ideals for science on Newtonian physics. Both emphasised the importance of establishing a cause. But Whewell thought a cause could be established solely on the basis of *consilience*, the feat of showing that a wide variety of apparently separate phenomena can be explained as a result of the same cause.[14] Darwin's claim, that phenomena ranging from embryology to biogeographical distribution can be explained in terms of transmutation by means of natural selection, adheres to Whewell's ideal of consilience. Ruse acknowledges that Darwin's appeal to the analogy between artificial and natural selection fitted Herschel's ideal for demonstrating a *vera causa*, but Ruse believes the chapters covering the analogy and the struggle for existence are not crucial elements of Darwin's argument.

Ruse's interpretation has textual support. In the third part of the *Origin*, Darwin claimed that the ability of his view to explain particular groups of facts would itself establish his theory: 'Finally, the several classes of facts which have been considered in this chapter, seem to me to proclaim so plainly, that the innumerable species, genera, and families of organic beings, ... have all descended, ... from common parents, and have all been modified in the course of descent, that I should without hesitation adopt this view, even if it were unsupported by other facts or arguments' (457–8). Nevertheless, such remarks do not alter the fact that Darwin structured the *Origin* in a way that adhered to Herschel's ideal of demonstrating the existence and adequacy of a cause independently of one's reasons for thinking the cause was responsible for particular phenomena. When Darwin claimed that his book was one long argument, he had Herschel's ideal in mind.

It appears, in sum, that if one's goal is to clarify Darwin's own reasoning, then the arguments in the *Origin* are best interpreted in terms of how they fit into the overall Herschelian scheme. Interpreted in this way, the *Origin* was indeed one long argument for evolution by means of natural selection. This interpretation is consistent with the argumentation of Darwin's most prominent critics, who frequently took aim at Darwin's claim that natural selection was adequate for transmuting species.[15] But many sympathetic readers, those who were presumably swayed by his reasoning, had a different understanding of Darwin's argumentation. For many of Darwin's supporters rejected the idea of natural selection even though they accepted the transmutation and common-descent theses. This would not make sense on the Herschelian interpretation. If natural selection is removed, the alleged *vera causa* vanishes, the Herschelian argument collapses, and there is no reason for accepting transmutation or common descent. This suggests that sympathetic readers found a different argument in the *Origin*, one that did not depend on the line of reasoning that natural selection existed, was adequate and actually caused the broad range of phenomena described throughout the third part of the *Origin*.

Although it is well known that many if not most nineteenth- and early twentieth-century evolutionists remained highly sceptical of natural selection, scholars have not analysed the *Origin*'s reasoning to determine whether it provides compelling arguments for transmutation and common descent that do not depend on the premise that natural selection is the underlying cause. In the analysis that follows, I will consider whether the *Origin*'s argumentation was sufficiently flexible to provide compelling arguments for evolution independently of natural selection. I will show that many of the arguments depend wholly upon natural selection (certainly those in the first part), but other arguments, if read from a Whewellian perspective, offer a strong case for transmutation and common descent regardless of whether natural selection is taken to be part of the *vera causa*.

IV REASONING IN THE FIRST PART OF THE *ORIGIN*: THE ARGUMENT FROM ARTIFICIAL SELECTION

The first part of the *Origin* contains four chapters, which discuss, in turn, artificial selection, variation in nature, the struggle for existence, and natural selection.[16] The reasoning in this part is organised around an analogical argument. This argument draws parallels between the components of artificial selection that are responsible for the development of domesticated races and components in nature. Darwin argues that the three components for natural selection are present in nature, hence demonstrating the existence of natural selection. Then he argues that since similar elements produce new breeds and cultivars in the domestic situation (by means of artificial selection) the corresponding conditions in nature are adequate for producing new species in nature (by means of natural selection).

Darwin's account of natural selection includes three causal components:

1. Variations appear within a species often with no relation to adaptive advantage.
2. Some variations provide their bearers with an advantage in the struggle to live and reproduce within their environment.
3. Variations are often transmitted to progeny through inheritance.

Darwin established the existence of the first component in the second chapter, by describing the ubiquity of variation among plants and animals in nature. He established the existence of the second component in the third chapter, where he pointed out that nature must provide checks to the potential geometric increase in population size and hence organisms must compete with one another for reproductive success. He examined the struggle for existence in this chapter as well, to show that minor advantages could tip the balance towards some organisms.[17] This established a connection between variation and the ability to leave descendants. The third component, the inheritance of variations, was dealt with in large part on the basis of artificial selection.

Although the analogy between artificial and natural selection is mentioned throughout the *Origin*, it is discussed most fully in the fourth chapter, on natural selection.[18] The primary role of the analogy in this chapter was to help Darwin establish the claim that natural selection could, over many generations, produce modifications of the magnitude that separate fully fledged species (Herschelian adequacy). Darwin's appeal to analogy fitted nicely with the leading accounts of scientific reasoning of his day. But Darwin had special reason to use an analogy: he had little knowledge of the laws governing the production and inheritance of variations. He had already admitted in the first chapter that the laws of variation were 'various, quite unknown, or dimly lit' (12) and that the laws concerning inheritance were 'quite unknown' (13). Darwin had no theoretical account in the *Origin* of why inheritance should support the accumulation of variations over successive generations. But the fact that the mechanisms of inheritance, whatever they were, had supported such

Table 5.2 *Darwin's analogy between artificial and natural selection*

Artificial selection	Natural selection
Variations produced (through unknown mechanism)	Variations produced (through unknown mechanism)
Man selects variations (sometimes by conscious efforts and often by unconscious means)	Nature selects variations (by providing conditions that give organisms with certain variations a better chance to live and reproduce)
Variations inherited (through unknown mechanism)	Variations inherited (through unknown mechanism)
The three factors above cause the production of domestic races	The three factors above cause the production of the natural counterpart to domestic races, which, Darwin inferred, were fully fledged species

accumulations when humans performed artificial selections implied that the same should happen with nature's selections: 'as man can certainly produce great results by adding up in any given direction mere individual differences, so could Nature' (82).

Darwin's strategy was to match specific information about artificial selection with information about its natural counterpart in order to infer that the results of the two processes must also correspond. Darwin's argument depended upon matching the elements of artificial and natural selection as illustrated in table 5.2.

By assuming that the factors underlying the production and inheritance of variations were the same for artificial and natural selection, Darwin could infer that whatever was brought about by these factors under artificial conditions could also be brought about under natural conditions. But the factors for selection were not the same and this posed a difficulty for the analogical argument.

Darwin dealt with this difficulty by carefully comparing the way man made selections with the way selections were made in nature. Although most commentators assume that Darwin based his analogical arguments on an analogy from the results of conscious efforts of man, he also appealed to a different kind of artificial selection:

> In man's methodical selection, a breeder selects for some definite object, and free intercrossing will wholly stop his work. But when many men, without intending to alter the breed, have a nearly common standard of perfection, and all try to get and breed from the best animals, much improvement and modification surely but slowly follow from this unconscious process of selection, notwithstanding a large amount of crossing with inferior animals. Thus it will be in nature [....] (102)

Darwin had already established in the first chapter that unconscious selection had resulted in significant modification of plants and animals under domestication. Hence, even though natural selection 'will always act with extreme slowness' and 'often be greatly retarded by free intercrossing', Darwin had reason to believe that, like unconscious artificial selection, it could still result in significant modification (108).

Darwin's analogical argument faced a second difficulty: the division between natural species is much greater than the division separating artificial varieties. Having matched the causal inputs, how did Darwin justify his conclusion that the causal outputs (natural species versus domestic varieties) would be so different? Darwin employed a dual strategy: first he argued that the differences between domestic races and natural species were not as great as many assumed (13–16), and then he reasoned that the actual differences in outcomes could be accounted for by differences in the selection processes:

> As man can produce and certainly has produced a great result by his methodical and unconscious means of selection, what may not nature effect? Man can act only on external and visible characters.... [Nature] can act on every internal organ, on every shade of constitutional difference, on the whole machinery of life.... How fleeting are the wishes and efforts of man! how short his time! and consequently how poor will his products be, compared with those accumulated by nature during whole geological periods. (83–4)

In a sense, Darwin was estimating what would result if man could make the same kinds of selections that were made in nature.[19] Many of Darwin's critics attacked this move and it is easy to understand why many of his sympathisers reserved judgement on the adequacy of natural selection.

The *Origin* did more than simply advance basic evolutionary claims; it also introduced new ways to investigate and explain biological phenomena. The first part of the *Origin* legitimised this, not just by arguing for the existence and adequacy of natural selection, but also by easing readers into Darwin's patterns of evolutionary reasoning. Darwin lured readers into his new ways of reasoning by introducing this type of reasoning in the uncontroversial setting of breeding techniques. Having established the coherence of his reasoning patterns in this uncontroversial context, he could more plausibly argue that the same patterns should be applied to nature.

For example, Darwin devoted nearly ten pages to tracing the ancestry of domestic pigeons. It was easy to show that several races were bred from common ancestors. Darwin denounced the view that domesticated races of pigeons were each derived from a separate aboriginal stock as 'rash in the extreme' (26). Through careful analysis, he determined ancestral relations among different races of pigeons. By starting with what must have seemed to be a perfectly respectable problem, even by the orthodox standards of his day, Darwin was able to illustrate the effectiveness of his investigative and explanatory strategies without relating them to controversial issues of evolution.

Intentional or not, the effect of applying his investigative and explanatory strategies to problems that seemed uncontroversial must have led readers to think that analogous problems concerning natural species and analogous strategies for solving them could be legitimate parts of scientific practice even if they did not accept his claim that transmutation in nature closely resembled artificial selection. His denunciation of those who would argue that each race of pigeon was independently derived from a separate aboriginal stock was perhaps a thinly veiled strike against those who believed in the independent creation of each species. Starting with artificial selection was a smart rhetorical move.

V A PREVIEW OF THE THIRD PART OF THE *ORIGIN*

Darwin began the tasks of showing what his view could explain and illustrating how it could be used to investigate a wide variety of phenomena in the fifth chapter (see table 5.1). Analysing this chapter sheds light on the issue of whether the *Origin* offers compelling arguments for transmutation and common descent that do not depend on natural selection. The issue comes down to the question of what has to be included in 'my view' when Darwin claimed that his view could explain phenomena that independent creation could not. Would such claims retain their plausibility if by 'my view' readers left out natural selection and plugged in only transmutation and common descent?

I will examine two arguments from chapter 5 to show that Darwin's use of 'my view' was ambiguous. Sometimes his reasoning depended on including natural selection as part of his view, but other times the reasoning required only transmutation and common descent. The first argument concerns a law attributed to the zoologist G. R. Waterhouse: 'A part developed in any species in an extraordinary degree or manner, in comparison with the same part in allied species, tends to be highly variable' (150; italics omitted). Darwin showed how his view could explain this law by appealing to the analogy between artificial and natural selection. He noted that when artificial selection is applied to bring about the rapid transformation of certain parts of a domestic breed, those parts are particularly liable to variation. There is, Darwin explained, 'a constant struggle going on between, on the one hand, the tendency to reversion to a less modified state, as well as an innate tendency to further variability of all kinds, and, on the other hand, the power of steady selection to keep the breed true' (152–3). So, Darwin concluded, 'we might, as a general rule, expect still to find more variability in such parts than in other parts of the organisation, which have remained for a much longer period nearly constant' (153). This is not the only place where Darwin appealed to artificial selection in order to establish how his view could explain various groups of facts that were otherwise inexplicable. When Darwin appealed to the analogy, readers needed to insert not just transmutation and common descent into 'my view', but also natural selection (or the argument would be weakened). But there were many cases where Darwin illustrated the investigative and explanatory powers of his view that did not depend on natural selection. One of those cases involved the law of use and disuse.

The law of use and disuse states that when organs are enhanced through use, the enhancements tend to be inherited by progeny; and when organs atrophy through disuse, progeny tend to inherit diminished organs. The *Origin*'s treatment of the law of use and disuse includes a discussion that explicitly shows how transmutation and common descent can explain facts on their own, that is, without natural selection. Darwin considered the lack of eyes in the cave fish of America and in the cave fish of the European continent. He noted that these fish live under extremely similar conditions of life ('limestone caverns under a nearly similar climate' (138)). Next, he granted that these animals lost their eyes through the law of disuse and not by means of natural selection ('As it is difficult to imagine that eyes, though useless, could be in any way injurious to animals living in darkness, I attribute their loss wholly to disuse' (137)).[20] Third, he argued that on 'my view' one would expect the animals in American caverns to resemble more closely animals in the surrounding American country than animals in Europe (and vice versa). Then he stated, citing observations of naturalists, that this is exactly what one observes. Darwin remarked: 'It would be most difficult to give any rational explanation of the affinities of the blind cave-animals to the other inhabitants of the two continents on the ordinary view of their independent creation' (139). Darwin was suggesting that his view was preferable to the view of independent creation because his view could explain this phenomenon while the alternative view could not. What was Darwin's 'view' in *this* discussion? It was not evolution by means of natural selection because he admitted that natural selection is not responsible for the disappearance of eyes. By 'my view' Darwin must have meant only the ideas of transmutation and common descent.

Darwin's discussion in this chapter is particularly revealing because it shows that, in many discussions, natural selection is not an essential part of his view. That is, it was not doing the explanatory work in his reasoning. He acknowledged the possibility of other causes (such as use and disuse) and he even presented an example (the loss of eyes in cave fish) illustrating how his central pattern of reasoning, to be repeated throughout the third part of the *Origin*, could be applied without appealing to natural selection. Darwin usually lumped the three ideas together and contemporary scholars often assume that the *Origin* must be read as an argument for all three. Perhaps Darwin assumed the same. But the cave fish example explicitly illustrates another option. Natural selection can be read out of many of Darwin's arguments about the superiority of his 'view' compared to the alternative of independent creation.

VI REASONING IN THE SECOND PART OF THE *ORIGIN*: DEFENDING AGAINST MISCELLANEOUS POSSIBLE OBJECTIONS

Darwin anticipated objections to his view and addressed them in four chapters in the middle portion of the *Origin*. The first of these chapters, the sixth, concerns tensions between Darwin's view that transmutation was a gradual process and the existence of numerous discontinuities in the biological realm such as those between contemporary species. The seventh and eighth chapters deal with the difficulties of explaining instincts and of explaining the sterility of interspecies hybrids. The ninth chapter deals with gaps in the fossil record. There is a common theme among these chapters, since many of the difficulties relate, as in the sixth chapter, to apparent tensions between, on the one side, Darwin's idea that transmutation is a gradual, continuous process, and on the other, the existence of discontinuities in nature. Nevertheless, Darwin's solutions do not fit into a uniform pattern. Three categories of solutions can be distinguished: (a) solutions expanding on his basic theory of natural selection (discussed below); (b) solutions involving approaches more fully presented in the third part of the *Origin* (these approaches are described in the next section); and (c) solutions involving accounts of processes that fall outside the domain of his basic theory.

Darwin's explanation of the gaps in the fossil record provides an example of the third kind of solution. These gaps seemed to contradict his gradualist account of evolution. He addressed this apparent contradiction by arguing that the discontinuities in the fossil record represent irregularities in fossilisation, not discontinuities in the process of species formation. That is, Darwin claimed that the process of transmutation was continuous, that all intermediate forms were represented by individuals living in the past, and that the reason these forms did not all appear in the fossil record is because many of them were not all fossilised. Hence, he did not solve the problem of fossil gaps by expanding on his basic ideas of transmutation, common descent or natural selection. He solved it by describing a process (fossilisation) that fell outside the domain of his basic theory.

Darwin often addressed difficulties for his view by expanding upon his theory of natural selection. Many of the difficulties he addressed centred on biological features that seemed to defy evolutionary explanation, especially explanation involving a gradual process of natural selection. When Darwin invoked natural selection to explain a difficult case of evolution, whether the case involved the complex structure of the eye or the intricate instinctive behaviour of insects, his reasoning typically followed the same pattern:

1. establish the existence of inherited variations of the trait as well as similar traits;
2. pick out a rudimentary example of the trait in some species and show how the rudimentary form might have first accidentally occurred;
3. explain how an individual with the original, rudimentary form of the trait might have benefited and describe how this trait could be inherited and established via natural selection;
4. argue that once the rudimentary form was established, additional variations of that trait could be selected in a gradual manner to establish the trait of interest.

This pattern of reasoning is exemplified many times in the *Origin*, but I will illustrate it with just one example, Darwin's explanation of instincts.

Instincts provided a difficult case for Darwin's theory because it is difficult to see how instincts could be established by a natural process of transmutation. Darwin initiated his discussion by distinguishing between instinct and habit and arguing that variations in instinctive behaviour could be inherited just as variations in physical attributes are inherited. Then he identified and explained three cases of instinctive behaviour by following the above pattern for each case. He started with the case that was easiest to investigate and account for on his view and concluded with the most difficult case. I will examine his account of the second case, which involved the slave-making instinct of various ant species.

Darwin's descriptions of the slave-making behaviour of ants, based on observations of Pierre Huber as well as his own, are intrinsically fascinating and it is easy to overlook the fact that Darwin's discussion follows a pattern of reasoning (sketched above) that occurs repeatedly when Darwin dealt with difficult cases. He began by describing the variation in behaviour among a number of ant species to establish that various behaviours are instinctive and inherited (step 1 above). His evidence included not just telling observations but also experimental results – his own observations and results as well as those of others. He then described the slave-making instincts of two different species, one of which relies on the work of slaves to a much greater extent than the other. After saying he would not guess how the less dependent species, *Formica sanguinea*, might have developed its slave-making instinct, he nevertheless did so (steps 2 and 3 from above):

> By what steps the instinct of F. sanguinea originated I will not pretend to conjecture. But as ants, which are not slave-makers, will, as I have seen, carry off pupae of other species, if scattered near their nests, it is possible that pupae originally stored as food might become developed; and the ants thus unintentionally reared would then follow their proper instincts, and do what work they could. If their presence proved useful to the species which had seized them – if it were more advantageous to this species to capture workers than to procreate them – the habit of collecting pupae originally for food might by natural selection be strengthened and rendered permanent for the very different purpose of raising slaves. (223–4)

Having made plausible the idea that the slave-making instinct of *F. sanguinea* might have been established by means of natural selection, he then suggests that natural selection could select for a series of additional variations that would result in the slave-making instinct of the second species, *F. rufescens* (step 4 from above):

> When the instinct was once acquired, if carried out to a much less extent even than in our British F. sanguinea, which, as we have seen, is less aided by its slaves than the same species in Switzerland, I can see no difficulty in natural selection increasing and modifying the instinct – always supposing each modification to be of use to the species – until an ant was formed as abjectly dependent on its slaves as is the Formica rufescens. (224)

The pattern of reasoning outlined above and exemplified by Darwin's account of instinct explicitly draws upon natural selection. We might wonder, however, whether sceptical readers thought these difficult cases could also be explained by other evolutionary mechanisms. In fact, it does not take much imagination to recast Darwin's account of the evolution of slave-making instincts in terms of use and disuse rather than natural selection. Clearly, Darwin thought of natural selection as the primary explanatory principle for dealing with difficult cases, but his arguments can be recast differently and probably were recast differently in the minds of readers who were persuaded about transmutation and common descent, but not about natural selection.

VII REASONING IN THE THIRD PART OF THE *ORIGIN*: INVESTIGATING AND UNDERSTANDING NATURAL PHENOMENA IN TERMS OF TRANSMUTATION, COMMON DESCENT AND NATURAL SELECTION

The third part of the *Origin* demonstrates what Darwin's 'view' could explain. This part includes five chapters: the fifth chapter, examined above; and the four chapters that come at the end of the book (excluding the final, summarising chapter). The tenth chapter continues Darwin's discussion of fossils, the eleventh and twelfth deal with geographical variation, and the thirteenth deals with systematics, morphology and embryology. The argumentation in these chapters is extraordinarily powerful. Insofar as the *Origin* provides logically compelling reasons for accepting evolution, these chapters play the crucial role. As will become apparent from the following account, natural selection did not play a dominant role in these chapters – even in the first edition.[21]

Whereas Darwin's ninth chapter addresses the objection that his view was incompatible with discontinuities in the fossil record, the tenth chapter shows how well his view can explain various generalisations about the fossil record.[22] The generalisations were diverse: that species appear one at a time, not suddenly in large batches; that some species last much longer than most do; that once extinct, species never return; that the later species in a group are often more specialised in structure and function than earlier species; and so on. The explanations were fairly uniform. Darwin explained nearly all of the generalisations by invoking transmutation and common descent, not necessarily natural selection. He explained, for instance, that once a species went extinct it did not reappear because the generational connection was broken. Clearly this explanation does not depend on natural selection. And neither did many of the others.

Darwin's eleventh and twelfth chapters provide a manual for investigating the geographical distribution of organisms. Darwin began the first of these chapters by identifying three curious facts: (a) the similarities and differences of organisms in various regions – for example, in the New World compared to the Old World – cannot be accounted for by differences in climate or physical conditions; (b) the various regions among which organisms differ are separated by barriers to migration (such as oceans and mountain ranges); and (c) organisms within the same region – on the same continent or in the same sea, say – exhibit an affinity to one another. He accounted for these facts in terms of a '*vera causa* of ordinary generation with subsequent migration' and claimed that anyone who rejected the view that each species was first produced within a single region 'calls in the agency of a miracle' (352). The basic idea is simple. New species arise from ancestral ones and hence their forms will resemble those of their ancestral species as well as those of their sister and cousin species that have also descended from the same ancestor. Geographic barriers that prevent the unlimited dispersion of the ancestral species will also prevent unlimited dispersion of its descendent species, and hence similar species will tend to be located in the same regions. Darwin developed a variety of ideas throughout these chapters to account for numerous nuances in geographical distributions. These accounts depended on details of geography and dispersion, not on the mechanism of species formation.

In the thirteenth chapter, Darwin dealt with three areas: systematics or classification, morphology and embryology. With regard to systematics, he showed how his view could explain the 'grand fact' of natural history, namely 'the subordination of group under group' (413). Again, the basic explanation was simple: the subordination of groups represents patterns of descent. Just as siblings resemble one another more than cousins, species with a more recent common ancestor resemble one another more than species more distantly related. Darwin acknowledged that most naturalists believed that the subordination of groups represented the Creator's plan, but he insisted that this belief adds nothing to our knowledge unless we can specify what is meant by the plan of the Creator.

Darwin remarked that this subordination of groups was so familiar that many assumed that it is not in need of explanation. But he identified features of the subordination that indeed called out for explanation. One of these was already well recognised by naturalists of Darwin's day: characteristics that establish the places that organisms occupy in the economy of nature are nearly useless for purposes of classification. One might well expect, Darwin reasoned, that grouping organisms by their special adaptive organs would provide the most natural classification scheme. If these organs are unimportant for classificatory purposes, what organs are important? Darwin answered that it is those organs that have 'greater constancy' throughout large groups of species. Under Darwin's view these are the organs that have been less subjected to adaptive change through the process of transmutation. Darwin then showed that his view could explain intricate practices for classifying organisms. He concluded that 'community of descent is the hidden bond which naturalists have been unconsciously seeking' (420).

Darwin's discussion of classification led him to morphology, the study of plant and animal forms. As his discussion of classification made clear, organisms that are grouped together resemble one another, not in their habits of life, but in their general organisation or their *unity of type*. 'What can be more curious', Darwin asked, 'than that the hand of a man, formed for grasping, that of a mole for digging, the leg of the horse, the paddle of the porpoise, and the wing of the bat, should all be constructed on the same pattern, and should include the same bones, in the same relative positions?' (434). He argued that the unity of type cannot be explained in terms of utility or the doctrine of final causes. All that could be said on the ordinary view of independent creation is that it pleased the Creator to create classes of plants and animals with distinctive unities of type. Darwin argued that his answer provided real knowledge: the curious unity of the human hand, the bat's wing and the porpoise's paddle was due to common descent. Darwin thought this explanation was so natural that morphologists could not help but use language suggestive of transmutation and common descent, speaking, for example, of 'metamorphosed' vertebrae, limbs and leaves. 'Naturalists, however, use such language only in a metaphorical sense .... On my view these terms may be used literally' (438–9).

Darwin raised a host of questions concerning embryology, the study of the development of individual organisms. Perhaps the most basic question concerned the fact that embryos of species tend to resemble one another much more closely than adults. He began his account by claiming a general principle: 'at whatever age any variation first appears in the parent, it tends to reappear at a corresponding age in the offspring' (444). He claimed that this is true even in cases where the variation might have appeared earlier or later in life. He then applied this principle, together with his theory of artificial selection, to explain why the embryos of particular domesticated races (selected from the same original species) resemble one another more closely than the adult forms of those domesticated races. Breeders typically select their dogs, horses and pigeons when they are nearly grown up and hence often select variations that do not appear until late in development. Hence the differentiation among breeds will be more pronounced at stages of development in which the selections are made. After introducing this mode of explanation in the context of artificial selection, he extended it to cases in nature. Darwin's explanations in the section on embryology explicitly invoked the process of selection (not just the term). This differs from the sections on classification and morphology where Darwin's explanation explicitly invoked the processes of adaptive transmutation and common descent, but not a particular mechanism of adaptive transmutation.

Darwin completed this chapter by discussing rudimentary or atrophied organs. He commented that rudimentary organs were sometimes said to have been created '"for the sake of symmetry"', or in order to '"complete the scheme of nature"' (453). Darwin insisted that such accounts explain nothing. 'Would it be thought sufficient', he asked, 'to say that because planets revolve in elliptic courses round the sun, satellites follow the same course round the planets, for the sake of symmetry, and to complete the scheme of nature?' (453). He then explained that in the course of transmutation, changes in the habits of life will sometimes render an organ useless and that through disuse the organ will become rudimentary (as in the case of eyes in cave fish).

Darwin summarised this chapter by stating that the several classes of facts considered clearly indicated that the innumerable species, genera and families of organisms on earth have all descended, each within its own class or group, from common parents, and have all been modified in the course of descent'. He did not mention selection here, which is only appropriate given that his explanations in this chapter rarely draw upon selection. He concluded: 'I should without hesitation adopt this view, even if it were unsupported by other facts or arguments' (458). Certainly it would be open to readers, even if Darwin had other intentions, to plug in for 'this view' transmutation and common descent, leaving aside the largely non-essential hypothesis of natural selection.

VIII CONCLUSION

The *Origin of Species* offers a flexible body of argumentation. Darwin apparently viewed this argumentation as a Herschelian demonstration of transmutation and common descent by means of natural selection. Read this way, natural selection is a *vera causa*. Under this interpretation, Darwin's analogical argument takes centre stage, as Herschel said analogical arguments should, to establish the adequacy of natural selection independently of the evidence that natural selection was indeed responsible for various phenomena. But Darwin's analogical argument was speculative. It included a leap of reasoning: that the magnitude of difference between the conditions of artificial selection and those of natural selection would lead to the magnitude of difference between artificially selected domestic races on the one hand and natural species on the other. The critics who Darwin took most seriously seized upon this weakness. Their criticisms seem to have assumed that if the argument from artificial selection was defeated, Darwin's whole argument would collapse. But many of Darwin's sympathisers took a different view. They accepted Darwin's ideas of transmutation and common descent without committing themselves to natural selection. This remained a common attitude well into the twentieth century.[23] This chapter shows how the *Origin* could support such a conclusion. By taking transmutation and common descent to be the cause of the various groups of phenomena that Darwin dealt with in the third part of the *Origin* (and in various sections of the second part), they could view the structure of the *Origin* as a Whewellian consilience of inductions.

NOTES

1. All page references in this chapter are to the 1859 edition of the *Origin*, reprinted as a Harvard University Press facsimile (1964).

2. The 1844 edition of *Vestiges* has been reprinted as a University of Chicago Press facsimile (1994). On *Vestiges* as a narrative work, see Secord 2000, ch. 3.
3. For an analysis emphasising narrational aspects of the *Origin*, see Beer 1983, esp. ch. 3.
4. On the scientific reception of the *Origin*, see Gayon, this volume.
5. S. F. Cannon 1978.
6. The 1842 *Sketch* and the 1844 *Essay* were published posthumously. See Darwin and Wallace 1958.
7. For further discussion of Darwin and Wallace, see Radick, this volume.
8. C. Darwin 1975; Darwin and Wallace 1859, reprinted in Darwin and Wallace 1958.
9. Hodge 1977.
10. On the publication and subsequent revisions of the *Origin*, see C. Darwin 1959, esp. 11–25.
11. See, e.g., Ruse 1979.
12. Hodge 1977, 1989, 1992b. For further discussion of Darwin and the *vera causa* ideal, see Sloan, Hodge, Radick and Hull, this volume.
13. Philosophers analysing the logic and structure (or the form and strategy) of the *Origin* have adopted two different approaches. Some have appealed to contemporary ideals of science to elucidate the deep logic of Darwin's argumentation (Lloyd 1983, Philip Kitcher 1993a, Thagard 1978, Waters 1986). Others stress the ideals of Darwin's day to clarify his reasoning and explain the structure of the *Origin* (Hodge 1992b, Recker 1987, Ruse 1979). In this chapter, I will take the latter approach. Nevertheless, readers may wish to draw connections between my account here and contemporary philosophical theories of scientific justification.
14. On Whewell and consilience, see Hull, this volume.
15. For a sampling of critical responses to Darwin, see Hull 1973.
16. For a complementary discussion of these chapters, see the Introduction to this volume.
17. Waters 1986.
18. For further discussion of the artificial selection–natural selection analogy, see L. T. Evans 1984, R. A. Richards 1997 and Sterrett 2002.
19. That is, he was tacitly considering a 'virtual analogue'. In the 1842 *Sketch*, Darwin explicitly imagined such a virtual analogue. Suppose, Darwin conjectured, that 'a being infinitely more sagacious than man (not an omniscient creator) during thousands and thousands of years were to select all the variations which tended towards certain ends.... Who, seeing how plants vary in [a] garden, what blind foolish man has done in a few years, will deny [what] an all-seeing being in thousands of years could effect.' Darwin and Wallace 1958, 45.

20. Darwin seems to contradict this point on p. 148, when he suggests that the nutrients wasted in the development of useless structures would provide a disadvantage.
21. It has often been noted that natural selection becomes less prominent in the successive editions of the *Origin*.
22. Jonathan Hodge clarified this point for me.
23. For further discussion, see Gayon, this volume.

Part II
Historical contexts

GREGORY RADICK

6 Is the theory of natural selection independent of its history?

I THE CULTURAL CONDITIONING OF DARWIN'S THEORY

Machines, competition, empire and progress fascinated the Victorians. One of the most famous scientific theories of the era, Charles Darwin's theory of natural selection, tells of machine-like organisms that compete, colonise and improve. To notice resemblances such as these, between the context of Darwin's theory and its content, is nothing new. In 1862, Karl Marx, in a letter to his collaborator Friedrich Engels, wrote: 'It is remarkable how Darwin recognises among beasts and plants his English society with its division of labour, competition, opening up of new markets, "inventions", and the Malthusian "struggle for existence". It is Hobbes' "bellum omnium contra omnes" ["the war of all against all"].'[1] In our own day, debates over the cultural conditioning of scientific knowledge have made this old insight newly problematic.[2] This chapter attempts to clarify these new problems. Drawing on recent thinking about culture and science, it looks at how Darwin's social, material and intellectual culture conditioned the form and content of his theory of natural selection.

One view may be dispensed with at the start: that Darwin developed the theory of natural selection because he was a genius, and, since geniuses do not belong to mundane history like most people, it is pointless to ask about the cultural conditioning of his theory. There is general consensus among historians of science that talk of 'genius' does not so much explain scientific innovation as redescribe it.[3] In Darwin's case, moreover, two generations of scholarship have revealed how much the history of the development of his theory is a social history. The pressing issue now is more subtle. We must ask whether, in fundamental ways, the theory of natural selection is nevertheless independent of the social history that brought it into being.

We can characterise two contrary theses. An *independence* thesis about the theory is the more traditional and intuitive of the pair. On this thesis, the resemblance between cultural context and theoretical content throws light on why a Victorian first developed the theory. Features peculiar to Victorian culture primed Darwin to recognise a timeless truth about nature. But the development of the theory was inevitable – the priming just accelerated the process.[4] There was only so much that could be learned about plants and animals before a conclusion in favour of natural selection became inescapable. Other individuals, belonging to different societies with different histories, would have developed the theory sooner or later. Since lots of different social histories would have yielded the theory, it is independent of any particular history, including the history that happened to yield it.

On the other side is an *inseparability* thesis. It is a deliberately provocative newcomer. On this thesis, the close match between context and content shows that the theory of natural selection was not at all inevitable, but a contingent result of a unique social history. The theory's existence depends crucially on features of the Victorian context unlikely to have been replicated elsewhere. Since the theory would never have existed apart from the trends and events that in fact led Darwin to develop it, the theory is not independent, but inseparable from its history. Furthermore, if Darwin, or someone much like him, with similar relations to a similar cultural context, had not developed the theory of natural selection, the biological sciences would now be different, but no less successful.

After first sketching the social history of Darwin's theory, I shall examine some arguments for and against its independence from its historical matrix. At bottom, to ask about the independence of the theory is to ask whether the assumptions and decisions that produced it were both necessary and such that no one outside Darwin's matrix would likely have made them. The third section below explores this point about assumptions and decisions in quite a general way. The fourth section looks at one of Darwin's assumptions in particular – his assumption that the concept 'adaptation', as he understood it, deserved to be at the centre of theorising about the origin of species. The fifth section then looks at one of Darwin's decisions in particular – his decision to concentrate on developing the Malthusian theory of natural selection once that theory had emerged in his notebooks. I argue that the stability of Malthusian struggle in Darwin's theorising is better accounted for on the inseparability thesis. In place of the standard, Marxian version of that thesis, however, the sixth section offers an alternative version, emphasising Darwin's views on method.[5] The chapter concludes with some reflections on how debate over the independence of Darwin's theory from its history relates to recent controversies in that most Darwinian science, evolutionary biology.

II VICTORIAN POWER, DARWINIAN KNOWLEDGE

Was Darwin a genius? Not in his own estimation.[6] His notebooks indeed show scant sign of those flashes of insight which, since the Romantic era, have been associated with the scientific genius.[7] But however high one's regard for Darwin's intellectual powers, those powers did not enable him to transcend his outward circumstances. He did not develop the theory of natural selection by communing with the truth about nature, isolated from the bustling world around him. At every step towards the mature theory, worldly power enabled cognitive advance.[8]

Three steps in particular can stand for the whole, complex sequence. First, there was Darwin's coming to believe, within half a year of his return from the *Beagle* voyage, that new species arose through natural causes acting on pre-existing species: the transmutation thesis. If Darwin had never persuaded himself that transmutation was true, it is hard to see why he would ever have bothered with theorising about its causes at all, much less with developing the theory that natural selection was its principal cause. Darwin seems to have committed himself to transmutationism in the course of reflections on some surprising news about his *Beagle* collections. In the Spring of 1837, the London-based Darwin learned, among other things, that many of his Galapagos specimens belonged to species found only on the Galapagos archipelago. Moreover, those species often belonged to genera peculiar not to other rocky oceanic islands around the world, but to the South American mainland, where the lush tropical conditions could hardly have been more different from the conditions on the Galapagos. For Darwin, the best explanation of this taxonomic and biogeographic puzzle was that the Galapagos species had arisen through transmutation from the nearby mainland species.[9]

Darwin had this crucial puzzle to ponder, then, because he had travelled on the *Beagle*, had collected certain birds from the Galapagos, and those birds had been classified in a certain way. Each element in this package has its place in a uniquely Victorian order. The *Beagle* voyage was not, after all, a quest to discover the origin of species. The idea for the voyage was Captain FitzRoy's. He had returned from a previous trip to South America with four Fuegians, and now wanted to take the three survivors back, to serve as Christian paragons among the savages. The Admiralty funded the new voyage for its own purposes, because better maps of the South American coastline would benefit trade and so increase national treasure. Darwin was no mapmaker, and the ship already had a naturalist; but Darwin was refined and rich – enough to pay his own way – and therefore a suitable dining companion for the aristocratic captain.[10] Once aboard, Darwin hired a crew member, Syms Covington, to act as a personal servant in collecting plants, animals and fossils.[11] Back in England, Darwin eagerly handed over his collections to museum-based experts in taxonomy. Such deference on the part of voyaging collectors had made the museum collections vast; and this vastness in turn underwrote the authority of expert classifications.[12]

Theoretical content and wider context likewise intertwine at a second step: Darwin's turning to the domestication of animals and plants for insights into transmutation. Darwin began making incursions into the breeding literature soon after opening his notebooks on the transmutation problem. Later, as an established gentleman of science, he went along to the breeders' meetings. The enterprise of plant and animal breeding was as far advanced in Darwin's Britain as anywhere else in the world. Well organised and intensely competitive, breeders kept tabs on their art and each other through periodicals, clubs, societies, exhibitions and prize competitions. Darwin's wealth enabled him to inquire about trade secrets without posing a threat to profits. The breeders may even have seen in Darwin's interest a means of elevating the cultural standing of breeding.[13] Famously, an analogy with stockbreeding would become the centrepiece of Darwin's public presentation of the theory of natural selection in the *Origin of Species* (1859).

A third and final step to consider is Darwin's so-called 'Malthusian moment'. Darwin developed the theory of natural selection over several months beginning in the autumn of 1838, after reading in the political economist Thomas Robert Malthus' *Essay on the Principle of Population*. Malthus had written in part to dampen utopian hopes aroused in the wake of the French Revolution. He had claimed to show that, other things being equal, human populations outgrow available subsistence, bringing hunger, war and other miseries.[14] Extrapolating from Malthus, Darwin came to believe that population pressures in nature were so intense that all plants and animals were locked in a struggle for existence. Given inheritable variation among those struggling plants and animals, over time there emerged, slowly but surely, new and better adapted species.

Later Darwin would recall picking up Malthus' *Essay* 'for amusement', as though, on a dull afternoon, he had reached for whatever was near to hand.[15] Maybe so. But Malthus was on a lot of minds at the time. The Whig party, political home for the Darwins, the Lyells and other gentlemanly families, had recently come to power, and in the name of Malthus was introducing harsher measures for the provisioning of the poor. Darwin had long been familiar with arguments in favour of these changes. While he was on the *Beagle*, his sisters sent him pamphlets full of pro-reform propaganda. Their author, Harriet Martineau, soon became an acquaintance. Malthusian doctrine was the stuff of dinner conversation at London parties – and Darwin was there. When Darwin at last read Malthus for himself, the London papers were full of news of riots, marches, workhouse burnings and other protests against laws acknowledged on all sides as Malthusian in spirit.[16]

So Darwin's theory of natural selection was no gift of sheer, sublime, solitary genius, but in several key respects a product of Victorian culture. This conclusion is not obvious. We have contextualist historians of science to thank for it. Their labours have not so much ended the debate over context and content, however, as raised its level. Aware as never before of the theory's ties to its historical matrix, we can now pose the difficult issue of the independence or inseparability of the theory from that matrix.[17]

III DARWIN'S ASSUMPTIONS AND DECISIONS

To bring this issue into sharper focus, it helps to examine Darwin's assumptions and decisions: assumptions about nature and knowledge, and decisions about, among other things, how to resolve conflicts between theories held and observations made. On the inseparability thesis, there was nothing inevitable about making just the assumptions Darwin made, or resolving conflicts in just the ways he did. But the assumptions made and the resolutions decided upon led Darwin to work out his theory of natural selection. This theory in turn set the biological sciences in certain directions rather than other ones.

What assumptions structured Darwin's investigations? One was that a true theory of species origins would explain adaptations.[18] Another was that a true theory would conform to the old *vera causa* ideal, referring only to presently acting and independently attested causes.[19] Neither of these assumptions was obviously reasonable to all those concerned with being scientific about the history and diversity of life. Consider the assumption about admissible causes. In Germany, following Goethe and others, the morphologists dealt in archetypal patterns. In France, Cuvier had urged that causes now diminished in power conditioned the succession of animal types recorded in the rock strata. Even in England, where the *vera causa* ideal was associated with the illustrious Isaac Newton, strict adherence was unusual, not least among geologists. Yet Darwin made the ideal his own, in imitation of his geological mentor Charles Lyell. We need, then, to ask whether something specific to Lyell's microcontext explains his *vera causa* enthusiasms. The sixth section of this chapter makes the case for the Whig reform drive, in the sciences and outside them, as the key.[20]

Underlying assumptions bind a theory to its context. So do resolutions of conflicts between theory and world. Darwin's reading of Malthus eased such a conflict, and in doing so directed Darwin's theorising towards natural selection. The conflict concerned the causes of species extinction. According to Lyell, the struggle for existence, driven by population pressures, was the *vera causa* of species extinction – that is, species become extinct when a delicate competitive balance is upset by environmental causes such as changes in climate. Throughout 1837 and 1838, Darwin was still questioning this theory as hard to reconcile with those cases, familiar from his observations in South America, of the big mammals of yesteryear becoming extinct apparently without any such changes. There did not seem to be evidence for Lyell's environmentalist explanation. After reading Malthus, however, Darwin changed his mind. With a newly vivid appreciation for how intense the struggle for existence was, he was able to excuse Lyell's theory its evidential problems, on the grounds that environmental changes far too small to leave evidential traces might nevertheless cause some species to drive others to extinction.

Darwin went on to develop the theory of natural selection – a theory complementing this account of extinction – by focusing on what happened not to the losing, extinct species, but to the winning, surviving species; in particular, to those individuals in the winning species whose variations made them especially strong competitors.[21] But suppose Darwin had not been immersed in Malthusian conversations in London, and had never happened upon Malthus' *Essay*. He might have resolved the conflict over extinction in the opposite way, concluding that, in light of the geological evidence, population pressure did not make species liable to extinction. He might then have continued working on his earlier theory of adaptive species formations. In Darwin's view at that time, this non-Malthusian theory, while evidentially problematic, did conform to the *vera causa* ideal. Perhaps he would eventually have published that theory. Or perhaps he would have judged the problems to be so severe that he would have given up on it, and abandoned theorising about species origins altogether.

Let us grant for the moment that no-one but Darwin, in his context, would have made just those assumptions about species origins, or decided, on Malthusian grounds, to resolve the conflict between Lyellian theoretical struggle and earthly evidence in favour of the former. What are the signs that, without those assumptions and that decision, the theory of natural selection would never have been developed? The need to show a one-to-one relationship between aspects of the theory of natural selection and the history of Darwin's development of it is the most formidable challenge confronting the inseparability thesis.

Not the least part of that challenge is to explain away the case of Alfred Russel Wallace. Wallace did not share Darwin's privileged background or steep himself in adaptationist natural theology at Cambridge. Yet Wallace formulated a theory of species origins close enough to Darwin's own that Darwin feared he had been scooped.[22] This famous example of simultaneous discovery in natural science appears to lend strong support to the independence thesis. Darwin found his way to natural selection by one route, and Wallace by a different route. The lesson seems to be: if you think hard about species origins, then it does not matter how you travel, you will reach the theory of natural selection in the end.

On closer inspection, however, the Wallace case offers at least a few openings to those sceptical about the independence of the theory from its history. One move would be to deny that Wallace did, in fact, 'co-discover' the theory of natural selection. Rather, he came up with a theory quite different from Darwin's, and Darwin's overreaction in 1858 has misled historians ever since.[23] Allowing instead that, as Darwin thought, the theories are indeed basically the same, one might conclude that, for all their differences, Darwin and Wallace were similar-enough products of Victorian culture. Wallace, after all, was not merely a student of biogeography, but, like Darwin, committed to Lyell's distinctive view that the history of changes on the surface of the earth held clues to animal and plant distribution. Indeed, like Darwin, Wallace arrived at a branching evolutionary tree from dissatisfaction with Lyell's account of the timing and placing of species origins as determined solely by the principle of adaptation to conditions.[24]

There are other common inheritances. Not long after discovering a geographic boundary between human races in the Malay Archipelago, Wallace recalled his own reading of Malthus, and articulated a new Malthusian explanation for adaptive evolutionary change. Wallace had with him the 1845 edition of Darwin's *Journal of Researches*, and may have been responding to a Malthusian passage on species extinctions in that book. Or perhaps a chain of association in Wallace's fevered mind – he was ill at the time – led his thoughts from the racial boundary he had just discovered to the boundaries he drew while working as a land surveyor in England and Wales in the early 1840s. It was around that time, amid general discontent over the Poor Law reforms and rising English–Welsh tensions, that Wallace had first read Malthus.[25] So the Wallace case, awkward though it is, may not be fatal to the inseparability thesis.

IV THE DARWINIAN CONCEPT OF ADAPTATION

Some of Darwin's assumptions concerned concepts, classifications, categories – or, in the philosopher's term, kinds. One kind, 'species,' figures in the title of the book that introduced the theory of natural selection, *On the Origin of Species*. Some say the title was false advertising, as Darwin denied that individual plants and animals come sorted into species. In his sceptical view, it was naturalists, not nature, that divided species from one another.[26] By contrast, he took for granted that the individual *traits* of plants and animals come sorted naturally, into traits that are adaptations and traits that are not. For Darwin, in other words, adaptations formed a natural kind.[27] Moreover, they represented one of the chief explanatory challenges before the transmutation thesis. In his introduction to the *Origin*, Darwin wrote that, however impressive the general grounds for favouring transmutation, a transmutation theory would be 'unsatisfactory' unless it could explain 'that perfection of structure and coadaptation which most justly excites our admiration'.[28] Later in the book, he addressed the challenge of an especially complex adaptive structure: the eye. 'It is scarcely possible to avoid comparing the eye to a telescope', he wrote. Just as humans have perfected the telescope gradually, so, Darwin argued, natural selection had gradually perfected – but to a much higher degree – 'a living optical instrument'.[29]

The mechanical concept of adaptation exemplified in Darwin's account of the eye has a history.[30] The idea that different traits suit different plants and animals – that fins suit fish to swimming, say, and wings suit birds to flying – goes back at least to the ancient world. Aristotle wrote of the purposes fulfilled by the parts of animals. Far from ancient or universal, however, is the idea that traits suiting their various bearers under their diverse conditions of life should be grouped *together*, privileged as the outstanding facts about organisms and conceived as mechanical contrivances. That idea is the product of one culture: early-modern Britain. To understand why Darwin gave pride of place to a mechanical conception of adaptive traits, we need to recall a British tradition of natural history and natural theology, its themes and its setting.[31]

In the late seventeenth century, two members of the Royal Society published influential works of natural theology. Robert Boyle's

A Disquisition about the Final Causes of Natural Things (1688) and John Ray's *The Wisdom of God Manifested in the Works of the Creation* (1691) argued that the abundant evidence of design in nature, and especially in animate nature, showed the existence, intelligence and goodness of God. Boyle and Ray set the model for subsequent natural historical and natural theological writing in Britain. From the Middle Ages to the early-modern period, the study of animals had been largely the study of revered texts and preserved specimens. Now it involved active observation of living creatures in the wild. As for natural theology, earlier design arguments had not dwelt especially on the adaptedness of the parts and instincts of organisms. As Boyle explained, however, the proposals of Descartes had made the regularly cycling heavenly bodies rather less attractive as evidence for design than they had been previously. Traits fulfilling some purpose in the lives of organisms became the best evidence by default.[32]

Adaptations were now regarded as constituting a kind in their own right, as the features of nature in which God's signature was most clearly legible. They were described as products of the highest possible order of craftsmanship. 'I never saw any Inanimate production of *Nature*', marvelled Boyle in his *Disquisition*, '... whose contrivance was comparable to that of the meanest Limb of the dispicablest Animal: and there is incomparably more Art express'd in the structure of a Doggs foot, then in that of the famous Clock at *Strasburg*.'[33] Devout naturalists in the eighteenth century catalogued the adaptive parts of organisms, describing those parts as machines engineered with admirable skill.[34] Talk of contrivance and clocks remained central, sustained in part by the success of British workshops at contriving the most precise clocks and watches in the world. Along with steam engines, spinning mules and other cunning devices, precision timepieces were instruments of British industrial and imperial expansion.[35] Again following Boyle and Ray, British writers on natural theology approved. In their view, the natural world had been designed so that industrious humans would benefit from its exploitation. To admire the craftsmanship of God was at the same time to admire the social and commercial arrangements that facilitated such efficient fulfilment of God's wishes for humankind.[36]

Boyle and Ray wrote at the end of a turbulent period in British history. In their books, the argument from design became a means of allying the new empirical science to Christian consensus and the prosperity it fostered. By emphasising the study of adaptive contrivance in living creatures, they created a useful role for British science in promoting national harmony. Men and women awake to the providential character of living nature and commercial society would be less prone to atheism and revolution.[37] Boyle and Ray's most famous successor, William Paley, continued these apologetic efforts, issuing his famous *Natural Theology* (1802) at a moment of renewed fear of revolution – this time imported from France.[38]

In his most famous argument, Paley concluded that organisms, with their many parts contrived to serve particular ends, could no more come into being without a designing intelligence than could functioning watches.[39] Paley's book was one of the few to make an impression on Darwin when he was a student at Anglican Cambridge.[40] Not least impressive, it seems, was Paley's comparison of the eye with a telescope.[41] From Paley, and from other authors writing along similar lines, Darwin learned to view organisms as assemblies of separate adaptations, and to view adaptations as remarkable contrivances. For Darwin, the facts about adaptations, so conceived, became the outstanding facts about organisms, the facts a theory of species origins had to account for satisfactorily. Boyle's celebration of the scrupulously attentive 'Author of Nature' echoed in Darwin's insistence, crucial to his case for natural selection, that Nature preserves even the slightest advantageous variation in structure and constitution.[42]

The Darwinian kind 'adaptation' thus has a history rooted in the soil of British scientific, religious, social, commercial and political life.[43] We can gloss this historicity in two ways, with different consequences for independence versus inseparability. We might conclude that, thanks to events that brought British natural theology into being, and Darwin into contact with this tradition, Darwin came to recognise what adaptations truly are – the as-if engineered contrivances of natural selection. That recognition would have come sooner or later, since the kind is part of the pre-social order of nature. How the British came to recognise it had no influence on the kind itself. To that extent, the kind is independent of its historical matrix. Or we might conclude, on the contrary, that history, not nature, made the kind what it is. The theory of natural selection assumes a view of organisms and their parts that is peculiar to a time and place. The Darwinian kind 'adaptation' is inseparable from

Britain in the age of complex machines and counter-revolutionary theology. Other histories produced, and continue to produce, alternative ways of sorting the traits of organisms, ways no more or less in keeping with what we observe. Adaptation is not a natural kind, but a social construct.[44]

V THE MALTHUSIAN STRUGGLE FOR EXISTENCE

In Darwin's day, and to his nineteenth-century Russian readers in particular, the stamp of his context was most visible in his appeal to a struggle for existence identified as Malthusian.[45] Describing that struggle in the *Origin*, Darwin wrote: 'It is the doctrine of Malthus applied with manifold force to the whole animal and vegetable kingdoms.'[46] He argued that the diversity and adaptedness of species were the consequence of generations of struggle among organisms who had passed at least some adaptive variations on to their offspring. This argument for natural selection, developed between September 1838 and March 1839, emerged only after much previous and wide-ranging theorising on the causes of adaptive change. Once he had the argument, however, Darwin's allegiance to it never seriously faltered. How, then, to explain this stabilisation of Darwin's theorising around a doctrine as contentious as Malthus' population principle?[47] Why the decision to stick with Malthus?[48]

For some commentators, then and later, the best explanation is that Darwin stuck with Malthus in order to legitimate hierarchical relations of power in Victorian Britain. The explanation has rarely been stated this baldly. It derives from an analysis of ideology associated now with Marx.[49] In a diffuse way, of course, Marx's influence extends over all the territory covered in this chapter. Soviet Marxist historians helped pioneer the anti-genius historiography of the sciences.[50] Marx's most famous comment on Darwin's theory and his society, quoted above, was in part a comment on the naturalness of the kinds that appear in the theory.[51] It was not Marx but Engels who gave the classic Marxian reading of Darwin's Malthusianism:

> The whole Darwinist teaching of the struggle for existence is simply a transference from society to living nature of Hobbes' doctrine of 'bellum omnium contra omnes' and of the bourgeois-economic doctrine of

competition together with Malthus' theory of population. When this conjuror's trick has been performed, ... the same theories are transferred back again from organic nature into history and it is now claimed that their validity as eternal laws of human society has been proved.[52]

If this was indeed what Darwin was doing, then his decision to stick with Malthus appears inseparable from its matrix. Making competitive struggle look natural is an ambition that makes little sense outside a social context where there is not only competitive struggle but potentially much discontent with the results. Nearer our own day, the historian Robert Young has similarly argued that, just as the theory of special creation was 'a theory suitable for a pastoral, agrarian, aristocratic world', so Darwinian natural selection, with Malthusian struggle at its core, was a theory 'which reflects a competitive, urban, industrial one'. For Young, the transition from natural theology to natural selection was but 'the substitution of one form of rationalization of the hierarchical relations among people for another'.[53]

To come to grips with this explanatory tradition, two quite different claims about Darwin, Malthus and legitimation need to be distinguished.[54] One is that Darwin in his theorising on species stuck with Malthus for reasons having nothing to do with legitimation, but that, in sticking with Malthus, Darwin happened to produce a legitimating theory. The other is that Darwin stuck with Malthus precisely *because* a Malthusian theory would be legitimating. Young equivocates between these two possibilities. So do Young's historiographic successors, Adrian Desmond and James Moore, in their biography of Darwin. In a representative passage, Desmond and Moore set the scene in 1842, when Darwin's Malthusian theorising was well developed: 'And with Chartists massing, it was time for middle-class Malthusians to stand up and show that nature was on the side of the bosses.'[55]

Does the equivocation matter? It does if we are after an explanation of why Darwin's theorising stabilised as it did. Suppose Darwin just happened to stick with Malthus at a time when middle-class Malthusians were keen to show the poor and powerless that a law of nature had ordained their position in the social hierarchy. In this case, there would be no explanation for the stability of Malthusian doctrine in Darwin's theorising on species. There would simply be a remarkable coincidence between what was happening in Darwin's notebooks and what was happening outside his window. I doubt that this is how Young or Desmond and Moore want to be read. Theirs are fighting words. Claims about coincidence do not raise the temperature of debate. Claims about explanation do.

Suppose their claim is indeed the explanatory one, that Darwin stuck with Malthus because his society needed a theory that legitimated competitive social struggle by naturalising it.[56] There are honourable reasons for interpreting Darwin's theorising along these lines. Almost from the outset, Darwinians have enjoyed tremendous cultural authority. Their science is so much a part of the established order that Darwin's portrait now adorns the British ten-pound note. So much authority lends itself to abuse. Directing attention to an ideological function for the theory of natural selection is one strategy for countering uncritical deference.[57] Moreover, as we have seen, some of the natural-theological writers who shaped Darwin's concept of adaptation did write with propagandist intent. Signs are good that, if Ray or Paley had been asked why they wrote about the divine design of animals, they would have said something about the need to forestall revolution. But there is no serious suggestion that Darwin, had he been asked, would have said that he stuck with Malthus to forestall revolution.[58] Rather, the claim must be that Darwin was not aware of the legitimating needs to which the stability of Malthusian doctrine in his theorising was a response.

There are at least three clusters of difficulties with a legitimation explanation so construed. First, there are historical difficulties. The closer we look at the Victorian scene, the harder it becomes to maintain the tidy generalisations on which the explanation depends. Consider that equation: Malthusian = middle-class = Darwin = bosses. Yes, Malthus had supported the middle-class cause of Poor Law reform. But he had opposed that other middle-class cause, reform of the Corn Laws. Those laws protected the domestic grain market from foreign competition. In opposing their reform, Malthus sided with the interests of aristocratic and gentlemanly landowners against middle-class factory bosses (who wanted grain costs to fall so that workers' wages could fall in consequence).[59] Indeed, for all the growth in industrialisation, the dominant elite in England in the 1830s were the land owners. The Darwin family's wealth came more from land and other property than from manufacture.[60] So Darwin's sticking with

Malthus was not straightforwardly in the interests of the Chartist-threatened factory bosses.

Second, there are evidential difficulties. A number of apparently relevant sorts of facts turn out, on inspection, to be irrelevant to evaluating the legitimation explanation's truth or falsehood. It is irrelevant, for example, whether the poor and powerless in fact became complacent upon encountering Darwin's Malthusian theory. Rather, if the theory pacified the poor, then it successfully fulfilled its function; and if not – as appears to be the case – then it simply failed to function properly.[61] It is likewise irrelevant what Darwin himself thought he was doing in sticking with Malthus. On the legitimation explanation, whatever Darwin's conscious motives in keeping with a Malthusian theory, it was at an unconscious level that he responded to the need for such a theory. If unconscious motives do not announce themselves in the documentary record, then, it seems, so much the worse for the documents, and the desire for explanations that draw upon them.

Third, there are ontological difficulties. If we accept the legitimation explanation, we accept a holistic ontology for social life, with collective needs that are unconsciously harboured, unconsciously communicated and unconsciously acted upon, by mechanisms wholly mysterious.[62] In one sense, to indicate this is merely to flag the point that, at present, there is an ontological job of work to do. But that would be disingenuous. There is a long tradition of Anglophone flinching from holism in social explanation. Indeed, it might well be – or so those who back the legitimation explanation could argue – that squeamishness about collective needs and unconscious lines of action is itself evidence of the legitimating power of Darwin's theory. Maybe people bred to Darwinian thinking, with its emphasis on the individual, ever after regard individualist explanations as sensible and holistic explanations as suspicious. The social function of the theory of natural selection may thereby have become invulnerable to exposure, for wherever the theory goes, it takes an obfuscating prejudice about ontology along with it.[63]

VI THE *VERA CAUSA* IDEAL AND THE SOCIAL USES OF MALTHUS

What are the alternatives? It is no explanation to say that Darwin's theorising settled on a Malthusian theory because, when he developed that theory, he hit upon the truth. If the independence thesis requires this view of Darwin's sticking with Malthus, then that thesis is a non-starter. People cannot be said to accept a theory *because* it is true. They may accept it because they believe the evidence shows the theory to be true, or because the theory is more parsimonious than its rivals, or because it fits well with prior beliefs and attitudes. They may accept it because those in authority have pronounced the theory 'true'. In the case of Darwin and Malthus, some combination of the above, properly understood, indeed constitutes a more satisfying version of the inseparability thesis than the Marxian one, or so I argue below. But the truth of a theory, any theory, has no power to explain why this or that individual or community accepts the theory.[64]

There is another reason, specific to the history of evolutionary biology, for dismissing the truth of the Malthusian theory of natural selection as explanatory. Since the synthesis of Darwinism and Mendelian genetics in the 1930s and 1940s, Darwinians have not regarded the struggle for existence as a cause of natural selection. As they now understand the theory, selection occurs whether or not resources are scarce. All that matters is that there are differences of fitness within a population. Commenting on the previously central role of Malthusian population pressure, Ronald Fisher, a preeminent synthetic theorist, wrote in 1930 that there was 'something like a relic of creationist philosophy in arguing from the observation, let us say, that a cod spawns a million eggs, that *therefore* its offspring are subject to Natural Selection...'[65] With the passing of Victorian society, struggle passed out of the foundation of Darwin's theory.

So Darwin cannot have stuck with Malthus because the Malthusian theory was the true theory. Nor can any other scientific seeker after truth, in whatever social context, have settled on a Malthusian theory because it was true. To explain the stability of struggle in Darwin's theorising, we need to look to a local and, quite probably, unique context. On this issue, the inseparability thesis appears to be the winner. But, as we have seen, the Marxian version of the thesis wins at high cost, demanding permanently blurred historical vision, cavalier disregard of Darwin's likely self-description and baroque ontological commitments.

A more attractive version of the thesis is now emerging. It centres on the principle that guided Darwin's reasoning, the *vera causa* ideal.[66] We have already seen how local was that ideal.[67] What we have not noticed thus far are its cultural politics. When Lyell published his three volumes of *vera causa* geology in the 1830s, the character of the sciences in Britain was beginning to change in a fundamental way. At that time, Anglican clerics alone held the small number of scientific posts at the two ancient universities, Oxford and Cambridge, that dominated the elite life of the nation.[68] Church, state and science thus enjoyed strong institutional links. However, thanks especially to Scottish dissatisfactions and to movements within the Whig party – now reaching out to groups in dissent from Anglican doctrine – those links were coming to be increasingly contested. In the late 1820s, when the self-consciously Scottish Lyell began to write his *Principles of Geology*, his sympathies were becoming ever more Whiggish; and he saw his books as an attempt to expunge biblical religion from geology.[69]

Geology in particular had attracted the devout. Lyell's first teacher in geology, the Oxford cleric William Buckland, had claimed to find evidence of the flood that bore Noah's ark. In Buckland's view, this flood was but the most recent in a series of catastrophes that God had visited upon the Earth in preparation for the arrival of humans. Where Buckland offered narratives that arguably harmonised with Scripture, Lyell – following a long tradition of Scottish liberals in his hostility to Tory, Anglican, Oxonian alliances – eschewed such narratives as altogether unscientific. According to Lyell, a scientific, *vera causa* geology did not admit the existence of catastrophes, the likes of which had never been observed. Lyell's reforms struck at the English elite and their complacencies. If the reforms succeeded, the views of the cleric-geologists would cease to count as scientific explanations. Just as important, the cleric-geologists, beholden to the Church of England for their livelihoods, would cease to count as men of science.[70]

Recall that Darwin, a disciple of Lyell, was searching for a *vera causa* theory of species origins. In the months following his reading of Malthus, Darwin believed he had found the beginnings of an even better version of the *vera causa* theory he already had. His theorising stabilised around a Malthusian core in part because he had read Malthus' *Essay* in the autumn of 1838, and in part because, in Darwin's estimation, the Malthusian theory he developed thereafter conformed more closely than any of his previous theories to the *vera causa* ideal. With the cultural setting of that ideal now in view, the two parts of this explanation can each be tied to the Whig reform drive, in and out of the sciences.

Let us take the reading of Malthus first. Commenting in his *Principles* on competitive struggle as the true cause of species extinction, Lyell had quoted, not Malthus, but the Swiss botanist Augustin de Candolle: 'All the plants of a given country are at war with one another.'[71] Lyell had made no reference to Malthus' *Essay* at all. At a moment of unrest over the Poor Law, however, Darwin – eager to resolve the conflict between his own observations and Lyell's theory of extinction – found a resolution in the writings of Malthus. The effect was to initiate that series of modifications in Darwin's thinking which, over the next months, would develop into the theory of natural selection. To the extent that Darwin's position among the Whig chattering classes predisposed him to associate Malthus with the idea of intense, competitive, providential struggle, Darwin's Whig affiliations thus help explain why he read Malthus' *Essay* when he did. As for Darwin's espousal of the *vera causa* ideal in the first place, it was not so much Darwin's as Lyell's Whig affiliations that matter. As we have seen, Lyell had advocated the ideal as part of the Whig drive to reform British institutions. When the Lyellian Darwin conformed his theorising on species to the *vera causa* ideal, he thus aligned his theories with Whig ambitions for British science and society generally.

The history of changing views on method can often seem remote from the social history of the sciences. When it comes to explaining the stability of struggle in Darwin's theorising, however, an attempt to integrate these histories offers several advantages. First, doing so enables us to explain Darwin's Malthusianism without explaining it away.[72] There is no denying or trivialising of the social uses of Malthus in Darwin's time and place. On the contrary, we see how crucial was Darwin's proximity to the Whig conversation about Malthus. Second, there is no need to ignore what Darwin thought he was doing. Darwin's self-conscious motives and allegiances are the starting point for the social-*vera causa* explanation. Third, we are saved from postulating obscure mechanisms of unconscious response to social needs. The explanation points towards mediated causal sequences, complicated but intelligible, leading from Darwin's Malthusian culture to the stable Malthusianism of his science. The upshot is a new option: inseparability without Engels.

VII DARWINIAN CONCLUSIONS

The question posed in this chapter about the independence of the theory of natural selection from its history can be posed of any successful scientific theory. It is nevertheless fitting that Darwin's theory in particular should come under scrutiny. As Philip Kitcher points out, the Darwinian view of life belongs to an era that saw the burgeoning of historical thinking across intellectual culture. Where history had previously been little noticed – in the composing of the Bible, in the heavens, in the structure of organisms – educated people began to see signs of historical process.[73] To look for those signs in the theory of natural selection itself is thus to take the historicist attitude home again.

Another consideration is that the independence and inseparability theses resemble, in a rough and ready way, divergent interpretations of the Darwinian history of life, now much debated. On the 'independence' side, there are arguments that life was constrained to evolve much as it has, that the trajectory of life was fairly robust in the face of contingent history. Even if much in the past had been otherwise, organisms would still have evolved eyes, wings and other familiar features. These are simply the best solutions to certain problems of survival on our planet. Natural selection has converged on them time and again, and would probably have done so however different the past. On the 'inseparability' side, there are arguments that the actual history of life was shaped fundamentally by contingent events, that it all – we all – could have turned out quite differently. An asteroid collision here rather than there, at this time rather than that, and the earth might now support radically different forms of life. Life as we know it is inseparable from the accidents that mark its history.[74]

The match between the inseparability thesis in the history of science and this contingentist thesis in evolutionary biology is no coincidence. One of the books that set historians of science posing sceptical, counterfactual, contextual questions about past scientific theories in the first place was Thomas Kuhn's *The Structure of Scientific Revolutions* (1962). In his conclusion, Kuhn famously urged readers to view the advance of scientific knowledge much as Darwin had viewed the advance of biological form. The message Kuhn drew from Darwin was contingentist. On Kuhn's account, the theory of natural selection made it possible to understand how life could evolve, diversify and complexify without there being a goal to evolve towards – and this was what most deeply unsettled Darwin's contemporaries. In similar fashion, Kuhn argued, historians could now write the history of science without supposing that there was a final goal towards which scientific knowledge was progressing. In science as in life, wrote Kuhn, the process was one of 'evolution *from* primitive beginnings', not 'evolution *toward* anything'.[75]

Those who view Darwin's theory as inseparable from its historical matrix will find it easy enough to develop the parallel between Darwin's theory and an inseparability thesis about the theory. The theory of natural selection, they will say, revealed species as contingent entities, born of chance variation and conditions of life that happened to prevail at a particular time and place. Likewise, outside his specific historical matrix, Darwin might well not have made his particular assumptions, or resolved a crucial conflict between theory and observation as he did. It is even possible to imagine alternative successful biologies which do not include the theory at all. Next take the matter of kinds. Darwin's theory revealed species to be non-natural kinds, invented not by God but by taxonomists. Now historians have thrown doubt on the naturalness of the Darwinian kind 'adaptation'. There is nothing in nature that requires us to conceive plants and animals as mosaics of mechanical contrivances. Darwin inherited that conception from a peculiarly British tradition. Finally, there are explanations of stability. To the extent that species appeared stable, Darwin's theory attributed that stability not to some inner coherence, but to the surrounding conditions of life. In a broadly similar move, historians have emphasised explanatory connections between the stability of Malthusian struggle in Darwin's theorising and the surrounding social context, in particular the Whig reform drive.

Is it really more in the Darwinian spirit to hold that Darwin's own theory is a contingent product of social history, rather than a timeless truth? Before they accept this surprising claim, those who favour the independence thesis will rightly ask for more. They will query the notion of a 'successful' biology, and ask to see in detail how a creationist or saltationist biology, say, could be such a thing.[76] They will cast doubt on whether Darwin and Wallace's co-discovery of the theory of natural selection – so patent an example of theorists converging independently on the truth – can be otherwise explained. They will rebuke as fallacious the inference that *because* the kind 'adaptation' emerged in one culture alone, *therefore* the kind is not natural. They will insist that Darwin's *vera causa* ideal, though local in certain respects, engendered a respect for empirical support that is common to all viable methodological ideals; and it was this respect that made Darwin stick with Malthusian struggle once he happened upon it. Making up our minds over the independence or inseparability of Darwin's theory from its history thus requires us at the same time to make up our minds about Darwin's intellectual legacies. We need to decide not only how best to honour them, but, indeed, what they are.

NOTES

Earlier versions of this chapter were presented in Cambridge, Leeds, York and St Louis in 1999 and 2000. I am grateful for the comments I received on those occasions, and, for detailed criticism of more recent versions, to Jon Hodge, Thomas Dixon, Lindsay Gledhill and John Christie.

1. K. Marx to F. Engels, 18 June 1862, quoted in Schmidt 1971, 46.
2. Hacking 1999, esp. ch. 3, provides the best overview of these debates. For a summary, see Radick 2002. The analysis of this chapter owes a great deal to Hacking's arguments and example. On the 'constructivist' or 'contextualist' turn among historians of science, see Golinski 1998 and Lightman 1997, Introduction. For another assessment in relation to Darwinian biology, see Ruse 1999b, discussed in Radick (in press).
3. On the history of such talk, see Schaffer 1990.
4. Inevitable, that is, so far as the scientific enterprise as we know it remained a going concern. See Hacking 2000.
5. One item on Marx's 1862 list that I shall not discuss here is the idea that competition in nature results in an increasing division of labour. For discussion, see, e.g., Ospovat 1981, chs. 7–9; Limoges 1994; Tammone 1995; Ruse 1999b, 241–5; Hodge, this volume; and the Introduction to this volume.
6. C. Darwin 1958, 140.
7. On the nature of Darwin's intelligence, see Gould 2000.
8. An old but still useful 'big picture' view of how capitalism begat Darwinism is Sandow 1938. On the social and economic history of Britain in this period, see Daunton 1995.
9. See Hodge, this volume.

10. On the run-up to the *Beagle* voyage, see Browne 1995, ch. 6. On the imperial context and content of Darwin's theorising, see Hodge, this volume.
11. McDonald 1998 is a novel about 'Mr Darwin's Shooter'. Covington's *Beagle* journal is currently available on the web. See Covington 1995.
12. For a study of authority, classification and museums in nineteenth-century natural history, see Barton 2000. On museums in science generally, see Pyenson and Sheets-Pyenson 1999, ch. 5.
13. On Darwin and the breeders, see Secord 1981, 1985. For general background on animal breeding in Victorian Britain, see Ritvo 1987.
14. Malthus 1826. Darwin read the sixth edition. The first, quite different edition was published in 1798. On Malthus, see Winch 1987.
15. C. Darwin 1958, 120.
16. Desmond and Moore 1991, 153–4, 196–7, 201, 216–18, 264–7. For a scathing indictment of 'Malthus' Law of Population and the New Poor Law framed in accordance with it', see Engels [1845] 1987, 281.
17. For an attempt to use computer modelling to settle similar issues about the history of quantum physics, see Pessoa 2001.
18. For discussion of this point, see the fourth section below.
19. See Hull, this volume, and Hodge 2000.
20. On pre-Darwinian theories of life's history and diversity, see Bowler 1989. On the 'singularity of Lyell', see Bartholomew 1979.
21. See Hodge, this volume, and Hodge and Kohn 1985.
22. Wallace's paper, 'On the Tendency of Varieties to Depart Indefinitely from the Original Type', was read at the Linnaean Society in London on 1 July 1858, jointly with a paper by Darwin and an excerpt from one of Darwin's letters. All are reprinted in Darwin and Wallace 1958. Two recent anthologies of Wallace's writings are Camerini 2001 and Berry 2002. A recent biography of Wallace is Raby 2001.
23. Kottler 1985.
24. Hodge 1991b, esp. 191–300. See also Beddall 1968 and, on the imperial context of Darwin's and Wallace's biogeographical views, J. R. Moore (in press).
25. J. R. Moore 1997. For Wallace on natural selection and political economy generally, see Coleman 2001. It has been alleged that Darwin was indebted to Wallace for the principle of divergence (see, e.g., Brooks 1984, esp. ch. 11, epilogue). The most careful discussions of the issues are Kohn 1981 and Beddall 1988. Neither finds the allegation persuasive. On Darwin's independent development of the principle – the most important addition to the theory of natural selection following its formulation in the late 1830s – see Ospovat 1981, chs. 7–8 and Kohn 1985b.

26. For Darwin on 'species', see Beatty 1985, Hodge 1986, Stamos 1996, Stamos 1999 and McOuat 2001.
27. Talk of 'natural kinds' dates from the Victorian era. See Hacking 1991, 111–12.
28. C. Darwin [1859] 1964, 3.
29. C. Darwin [1859] 1964, 188–9.
30. The most complete history of the concept to date is Amundson 1996, though it pays scant attention to contextual issues.
31. What of France? Darwin learned from Lamarck and Cuvier, both of whom dealt with adaptations. As Toby Appel has argued, however, the French naturalists of the late eighteenth and early nineteenth centuries 'had none of the British obsession with contrivance', perhaps because machines were less conspicuous in French economic life (Appel 1987, 57).
32. Boyle 1688, section 11; Ray 1692; Gillespie 1987. Excellent introductions to the historical literature on natural theology are Brooke 1991, ch. 6 and Brooke and Cantor 1998, ch. 5.
33. Boyle 1688, 47, spelling and italics in original; discussed in Gould 1998, 13. On the Strasburg clock and Boylean natural philosophy, see Shapin 1996, 32–7. On the cultural history of clock imagery, see O. Mayr 1986.
34. On the development of British natural theology between Boyle and Paley, see Brooke 1974.
35. On the British lead in horology in the eighteenth century and its social and economic consequences, see Landes 1983, ch. 14; Schaffer 1996.
36. Turner 1993, ch. 4, esp. 101–9.
37. Gillespie 1987.
38. Gillespie 1990, esp. 225–6.
39. Paley 1819, ch. 1.
40. On the influence of Paley on Darwin, see Brooke, this volume. On Paleyan Cambridge in Darwin's student days, see Fyfe 1997.
41. Paley 1819, 23–39.
42. C. Darwin [1859] 1964, 83–4; Boyle 1688, 43. Richards, this volume, argues for a Humboldtian rather than a Boylean–Paleyan genealogy here. On continuities and discontinuities between Boyle's *Disquisition* and Darwin's *Origin*, see Gould 1998.
43. Cf. Ospovat 1981, 35–7. On Darwin on adaptation, see Amundson 1996, 27–32. On the modern-day Darwinian concept of adaptation, see Sober, this volume.
44. Among the sceptics about the Darwinian concept of adaptation, see esp. Depew and Weber 1995, who argue that, contrary to the British tradition from Boyle to Dawkins, 'there is no watchmaker, blind or sighted, for

the simple reason that there is no watch. Natural organization is not an artifact, or anything like it, but instead a manifestation of the action of energy flows in informed systems poised between order and chaos' (477–8).

45. Todes 1989, chs. 1–2.
46. C. Darwin [1859] 1964, 63.
47. Here I shall not address the separate problem of how to explain the stability of Darwinian theory within the biological sciences. My primary concern is with Darwin's own theorising, not with the public reception of his theory.
48. The Darwin–Malthus relationship has been much examined. For a survey of the literature up to the mid-1980s, see La Vergata 1985, 953–8. Notable among more recent efforts are Gordon 1989 and Benton 1995.
49. See esp. Marx's preface to *A Contribution to the Critique of Political Economy* (Marx [1859] 1959). One of the most influential philosophical discussions is Cohen 1978.
50. See the papers collected in Bukharin [1931] 1971.
51. On Marx's ambivalence towards Darwin's theory of natural selection, see Weikart 1998b, ch. 1.
52. F. Engels to P. L. Lavrov, 12–17 November 1875, quoted in Schmidt 1971, 47.
53. Young 1985a, 240. Young explicitly allied himself with the interpretative tradition of Marx and Engels. See, respectively, Young 1985a, 239 and Young 1985b, 631–2.
54. My analysis here is indebted to the example of Rosen 1996, esp. 52, 184–200.
55. Desmond and Moore 1991, 294. On the Desmond–Moore map of the Victorian transmutation debates, Tories backed special creation (no natural/social change), Whigs backed natural selection (lawful, slow, gradual natural/social change) and radical revolutionaries backed Lamarckism (rapid, up-from-below natural/social change). Desmond develops the Lamarckian-radical connection in Desmond 1989. For alternative maps, see Rupke 1994 and Secord 2000.
56. Muñoz-Rubio 1999 is in much the same vein.
57. Hilary Rose, for example, adduces the Darwin–Malthus connection as part of a critique of evolutionary psychology (H. Rose 2000, esp. 107–10). For similar attacks on the older sociobiology, see Lewontin 1993, ch. 1, esp. 9–10; Sahlins 1976, xv, ch. 4.
58. Asking Darwin why he stuck with a Malthusian theory is, of course, not the same as asking him whether, in the light of his Malthusian theory, competitive struggle is a social good. See Paul, this volume, for Darwin's affirmative response to the latter question.

59. Winch 1987, esp. ch. 5.
60. Hodge 1994 and this volume.
61. The miner Chester Armstrong read Darwin en route to reading Marxist economics. See J. Rose 2001, 74.
62. Rosen 1996, 197.
63. Roughly the same difficulties attach to the legitimation explanation of Darwin's public claims that natural selection is progressive (as in Gould 1996, ch. 12). For a critique, and an attempt to supply a better explanation, see Radick 2000. On the general history of theorising about evolutionary progress, see Ruse 1996.
64. Hacking 1992, 14; 1999, 81–2, 232 (note 13).
65. Fisher 1930, 43–4, quote on 43, italics in original. For discussion, see Depew and Weber 1995, 269 and Gayon, this volume.
66. What follows is a modified version of the argument in Depew and Weber 1995, esp. chs. 3 and 5. For discussion, see Radick 1998, 353–5.
67. For the history of the ideal from Newton to Darwin, see Kavaloski 1974. See also L. Laudan 1981, ch. 7.
68. Turner 1978.
69. Secord 1997.
70. On scriptural geology and its opponents, see Gillispie [1951] 1996. Rupke 1996 helpfully summarises later historical work on this topic. On Lyell's *vera causa* geology, see R. Laudan 1982.
71. Lyell [1830–3] 1990, II, 131.
72. Cf. the strictures in Shapin 1982, 178; Shapin and Barnes 1979.
73. Kitcher, this volume.
74. For the convergentist case, see Conway Morris 1998; for the contingentist case, see Gould 1989. For an overview, see Sterelny and Griffiths 1999, ch. 12. On the theological dimensions of this debate, see Ruse, this volume.
75. Kuhn 1970, ch. 13, esp. 170–3, quote on 170–1, italics in original. For Kuhn as inspiration for theory–history inseparability theses, see Hacking 1999, 96–9. So far as Kuhn's book influenced Stephen Jay Gould, the most prominent contingentist, it may be that Kuhn lies behind the evolutionary-biological side of the symmetry as well as the history-of-science side. See Gould 2002, 967, and, for a distinct echo of Kuhn on evolution-away-not-towards, Gould 1996, 173.
76. For an attempt to make sense of 'success', see Hacking 1999, 69–70,74–8. On saltationist tendencies in the history of evolutionary biology, see Schwartz 1999 and Gould 2002, ch. 5.

DAVID L. HULL

7 Darwin's science and Victorian philosophy of science

I SCIENTIFIC METHOD IN THE DEBATES OVER THE *ORIGIN*

Soon after the publication of the *Origin of Species* (1859), Darwin sent out over a hundred complimentary copies to a variety of contemporaries, including his former geology teacher, Adam Sedgwick. Darwin was prepared for attacks on the content of his theory. What he had not expected were attacks on his methods. Sedgwick, for example, writing in the *Spectator* in March 1860, complained that 'Darwin's theory is not *inductive*, – not based on a series of acknowledged facts pointing to a *general conclusion*, – not a proposition evolved out of the facts, logically, and of course including them. To use an old figure, I look on the theory as a vast pyramid resting on its apex, and that apex a mathematical point.'[1]

In other words, for Sedgwick, the problem with the theory of natural selection was that Darwin had not supported it in the right way. The right way was to show that the theory was a generalisation from a wide range of particular facts. That was induction. The wrong way was to invent the theory as a hypothesis and then deduce from it particular facts. That was the method of hypothesis. In Sedgwick's estimation, the theory of natural selection was not an inductive generalisation, but an invented hypothesis, and as such could claim no support from the facts. His image of the pyramid is telling. As he saw it, in induction, a wide base of particular facts supported a single theory up top, just as the base of a pyramid supports the rest of the structure. Darwin had produced an upside-down pyramid of a theory, inverting the relations that ought to obtain between theory and facts. The resulting structure was accordingly doubtful.

Sedgwick was far from alone in finding fault with Darwin on methodological grounds. The three best-known theorists of scientific method in the mid-Victorian era, John Herschel, William Whewell and John Stuart Mill, likewise weighed in with verdicts on the theory of natural selection. Each theorist had his own line on invented hypotheses versus inductive generalisations in science. In the light of Sedgwick's remarks, one might expect that those who regarded invented hypotheses as legitimate would have been more open to Darwin's theorising than those who did not. But just the opposite seems to be the case. Mill, the most wary of the method of hypothesis, looked more favourably upon Darwin's theory than either Herschel or Whewell did (although not much more favourably). For all their philosophical differences, Herschel, Whewell and Mill found themselves in basic agreement about the theory of natural selection. At best, it was not good enough, and certainly not as credible as the theory of creation by a designing intelligence. At worst, it was not a legitimate scientific theory at all.

This chapter explores the methodological issues that arose in the debate over Darwin's theory in the nineteenth century. There will be no attempt to deal with all the issues that mattered in the philosophy of science of the era, nor with the full range of opinions on what Darwin called 'the right principles of scientific investigation'. Rather, the emphasis will be on those aspects of the Victorian discussion on method that illuminate the responses of Herschel, Whewell, Mill and Darwin himself. In part such an emphasis makes biographical sense, since Herschel and Whewell influenced Darwin's views on method. No evidence exists to show that Mill also influenced Darwin in this respect. The writings of all of these men, however, shaped the reception of Darwin's theory.[2]

The mid-Victorian era was not the only time, of course, that the theory of natural selection provoked methodological debate. Generational change later in the century brought new philosophical preoccupations in relation to Darwin's theory. Some of these changes will be discussed in the final section. But the earlier era is of special interest. It was then that public discussion of methodological issues occurred on a remarkable scale, especially in response not to the biological but to the physical sciences of the day.

II THE FERMENT IN METHODOLOGICAL THINKING IN MID-VICTORIAN BRITAIN

For mid-Victorian British men of science, the best, shining example of inductive science was Isaac Newton's gravitational mechanics for earthly and celestial motions. Newtonian mechanics had two great inductive strengths. First, the action of the gravitational force came within observational witness here on earth, in falling, rolling and swinging bodies. By extrapolating this force to terrestrial tides as caused by lunar motions as well as to the planets' orbits around the sun, this science proceeded, it was held, by inductive generalisation from observed facts. Second, the law of gravitation was quantitative – the attractive force was inversely proportional to the square of the distance between any two bodies. Not only was this law capable of explaining and predicting precise properties of planetary orbits, but also it seemed demonstrable that no other law for the force, an inverse cube law say, could do so.

As an example of success in inductive science, this Newtonian triumph was hard to emulate. Ever since Newton's own day, various theorists, including reputable savants seeking to account for electrical, magnetic, thermal, optical and chemical phenomena, had put forward hypotheses admittedly not meeting these standards: hypotheses, especially, about fluid or solid media, often called ethers, that were impossible to observe directly by sight or touch. These hypothetical entities seemed to be fictions or figments of inventive conjecture rather than securely inferred factual generalisations. And if they provided possible explanations and predictions, they did not provide the only possible ones.

In Britain in the 1820s, this gap between hypothetical practices and inductive ideals was raised to special urgency by controversies concerning the very nature of light and so the explanation of all optical phenomena. Optics was seen as central and consequential for all natural science. For there was not merely a desire to explain rainbows or predict eclipses, but also to understand the instruments decisive for much science, and to comprehend sight itself. On one theory, favoured by Newton, a beam of light consisted of a stream of particles whose diverse motions caused different sensations. These particles, it was granted, were too small to be directly observable; but their powers and actions were supposed to differ only in degree from the observable powers and actions in bodies large enough to be observed. The particle theory of light was, to that extent, taken to be supported inductively by facts within experience.

The rival wave or undulatory theory of light could hardly be defended that way. For it supposed that light is propagated as waves in an ethereal medium which is not only invisible, intangible and imponderable, but can permeate where ordinary gases and fluids cannot, being present therefore in vessels evacuated with the best air pumps and in the voids between the stars. Worst of all, whereas the particles of the particle theory had none of their bodily properties totally diminished, the ether, in some versions, had all of its characteristics reduced to zero. Not merely an extremely elastic medium, it was a perfectly elastic one. Unsurprisingly, then, even partisans of the wave theory conceded that it was far from being a generalisation from experience, or defensible as the only possible explanation for optical facts. Hypothetical not inductive, it seemed to offer not knowledge, but conjecture. And yet, by the 1820s, its record of explanatory and predictive successes seemed, to many authoritative minds, far more impressive than the rival particle theory. This success raised the issue of a clash between standards and achievements. The theory having the most success with the newest challenges was still unable to meet traditional criteria for theory appraisal as natural knowledge. If the wave theory was good science, then perhaps those criteria were discredited; conversely, if those criteria were upheld, then the theory had to be rejected despite its manifest virtues.

John Herschel, astronomer son of William Herschel, the famous émigré astronomer from Germany, was England's most admired man of science in 1830. His *Preliminary Discourse on the Study of Natural Philosophy*, appearing that year in a prominent encylopaedic series of books for a wide readership, was then a commanding text. However, in this text Herschel provided no sustained unequivocal resolution of the roles of induction and hypothesis in science. He reaffirmed the impeccable inductive credentials of Newtonian gravitational mechanics. Considering optics, he admitted that, even though the wave theory of light did not possess the proper inductive credentials, it was much the best theory of light because of its explanatory and predictive successes. These successes suggested, albeit very uncertainly, that its postulates might come close to being truths about the physical world, although no one could be sure.

Ten years later, Herschel's good friend William Whewell presented a new doctrine in his *Philosophy of the Inductive Sciences* (1840) – the 'consilience of inductions' – that was designed to make gravitational astronomy and undulatory optics look more similar in their credentials than they were usually taken to be. By contrast, the *System of Logic* of 1843, from John Stuart Mill, a liberal man of letters and politics, upheld the traditional insistence that inductions and hypotheses must never be confused with one another, and that even hypotheses that are good, as hypotheses, do not constitute inductive knowledge. Whewell's and Mill's divergences on this issue were related to their divergences on others. Whewell was a prominent Anglican, Platonist, Kantian Tory; while Mill was a direct philosophical descendant of Hume. Like the French philosopher Auguste Comte before him, Mill had positivist sympathies and proposed to extend the methods of natural science to human minds and societies. Mill's inductivism reflected his empiricism and his positivism – doctrines Whewell was resolved to oppose and replace. Darwin was publishing, then, at a time of acute, collective methodological self-consciousness.

In what follows I am concerned with the influence that philosophy of science had on the reception of Darwin's theory of evolution. Assuming that Darwin's contemporaries were influenced by the views of these nineteenth-century philosophers of science, what were these views? Some will say the assumption is unwarranted. Jed Buchwald, among others, doubts whether arguments over issues such as these 'did much historical work at all – whether, that is, anyone ever actually persuaded anyone else to change a belief'.[3] At times I share Buchwald's cynicism. Too often it seems that good arguments never convince anyone. Even so, Buchwald and I must see some point in good arguments because we attempt to provide them in our own work. If we think that argumentation can convince our readers, then we are in no position to reject out of hand the effects of such argumentation on the subjects of our enquiry.[4]

III INDUCTION

Within the works of Whewell, Herschel and Mill certain persistent tensions can be found. One concerns the role of deduction in the method of induction. Even Francis Bacon, the patron saint of induction, acknowledged a role for deductive reasoning. While emphasising the need to ascend carefully and gradually from particulars to generalisations of increasing scope, Bacon allowed that, 'from the new light of axioms, which have been educed from those particulars by a certain method and rule... greater things may be looked for', not least new particulars. On Bacon's view, the road to knowledge 'ascends and descends; first ascending to axioms, then descending to works'.[5]

Two centuries later Herschel repeated Bacon's praise of induction in science,[6] but then went on to remind the reader that 'the successful process of scientific enquiry demands continually the alternative use of both the *inductive* and *deductive* method'.[7] In the study of nature, 'we must not, therefore, be scrupulous as to how we reach to a knowledge of such general facts: provided only we verify them carefully when once detected'.[8] Whewell likewise insisted on the need to use both induction and deduction in science. In Whewell's view, this 'mutual dependence and contrast of induction and deduction, this successive reasoning up to principles and down to consequences, is one of the most important and characteristic properties of true science'.[9] Mill, too, despite his reputation as an arch-inductivist, had a similar opinion. For Mill, it was a mistake to celebrate Bacon for 'exploding the vicious method pursued by the ancients of flying to the highest generalizations first, and deducing the middle principles from them', since 'this is neither a vicious nor an exploded, but a universally accredited method of modern science, and that to which it owes its greatest triumphs'.[10]

One need not be a pedant to see some problems with respect to the 'inductive' methods being urged by Herschel, Whewell and Mill. All three repeatedly invoke the importance of observations over hypotheses. If no errors are allowed into one's system of belief, no errors have to be eliminated later. But no sooner do they emphasise the role of observations in science than they recant, pointing out the crucial role played by hypotheses. They counselled the investigator to 'look before you leap', but then immediately warned that 'he who hesitates is lost'. Regardless of what Herschel, Whewell and Mill may have intended, the message that their readers took away was that genuine science had to be built on an extensive evidential base. Anything else was not genuine science.

Nineteenth-century philosophers of science wanted certainty. There was some debate, however, over the proper roles for different forms of induction in securing certainty. For Herschel and Whewell, eliminative induction was preferable to enumerative induction. In induction by simple enumeration, one proceeds to a generalisation from observed actual instances of causal connections. For example, the finding that all cases of smallpox diagnosed thus far – all the positive enumerative instances – are caused by contagion from prior cases justifies the conclusion that this disease is always caused in this way. In eliminative induction, one proceeds not from observed actual instances of causal connections, but from possible causes. The changes in relative level of sea and land studied by geologists could be due to the land rising, the sea sinking or both together. Further facts about these changes may serve to eliminate all but one of those three possibilities, thus making it inductively proven. Initially a number of possible causes are considered, but eventually only a single cause remains.

At the time, the number of known kinds – and so the number of actual causes, let alone possible ones – was huge. For example, from fifty to sixty physical elements were known, and over a hundred thousand biological species. The number of particulars was orders of magnitude greater.[11] Mill was not intimidated by such large numbers of particulars. For him, enumerative induction was the basic form of reasoning. Nevertheless, he saw some role for eliminative induction. Mill's overall method of science had three parts: enumerative induction, ratiocination and verification. In the hypothetical method the first of these three steps – enumerative induction – is suppressed. Such a suppression is legitimate, in Mill's view, only when the hypothesis in question has already been shown by eliminative induction to be the only hypothesis consistent with the facts.[12]

Much of the debate between Whewell and Mill was over ownership of the term 'induction' and its cognates. Both men extended the meaning of the term, but in different ways. According to Herschel, Whewell viewed induction as the process by which minds 'construct general propositions themselves from the contemplation of particulars, and attribute to them a universality which experience alone is incapable of warranting'.[13] In Whewell's view, induction was not a logical process of totting up particulars or eliminating possible causes, but a process by which minds superinduced generality on particulars. Reading Whewell as a strict inductivist was difficult, no matter how frequently he used the term 'induction'; and this lack of strict inductivism was one thing that his contemporaries disliked about his theory of science. Mill, on the contrary, bent over backwards to give the impression that his was the philosophy of the particular. To be sure, he acknowledged that investigators can legitimately reason from particulars to generalisations and from these back to particulars; but, according to Mill, generalisations were nothing but 'collections of particulars, definite in kind but indefinite in number'.[14] Thus, all inference for Mill was really from particulars to particulars.[15] As a result, Mill's contemporaries interpreted him as being an inductivist, and rightly so. If Mill had not existed, historians of philosophy would have been forced to invent him.[16]

IV *VERAE CAUSAE*

No matter what methodological tenets one espoused at this time, they had to be described as 'inductive', and have as their source Bacon and Newton. Hypotheses were suspect. After all, the great Newton never feigned such things. Direct experience was sacred. There was to be no appeal to the occult qualities of the medieval Schoolmen. Rather, the causes used to explain natural phenomena had to be true causes – '*verae causae*,' as Newton's admirers called them. According to Herschel, theorists had to limit themselves to 'causes recognized as having a real existence in nature, and not being mere hypotheses or figments of the mind'.[17] Of course those causes should have a 'real existence in nature'. The problem was deciding how the status of being a true cause was to be established.

That problem in turn raised the question of how the *vera causa* requirement related to the ideal of being inductive rather than merely hypothetical. Traditionally, the answer concentrated on requiring independent evidence for the existence of the cause invoked by a theory. If the existence of the cause could be evidenced by facts other than those facts it was used to explain, then that was evidence independent of explanatory virtue. Such a cause was a real, known, existing or true cause, not a supposed, fictional, conjectural or hypothetical cause; and, to that extent, the theory was no invented hypothesis but an inductive theory. An additional requirement was that the cause invoked by a theory had to be adequate to produce the effects to be explained by the theory. In brief, then, the *vera causa* ideal traditionally specified that both the existence and the adequacy of a cause should be evidenced independently of the facts explained.

But how, precisely, were these evidential requirements to be met? How could one be sure that the cause invoked by a theory was indeed a true cause? Herschel's initial suggestion was that true causes lead to a great multitude of effects in addition to those that gave rise to our knowledge of the cause in the first place. Certain facts are already known. They indicate a possible cause. If this cause gives rise to numerous additional effects that are found to exist, then this cause is likely to be a true cause. But when Herschel turned to giving examples of true causes, other considerations came into play. For example, numerous seashells could be found in rocks at a great height above the sea. Several causes had been suggested at the time for the presence of these seashells: a plastic virtue in the soil, the influence of celestial bodies, fermentation, transport by pilgrims or birds, and the encapsulation of shells by sedimentation before the land mass was elevated. Herschel dismissed plastic virtues and celestial influence as 'figments of fancy'. Transportation by pilgrims and birds could account for a small number of shells but that was all. Fermentation was a genuine cause for a variety of phenomena, but no one had ever witnessed fermentation producing anything like shells. However, sea creatures dying and settling into the mud at the bottom of the sea happened all the time; and the elevation of the sea to become dry land, though it occurred over a more protracted period of time, had also been *witnessed*.

As in the case of induction, a tension can be found in Herschel's criteria for true causes: one is direct experience, the other is inference to additional effects. Herschel can be found saying that experience is the 'only ground of all physical enquiry'.[18] For example, if you want to experience force, just whirl a stone around your head in a sling. Without such direct evidence, science would be impossible. However, Herschel also acknowledges that some phenomena are too small or too large to be experienced in such a direct way. For example, one can perceive electricity directly by an electric shock. From this direct perception one can then reason about electricity in general. The danger is letting *ad hoc* hypotheses intrude. Herschel designed his version of the *vera causa* principle to eliminate hypotheses that would turn out to be *ad hoc*. In his view, one sign that one has identified a true cause was the ability to infer unanticipated phenomena – phenomena that no one had yet experienced. On the basis of one's theoretical understanding, an as-of-yet unexperienced phenomenon was predicted, pursued and discovered. Nothing could be more convincing than that!

Whewell's writings show similar tensions.[19] As might be expected, Whewell's Kantian philosophy posed problems for anything like direct experience. For Whewell, all observations were to some extent, as we would now say, 'theory-laden'; or to use Whewell's frequently quoted aphorism, there was a 'mask of theory over the whole face of nature'. Whewell reinterpreted Newton's *verae causae* as being embodied in his own consilience of inductions.[20] Whewell did not urge 'scientists' (his coinage) to abandon the search for true causes. He simply downplayed the role of direct experience with respect to true causes. In the consilience of inductions, the 'theoretical cause takes its place among the realities of the world, and becomes a *true cause*'.[21] Certainly the relaxation of the requirement of direct experience allowed Whewell to countenance all sorts of theoretical entities, such as the ether. As he put it, the science of optics was 'traveling rapidly towards a single theoretical view – the theory of undulations'.[22]

Whewell also disagreed with Herschel's uniformitarian view of the past. Herschel had argued that, in deciding which causes acted in the past, one can infer from a perceived cause to other causes *of the same kind* but not to causes of *different kinds*. Whewell saw no reason for this exclusion. In particular, he was willing to countenance 'catastrophes' – causes that do not differ just in degree from experienced causes (for instance, earthquakes of a much larger scale than those occurring nowadays), but also causes of the sort never experienced by human beings, including supernatural ones. Species going extinct might well be explained by natural causes of the sort still in evidence; but, in Whewell's view, their initial wholesale appearance at the beginning of geological cycles could not be explained naturalistically. The causal chains could be traced back only so far in time. Hence, Whewell concluded, 'we must contemplate supernatural influences as part of the past series of events, or declare ourselves altogether unable to form this series into a connected chain'.[23]

Whewell's references to God and supernatural causes in his work on the history and philosophy of science were not in the least unusual at the time. Herschel began his *Preliminary Discourse* with an extensive discussion of the Power and Intelligence responsible for the universe exhibiting Order and Design. He argued that, contrary to what many people thought, religion and science were not in opposition, for 'truth can never be opposed to truth'. Indeed, the study of science rendered 'doubt absurd and atheism ridiculous'.[24] Immediately after extolling religion, Herschel launched into an equally laudatory celebration of the practical applications of science from the pendulum to the steam engine. Science was to be honoured for supporting the Christian faith and providing practical results.

V DARWIN ON THE METHODOLOGICAL VIRTUES OF HIS THEORY

Darwin thought that he had gone about formulating, testing and enunciating his theory of evolution according to the best canons of science held at the time – chiefly those he derived from reading Herschel's *Preliminary Discourse*.[25] With respect to true causes, Darwin thought that he was on safe ground.[26] His theory of evolution appealed to such uncontentious facts as the variations seen in living creatures. Offspring looked much like their parents, and siblings were more similar to each other than to other organisms in their species. It was likewise a matter of common experience that not all organisms survived long enough to reproduce themselves, and that just which organisms survived to reproduce was a result in part of how well adapted they were to their environments. So far as successive changes in the environments could result in successive changes in the organisms, the evolution of species seemed at least plausible. Darwin also placed considerable weight on the analogy from artificial to natural selection. If plant and animal breeders could introduce so much change in such a short time, how much more change could nature have been able to introduce over the long expanses of time that geologists such as Lyell postulated?[27]

Darwin had gathered massive amounts of data in support of his theory that species evolve through descent with modification by means of natural selection. Although he could not include all this data in the *Origin of Species* – an abstract of a much longer work – he did incorporate quite a bit and alluded to additional evidence elsewhere.[28] Some of the phenomena that Darwin cited were, he suggested, phenomena that he had recognised because his theory indicated that they should exist, most notably certain correlations between embryonic development and species evolution. (Herschel and Whewell both prized the prediction of unexpected phenomena, though Mill did not.[29]) Darwin also drew attention to the evidential support deriving from the classification of animals and plants. He acknowledged that, while many species were clearly distinct, just as many graded imperceptibly into each other. Brambles were especially brambly in this respect, as were oaks. Moreover, in Darwin's view, the groups-within-groups classifications which had been produced over the years supported belief in the evolution of species. This pattern is exactly what one would expect if species gave rise to species in an ever-expanding tree of life.[30]

In short, Darwin thought that he had met the standards of induction set by the philosophers of science of his day. Natural selection was clearly a true cause. Responding to Sedgwick's condemnation, Darwin asked another teacher from his Cambridge days, the botanist John Stevens Henslow, to ask Sedgwick, the next time the two men met,

> whether it was not allowable (& a great step) to invent the undulatory theory of Light – ie hypothetical undulations in a hypothetical substance the ether. And if this be so, why may I not invent hypothesis of natural selection (which from analogy of domestic productions, & from what we know of the struggle of existence & of the variability of organic beings, is in some very slight degree in itself probable) & try whether this hypothesis of natural selection does not explain (as I think it does) a large number of facts in geographical distribution – geological succession – classification – morphology, embryology &c. &c.– I shd really much like to know why such an hypothesis as the undulation of the ether may be invented, & why I may not invent (not that I did *invent* it, for I was led to it by studying domestic varieties) any hypothesis, such as natural selection. . . . I can perfectly understand Sedgwick or any one saying that nat. selection does not explain large classes of facts; but that is very different from saying that I depart from right principles of scientific investigation.[31]

Darwin's argument here may seem quite straightforward. Sedgwick, he assumes, accepts that the wave theory is both good science and an invented hypothesis not an inductive theory. So Darwin's own theory should not be condemned totally for being likewise. It should be assessed, not solely and adversely for introducing hypothetical causes, but, rather, solely on its ability to explain many facts of many kinds. So read, Darwin's response seems to concede the correctness of Sedgwick's view that his theory was not inductive but hypothetical, and to resort to retorting that, nevertheless, as such it can be of value, witness the unassailable precedent from the high-ranking science of optics. However, the two longest parenthetical passages show this reading to be misleading. For Darwin says that his hypothesis is made in itself slightly probable at least, by analogy and by two bodies of knowledge about the struggle for existence and the variability of organisms.

Now, this is probable support independent of explanatory virtue. And, indeed, in Darwin's *Origin*, the existence of natural selection and its ability to produce and diversify species are given evidential support in the early chapters before the theory is put to explanatory work in the later chapters. So, the theory is not argued for as one would argue for a mere hypothesis, solely on its explanatory virtue. To that extent, Darwin in the *Origin* and in this letter is far from conceding that his theory is not inductive but hypothetical. Moreover, as the later parenthetical passage shows, Darwin was insistent that rather than inventing his theory as one would have to invent a hypothesis, he had in fact been led to it by comparing the origin of species in nature with the making by man of domesticated races of animals. Not only, then, *could* his theory have been reached by an inductive rather than an inventive process; it *had* been.

Some years later, Darwin included a revised version of his reply to Sedgwick in the introduction to his *Variation of Animals and Plants under Domestication* (1868). This version may seem to concede even more fully that he saw natural selection as having, like the wave theory, only the credentials of an invented hypothesis. However, Darwin says only that it may be looked upon that way, not that it must be or that he himself views it so; and, again, he insists that his hypothesis is made probable by what is positively known of the struggle for existence and domesticated races. That kind of probable support, independent of explanatory virtue, was, again, what traditionally made a theory inductive and so not merely inventive or hypothetical. In continuing to insist on this claim, Darwin was reaffirming his conviction that he had always aligned his theorising with the evidential ideals for inductive science codified, for his generation, by Herschel and exemplified by Lyell.

VI HERSCHEL ON THE *ORIGIN*

When we turn to how Herschel, Whewell and Mill responded to the *Origin of Species*, one fact becomes especially noteworthy – they said almost nothing about it in print. During the thirteen years after the appearance of the *Origin*, Herschel saw fit to include a single footnote to his *Physical Geography of the Globe*,[32] while Whewell added a short discussion to the preface of the seventh edition of his *Astronomy and General Physics*.[33] Prior to his death, all Mill published was a footnote in his *System of Logic*.[34] After his death there appeared a short discussion of evolution in his *Three Essays on Religion*.[35] Other than several paragraphs in their private correspondence, that was it. As far as the three major philosophers of science at the time are concerned, Darwin's major achievement warranted only two footnotes, a revised preface, and a short discussion in a posthumously published work. Darwin's own examination of the role of philosophy of science in the reception of his theory was, to the contrary, a good deal more extensive.

Darwin sent a copy of the *Origin* to Herschel, to see 'whether I produce any effect on such a mind'.[36] It did not take long for Darwin to find out. In a roundabout way, Darwin heard that Herschel thought that his theory is the 'law of higgledy-pigglety'. Darwin went on: 'What this exactly means I do not know, but it is evidently very contemptuous. – If true this is [a] great blow & discouragement.'[37] It was a great blow both because Darwin thought that he had adhered to Herschel's methods in the *Origin* and because Herschel, as early as 1837, could be found saying that the introduction of new species is a 'natural in contradistinction to a miraculous process'.[38] In his *Physical Geography of the Globe*, Herschel repeated his earlier views that new species appear gradually in a 'series of overlappings, leaving the last portion of each in co-existence with the earlier members of the newer species'.[39]

In the 1861 edition, Herschel appended a footnote to this discussion on Darwin's theory. Instead of commenting on Darwin's method, Herschel expanded on his complaint about Darwin's theory being the law of higgledy-piggledy. As one might expect from his comments in the first chapter of his *Preliminary Discourse*, the problem was 'intelligent design'. On Darwin's theory, variations occurred 'in all directions', not just in those directions that might help organisms cope better with their changing environments. According to Herschel:

> We can no more accept the principle of arbitrary and casual variation and natural selection as a sufficient account, *per se*, of the past and present organic world, than we can receive the Laputan method of composing books (pushed *a l'outrance*) as a sufficient one of Shakespeare and the *Principia*. Equally in either case, an intelligence, guided by a purpose, must be continually in action to bias the directions of the steps of change – to regulate their amount – to limit their divergence – and to continue them in a definite course.[40]

One thing that Darwin had learned from Herschel is that men of science were committed to discovering secondary laws, not primary laws. Darwin acknowledged that God, the primary cause, may well work by means of secondary laws; but he did not see why he had to include reference to God in his explanations of these secondary laws, any more than astronomers had to in explaining how the planets circle the sun. Herschel did not object to Darwin introducing secondary laws, but to the *character* of the secondary laws he introduced. For Darwin, variations were in no sense preordained. The fact that an organism might need a particular variation did not increase the likelihood that it would get that variation. To make matters worse, selection looked equally indifferent to the good of individuals, including people.

Herschel had warned that to ascend to the 'origin of things, and speculate on the creation, is not the business of the natural philosopher'.[41] Darwin had made no such ascent.[42] The first origins of life were not part of his theory. Indeed, he ended the *Origin* with the claim that there is 'grandeur in this view of life, with its several powers, having been originally breathed into a few forms or into one'.[43] But this single reference to God was not good enough for Herschel, especially since the laws that Darwin proposed gave no indication of the Creator's foresight. In Herschel's view, God may act by secondary laws to create new species, but not by Darwin's secondary laws:

> We do not believe that Mr. Darwin means to deny the necessity of such intelligent direction. But it does not, so far as we can see, enter into the formula of his law; and without it we are unable to conceive how the law can

have led to the results. On the other hand, we do not mean to deny that such intelligence may act according to a law (that is to say, on a preconceived and definite plan). Such law, stated in words, would be no other than the actual observed law of organic succession; or more general, taking that form when applied to our planet, and including all the links of the chain which have appeared. But the one law is a necessary supplement to the other, and ought, in all logical propriety, to form a part of its enunciation.[44]

In the early part of his footnote, Herschel is worried about the forces that produce the evolution of species. They need to be in some sense directed. In the later part he turns to the sequences of species that these forces produce. They too must exhibit a direction, preferably one that leads ineluctably to the human species. According to Herschel, statements of such sequences are themselves laws of nature. Herschel then draws his footnote to a close with the following observation: 'Granting this, and with some demur as to the genesis of man, we are far from disposed to repudiate the view taken of this mysterious subject in Mr. Darwin's work.'[45]

Darwin was reassured to some extent by Herschel's concluding remarks. After all, it would take Darwin's mentor, Charles Lyell, almost a decade to go as far. Eventually, Darwin himself admitted that my 'theology is a simple muddle; I cannot look at the universe as the result of blind chance, yet I can see no evidence of beneficent design, or indeed of design of any kind, in the details'.[46] He had earlier exhibited even greater scepticism.[47] On teleology, he was siding with Bacon, who had famously remarked that enquiries into final causes were as unproductive as barren virgins dedicated to God. Bacon's nineteenth-century disciples had a difficult time working their way around this judgement since, as far as they were concerned, God was the ultimate final cause.[48]

VII WHEWELL ON THE *ORIGIN*

When the *Origin* was published, Whewell was no longer active in debating the sorts of issues that he discussed in his *History of the Inductive Sciences* (1837) and *The Philosophy of the Inductive Sciences, Founded upon Their History* (1840). The only acknowledgement that Whewell made in print of Darwin's theory was in the preface of the seventh edition of his Bridgewater Treatise on astronomy and physics, published in 1864. In this preface, Whewell contrasted explanations of the organisation of living creatures in terms of design with the view of Democritus that these all came into existence through the chance encounters of atoms. Whewell asked incredulously whether there were 'any persons who, in modern times, assert that the world was produced by a fortuitous concourse of atoms?'[49] Though Darwin was not mentioned by name, Whewell's subsequent references to 'recent' arguments and his comparison of telescopes to eyes clearly indicated that Whewell was talking about Darwin.[50] In this preface Whewell specified two objections to Darwin's theory: that it showed the mere *possibility* of *imagining* the transition of one organ into another, not that such transitions had in fact taken place; and that the amount of time needed for such transitions was not shown to have been available.

Why such reticence? One explanation is that Whewell had already discussed all of these issues at great length in his debates with Lyell and could see no reason to rehearse them once again. In an October 1863 letter to the Reverend D. Brown, Whewell stated once again that no one had been able to trace all sequences of species back in time to their first origins. Hence, he concluded, the 'absence of any conceivable natural beginning leaves room for, and requires, a supernatural origin'.[51] To this objection, Whewell added that Darwin could not adduce a single example of one species evolving in nature into another. Nor had plant and animal breeders, through all their efforts, succeeded in producing a single new species.

If one took the 'witnessing' requirement of the *vera causa* ideal seriously, then Darwin was potentially in real trouble. He had never observed one species evolving into another, nor had anyone else. Even worse, if the evolutionary process was as protracted as Darwin thought, then no one would ever witness one species evolving into another, and the inductive foundations of his theory would forever remain insecure. For a variety of reasons, however, all three British philosophers, and especially Whewell, had watered down the witnessing requirement considerably. Whewell's resurrecting it in Darwin's case might be put down to his general animosity towards the idea of species evolving. But Thomas Henry Huxley had no such animosity, and he too insisted that 'until selective breeding is definitely proved to give rise to varieties intersterile with one another, the logical foundation of the theory of natural selection is incomplete'.[52] Darwin responded to Huxley on this point that we 'differ so much that it is no use arguing'.[53]

Although Whewell did not say so in his letter, he had an additional reason for rejecting the evolution of species – one that is absolutely fundamental to his theory of science. According to Whewell, species were 'natural classes', and a 'natural class is neither more nor less than the observed steady association of certain properties, structures, and analogies, in several species and genera'.[54] These were the classes connected in general laws. The object of the classificatory sciences was to discover the natural classes that make the formation of general laws possible.[55] Whewell was willing to countenance the supernatural suspension of laws of nature at each geological period when new species were introduced. But he was not willing to have laws themselves change through time. Perhaps they might vary in their intensity; but that would not bring their permanence into question.[56]

From Whewell's point of view, if species evolved, with one species changing gradually into another, then it followed that the laws of nature themselves were evolving. That was a proposition Whewell just could not accept.[57] He could not conceive a greater violation of the known laws of nature than new species appearing in successive geological strata. But since new species did appear in successive strata, Whewell concluded, a creative agency had to be perpetually at work bringing new species into existence as old ones went extinct.[58]

VIII MILL ON THE *ORIGIN*

The final member of this British triumvirate of philosophers was Mill, and, according to popular conception, he alone saw the true value of Darwin's theory. In later editions of his *System of Logic*, Mill introduced a long footnote in which he discussed 'Mr. Darwin's remarkable speculation'.[59] This footnote occurred in Mill's discussion of the method of hypothesis. Contrary to what Newton seemed to be saying when he proclaimed 'Hypotheses non fingo', Mill argued that hypotheses play a central role in the process of discovery. For example, in Mill's view, Descartes' hypothesised vortices would have been legitimate if he or his followers had been able to bring them to the test of observation, as advocates of the undulatory theory of light had been able to do.

Mill began his famous footnote by listing additional examples of hypotheses that were legitimate when they were first introduced, regardless of whether they turned out to be true or false: Broussais' mistaken hypothesis that every disease originates in some one part of the organism; the doctrine that the earth is a natural magnet; the claim that the brain is a voltaic pile; and the phrenologists' view that the various mental functions were localised in different regions on the surface of the brain. Mill lauded the first three hypotheses because they were set out in ways that they could be tested. In the case of the phrenologists, Mill argued, testing had thus far turned out to be beyond them. Nevertheless, for Mill, all four of these uses of the method of hypothesis were legitimate. Mill then turned to Darwin:

> Mr. Darwin's remarkable speculation on the Origin of Species is another unimpeachable example of a legitimate hypothesis. What he terms 'natural selection' is not only a *vera causa*, but one proved to be capable of producing effects of the same kind with those which the hypothesis ascribes to it: the question of possibility is entirely one of degree. It is unreasonable to accuse Mr. Darwin (as has been done) of violating the rules of Induction. The rules of induction are concerned with the conditions of proof. Mr. Darwin has never pretended that his doctrine was proved. He was not bound by the rules of Induction, but by those of Hypothesis. And these last have seldom been more completely fulfilled. He has opened a path of enquiry full of promise, the results of which none can foresee. And is it not a wonderful feat of scientific knowledge and ingenuity to have rendered so bold a suggestion, which the first impulse of every one was to reject at once, admissible and discussible, even as a conjecture?[60]

Darwin's allies had earlier been looking to Mill for support.[61] However, Mill is plainly saying here that while Darwin's theory is fine as a hypothesis, his evidence goes no way towards inductive proof. Mill grants that natural selection is shown to be a *vera causa*, meaning here presumably an existing, a real, not fictional causal process. Moreover, he thinks it is proved capable of the same kind of effects that Darwin ascribes to it, although not effects of the same degree; meaning, apparently, that it is proved capable of producing intraspecific adaptive divergences but not the larger, interspecific diversifications that Darwin would invoke it to explain. This question of degree is left open. So, by contrast with Darwin's own claims for his theory, Mill's judgement here is far from favourable, treating it as an example of the method of hypothesis, as part of the logic of discovery, not of final proof. Darwin had put forth a promising hypothesis, but all of the efforts that he and his fellow Darwinians had exercised to test the theory were insufficient for anything that might be termed proof. Newton had proved his theory, Kepler had proved his laws, advocates of the undulatory theory of light were close to proving their theory, but Darwin and his followers had not provided any proof at all for evolutionary theory.

Prior to his death in 1873, Mill made his negative evaluation more emphatic. In his *Three Essays on Religion*, published in 1874, he argued that in the fourteen years since Darwin published the *Origin* the weight of evidence still remained on the side of intelligent design. Taking the example of the eye, Mill upheld the traditional view that, since sight is subsequent to the putting together of the structures of the eye, the fact of sight cannot serve as an efficient cause of those structures.[62] Instead, something else must function as the efficient cause of the eye; and the most likely candidate for Mill was 'intelligent will'. He continued:

> I regret to say, however, that this latter half of the argument is not so inexpugnable as the former half. Creative forethought is not absolutely the only link by which the origin of the wonderful mechanism of the eye may be connected with the fact of sight. There is another connecting link on which attention has been greatly fixed by recent speculations, and the reality of which cannot be called into question, though its adequacy to account for such truly admirable combinations as some of those in Nature, is still and will probably long remain problematical. This is the principle of 'the survival of the fittest'.[63]

Mill then concluded that the 'adaptations in Nature afford a large balance of probability in favour of creation by intelligence'.[64]

In sum, both Herschel and Mill published footnotes in later editions of their respective works that appeared to their readers as providing equivocal, hesitant support for Darwin's theory of evolution as an 'hypothesis' or 'speculation', while Whewell came out solidly against Darwin. By the time Mill died, his doubts about the adequacy of natural selection when compared to creative intelligence had if anything intensified. What is most damning, however, is how little these philosophers had to say in print about one of the most important theories in Western science – a half dozen or so printed pages, that is all.

IX THE NEXT GENERATION

A generation later the scene seems to have changed radically. Such philosophers as Chauncey Wright, William Stanley Jevons and Charles Saunders Peirce not only claimed to accept Darwin's theory but also voiced approval of his methodology. In the case of Wright, these claims were well founded. Wright both understood Darwin's theory and accepted it. Darwin went so far as to finance the publication of a pamphlet by the young American defending Darwin and his theory.[65] More importantly, Wright used Darwin's theory in research, observing, moreover, that a 'theory which is utilized receives the highest possible certificate of truth'.[66] At a time when the views of Herbert Spencer had surpassed those of Darwin in popularity, Wright saw a marked difference between the methods that Darwin used and those of Spencer. For Wright, Darwin's methods were genuinely scientific; Spencer's were not.[67]

The English logician and economist Jevons championed evolutionary theory with little in the way of reservations.[68] The theory of evolution he championed, however, had a lot more to do with Spencer than with Darwin. Although Jevons defended Darwin's methodology, finding it perfectly acceptable, Darwin took little comfort from this support, because Jevons defended Spencer's methodology as well. Darwin thought the latter was more 'philosophy' than science. Nor did Darwin's theory play all that much of a role in Jevons' own research. Nevertheless, Jevons did acknowledge that traditional principles of classification as explicated by generations of logicians were incompatible with genealogical classifications.[69]

Along with his debating partners Wright and William James, Peirce today is regarded as one of the founders of American pragmatism. He was initially impressed by Darwin's theory, finding it a legitimate application of statistical methods to biology, at a time when statistics was rapidly coming into its own. As Wright had argued, although Darwin could not say what would happen in any one case, he showed that, in the statistical long run, organisms would become adapted to their environment.[70] Peirce contrasted Darwin's methodology with that of Spencer, finding Spencer much more 'philosophical' than Darwin. Being philosophical was no bad thing for Peirce, and he preferred Spencer's views to those of Darwin. Moreover, according to Peirce, evolution was not gradual, but involved a series of minor catastrophes. Those species that were able to change most rapidly survived to reproduce. He also noted, as Whewell had done before him, that the idea of species evolving implied that laws of nature themselves change through time. Whewell rejected the evolution of species on that account. Peirce, on the contrary, embraced the evolution of laws in his grand cosmic theory of Evolutionary Love.[71]

To the extent that Peirce fostered the acceptance of any theory of evolution, it was not Darwin's theory. Yet again, one sees a philosopher not simply accepting Darwin's theory as Darwin himself might have hoped, but adapting it to new and specific purposes. Not that this phenomenon should surprise us; those who produce arguments very rarely succeed in controlling what others do with those arguments.

NOTES

1. Sedgwick [1860] 1973, 160.
2. For the development of Darwin's theory, see Ruse 1975, 2000c; Hodge 2000; Hodge and Waters, this volume. Hull 1973 contains a large number of reviews of the *Origin*. For other treatments of the topics in this chapter, see, e.g., Hull 1995 and Ellegård [1958] 1990, ch. 9.
3. Buchwald 1993, 205.
4. For further discussion of the controversy over the wave theory of light, see Achinstein 1993; Buchwald 1993; L. Laudan 1993; and, more generally, Schuster and Yeo 1986.
5. Bacon [1620] 1960, I, 97, aphorism CIII.
6. Herschel [1830] 1987, 104.
7. Herschel [1830] 1987, 174.
8. Herschel [1830] 1987, 164.
9. Whewell 1831, 381.
10. Mill [1843] 1973, VIII, 871; also in 8th edn, 1872, 568–9.
11. Whewell 1831, 391.
12. Mill [1843] 1973, VII, 492; also in 8th edn, 1872, 323.
13. Herschel 1841, 193.

14. Mill [1843] 1973, VII, 284; also in 8th edn, 1872, 186.
15. Mill [1843] 1973, VII, 203; also in 8th edn, 1872, 133.
16. On Mill's inductivist philosophy of science, see Scarre 1998.
17. Herschel [1830] 1987, 144.
18. Herschel [1830] 1987, 80.
19. On Whewell more generally, see Yeo 1993 and Fisch and Schaffer 1991.
20. Whewell 1849, 64.
21. Whewell 1840, II, 447.
22. Whewell 1831, 395.
23. Whewell 1840, 116.
24. Herschel [1830] 1987, 9 and 7.
25. Hodge 2000.
26. Darwin to C. J. F. Bunbury, 9 February 1860, in Burkhardt *et al.* 1985–2001, *Correspondence* VIII, 76 (hereafter *CCD*).
27. On the analogy between artificial selection and natural selection, see Waters 1986; Sterrett 2002; Waters, this volume; and the Introduction to this volume.
28. For the longer work, see C. Darwin 1975.
29. L. Laudan 1981, chs. 8 and 10.
30. The widespread belief that traditional Linnaean classifications exhibit a structure that can be easily adapted to reflect the successive branchings of phylogenetic trees turns out to be an illusion. See Hull 1964, 1979.
31. Darwin to J. S. Henslow, 8 May 1860, in *CCD* VIII, 195.
32. Herschel 1861, 12.
33. Whewell 1864.
34. Mill 1872, 328. This footnote first appeared in the book's fifth edition, published in 1862. See *CCD* IX, 205.
35. Mill 1874.
36. Darwin to Charles Lyell, 23 November 1859, in *CCD* VII, 392.
37. Darwin to Charles Lyell, 10 December 1859, in *CCD* VII, 423.
38. Babbage 1837, 204. See also the letter from Darwin to Baden Powell, 19 January 1860, in *CCD* VIII, 41, and the remarks in the same volume, 575.
39. Herschel 1861, 11–12.
40. Herschel 1861, 12.
41. Herschel [1830] 1987, 38.
42. C. Darwin [1859] 1964, 490.
43. C. Darwin [1859] 1964, 490.
44. Herschel 1861, 12.
45. Herschel 1861, 12.
46. Darwin to Joseph Hooker, 12 July 1870, in F. Darwin and Seward 1903, I, 321.

47. Darwin to Asa Gray, 5 June 1861, in *CCD* IX, 162; Darwin to Charles Lyell, 1 August 1861, in *CCD* IX, 226.
48. Hull 1973, 55–66.
49. Whewell 1864, xv.
50. Cf. C. Darwin [1859] 1964, 137, 188.
51. Whewell to D. Brown, 26 October 1863, in Todhunter 1876, II, 433–4.
52. T. H. Huxley 1896, vi.
53. Darwin to T. H. Huxley, 28 December 1862, in *CCD* X, 633.
54. Whewell 1831, 392.
55. Whewell 1831, 392.
56. Whewell 1835, 448.
57. Hodge 1991a, 275.
58. Whewell 1853, 92.
59. Mill 1872, 327. For further discussion of Mill on Darwin, see Hull 2000.
60. Mill 1872, 328.
61. Letters from Darwin to T. H. Huxley, 5 December 1860, in *CCD* VIII, 514, and to Henry Fawcett, 16 July 1861, in *CCD* IX, 204. See also Mineka and Lindley 1972, XIV, 695, 1505, 1553.
62. Mill 1874, 172.
63. Mill 1874, 172.
64. Mill 1874, 174.
65. C. Wright 1871.
66. Madden 1963, 78.
67. C. Wright 1865. A recent collection of writings by and about Wright is C. Wright 2000.
68. Jevons 1874.
69. Jevons 1869, 231.
70. C. Wright 1871.
71. On Peirce's 'universe of chance', see Hacking 1990, ch. 23.

JOHN HEDLEY BROOKE

8 Darwin and Victorian Christianity

I THE DARWINIAN CHALLENGE

During his Cambridge years, Darwin was preparing to become a priest in the Anglican Church. Later in life he saw the irony: 'Considering how fiercely I have been attacked by the orthodox it seems ludicrous that I once intended to be a clergyman'.[1] Why he was attacked by the orthodox has never been difficult to explain. Offering a naturalistic account of the emergence of human beings from ape-like ancestors, Darwin offended religious sensibilities as well as common sentiment. His theory of evolution by natural selection reinforced doubts about biblical authority at a particularly sensitive time. It could easily be interpreted as an affront to human dignity and it called for a serious re-thinking – not necessarily a rejection – of traditional Christian doctrines.

Despite friction between competing Christian traditions, and despite political tensions in England between the established Anglican Church and socially disadvantaged dissenters, there were features of a Christian creed that transcended party lines. These were belief in an all-powerful, merciful God on whom the world depended for its creation and continued existence. Humankind had been made in God's image and had been granted the privilege of free will. The privilege extended to dominion over, and responsibility for, the rest of creation. The Christian God was an active, living God, to whom prayers were directed and whose providence was not confined to an original creative act. Central to most Christian belief was the doctrine that human nature had been tainted through Adam's disobedience and that in the life of Jesus Christ was a special revelation of the nature of God. Christ was envisaged as both human and divine, as the

Messiah whose coming had been prophesied in the Hebrew Scriptures. In evangelical preaching familiar to Darwin, Christ's death was an atonement for human sin, his resurrection a source of hope for all who trusted in his teaching, love and forgiveness.

Most Victorian intellectuals were not taking the *Genesis* creation narratives literally. Advances in the understanding of both earth history and the Bible had already called for symbolic readings of the *Genesis* 'days'.[2] There were even ancient precedents for non-literal readings of Scripture. Augustine had warned against taking the 'days' of creation literally. Nevertheless, among unsophisticated religious folk, Darwin was often seen as threatening a sacred text.[3]

To make matters worse, the historical nature of the creation narratives entailed other theological issues, such as the consequences of Adam's 'fall' and the biblical description of Jesus Christ as the 'second Adam' atoning for the sins of the first. Had Darwin not shown that man had risen, not fallen? And what of divine activity in the world? Even among Darwin's peers were some who believed that the origin of human beings would remain beyond the limits of science.[4] Darwin's contrary view challenged the picture, familiar from Milton's *Paradise Lost*, of a Creator who miraculously conjured new species into existence. Darwin did not close all the gaps. Unlike Robert Chambers, the anonymous author of *Vestiges of the Natural History of Creation* (1844), Darwin wisely refrained from speculating how the first few living forms had originated. Nor did he claim any insight into how the earth, much less the solar system and least of all the entire universe itself had come into being. Nevertheless, his account of species formation as resulting from the gradual accumulation of minor modifications was embarrassing for those who habitually found solace in the inexplicable. Darwin removed much of the mystery from what, following John Herschel, he called the 'mystery of mysteries', the origin of new species.

There were deeper questions, too. What did it mean for humankind to be made in the image of God if we shared ancestors with other primates? Had the human 'soul' been added during the evolutionary process, or was it more appropriate to speak of our *being* souls rather than *having* them? What was the ultimate ground of moral values if the evolution of the moral sense could be explained simply in terms of survival value, without reference to the transcendent? When Darwin wrote his *Descent of Man* (1871) he did not intend to proclaim the relativity of moral values. He wanted to explain how the highest form of moral sensibility (that we should behave to others as we would have them behave towards us) had developed naturally. But it was easy to read his theory as disruptive of moral responsibility and, by implication, of the stability of society. Put crudely, if men and women were told that they were essentially no different from animals, would they not start behaving like them? That was a common fear, hardly diminished by references to a 'struggle for existence' that could easily be translated into aggressive individualism. Within the Christian traditions, might was not supposed to be right. It was the meek who would inherit the earth.

Darwin's emphasis on continuity between *Homo sapiens* and ape-like ancestors could be offensive even to those without Christian convictions. Cartoonists had a field day. Apes in their cages allegedly enquired whether they were their keeper's brother. Monkeys were depicted with their tails about to be shorn: 'cut it off short', says one, 'I can't afford to await developments before I can take my proper position in Society.' Darwin came close to saying that those who opposed his theory by snarling and baring their teeth only confirmed thereby their canine origins. Underlying the jokes were matters of deadly earnest. Victorian prudery and animal lewdness were not the best of bedfellows. But there was more to it than that. If Christian commentators were not amused, it was because they saw the new theory as a powerful tool for those wishing to wrest control of education from religious institutions.

As if this were not enough, Darwinism challenged natural theology – the attempt to infer the existence and attributes of a deity, independently of revelation. In England especially, confidence had often been placed in arguments for design, comparing intricate organic structures and their marvellous adaptive functions with the work of human artisans, as in the design of magnificent clocks. Such analogies pointed to the wisdom and power of God, the refinement of whose creatures far transcended anything mere mortals could make.[5] The inference to a Designer was not peculiar to Christian traditions. It appeared in antiquity and was sometimes embraced by critics of Christianity in their quest for an alternative and, in their estimation, more rational religion.

This argument for design had often incorporated the latest science and had been reinforced by it. In the second half of the seventeenth century the microscope had disclosed a new world of great beauty and precision in minute organic structures. For Robert Boyle the way the Creator had packed life into the merest mite was awe inspiring. The physical sciences had also testified to divine precision – in the exquisite calculations made by Isaac Newton's God to ensure that the planets had gone into stable orbits. Because the sciences had so often supported religious belief, the Darwinian challenge was particularly poignant. Darwin never denied the appearance of design in the wonderful adaptations he studied; but his causal process of natural selection enabled one to see, almost as in a conversion experience, how nature could counterfeit design. For the Princeton theologian Charles Hodge the conclusion was inescapable. In his book *What is Darwinism?* (1874) Hodge did not regard the idea of evolution as necessarily atheistic. Nor did he accuse Darwin himself of atheism. But, for Hodge, Darwin's theory of evolution by natural selection, through its emasculation of design, amounted to atheism.

To compound the problem, Darwin's emphasis on divergent lines of evolution from common ancestors, represented by the image of a branching tree or branching coral, made it difficult to believe in the unfolding of a divine plan. The only diagram in the *Origin of Species* depicted this repeated forking and branching, enabling Darwinians with atheistic leanings to say that we are the product of a process that never had us in mind.[6] Add to this the accidental features of the evolutionary process, for example the demise of the dinosaurs making our own evolution possible, and the full force of the Darwinian challenge can then be appreciated.[7]

Given the widespread use of Darwinism in secular critiques of religion, it is not surprising that some Christians feel threatened by it. Historically, however, the relations between Darwinism and Christianity have been more diverse than the idea of continuous conflict would suggest. There is a richer, more fascinating story to be told. Darwin himself began as a reformer, not a destroyer of natural theology. His biography is revealing because his eventual agnosticism was not simply a result of his science. Family tragedy crushed his faith as did moral objections to certain Christian doctrines. Examining religious responses to his theory in Victorian England we shall find that they were sometimes surprisingly positive. Many did see opposition between evolution and creation; but it was also possible to see evolution as God's method of creation. The variety of response raises important questions about the models we use to describe the relations between science, religion and modernity. These will be discussed in the closing section.

II DARWIN AND NATURAL THEOLOGY

Within Christianity, knowledge of God was derived from two principal sources: revelation, which might include forms of religious experience, and natural reason. The precise relationship between the two had often been controversial. Eighteenth-century critics of Christianity had argued that knowledge of the deity derived from reason was more reliable than that based on the Scriptures or on Church tradition. For Christian writers a theology based on reason alone would always be deficient because it could never show that God had entered into a special covenant with humankind. Nevertheless, natural theology did have a place in defending the faith, providing arguments against atheism and for an immortal soul. Informally it helped to reinforce belief by evoking a sense of awe at the wonders of the natural world. In William Paley's popular *Natural Theology* (1802), it was argued that rational proof of a deity was a first step towards believing that, from the same deity, a revelation might be expected.

The Darwinian challenge to natural theology was expressed by Darwin himself: 'the old argument from design in nature, as given by Paley, which formerly seemed to me so conclusive, fails, now that the law of natural selection has been discovered'.[8] The contrast is such that it can be a profound existential experience when one first sees the world not as Paley saw it but through the eyes of Darwin. God's well-adapted creatures suddenly become nature's products that happen to be the survivors of a long, tortuous, bloodstained process. For Darwin himself the sheer volume of extinction was staggering; and if one had not been staggered one had not understood the theory.[9]

Had natural theology been completely sterile; had Darwin learned nothing from it? Opinion is divided on this question; but there certainly exists a revisionist literature in which Darwin's debt to natural theology is explored.[10] Through reading Paley, Darwin became fascinated by the intricate adaptations he would eventually ascribe to natural selection. It has been claimed that the only universe in which natural selection could work was the universe Darwin inherited and then stole from the natural theologians.[11] Even his debt to Malthus' argument that, in the absence of checks, population growth would tend to outstrip food supply, was a debt to a work of natural theology; for Malthus had been defending a God-given natural order within which secular hopes of a social utopia were purely visionary.[12] For Malthus the laws of nature were designed to promote the Christian virtues of diligence, industry and sexual abstinence until one could afford marriage and a family. His famous essay on population focused Darwin's mind on a struggle for survival throughout nature.[13]

Opinions differ on the extent of Darwin's debt to natural theology because two contrasting views have emerged concerning his intellectual formation. In the first he is a peculiarly English reformer of the language of design that he had encountered in Paley. In the second he is a Romantic naturalist, excited by the travels of Alexander von Humboldt, eager to experience the flora and fauna of exotic landscapes. On the first view the reform that Darwin favoured was that of the astronomer John Herschel and adopted in part by the philosopher William Whewell. Their emphasis fell on beneficent laws of nature rather than divine intervention. In Whewell's account, design was visible in propitious *combinations* of laws rather than in anthropomorphic images of contrivance.[14] Darwin looks to be just such a reformer of natural theology in the 1830s. A notebook entry reads: 'the Creator creates by laws'. Darwin supposed that the 'end of formation of species & genera, is probably to add to quantum of life possible with certain preexisting laws'. He also referred to 'laws of harmony' in the system.[15] Design was to be seen in providential combinations of laws rather than in specific organic structures.

In the alternative view, where the young Darwin is recast as a Romantic naturalist, he is entranced not so much by Paley's mechanistic anatomy as by an emotive response to the beauties of nature, enticed by the vision of tropical rain forests, intoxicated by what he reads of Humboldt's travels, desolated when his ship could not land on Tenerife.[16] This was the young man who would eventually breathe the word 'hosannah' when finally experiencing the Brazilian jungle for himself: 'Twiners entwining twiners, tresses like hair – beautiful lepidoptera – Silence, hosannah.'[17] On this interpretation the young Darwin found God *in* nature rather than deduced God's existence *from* it. On neither view was nature bereft of religious meaning.

Darwin's reference to 'ends' in creation suggests that at the time his theory took shape he was not erasing divine purposes. In an early *Sketch* of his theory (1842) the divine laws leading to 'death, famine, rapine, and the concealed war of nature' were justified because they produced 'the highest good, which we can conceive, the creation of the higher animals'.[18] There were even hints of a theodicy – an attempt to rationalise the existence of pain, suffering and the uglier features of creation. Might something be gained by having the Creator create through intermediate processes? The deity would not then be directly responsible for what Darwin called a 'long succession of vile molluscous animals'. From this perspective, it was separate creation that he deemed 'beneath the dignity of him, who is supposed to have said let there be light and there was light'. To deny that God was capable of producing 'every effect of every kind' through 'his most magnificent laws' Darwin described, in strong language, as an act of profanity.[19]

Seeing Darwin as a reformer of natural theology may help us understand certain constraints on his theory of natural selection. If the laws of nature were of divine origin, one might expect the improvement of organic forms to reach such levels of perfection that a continuous action of natural selection would cease. If environmental changes subsequently produced new pressures, then (and only then) would natural selection cut in again. It has been argued that such a constraint on the continuous action of natural selection was not lifted until Darwin began to think in terms of relative rather than absolute or perfect adaptation.[20] Darwin admitted that other legacies from natural theology had also shaped his thinking. In his *Descent of Man* there was a frank confession: 'I had not formerly sufficiently considered the existence of many structures' which are 'neither beneficial nor injurious; and this I believe to be one of the greatest oversights as yet detected in my work'. What reason did he give for this oversight? 'I was not able to annul the influence of my former belief, then widely prevalent, that each species had been purposely created; and this led to my tacitly assuming that every detail of structure, excepting rudiments, was of some special, though unrecognised, service.'[21] Darwin corrects his former self, and we may recognise both Darwins in current evolutionary debates.

III DARWIN'S RELIGIOUS ODYSSEY

What were Darwin's private religious beliefs and how did they change? A possible *ending* of the story is contained in a letter from Julia Wedgwood to Darwin's son Frank: 'Everyone who feels Religion infinitely the most important subject of human attention would be aware of a certain hostility towards it in [your father's] attitude, so far as it was revealed in private life.' She continued with the arresting remark that he felt he was confronting some influence that adulterated the evidence of fact.[22] The strength of this remark suggests that in the course of his spiritual trajectory Darwin had reached some conclusions he was unlikely to renounce.

The standard view is of a neat linear progression: from his early Christianity, in which he would astonish members of the *Beagle* crew by quoting the Bible to settle a point of morality, to a deistic position when he wrote the *Origin*, to his later agnosticism.[23] This is an attractive formula because of another seemingly irreversible process at work: the loss of an aesthetic sensibility that Darwin confessed had been 'intimately connected' with his belief in a deity.[24] Such a neat progression also harmonises with standard models of secularisation. However, it has become less clear that Darwin can be pigeon-holed at each stage of his intellectual development. On reflection it would be surprising if the man who showed us that we cannot pigeon-hole pigeons could be pigeon-holed himself. He spoke of *fluctuations* of belief.[25] The materialism with which he flirted in the late 1830s, even if sustained, may not have precluded a Christian sensibility of sorts. There were certainly monistic models of mind and body within Unitarianism – that tradition within Christianity, exemplified by Joseph Priestley, which denies the orthodox doctrine that Christ is as divine as God.[26] Much later, when Darwin preferred to think of himself as an agnostic, he still insisted that there were days on which he deserved to be called a theist.[27] Even his atrophied sensibilities were perhaps not as deadened in later life as he pretended.[28]

Consequently we may need to revise our understanding of Darwin's loss of faith. There were many cultural resources on which he could have drawn for his eventual agnosticism. These included the scepticism of David Hume and the positivism of Auguste Comte.[29] We have long known of his early doubts about sacred texts and how on the *Beagle* voyage he came to doubt whether an intuitive sense of God was a universal human characteristic. His cousin, Hensleigh Wedgwood, tried to persuade him that this innate sense of God differentiated us from the animals. Darwin disagreed. On his voyage he had discovered that a sense of God was not pronounced in a Fuegian or in an Australian.[30]

A radical hypothesis would be that Darwin's loss of faith had little or nothing to do with his science. This would be to go too far. Darwin emphatically did make connections *between* scientific and other reasons for his religious doubts. Extending the domain of natural law did make miracles more incredible.[31] The extent of human suffering threatened belief in a beneficent God but was consonant with his theory of natural selection.[32] Randomness in the production of variation was difficult to square with divine control. There was also the concern his wife Emma had expressed just before their marriage – that the critical, questioning mentality appropriate to a life in science might encourage scepticism on matters of faith.

Nevertheless, the most sensitive accounts of Darwin's doubts have stressed their origins in experiences and traumas common to the human condition. There was the death of his infidel father, forcing him to confront once again that 'damnable doctrine' of eternal damnation. 'I can hardly see how anyone ought to wish Christianity to be true', he would later write in a passage that his wife considered so 'raw' that she wished to have it excised from his *Autobiography*.[33] Excised because, in her opinion, Charles' characterisation of Christian doctrine had become a caricature. Then there was the tragedy of his daughter Annie's death in 1851 – the cruel death of an innocent ten-year-old, which marked for Darwin the crucifixion of all his hopes.[34]

Many of the ingredients of Darwin's agnosticism sprang from incidents easily missed if one looks only to his science. An important step was his realisation that the radical friends with whom he associated in his London years – members of the circle of Harriet Martineau – could lead an exemplary moral life without embracing the Christian religion.[35] This challenged a common cultural assumption that atheists could not be trusted because any oath they might take would not be binding. Darwin's religious slide was perhaps not so different from that of Francis Newman, brother of the more famous, and much more orthodox, John Henry Newman, and one of the 'honest doubters' whom Darwin studied in the early 1850s.[36]

What of Darwin's public utterances? It has become increasingly clear how carefully they must be read. From his notebooks we know that he had to calculate what he should *not* say.[37] It was also expedient to keep what he said about religion to a minimum. 'Many years ago', he reminisced, 'I was strongly advised by a friend never to introduce anything about religion in my works, if I wished to advance science in England.'[38] There may have been expediency, too, in protecting himself from censure. But it is a complex matter because he also shared the belief that it was ungentlemanly to disturb the faith of others. This means there can be a greater ambiguity in his public remarks on religion than in private. Here is Darwin confiding to Joseph Hooker in March 1863: 'I have long regretted that I truckled to public opinion, and used the Pentateuchal term of creation, by which I really meant 'appeared' by some wholly unknown process.'[39]

Because he regretted having used biblical language it does not follow that he was admitting to atheism. It is even possible he was truckling to Hooker! But it is indisputable that he lost a specifically Christian faith. He could write that science itself had 'nothing to do with Christ, except in so far as the habit of scientific research makes a man cautious in admitting evidence'. But that very caution, just as Emma had feared, took its toll: 'For myself I do not believe that there ever has been any revelation.'[40] It has been suggested that Darwin's evidentialist view of Christianity goes back to another work of Paley, his *Evidences of Christianity*. If that is correct there is a subtle irony. The Anglican Church itself had taught him to test the rationality of faith through the study of evidence – a lesson that he so took to heart that it cost him the beliefs he had earlier espoused.

Writing to the American botanist Asa Gray, Darwin confessed that he could not see evidence for design in nature as clearly as Gray apparently could. Whereas Gray supposed that the variations on which natural selection worked were led by providence in propitious directions, Darwin interpreted them as appearing at random without any prospective use in mind. For Darwin the case was like that of a builder who might use stones to build a house but where it would be impossible to claim that the stones had come to be as and where they were for that purpose. In a revealing reply, Gray conceded that he had no answer to such an argument – except that the perception of design in nature was, after all, based on faith and not reason alone.[41] In his private correspondence Darwin exulted in his victory.[42] Yet, even for Darwin himself, the issue was not transparent. On several occasions he said that he could not believe so wonderful a universe is the product of chance alone. He was attracted to the formula that it was the result of designed laws, with the *details* left to chance. But then the distinctiveness of his agnosticism shines through. He had convictions that the universe in its main lines of development was not the product of chance. Convictions of that sort were what agnostics were not supposed to have. Yet, disarming as ever, Darwin asked whether he should trust his own convictions – especially if his own mind was the product of evolution: 'Can the mind of man, which has... been developed from a mind as low as that possessed by the lowest animals, be trusted when it draws such grand conclusions?'[43]

In Darwin's *Descent of Man* (1871) a naturalistic account was given of the moral sense and its origin. This could be deeply wounding for his contemporaries. In an age that experienced a crisis of faith, belief in moral absolutes had sometimes been a lifeline. Darwin's account certainly wounded his wife. To her son Francis she spoke frankly: 'your father's opinion that *all* morality has grown up by evolution is painful to me'. The offending suggestion was that a child's belief in God might be compared with a monkey's fear of a snake – inculcated until it almost became an instinct.[44] Because Darwin's work could be so wounding, we should turn to its reception.

IV RELIGIOUS RESPONSES TO DARWIN'S THEORY

Darwin's theory was bound to be a divisive issue within the Churches because it was so easily transformed into a naturalistic worldview, in which references to a deity were marginalised or excluded. Scholars have spoken of a clash between positivism and creationism, between chance versus design, between contending appeals to authority, the scientific versus the clerical.

To place the clash of ideas in a social and political context, two theses have become prominent. Frank Turner has seen the Darwinian debates as symptomatic of a profound social change in which scientific amateurs (epitomised by clerical naturalists) were displaced by a younger generation of professional scientists (typified by Thomas

Henry Huxley) eager to assert their rigorous standards and cultural authority.[45] Not without provocation, advocates of scientific naturalism sometimes went on the offensive, as when the physicist John Tyndall at the 1874 Belfast meeting of the British Association for the Advancement of Science declared that 'we shall wrest from theology the entire domain of cosmological theory'.[46]

The second thesis is that of Adrian Desmond and James Moore who ask from where Darwin derived his predilection for causal explanations of animal distribution. They point to the influence of scientific mentors: Robert Grant, Charles Lyell, John Herschel. But, they add, 'all these were particulate influences within a much wider and deeper sea-change. The tide was running towards naturalism in an age rejecting Oxbridge Anglicanism for Dissenting industrialism. Nature was being reformed – purged of miracles, subjected to law – and the message was rife in radical literature around the time of the first Reform Act.'[47]

As with all such general theses there is room for nuance. In the physical sciences of Darwin's era, one could be a thoroughly professional scientist, wedded to rigorous standards in one's work, and still prefer a theistic worldview to one purged of design. This would be true of James Clerk Maxwell and William Thomson (Lord Kelvin), of whom it has recently been said that they 'not only embedded their new natural philosophy in the cultures of Presbyterianism but had also been ready to deploy that natural philosophy in the service of a Christianity suitable to the wants of Victorian Britain'.[48] Energy sources were conceived as gifts analogous to the spiritual gift of grace, which when accepted carried an obligation to ensure they were not wasted. There were physicists who suspected that secular thinkers were falling for Darwinism because it suited their purpose, not for solid reasons.[49] It is a mistake to assume that the scientific community was united behind Darwin, just as it would be a mistake to imagine that all Christian theologians lined up against him.

As a qualification to the thesis of Desmond and Moore, it has been suggested that the politics of evolution may have been less radical – at least in England and Scotland – than these authors imply.[50] There was no lack of evolutionists or fellow-travellers in the late 1830s: Baden Powell, William Carpenter, Robert Chambers and Francis Newman would be examples. Darwin may have felt that to confess his 'murder' (admitting the mutability of species) would have led to his being stigmatised along with artisan radicals; but the suggestion is that he might have been mistaken in that belief. How one was treated depended on who one was, not simply on what one said.

To impose social and political dichotomies on the Darwinian debates can be misleading if no space is left for intermediate positions. A large space was created by Baden Powell, Oxford's Professor of Geometry, who wished to protect the autonomy of both science and theology by giving to men of science all the freedom they needed to investigate nature, at the same time assigning jurisdiction over moral issues to the theologian.[51] Even Darwin's advocates often preferred to see their science as a-theological rather than anti-theological. T. H. Huxley referred to the sciences as neither Christian nor un-Christian but extra-Christian.[52] He found nothing in Darwinian evolution to exclude the possibility of an original design in a primordial state of the universe.[53]

Some modern writers suggest that, by destroying Paley's argument for design, Darwin deprived Christianity of its rational foundation. This is a serious mistake because there were theological perspectives from which the design argument was of minor importance. It was seen by some High Church Anglicans as little more than the ideological construct of a scientific community seeking to promote itself by claiming that the sciences were spiritually edifying. This scientific rhetoric found little favour with John Henry Newman, one of the most influential theologians of the mid-nineteenth century, who famously deserted the Anglican Church for the Church of Rome. In his vision of an ideal university Newman conceded that the design argument may teach God's power, but 'What does Physical Theology tell us of duty and conscience? Of a particular providence and, coming at length to Christianity, what does it teach us even of the four last things, death, judgment, heaven and hell, the mere elements of Christianity?' Newman's conclusion was that 'it cannot tell us anything of Christianity at all'.[54] There is a sense in which he was more critical of Paley than he was of Darwin.

For religious thinkers who focused on evolutionary progress there were ways of integrating the physical development of humankind with a spiritual development that crowned the process. Such evolutionary schemes were often facile. Henry Drummond, minimising the waste and carnage in nature, shifted attention from the struggle for existence to an altruistic struggle for the life of others. And in his immortal words it was better to have lived and been eaten than not to have lived at all! It may, however, be too easy to ridicule the theologians who minimised the nastiness of natural selection. Even among Darwinian biologists, natural selection remained highly controversial. Darwin himself acknowledged that he probably gave it too much prominence in the first edition of his *Origin*, while Huxley always thought new species arose by 'saltations' (large sudden changes). If natural selection was eclipsed by other evolutionary causes even among naturalists themselves, we should exercise caution before accusing the theologians of distortion. Scientific disagreement over the relative importance of natural selection and the inheritance of characteristics acquired by use and disuse created the space for schemes of theistic evolution in which teleological factors were retained.[55] Reconstructing the fossil record to display independent lines of convergence towards a few archetypal structures (rather than Darwin's process of increasing divergence), one could argue, as did J. H. Newman's protégé St George Mivart, that the evolutionary process was indeed under divine control.[56]

Because religious sensibilities depended on location as well as tradition, it is impossible to generalise about Christian responses. Even within the same Christian denominations there was diversity. Whereas the Anglican bishop of Oxford, Samuel Wilberforce, thought he could demolish Darwin's theory on scientific and philosophical grounds, another Anglican divine, Frederick Temple, was receptive to the new science as early as 1860. Whereas in Belfast a traditional Calvinism was used to refute the precepts of evolution, at Calvinist Princeton, under the leadership of James McCosh, biological evolution was accepted.[57] One reason for the contrast was the legacy in Belfast of John Tyndall's 1874 address as President of the British Association. His aggressive remarks that we noted earlier encouraged the view that Darwinism, atheism and materialism went hand in hand.

To add to the diversity there were prominent scientists who doubted whether the development of the human mind could be reduced to the action of natural selection. Darwin's mentor Charles Lyell is one example: a convert to evolutionary theory who nevertheless held back when it came to the uniqueness of the human mind. Darwin's co-founder of the theory of natural selection, Alfred Russel Wallace, is another. Wallace had rejected an evangelical Christianity early in life but later became enthralled by a spiritualist philosophy, even seeking to test it experimentally.[58] To Darwin's regret, Wallace insisted that certain attributes of the human mind, notably its aesthetic, musical and mathematical powers, defied explanation by natural selection.

Neither Lyell nor Wallace was orthodox in his religious beliefs. By contrast there were respectable Christian clerics who encouraged Darwin with their support. One of the first was the Christian socialist Charles Kingsley; another was Frederick Temple, whose advocacy did not prevent him from becoming Archbishop of Canterbury. Both decided that it required more wisdom in a deity to make all things make themselves than to make all things directly. Kingsley's point was that, on Darwin's view, one could safely reject the image of an interfering deity – a magician who had conjured new species, as it were, out of a hat. There was now the prospect of emancipation from such a childish vision and that would strengthen a mature Christianity. Temple held a similar view, rebuking those theologians who had so often built on the shifting sand of what science could not yet explain. He welcomed the extension of natural law because this made it more probable that the world was also governed by moral law.[59]

Other advantages were seen in a Darwinian theology. Asa Gray, who championed natural selection in America, argued that the problem of suffering, so difficult for Christian theologians, was mitigated rather than magnified by Darwin's theory. His point was that, if pain and suffering were necessary concomitants of a struggle for existence that was itself a precondition of the emergence of complex beings like ourselves, then this was the price that had to be paid for a truly creative process. The argument could be given another twist, in keeping with Darwin's early speculations. A process in which the laws were designed but the details left to chance might explain nature's more repulsive products without having to ascribe them directly to divine action.

A different move was made by some Oxford theologians towards the end of the nineteenth century when they reasserted the Christian doctrine of the Incarnation – that God had taken human form in the person of Jesus Christ. This led them to stress divine participation in an evolving world rather than the interfering *deus ex machina* of a clockwork universe. One of their number, Aubrey Moore, insisted that under the guise of a foe Darwin had done the work of a friend.

Instead of an absentee deity who occasionally intervened, one had to choose now between a God who was in all or in nothing.[60] By using evolutionary theory as a theological resource, writers such as Kingsley, Temple and Moore baptised it in Britain.

V DARWINISM AND RELIGION IN BROADER PERSPECTIVE

Because evolution could be regarded as a creative process, the damage inflicted by Darwin on open-minded Christian believers can easily be exaggerated. The Victorian crisis of faith had other roots, extending back to the Enlightenment. In France Voltaire had attacked the morality of a faith grounded in Old Testament conceptions of a partisan and vengeful deity. Other voices, too, had protested against the intolerance, especially of the Catholic Church, towards any form of religious dissent. In England Joseph Priestley had stood up for 'rational dissent', a philosophical position from which he attacked Calvinist theology, the doctrine of the Trinity, the duality of matter and spirit and the idea that the Deity could directly influence the human mind.[61] From Germany had come methods of biblical criticism that in their most radical forms stripped Christ of his miracles. While David Strauss' *Das Leben Jesu* [*Life of Jesus*] (1835) did not outright accuse the gospel writers of deliberate falsification, it argued that they had written after the events they described, and within a tradition of prophetic literature that associated the Messianic era with signs and wonders. This did not have to mean that these biblical writers lacked special inspiration; but it implied that they had been ordinary, fallible men, whose beliefs reflected their own times. One could still argue, as liberal Anglican Christians did, that the Bible should not be understood as the unmediated word of God but as an inspiring record of a developing spirituality, of progressive religious discernment. Nevertheless, when advocated in *Essays and Reviews* (1860), this thesis angered conservative churchmen.

Other forces had thrown the English Church on the defence. Urbanisation and industrialisation had encouraged the spread of new secular values. An expanding literacy and a voracious demand for reading matter had created a situation in which, by 1853, one clergyman estimated that 28.5 million publications were appearing annually from secular presses against 24.5 million from religious publishers.[62] It looked as if the devil was winning. Adding to the concern, intellectuals within the Church were among the honest doubters – at least on certain points of doctrine. When, in his *Theological Essays* (1853), F. D. Maurice criticised the doctrine that the spiritually unregenerate would endure eternal damnation, his liberalism cost him his Chair at King's College London. His courageous expression of doubt acted as a catalyst for others who wished to reform the Christian faith. Charles Kingsley, for example, was as receptive to Maurice's teaching as he was to Darwin's. He told Maurice that he 'was utterly astonished at finding in page after page things which I had thought, and hardly dared to confess to myself, much less to preach'.[63]

These were trends that owed little to Darwin, who on eternal punishment shared the moral repugnance of others. In an important respect, however, Darwin's science reinforced the impact of biblical criticism. Darwin made the same assumptions as Strauss about the continuity of nature and the incredibility of miracles. 'The more we know of the fixed laws of nature', Darwin wrote, 'the more incredible do miracles become'.[64] Darwin's science also contributed to what for many Victorians became a substitute religion – a religion of human perfectibility and technological progress, consonant with Darwin's belief that natural selection worked only for the improvement of species.[65]

The assumption of inevitable conflict between 'science' and 'religion' pervades modern Western culture. It has sponsored a view of history in which Christian clerics are the villains seeking to suppress, as in the case of Galileo, the well-founded knowledge of scientific heroes. Darwin's theory and the negative responses to it might seem to corroborate the model. Yet the conflict thesis was largely a product of the nineteenth century, its champions having personal reasons for mocking ecclesiastical authority. John Draper's *History of the Conflict between Religion and Science* (1875) was a diatribe against the Roman Catholic Church, prompted by recent proclamations that public institutions teaching literature and science should not be exempt from the Church's authority and that the pope was infallible when speaking *ex cathedra* on matters of faith and morals. Andrew White's *A History of the Warfare of Science with Theology in Christendom* (1896) was written in reaction to stinging criticism he received from Christian clerics when his charter for Cornell

University placed it under the control of no one religious sect. Both Draper and White projected a 'conflict between science and religion' backwards in time, using categories that were anachronistic.[66] They were not alone in constructing sweeping narratives in which science was defeating dogmatic theology. In France Auguste Comte had already advertised his three-stage model for the progress of human civilisation – from a theological stage, when natural phenomena had been ascribed to gods, to a metaphysical stage when abstract concepts (such as Newton's force of gravitation) had been explanatory resources, to the present scientific or 'positive' stage represented by verified facts and laws. Comte had his reasons: he wished to set up a 'religion of humanity' to displace that of the Catholic Church in France.[67]

Religious battles over evolution seemed to support these master narratives. Draper observed that there was a controversy raging over the method of divine government of the world – whether this was by direct intervention or through the rule of law. This was one of the primary issues in debates over evolution. White saw in clerical opposition to Darwin the last throes of the Church in a battle she was destined to lose. Darwin may have perceived himself as ushering biology into Comte's 'positive' stage, leaving metaphysical and theological concerns behind.

There are, however, problems with the 'conflict' model. It conceals the fact that many scientists have had deep religious convictions and that within religious traditions there have usually been liberal as well as conservative forces. Conflicts in the past have sometimes arisen because religious thinkers have embraced new science too enthusiastically, only to find themselves stranded when their sanctified science becomes obsolete. A conflict model also conceals the efforts of mediators to achieve harmony or integration. In the case of the Darwinian debates it would conceal men of science, such as Richard Owen and St George Mivart, who argued for evolution as an unfolding of a divine plan, just as it would conceal advocates of theistic evolution among the theologians.

If the conflict model is defective, are there other ways of relating science and religion? Some scholars have gone to the other extreme, arguing that a doctrine of Creation positively contributed to the rise of modern science.[68] This may sound implausible, but pioneers of Western science, such as Copernicus, Kepler and Newton certainly thought of themselves as uncovering a mathematical harmony in nature that had been the product not of chance but of divine choice. The rationality of science required that nature be orderly and intelligible. These two assumptions were reasonable if an intelligent Creator had prescribed the laws of nature. Physical scientists to this day sometimes speak as if they are privy to the mind of God, echoing Kepler's belief that, through the language of mathematics, he could think God's thoughts after Him. The quest for elegance, symmetry and harmony in scientific theories can be understood theologically. Einstein once said that when asked to evaluate a physical theory he would always ask himself whether, if he had been God, he would have made the world that way.[69]

A revisionist historian might observe that, in his *Origin of Species*, Darwin spoke of 'laws impressed on matter by the Creator'. In private correspondence Darwin declared that he had never been an atheist in the sense of denying the existence of a deity. His confidence that his theory disclosed hidden realities behind the mask of nature was conceivably a legacy from a theistic position in which the human mind was privileged to know such things.[70] On the revisionist view, one would focus on the Christian thinkers who have insisted on compatibility rather than conflict between Darwinian science and their faith.

Just as the conflict thesis ignores many instances of harmony between science and religion, the revisionist response tends to minimise the dissonance.[71] There are certainly popularisers of Darwinian evolution today who, reconstructing the tortuous path by which humans have evolved, would say that, had they been God, they would not have made the world this way. However, no unanimity exists on such metaphysical questions. Among evolutionary biologists there are Christians who recognise that a religious faith can answer a person's moral and existential concerns in ways that scientific knowledge alone cannot.

Responses to Darwinian evolution have varied from context to context and still do. We saw something of this in the previous section when examining the range of early reactions. The anti-Darwinian lobby in North America has been more vociferous in some states than others. One of the appealing features of a postmodern approach to issues in science and religion is that it invites the careful study of local contexts and what differentiates one from another. In the famous Scopes trial (1925), William Jennings Bryan came to Dayton, Tennessee, to defend the power of local majorities to enact a law – in this case a law against teaching human evolution in public schools. Recent research has shown how far the historical reality differed from the legend. One reason why Bryan wished to ban the teaching of human evolution was that it had come to be associated with what he saw as a distasteful commitment to eugenics.[72]

Does this mean that any reputable account of the impact of Darwin's theory on religious sensibilities has to fragment into many disconnected stories? Yes and no. To escape from the crude master-narratives and to appreciate the diversity of response, it is essential to undertake comparative studies of different national and local contexts.[73] More work needs to be done on contrasts between North America and Britain, where an anti-Darwinian right-wing Christianity has never been a serious political force. Still more needs to be done on responses to Darwin in other world religions.[74] On the other hand, it is possible to identify recurring metaphysical and theological issues wherever Darwinism is discussed – whether, for example, nature is fully autonomous; whether there are identifiable and perhaps even convergent trends in evolutionary processes; whether there might be design in the laws governing evolution; whether all mental capacities, even religious sensibilities themselves, can be fully explained by natural selection; and whether the quintessentially Darwinian concept of natural selection can be applied to the development of other systems, including entire universes. Such questions will continue to produce disparate answers; but it would be difficult to deny that Darwin contributed decisively to an intellectual trend, in both Europe and America, which led to the exclusion of God-talk from technical scientific texts.

NOTES

1. C. Darwin 1958, 57.
2. Rudwick 1986.
3. Ellegård [1958] 1990, 155–73.
4. Gillespie 1979, 19–40.
5. Brooke and Cantor 1998, 207–35.
6. Simpson 1967; Dawkins 1986.
7. Gould 1989.
8. F. Darwin [1888] 1969, 1, 309.

9. F. Darwin [1888] 1969, II, 218.
10. Ospovat 1980 and 1981; Brooke 1985.
11. W. Cannon 1961.
12. La Vergata 1985, 957.
13. Browne 1995, 385–90.
14. Yeo 1979 and 1993.
15. Brooke 1985, 46–7.
16. Sloan 2001.
17. Desmond and Moore 1991, 122.
18. Darwin and Wallace 1958, 87.
19. Brooke 1985, 47.
20. Ospovat 1981.
21. C. Darwin [1871] 1981, I, 152–3.
22. Brooke 1985, 41.
23. Burch Brown 1986; Mandelbaum 1958.
24. F. Darwin [1888] 1969, I, 311–12.
25. F. Darwin [1888] 1969, I, 304.
26. Brooke 1990; Desmond and Moore 1991, 7–9.
27. F. Darwin [1888] 1969, I, 312–13.
28. Sloan 2001.
29. Manier 1978.
30. Barrett *et al.*, 1987, *Charles Darwin's Notebooks, Notebook* C, MS p. 244; C. Darwin [1871] 1981, 65–9.
31. C. Darwin 1958, 86.
32. F. Darwin [1888] 1969, I, 311.
33. C. Darwin 1958, 87.
34. Desmond and Moore 1991, 375–87.
35. Erskine 1987.
36. Desmond and Moore 1991, 376–8.
37. Kohn 1989, 224.
38. Brooke 1985, 41.
39. Gillespie 1979, 134.
40. F. Darwin [1888] 1969, I, 307.
41. J. R. Moore 1979, 276.
42. F. Darwin [1888] 1969, I, 314.
43. F. Darwin [1888] 1969, I, 313.
44. C. Darwin 1958, 93.
45. Turner 1978 and 1993.
46. Tyndall [1874] 1970, 474–5.
47. Desmond and Moore 1998, 159
48. C. Smith 1998, 307.
49. D. B. Wilson 1984.

50. Corsi 1998, 135.
51. Powell 1861, 127–8; Corsi 1988, 218–19.
52. Dixon 1999, 322.
53. F. Darwin [1888] 1969, II, 201–2.
54. Rupke 1983, 271.
55. Gregory 1986, 374.
56. Desmond 1982, 183.
57. Livingstone 1992.
58. Kottler 1974.
59. Elder 1996.
60. Peacocke 1985, 110–11.
61. Brooke 1990.
62. Fyfe 2000, 80.
63. Kingsley 1883, 146.
64. C. Darwin 1958, 86.
65. Passmore 1970, 239–40.
66. Brooke 1991, 33–42.
67. Brooke and Cantor 1998, 47–57.
68. Jaki 1978; Klaaren 1977; Milton 1981.
69. Chandrasekhar 1990, 68.
70. Gillespie 1979, 144–5.
71. Gruner 1975; Brooke 1991, 42–51.
72. Larson 1998, 6 and 28.
73. Cantor 2001.
74. Bezirgan 1974; Killingley 1995; Swetlitz 1999.

DIANE B. PAUL

9 Darwin, social Darwinism and eugenics

I AMBIVALENCES AND INFLUENCES

How does Darwin's Darwinism relate to social Darwinism and eugenics? Like many foes of Darwinism, past and present, the American populist and creationist William Jennings Bryan thought a straight line ran from Darwin's theory ('a dogma of darkness and death') to beliefs that it is right for the strong to crowd out the weak, and that the only hope for human improvement lay in selective breeding.[1] Darwin's defenders, on the other hand, have typically viewed social Darwinism and eugenics as perversions of his theory. Daniel Dennett speaks for many biologists and philosophers of science when he characterises social Darwinism as 'an odious misapplication of Darwinian thinking'.[2] Few professional historians believe either that Darwin's theory leads directly to these doctrines or that they are entirely unrelated. But both the nature and significance of the link are disputed.

This chapter examines the views held by Darwin himself and by later Darwinians on the implications of his theory for social life, and it assesses the social impact made by these views. More specifically: section II discusses the debates about human evolution in the wake of Darwin's *Origin of Species* (1859).[3] Sections III and IV analyse Darwin's ambiguous contribution to these debates. Sometimes celebrating competitive struggle, he also wished to moderate its effects, but thought restrictions on breeding impractical and immoral. Sections V and VI see how others interpreted both the science and social meaning of Darwinism. Darwin's followers found in his ambiguities legitimation for whatever they favoured: laissez-faire capitalism, certainly, but also liberal reform, anarchism and socialism; colonial conquest, war and patriarchy, but also anti-imperialism, peace and feminism. Section VII relates Darwinism to eugenics. Darwin and many of his followers thought selection no longer acted in modern society, for the weak in mind and body are not culled. This raised a prospect of degeneration that worried people of all political stripes; but there was no consensus on how to counter this threat. In Nazi Germany, eugenics was linked to an especially harsh Darwinism. Section VIII sees 'Darwinismus' embraced initially by political progressives, and only later by racist and reactionary nationalists. Section IX concludes by assessing Darwin's impact on social issues and by reflecting on where we are now.

II IN THE WAKE OF THE *ORIGIN*

The *Origin* did not discuss human evolution; but Darwin's peers were less reticent, and within a month debate focused on the implications of Darwin's theory for human biological and social progress. Darwin eventually published his major work on social evolution, *The Descent of Man, and Selection in Relation to Sex*, in 1871. In the *Descent*, Darwin engaged these controversies, especially as they had proceeded in Britain.

Alfred Russel Wallace, co-discover of the principle of natural selection and one of the very few British naturalists from a non-elite family, was among the first to discuss its social implications. Like Darwin, he had been wrestling with the issue for a very long time.[4] In an influential 1864 paper, Wallace argued that selection would cause rationality and altruism to spread. Once this process became well developed, individuals with weak constitutions would be cared for; thus selection would come to focus on mental and moral, rather than physical, qualities. In the struggle for existence among tribes, those whose members tended to act in concert and show foresight, self-restraint and a sense of right, would have an advantage over tribes in which these traits were less developed. The former would flourish, resulting in constant mental and moral improvement. Ultimately, the whole world would consist of one race, and the need for government or restrictive laws would vanish.

The process that led to utopia would also guarantee the extinction of native populations such as American and Brazilian Indians, Australian aborigines and New Zealand Maoris. According to Wallace, 'savage man' would inevitably disappear in encounters with Europeans whose superior intellectual, moral and physical qualities make them prevail 'in the struggle for existence, and to increase at his expense', just as the more favoured varieties increase among animals and plants, and 'just as the weeds of Europe overrun North America and Australia, extinguishing native populations' thanks to their inherently more vigorous 'organization' and 'their greater capacity for existence and multiplication'.[5]

Wallace's focus was on the struggle among societies. But many of his peers were more concerned with whether selection still operated at home. Lesser races would not survive the brutal but ultimately beneficent (and in any case inexorable) struggle with their superiors, but in Britain and other 'civilized societies' it seemed that the process of selection had been checked. Modern medicine and humanitarian measures prevented elimination of the physically and mentally weak. Moreover, the least desirable elements in society were apparently outbreeding the best, prompting fears that the direction of evolution might actually reverse. The first to sound an alarm about the 'differential birthrate' was Darwin's cousin, Francis Galton.

In his 1865 essay, 'Hereditary talent and character', Galton argued that human intellectual, moral and personality traits – especially those making for success in life – were transmitted from parents to offspring.[6] Consulting biographical dictionaries, Galton demonstrated that men who had achieved eminence in various fields were more likely than members of the public at large to have had close male relatives who were themselves distinguished. Although conceding that the inheritance of social advantage might explain success in some fields, he insisted that most were open to talent. Certainly in science, literature and the law, talented individuals would succeed, no matter how unfavourable their background, while the untalented would fail, whatever their social connections.

Unfortunately, it seemed that the intelligent, industrious and foresighted were being outbred by the stupid, lazy and reckless. Given the complexity of modern life, this trend, if unchecked, could only end in disaster. The decline in intelligence would be especially harmful. How could this tendency be reconciled with Darwin's claim that the struggle for existence tended to the constant improvement of organic beings? Galton wrote to his cousin that natural selection 'seems to me to spoil and not to improve our breed' since 'it is the classes of coarser organisation who seem on the whole the most favoured... and who survive to become the parents of the next [generation]'.[7] The obvious solution was for humans to take charge of their own evolution, doing for themselves what breeders had done for horses and cattle. But as to how exactly the stockbreeders' methods should be applied, Galton had little to say. He did not propose any specific measures to improve human heredity. Galton's hopes lay in changing mores. If people could only be made to see the importance of breeding, a way would surely be found to get the job done.

The retired millowner William Greg largely agreed with Galton and insisted that, unlike the lower orders, it is the middle classes – energetic, reliable, improving themselves and choosing to rise not sink – who delay marriage until they can support a family. But, on how the resultant swamping of these good elements by bad is to be prevented, Greg was no more specific than Galton. In an ideal world, only those who passed a rigorous competitive examination would be allowed to breed, but admitting this was not a realistic plan, Greg was left, like Galton, hoping that mores would slowly change in the right direction.[8]

At about the same time, Walter Bagehot, a banker and editor of the *Economist*, argued that human history, at least in its early stages, was a bloody and brutal affair. The origins of civilisation lay in the forming in intertribal warfare of the more cohesive tribes. But this progress ends unless a state can go beyond coherence and tameness, to the variability that 'oriental' despotism crushes; for variability brings fitness for that slow and gradual progress which Europeans have achieved in benefiting from innovation generated by warfare and racial mixing.[9]

In 1868 Wallace announced an about-face, denying that natural selection could account for humans' higher mental or moral qualities, and crediting their evolution to guidance by forces from a higher world of the spirit.[10] Wishing to distinguish his position from Wallace's, Darwin finally finished *The Descent of Man*, which was published in two volumes in 1871.[11] It did not make nearly as much of a splash as had the *Origin*, perhaps because it was not nearly as novel. In its applications of the theory of natural selection, his *Descent* drew heavily on Malthus, Spencer, Wallace, Galton, Greg, Bagehot and other contemporary social theorists.[12]

III DARWIN ON HUMAN BIOLOGICAL AND SOCIAL PROGRESS

Darwin's reading reinforced views he had developed during the five years (1831–6) he spent circumnavigating the globe on HMS *Beagle*. Darwin hated slavery and his comments on the black people he met, both slave and free, were sympathetic and respectful. He was also repelled by the cruelty of European conquest, and often had a low opinion of settler populations.[13] But although shocked by the colonists' methods, Darwin assumed that conquest itself was inevitable. In the second, 1845, edition of his *Journal of Researches*, he wrote that, although it is not only the white man who acts as a destroyer, '[w]herever the European has trod, death seems to pursue the aboriginal.... The varieties of man seem to act on each other in the same way as different species of animals – the stronger always extirpating the weaker.'[14] And while the means might be repellent, he was sure the results would be beneficent.[15]

Darwin's views on human evolution were strongly influenced by his encounters with the inhabitants of Tierra del Fuego. On board the *Beagle* were three Fuegians whom its captain, Robert FitzRoy, had captured and brought back to England on an earlier visit. Darwin was impressed both by their acute senses and the extent of their cultural transformation.[16] But on encountering Fuegians in their native land, he found them unbelievably strange, and was shocked by their aggressive behaviour and apparent cruelty.[17]

Remote as these Fuegians seemed from Englishmen, Darwin would always see continuous gradations 'between the highest men of the highest races and the lowest savages'.[18] Rating animals, especially under domestication, highly and savages lowly, he could close any gap in intelligence between the Fuegians and the orang-utan as early as 1838.[19] He would eventually claim to prefer descent from the heroic monkey that risked its own life to save its keeper's, or the old baboon that rescued a comrade from a pack of dogs, as 'from a savage who delights to torture his enemies, offers up bloody sacrifices, practices infanticide without remorse, treats his wives like slaves, knows no decency, and is haunted by the grossest superstitions'.[20]

Darwin was thus receptive to Wallace's argument that selection guaranteed the extinction of all the primitive peoples with whom Europeans came into contact. In the *Descent*, Darwin drew on

Wallace's 1864 paper and also Bagehot's series of articles to argue that tribes which included the largest proportion of men endowed with superior intellectual qualities, sympathy, altruism, courage, fidelity and obedience would increase in number and eventually displace the other tribes. 'Obedience, as Mr. Bagehot has well shewn, is of the highest value', wrote Darwin, 'for any form of government is better than none.'[21] The process of improvement continues to the present, as 'civilised nations are everywhere supplanting barbarous nations'. Since morality is an important element in their success, both the standard of morality and number of moral men will 'tend everywhere to rise and increase'. Inheritance of property contributes to this process, since without capital accumulation 'the arts could not progress; and it is chiefly through their power that the civilised races have extended, and are now everywhere extending their range, so as to take the place of the lower races'.[22]

But in his own society, progress is not assured. In the *Descent*, Darwin noted that whereas among savages the weak in mind and body are soon eliminated, civilised societies do their best to check this selection. Asylums for the 'imbecile, the maimed, and the sick'; poor laws; medical efforts to preserve every life; vaccination against small pox – all entail that the 'weak members of civilised societies propagate their kind'. Anyone who has studied 'the breeding of domestic animals' cannot doubt 'that this must be highly injurious to the race of man'. Want of care, or care wrongly directed, leads to the 'degeneration of a domestic race'. But except 'in the case of man himself, hardly any one is so ignorant as to allow his worst animals to breed'.[23] Darwin immediately remarks, however, that the sympathetic instincts that lead us to aid the helpless are themselves the product of natural selection. Moreover, we could not suppress these instincts without damaging the 'noblest part of our nature'. To ignore the weak and helpless purposely would be to commit a certain and great evil in return for what is only a possible future benefit. 'Hence we must bear without complaining the undoubtedly bad effects of the weak surviving and propagating their kind.'[24] Moreover, while selection has been checked in many ways, it continues to operate in others. Thus it works to develop the body, as can be seen in the fact that civilised men are stronger than savages and have equal powers of endurance. It favours the intellectually able, even amongst the poorest classes. And it tends to eliminate the worst dispositions. Criminals are executed or sent to jail, and so are unable to pass on their bad qualities. The insane kill themselves or are institutionalised. Violent men die violently, and prematurely. The restless emigrate. The intemperate die young and the sexually profligate are often diseased.

On the other hand, the very poor and the reckless almost always marry early, while those who are virtuous enough to wait until they can support a family in comfort do so late in life. The former produce many more children who also, being born during their mothers' prime of life, tend to be more physically vigorous. Quoting Greg, Darwin regrets that the vicious members of society tend to reproduce more rapidly than the virtuous. There are, however, counters to this process too: mortality among the urban poor and among women who marry at a very early age is (it seems fortunately) high. But if these and other checks 'do not prevent the reckless, the vicious, and the otherwise inferior members of society from increasing at a quicker rate than the better class of men', Darwin warns, thinking of Bagehot and Henry Maine, 'the nation will retrograde, as has occurred too often in the history of the world. We must remember that progress is no invariable rule.'[25] This prospect remained a lifelong concern. Wallace noted that in one of their last conversations, Darwin had expressed gloomy views about the future because 'in our modern civilization natural selection had no play, and the fittest did not survive'. Those winning wealth are not 'the best or the most intelligent' and 'our population is more largely renewed in each generation from the lower than from the middle and upper classes'.[26]

IV THE WAY FORWARD

But what to do? Here Darwin, like Galton and Greg, had little to say. Advancing the welfare of mankind is a most 'intricate' problem. Population pressure has been an essential element in mankind's advance. 'Natural selection follows from the struggle for existence; and this from a rapid rate of increase. It is impossible not bitterly to regret, but whether wisely is another question, the rate at which man tends to increase; for this leads in barbarous tribes to infanticide and many other evils, and in civilised nations to abject poverty, celibacy, and to the late marriages of the prudent.'[27] But if man had not been subject to such pressure, he would not have attained his present rank. At the close of the *Descent*, Darwin considers the contemporary implications of this principle. On the one hand, he reasons, those who are unable to avoid abject poverty for their children should not reproduce. But on the other, if only those who are prudent refrain from marriage, the inferior members of society will supplant the superior. Malthusian 'moral restraint' is thus a counter-selective factor. He concludes with a reminder that: 'Man, like every other animal, has no doubt advanced to his present high condition through a struggle for existence consequent on his rapid multiplication' and warns that the advance will be halted unless he remains subject to severe struggle.

> Otherwise, he would soon sink into indolence, and the more highly-gifted men would not be more successful in the battle of life than the less gifted. Hence our natural rate of increase, though leading to many and obvious evils, must not be greatly diminished by any means. There should be open competition for all men; and the most able should not be prevented by laws or customs from succeeding best and rearing the largest number of offspring.[28]

However, immediately after voicing that classically 'social Darwinist' sentiment, he notes that moral qualities are advanced much more by habit, reason, learning and religion than by natural selection.

Darwin's views on inheritance of property and suspicion of labour unions clearly mark him as a Whig. He condemned primogeniture, on the grounds that it enabled the eldest sons, no matter how weak in mind or body, to marry, while often preventing superior younger sons from doing likewise. But here, too, there were compensatory checks.[29] Darwin did unambiguously favour allowing inheritance of moderate amounts of wealth. Holding capital accumulation to be partly responsible for the success of European colonisation, he also thought it necessary for continued domestic progress.

Darwin himself had been generously supported by his father, who provided not just an allowance but Down House as a gift and a large inheritance at his death in 1848. Combined with income from royalties, rents, and especially investments, a marriage gift, and an inheritance from his older brother, his estate at his death was worth over a quarter of a million pounds, apart from a trust established for his wife Emma.[30] His family's wealth had enabled Darwin to pursue his career, an experience reflected in his comment that, while inheritance of property means that children will not start at the same place in the 'race for success', capital accumulation is nevertheless necessary for progress both in the arts and intellectual work. Indeed, 'the presence of a body of well-instructed men, who have not to labour for their daily bread, is important to a degree which cannot be overestimated'.[31] Perhaps unsurprisingly, Wallace, whose family could not afford to keep him in school past the age of fourteen, came to the opposite opinion. He thought that inheritance in property should be abolished.

Shortly after the *Descent* appeared, Heinrich Fick, a law professor at the University of Zurich, sent Darwin a copy of an essay he had written urging restrictions on marriage for men ineligible for military service (to counter the dysgenic effects of war) and opposing egalitarian social policies (since they advantage the weak). In reply, Darwin voiced a hope that Fick would at some point discuss what he considered a serious problem in Britain: the insistence by trade unions that all workmen, 'the good and bad, the strong and weak', should all work the same hours for the same wages. 'The unions are also opposed to piece-work, – in short to all competition.' He fears, too, that Cooperative Societies 'likewise exclude competition.' This seemed 'a great evil for the future progress of mankind'. But he never published such sentiments, perhaps partly out of caution, but also because with Darwin there was always an 'on the other hand'. In this case, Darwin continues: ' – Nevertheless, under any system, temperate and frugal workmen will have an advantage and leave more offspring than the drunken and reckless.'[32]

Nor did Darwin propose any practical measures to control human breeding. Even in his own life, Darwin's worries did not translate into action. The Darwin–Wedgwood family was highly inbred, and, perhaps as a result, experienced more than its share of mental and physical infirmities. Charles, despite anxieties about the ill-effects of inbreeding, did marry his first cousin, Emma Wedgwood. Moreover, his nearly lifelong battle with ill-health began three years before his marriage, and he worried constantly about inflicting hereditary illness on his children. But this did not inhibit him from siring nine of them.[33] In the public as well as private sphere, Darwin's anxieties found little tangible expression. Like Galton, he urged his readers to pay at least as much attention to the pedigrees of their prospective mates as to those of their horses and dogs. For he was emphatic about the operation of sexual selection in humans. Males selected females for physical beauty and emotional qualities, while females selected males for their strength, intellect and status. This explains why women surpass men in tenderness, intuition and selflessness, but have less energy, courage and intelligence. Darwin concluded that, although they should be educated, women cannot compete successfully with men, and are, by nature, best suited to domestic life.

But all the concrete suggestions for encouraging reproduction of the valuable members of society or discouraging it by the undesirable members seemed to Darwin either impractical or morally suspect. He thought it unlikely that the reckless could be convinced to refrain from breeding, and he was too much of a Whig even to contemplate using the power of the state to segregate them from the rest of society. Nor did he think that the gifted would respond to appeals to have more children. Like Galton, he was left to hope that education would produce a change in mores. Unlike Galton, he does not seem to have been very optimistic about the chances of such changes taking place.

V SOCIAL DARWINISM AND SOCIALIST DARWINISM

Darwin's waverings certainly contributed to the diverse readings of Darwinism, as did ambiguities in the *Origin* about the locus and meaning of struggle. Darwin had stressed the importance of struggle within species, believing it to be the most severe since these individuals lived in the same places, ate the same food and faced the same dangers. Advocates of laissez-faire tended to follow suit. But Darwin also noted that he used the term 'Struggle for Existence in a large and metaphorical sense, including dependence of one being on another.'[34] Some of his followers read him as deprecating intra-specific struggle, at least among the social species, and as emphasising the value of within-group cooperation instead – a reading bolstered by Darwin's account of human evolution. Mutualistic readings tended to appeal to socialists, anarchists and liberal reformers, as well as (or including) those who appropriated Darwin to argue for racial, national or class superiority. Of course there was no need to choose, and many writers invoked natural selection to argue for laissez-faire at home and imperial conquest abroad.[35]

Certainly, apologists for dog-eat-dog capitalism easily found elements to their liking. As early as 4 May 1860, Darwin famously remarked in a letter to Charles Lyell: 'I have received in a Manchester Newspaper rather a good squib, showing that I have proved "might is right," & therefore that Napoleon is right, & every cheating Tradesman is often right.' It is notable that the reference was to a commentary on the *Origin* that appeared in the *Manchester Guardian* under the title 'National and Individual Rapacity Vindicated by the Laws of Nature.'[36] The commentary obviously involved a crude extrapolation. Nevertheless, the *Origin* was easily appropriated for such purposes, as the writings of Greg and other early commentators attest.

That reading of Darwinism – as a biologistic justification for laissez-faire and colonialism – is what is generally implied by the term 'social Darwinism'. It was a term that would have baffled Darwin. In Victorian England, scientists took for granted that biological facts mattered for social theory and policy. As James Moore has noted: ' "Darwinismus" in Germany and "Darwinism" in the English-speaking world quite sufficed to express Darwin's intentions, all his allies' hopes, and all his critics' fears.'[37]

Coined around the turn of the century, the phrase 'social Darwinism' was popularised in the mid-1940s by the American historian Richard Hofstadter. It has ever since been a term of abuse, applied to people, policies and ideas of which the writer disapproved. (People do not identify themselves as 'social Darwinists'.) A New Deal liberal, Hofstadter's target was laissez-faire conservatism. In his historical account, social Darwinism was an essentially conservative ideology and social movement, which appropriated the theory of evolution by natural selection to support unrestricted laissez-faire at home and colonialism abroad. It ostensibly flourished in the late nineteenth century, reaching its zenith in Gilded-Age America, where it appealed not just to professional social thinkers, but to a wide swath of the middle class. Its proponents held that it was only natural that 'the best competitors in a competitive situation would win', that this process would lead to continuing (if slow) improvement, and that efforts to hasten improvement through social reform were doomed to failure.[38]

But as Hofstadter himself acknowledged, the *Origin* was also appropriated for quite different ends. Socialists found in Darwinism support for religious scepticism and belief in the inevitability of change. Some (but not Marx) also found in his theory a direct basis for socialist principles. One socialist strategy was to elide the struggle for existence with the struggle among classes, arguing that the proletariat would inevitably triumph. Another was to claim that the struggle now was among societies, nations or races, a battle that would be undermined by class conflict. A third was to de-emphasise individual struggle, finding in Darwinism a basis for altruistic and cooperative behaviour. (Occasionally, these themes would combine, as in August Bebel's *Die Frau and der Sozialismus*, which argues that a fierce struggle for existence will prevail until the victory of the proletariat, after which social solidarity will reign.)

Anarchists such as Prince Peter Kropotkin (1902) and liberal reformers in the US and Britain also de-emphasised individual struggle, finding in the *Origin* support for a holistic view of nature as a 'tangled bank' characterised by a complex web of relations. Often drawing as much on Herbert Spencer as Darwin, they argued that the struggle for existence was not primarily about combat, at least among members of their own group, but coexistence.[39] Some cited Darwin's argument in the *Descent* that the development of reason, feelings of sympathy, and cooperation were key to human evolution. Moreover, by emphasising the Lamarckian elements in Darwin, they were able to claim that humans could escape the grip of biology and create social organisations which fostered desirable traits.

The softer, anti-deterministic view of Darwinism was also shared by the 'peace biologists'. Darwinism was, of course, used to justify warfare and imperial conquest. In the dominant motif, nature was brutal and humans were beasts. Humans were part of a natural world, which is characterised by a relentless struggle for existence, in which the strongest, fleetest, most cunning prevail. Human behaviour reflects man's animal origins. Belligerence and territoriality are ineradicable instincts, deeply rooted in human nature. Humans are 'fighting apes', as nineteenth-century popularisers had it, and war an essential part of the evolutionary process. British anthropologist Sir Arthur Keith famously asserted: 'Nature keeps her human orchard healthy by pruning; war is her pruning-hook.'[40] Moreover, if life is warfare, then discipline and obedience are cardinal virtues.[41] But pacifists also found resources in Darwin. They argued that murder and war were rare among animals within their own species. Only man regularly killed his own kind. They challenged the assumption that beasts were bestial, citing Darwin's examples of cooperative behaviour among animals, as well as evidence of their intelligence, loyalty, bravery, affection and self-sacrificing behaviour. And they could cite Darwin's comments in the second edition of the *Descent*, where he criticised conscription and war on the grounds that the former prevented healthy males from marrying during their prime, while the latter exposed them to the risk of early death. Following this line of argument, some anti-militarists claimed that even if war had once been a progressive force, it was now dysgenic.[42] In Britain, the slaughter of fit young men in the First World War led many Darwinians to rethink the evolutionary value of warfare and ultimately to reject the idea that it was beneficial.[43]

Darwinism was similarly used to legitimate every view of women's abilities and appropriate roles. Darwin's authority was invoked in support of the claim that women's place was in the home, not the school or the workplace.[44] But the theory of sexual selection, which for Darwin accounted for gender differences, was also turned to radical uses. Socialists and feminists could argue that, in contemporary society, sexual selection had been thwarted. Men who were stupid and vicious had no trouble finding mates, as long as they were rich. Women were forced by social circumstances to choose as husbands men who could support them, however inferior their personal qualities. A character in *Looking Backward*, an influential novel by the American utopian socialist Edward Bellamy, explained that, in the new Boston of the year 2000, sexual selection has full play. Thus poverty no longer induces 'women to accept as the fathers of their children men whom they neither can love nor respect. Wealth and rank no longer divert attention from personal qualities. Gold no longer "gilds the straitened forehead of the fool". The gifts of person, mind, and disposition . . . are sure of transmission to posterity.'[45] Many social radicals – including Wallace in Britain and Victoria Woodhull and Charlotte Perkins Gilman in the US – argued that the continued subjugation of women thwarts sexual selection and thus endangers the future of the race.[46]

VI DARWINISM, LAMARCKISM AND SOCIETY

The meaning of 'social Darwinism' is muddied not just by the use of Darwinism to justify a variety of existing or proposed social arrangements, but by the fact that many advocates of laissez-faire rejected the principle of natural selection or minimised its significance. Indeed, some stereotypical 'social Darwinists' preferred the theory, associated with Lamarck, that organisms acquire new characteristics as the result of a process of active adaptation to their environments. These 'neo-Lamarckians' included the British philosopher Herbert Spencer, who argued that unfettered economic competition would cull the unfit and also act as a spur to improvement. For Spencer, competition functioned to make creatures work harder, and thus to exercise their organs and faculties (in contrast with Darwin, for whom competition worked mainly to spread minority traits throughout a population). The mental powers, skills and traits of character fostered by this struggle would be transmitted to future generations, resulting in constant material and moral progress. Ultimately (and inevitably) the evolutionary process would produce a perfect society characterised by stability, harmony, peace, altruism and cooperation. Land would be held in common, women would have the same rights as men and government would become superfluous, and ultimately disappear.[47] In the meantime, the state should do nothing to alleviate the sufferings of the unfit. After all, as Spencer wrote in 1850, 'the whole effort of nature is to get rid of such, to clear the world of them, to make room for better'.[48]

Peter Bowler argues that Spencer's emphasis on the value of self-help was much closer to the spirit of competitive capitalism than Darwin's more fatalistic principle of natural selection of chance variations.[49] In any case, many social theorists, especially in America, owed more – sometimes much more – to Spencer than to Darwin.[50] Indeed, in 1907, the American sociologist Lester Frank Ward declared that he had 'never seen any distinctively Darwinian principle appealed to in the discussion of "social Darwinism"'.[51] (More recently, Antonello La Vergata jokingly suggested that 'Darwin was one of the very few Social Darwinists who was really a Darwinian'.[52])

Given that Spencer both minimised the role of natural selection and developed much of his theory before 1859, is it reasonable to classify him and his followers as 'social Darwinists'? Or if the term has value at all, should it be reserved for those who explicitly invoked Darwin's own theory? That issue is complicated by the fact that what counts as 'Darwin's theory' in the late nineteenth century is far from obvious, both because Darwin's own views shifted over time, and because 'Darwinism' was often employed interchangeably with 'evolutionism'. In particular, the boundary between Lamarckism and Darwinism was blurred. Many scientists who downplayed the role of natural selection were nonetheless considered Darwinians; indeed, Darwin himself accorded significant (and over time, increasing) scope to Lamarckian factors. The confused relationship between 'Darwinism' and 'Lamarckism' is nicely illustrated by Bagehot's *Physics and Politics*, which was subtitled 'Or Thoughts on the Application of the Principles of "Natural Selection" and "Inheritance" to Political Society'. According to Bagehot, the traits favoured in warfare are produced by a Lamarckian process in which changing desires produce changes in habits, which are transmitted to the next generation: 'it is the silent toil of the first generation that becomes the transmitted aptitude of the next'. Indeed, history is 'a science to teach the law of tendencies – created by the mind, and transmitted by the body – which act upon and incline the will of man from age to age'.[53]

Thus efforts to stipulate a definition of 'social Darwinism' are frustrated both by Darwinism's association with contradictory causes and the lack of specifically Darwinian content in the views of many classical 'social Darwinists'. Historians have weighted these factors differently, resulting in a plethora of definitions, ranging from the very narrow – the conventional identification of 'social Darwinism' with the legitimation of laissez-faire capitalism – to the very expansive – its application to any social use of Darwin's theory (or even to any social use of evolutionary theory, irrespective of its debt to Darwin). Steering a middle course are historians who recognise the multivalent character of the theory, but believe they can identify some core doctrine uniting the various strands.[54]

The absence of agreement on the meaning of social Darwinism (or even whether it has one) assures that there will be different views of its relation to eugenics. If social Darwinism is equated with laissez-faire, a programme to intervene with individual reproductive decisions may seem its obverse. If the term applies to collectivist as well as individualist ideologies, eugenics is more plausibly viewed as one form of social Darwinism.[55] But at least there is virtual consensus among historians that eugenics was linked in some important way to Darwin's theory. Even Robert Bannister, who dismisses social Darwinism as a myth, accepts that, 'the idea of pruning humanity like so many roses was indeed a logical deduction from the *Origin of Species*, *if* one could stifle the moral sensibilities that troubled Darwin himself'.[56]

VII NATURE, NURTURE AND EUGENICS

Darwin and his nineteenth-century compatriots worried that, if traits making for social success and failure were heritable, and if the failures were producing more children than the successful, the result would be degeneration. But in Darwin's day, the view that heredity held the key to social success was not widely accepted. Indeed, Darwin himself, while claiming to have been converted to Galton's perspective on the importance of inherited intellect, continued to believe that zeal and hard work also mattered. Moreover, while Lamarckism reigned, hereditarian beliefs did not necessarily imply support for programmes of selective breeding. Even those who assumed that social problems were due to bad heredity often concluded that the solution lay in social reform. As long as the Lamarckian view held sway, it made no sense to counterpose nature and nurture.

By the turn of the century, however, Lamarckism – while far from dead, even in scientific circles – was in decline. A corollary of the increasingly popular view that heredity was hard (that is, non-Lamarckian) was the belief that the only solution to social problems was to discourage reproduction by those with undesirable traits, while encouraging reproduction by society's worthier elements. In 1883, Galton coined the word 'eugenics' to describe this programme.

It would soon acquire a wide and enthusiastic following, which cut across the usual political divisions. Middle-class people of every political persuasion – conservative, liberal and socialist – were alarmed by the apparently profligate breeding of what in Britain was called the 'social residuum'. Galton, Greg and Darwin lacked any real evidence to support their intuitions that the least able elements in society were outbreeding the capable. However, a raft of reports and demographic studies seemed to confirm their worst fears. In Britain, the large number of recruits rejected for military service in the Boer War, and statistical studies demonstrating a correlation between large families and poor social conditions were taken as proof that the nation was deteriorating. This disturbing trend was exacerbated by the First World War, which resulted in the deaths of the fittest young men, and was widely viewed as a eugenic disaster.

How to counter this trend? Galton had been principally concerned to encourage the talented to have large families; that is, with what he termed 'positive' eugenics. But in the twentieth century, 'negative' measures came to seem much more urgent. In the United States, Canada and much of Northern Europe, as well as Britain, the central question was how best to discourage breeding by moral and mental defectives.

In the 1870s, when Darwin wrote the *Descent*, education and moral suasion appeared even to most alarmists as the only acceptable means of preventing the swamping of the better by the worse. But by the turn of the century, new views of heredity had converged with a heightened sense of danger and changing attitudes towards the state to make active intervention more acceptable. Darwin, Greg and even Galton were too imbued with Whig distrust of government to propose that it restrict human breeding. As a commitment to laissez-faire gave way to acceptance of collectivist-oriented reform, efforts to intervene actively with reproduction in the interests of the community acquired greater legitimacy. To those who had faith in disinterested expertise and the virtues of state planning, control of breeding seemed only common sense.[57]

Initially, intervention took the form of segregation of 'defectives' during their reproductive years. Since institutionalisation was expensive, sterilisation (vasectomy in men, tubal ligation in women) became an increasingly popular alternative, especially with the advent of the world-wide economic depression of the 1930s. Sterilisation was opposed, along with contraception and abortion, by the Catholic Church and, in Britain, by the Labour Party (which saw its members as potential targets). But by 1940 sterilisation laws had been passed by thirty American states, three Canadian provinces, a Swiss canton, Germany, Estonia, all of the Scandinavian and most of the Eastern European countries, Cuba, Turkey and Japan. In the United States, advocates of immigration restriction argued that newcomers from Southern and Eastern Europe were both biologically inferior to 'old stock' Americans and rapidly multiplying. In 1924, the Immigration Restriction Act sharply reduced the total number of allowable entrants, and, through adoption of a quota system, reduced to a trickle new entrants from Russia, Poland, the Balkans and Italy.[58]

The most extensive and brutal eugenic measures were adopted in Germany. The 1933 Law for the Prevention of Genetically

Diseased Offspring, passed soon after Hitler's ascent to power, encompassed a wide range of ostensibly heritable conditions, and applied also to the non-institutionalised; it ultimately affected about 400,000 people (compared with about 60,000 in the United States). But German *Rassenhygiene* involved much more than a massive programme of sterilisation. The Nuremberg Laws barred Jewish–German marriages. The *Lebensborn* programme encouraged racially 'pure' German women, both single and married, to bear the children of SS officers. The Aktion T-4 programme and its various sequels 'euthanised' (the euphemism for murder by gassing, starvation and lethal injection) up to 200,000 of the country's institutionalised mentally and physically disabled, sometimes with the tacit consent of their families.[59] The penal system was reformed so that many minor offenders were punished with death in order to counter the dysgenic effects of war.[60] These policies of ruthless selection were a prelude to extermination of Jews and other racial and political undesirables. Efforts to maintain racial purity and rid the country of 'useless eaters' often employed Darwinian rhetoric: survival of the fittest, selection and counterselection. That language had wide resonance, for Darwinism was particularly popular in Germany.

VIII FROM DARWIN TO HITLER?

Nowhere did the *Origin* have a greater initial impact than Germany, where the book appeared in translation within a year of its publication in English. Many scientists endorsed Darwin's theory, which was also widely popularised, most effectively by the University of Jena zoologist, Ernst Haeckel. Both liberals and Marxists were enthusiastic. Indeed, Karl Marx's friend Wilhelm Liebknecht reported that, following publication of the *Origin*, he and his comrades 'spoke for months of nothing else but Darwin and the revolutionizing power of his scientific conquests'.[61] The response in Germany was so enthusiastic that in 1868 Darwin wrote that, 'the support which I receive from Germany is my chief ground for hoping that our views will ultimately prevail'.[62]

In the 1860s and 1870s, the political uses of Darwinism in Germany had been predominantly subversive.[63] Given the failure of the Revolution of 1848, the aristocracy and the Catholic Church remained powerful forces, especially in Prussia, the most important of the German states. Socialists of all stripes saw that Darwin's theory could be appropriated both to argue for the inevitability of progressive change and against religion. Marxian socialists (including Marx himself) were often uncomfortable with the Malthusian element in Darwinism. As with many of Darwin's interpreters elsewhere, they tended to downplay natural selection in favour of Lamarckian and other evolutionary mechanisms, and also to deny that biological laws could be directly applied to society. Other Marxists and many non-Marxists read socialism directly from Darwinism. But irrespective of their specific interpretations of Darwin, nearly all socialists saw him as an ally. Works on his theory flowed from the German socialist press; it was the most popular non-fiction topic among workers.[64] Indeed, workers were generally more inclined towards scientific than economic and political titles, and vastly more interested in Darwin than the difficult-to-understand Marx.[65] The embrace of Darwinism by the Left led a puzzled Darwin to comment in 1879: 'What a foolish idea seems to prevail in Germany on the connection between Socialism and Evolution through Natural Selection.'[66]

Liberals also viewed Darwinism as an ally in their war with the Catholic Church, the monarchy and the *Junkers* (conservative noble land-owners). Haeckel's popular writings of this period express primarily liberal ideals and aspirations: laissez faire, anti-clericalism, intellectual freedom, anti-militarism, an end to inherited privilege. The nobility has no right to feel privileged, he argues, given that all human embryos – of nobles as well as commoners – are indistinguishable in their early stages from those of dogs and other mammals, while war causes the deaths of the bravest and strongest German youths.[67] The 'Monist League' Haeckel founded was a pacifist organisation.[68]

But there had always been an authoritarian and nationalist element in the German liberal programme, which gave it a distinctive character. After the failure of the 1848 revolution, German liberals supported not only economic laissez faire but a strong state and national unity, which they thought feasible only under the under the leadership of authoritarian Prussia.[69] Otto von Bismarck, Prussia's chief minister, also won liberal approval with his *Kulturkampf* of the 1870s against the Catholic Church. The achievement of national unity under Bismarck converged with the growing power of the working class, especially after the unification of the two working-class parties in 1875, to move liberals further to the right. Even in the 1860s, Haeckel had denounced the use of modern medicine to enable the diseased to survive and pass on their afflictions. By 1877, he was engaged in a vicious debate with Rudolf Virchow over the connection between Darwinism and socialism, asserting that 'if this English hypothesis is to be compared to any definite political tendency... that tendency can only be aristocratic, certainly not democratic, and least of all socialist'.[70] (After reading an English translation of Haeckel's anti-Virchow polemic, Darwin wrote to the author that 'I agree with all of it.'[71])

German Darwinism would become increasingly – though never uniformly – reactionary. By the 1890s, it was most often read to imply the necessity of competitive struggle, especially among groups, and linked to racism, imperialism and suppression of working-class demands. Modern society was now seen as counter-selective; degeneration could be reversed only through the active efforts of the state. In 1892, when Bismarck visited the University of Jena, he was embraced by Haeckel, who awarded him an honorary doctorate.[72] Particularly revealing is the outcome of the famous essay competition sponsored by the German munitions manufacturer and amateur zoologist, Friedrich Alfred Krupp. In 1900, Krupp offered the huge prize of 10,000 marks for the best essay on the question: 'What can we learn from the theory of evolution about domestic political development and state legislation?' Deeply hostile to socialism, his aim was apparently to demonstrate that Darwinism was not a threat to the state.[73] Most of the sixty entrants (including the forty-four from Germany) read Darwin as legitimising state intervention, both in the economy and breeding. Only a few essays were written from a socialist perspective, and a lonely one from a classical liberal perspective.[74]

Whereas in Britain, the First World War provoked many Darwinians to reevaluate the evolutionary consequences of warfare, in Germany, it reinforced the view of war as nature's way of ensuring the survival of the fittest. As a representative of the neutral commission for civilian relief, the American evolutionist Vernon Kellogg was assigned to the Headquarters of the German army in France and Belgium. From this unusual vantage point, he observed that German officers openly defended aggressive militarism as a corollary of Darwinism:

> The creed of the *Allmacht* of a natural selection based on violent and competitive struggle is the gospel of the German intellectuals; all else is illusion and anathema. . . . as with the different ant species, struggle – bitter, ruthless struggle – is the rule among the different human groups. This struggle not only must go on, for that is the natural law, but it should go on, so that this natural law may work out in its cruel, inevitable way the salvation of the human species.[75]

In the devastating aftermath of that war, eugenics came to be seen as crucial to collective survival. German eugenicists had earlier focused on positive eugenics – efforts to encourage breeding by the more desirable types. But as the economic crisis deepened, the cost of caring for the disabled in hospitals and asylums became an obsession, and the racist element in eugenics came to the fore. The Society for Racial Hygiene was once dominated by technocratic elitists, who struggled with Nordic supremacists. By the 1920s, the latter were in the ascendancy.

Thus, as many historians have stressed, the path from Darwin to Hitler was hardly a straight one.[76] In Germany, as elsewhere, evolutionary theory provided a resource for groups with disparate agendas, including socialists and other radicals, free-market and collectivist-oriented liberals, Fascists, eugenicists who opposed racism and racial purists. Indeed, it was the variety of interests which Darwinism initially served in Germany that explains why the theory was so widely and enthusiastically embraced. The continuing association of evolutionism with progressive causes, especially anti-militarism, explains why in 1935 the Nazis ordered that the works of nearly all the popular Darwinists, including Haeckel, be purged from libraries.[77]

That is not to say that Darwinism was infinitely plastic. In Germany as elsewhere, the social and religious views of classical conservatives made Darwinism hard to digest; the Catholic Church in particular remained a potent foe. But nearly every other group found what it needed in Darwin. Of course their ability to impose their particular reading depended on specific social conditions. In the immediate aftermath of the *Origin*, Darwinism was generally read as undermining religion and, for liberals, as legitimising laissez-faire. By the turn of the century, it was seen to justify collectivist-oriented social reform, colonialism and eugenics. While there were national variations, the trend from individualist to collectivist readings of Darwin was general. But only in Germany would Darwin come to be widely read as vindicating an active programme of extermination of the physically and racially 'unfit' – demonstrating how crucial is context. Darwin's metaphorical style and the ambiguities in his writings made many readings possible, but particular social and political circumstances determined which reading would prevail.

IX CONCLUSION

Darwin was not an original social thinker. His writings reflect assumptions conventional for a man of his time and class. Virtually everything he had to say on social matters – concerning the value of population pressure and inheritance of property, the naturalness of the sexual division of labour, and the inevitability of European expansion – can be found in Malthus, Spencer, Wallace, Greg, Bagehot and other contemporary writers.

Darwin's importance for social thought and institutions lay elsewhere. First, publication of the *Origin* was a crucial step on the road to modern eugenics. Darwin as well as his readers assumed that natural selection resulted in the constant improvement of organic beings. Thus progress depends on struggle for existence. When applied to humans, it followed that interference with this struggle would prove harmful. If improvement were to continue, it would either be necessary to withdraw the humanitarian measures that interfered with selection, or to counter their effects through a programme of artificial selection, or both. The alternative was degeneration.

That was the conclusion reached by most Darwinians in the decade following publication of the *Origin*, and also by Darwin, after much wavering, in the *Descent of Man*. Darwin himself opted for living with the bad consequences of the less capable outbreeding what he called 'the better class of men'. In the end, he could sanction neither a withdrawal of charity nor active intervention with human breeding. Darwin was thus not a 'eugenicist', or certainly not a fully-fledged one. But his theory fuelled fears that made the need for a programme of selective breeding seem dire. It is no coincidence that Galton, the founder of modern eugenics, was his cousin – or that Leonard Darwin, President of the Eugenics Society in Britain in the 1910s and 1920s, was his son.

Eugenics was only translated into a practical programme when it was linked to modern genetics, evidence of the high fertility of those at the bottom of the social scale, and a more positive view of the functions of the state. Support for eugenics has waxed and waned over the succeeding years, but the concerns that inspired it have never disappeared. For example, the authors of *The Bell Curve* (1994) warn of the threat to modern society represented by the profligate breeding of an underclass. They attribute social failure to low intelligence, which they believe is largely determined by heredity. Should members of this underclass continue to breed at a more rapid rate than their intellectual superiors, the general cognitive level of the population will inevitably decline, resulting in a host of social problems.[78] The huge sales of the book indicate that old fears linger, and are easily ignited.

Darwinism also continues to furnish a resource for advocates of diverse political and social causes. In the works of some professional and many popular sociobiologists and evolutionary psychologists, it is deployed to argue for the naturalness of territoriality, competition and traditional gender roles. Others read in Darwin the opposite messages. The philosopher Peter Singer has recently called for a new Darwinian Left, which 'takes seriously the fact that we are evolved animals'.[79] It should acknowledge that there is a real human nature, which constrains our behaviour. This nature includes competitive but also social and cooperative tendencies on which the Left can build. (Singer also hopes that recognition of our continuity with other animals will make us less likely to exploit them.)

As a resource, has Darwinism mattered? In 1906, Graham Wallas reported on a clergyman's response to his remark that many people now accepted Darwin's view of human evolution. 'Yes', he said, 'we all accept it, and how little difference it makes.'[80] Some scholars agree that its actual impact has been slight. In their view, Darwinism merely provided window-dressing for social theories that predated it and would surely have flourished in its absence.[81] Thus, writing on British imperialism in the late nineteenth century, Paul Crook notes that 'Darwinistic themes were used primarily as slogans, propaganda, crude theater, cultural extravaganza', and that it is possible to find only a very few 'serious' theoretical works (and those little read) linking Darwinism to empire.[82]

It is doubtless true that many popularisers misunderstood Darwin. (Darwin's own ambiguities, hesitations and waverings made that easy.) Some might not even have read him. That would also be true for Marx, Freud and many other major thinkers. But the social power of a theory has never depended on a detailed or correct understanding by its interpreters. In particular contexts, the Darwinian discourse of struggle and selection gave old ideas about competition, race and gender a new credibility. In Germany, as the historian Richard Evans has argued, what the Nazis obtained from Darwin was not a coherent set of ideas or well-developed ideology but a language. The rhetoric associated with the Nazi variant of social Darwinism was effective in justifying Nazi policies, for it 'helped reconcile those who used it, and for whom it had become an almost automatic way of thinking about society, to accept the policies the Nazis advocated and in many cases to collaborate willingly in putting them into effect'.[83] It is true that every social idea justified by reference to Darwin predated his work, and that many who invoked him lacked a firm grasp of his views. Darwinism's main contribution to social theory has been to popularise certain catchwords. But this is not to minimise its importance. Today, as in the past, rhetoric can be a potent resource.

NOTES

1. Bryan [1924] 1967, 547–8.
2. Dennett 1995, 393.
3. Greene 1981 remains the most balanced account of Darwin's social views.
4. C. H. Smith 1991, 13–14.
5. Wallace [1864] 1991, 21.
6. Galton 1865.
7. Quoted in Jones 1998, 9.
8. Greg 1868.
9. Bagehot [1872] 1974, 47–8, 55–8.
10. Wallace 1870.
11. Marchant 1916, 199; R. J. Richards 1987, 186.
12. Durant, 1985, 293–4; Desmond and Moore 1991, 579. For further complementary discussion of Greg and Wallace on these topics, see Richards, this volume.
13. See Keynes 1988, 45, 58, 79–80, 173–4; Barrett *et al.*, 1987, *Charles Darwin's Notebooks, Notebook* C, MS p. 154 – hereafter C154; Gruber, 1981, 18.
14. C. Darwin [1860] 1962, 433–4.

15. See Keynes 1988, 172, 408; F. Darwin [1888] 1969, I, 316.
16. Browne 1995, 237–8.
17. Keynes 1988, 139.
18. C. Darwin [1871] 1981, I, 35.
19. C79; C. Darwin [1871] 1981, I, 62; Knoll 1997, 14.
20. C. Darwin [1871] 1981, I, 404–5.
21. C. Darwin [1871] 1981, I, 162.
22. C. Darwin [1871] 1981, I, 160, 166, 169.
23. C. Darwin [1871] 1981, I, 167–8.
24. C. Darwin [1871] 1981, I, 168–9.
25. C. Darwin [1871] 1981, I, 174, 77.
26. Wallace 1905, 509.
27. C. Darwin [1871] 1981, I, 180.
28. C. Darwin [1871] 1981, II, 403.
29. C. Darwin [1871] 1981, I, 170.
30. Desmond and Moore 1991, 327, 396–8, 648, 655.
31. C. Darwin [1871] 1981, I, 169.
32. Weikart 1995, 610–11.
33. J. R. Moore 2001, 12–16.
34. C. Darwin 1859, 62.
35. Weikart 1998a.
36. F. Burkhardt *et al.*, 1985–2001, *Correspondence* VIII, 189.
37. J. R. Moore 1986, 62; cf. Shapin and Barnes 1979; Young 1985b.
38. R. Hofstadter 1944, 6–7.
39. Mitman 1997.
40. Quoted in Stepan 1987, 137.
41. Crook 1994, 7.
42. Stepan 1987, 140–1.
43. Stepan 1987, 138–42.
44. Hawkins 1997, 251–7; see also Russett 1989.
45. Bellamy 1888, 179.
46. On Gilman, see Doskow 1997.
47. See R. J. Richards 1987, 243–313, 325–30; also Wallace 1905, 27.
48. Spencer [1851] 1970, 379.
49. Bowler 1990, 170–1; for a similar view, see Kaye 1997, 26–35.
50. Hofstadter 1944; J. R. Moore 1985.
51. Quoted in Degler 1991, 12.
52. La Vergata 1985, 960.
53. Bagehot [1872] 1974, 22–3.
54. Jones 1980; Hawkins 1997, especially 26–35; and J. R. Moore 1986, 35, 65.
55. Jones 1980, 108; Bellomy 1984, 118.

56. Bannister 1979, 166.
57. For a more detailed account of these developments, see Paul 1995.
58. Perhaps the most direct evolutionary arguments on behalf of immigration restriction were by socialists. See Pittinger 1993.
59. On the 'euthanasia' programme, see Burleigh 1994.
60. R. J. Evans 1997, 55–6.
61. Liebknecht 1901, 91–2.
62. Quoted in Weikart 1993, 471.
63. Benton 1982, 89–91; Weikart 1993, 472–3; Weindling 1991, 16; Weindling 1998.
64. Weikart 1998b, 2.
65. For a detailed discussion of German workers' reading preferences, see Kelly 1981, 128–41.
66. F. Darwin [1888] 1969, III, 237.
67. Benton 1982, 92, 94.
68. R. J. Evans 1997, 64.
69. Benton 1982, 90.
70. Haeckel 1879, 92.
71. Quoted in Weikart 1998a, 25.
72. de Rooy 1990, 15.
73. Weiss 1987, 68.
74. de Rooy 1990, 14; Weiss 1987, 72, 74.
75. Kellogg 1917, 28–9.
76. Perhaps the only historian to argue that there *was* a straight path from Darwin to Hitler (via Haeckel) is Gasman 1971.
77. de Rooy 1990, 16.
78. Herrnstein and Murray 1994. For a nuanced discussion of the relation of their work to 'social Darwinism', see Dickens 2000, 64–80.
79. Singer 1999, 6.
80. Quoted in Bellomy 1984, 126.
81. Burrow 1966; Bannister 1979.
82. Crook 1998, 1.
83. R. J. Evans 1997, 78.

JEAN GAYON

10 From Darwin to today in evolutionary biology

I THE PERSISTENCE OF DARWINISM

For nearly one-and-a-half centuries, biologists interested in evolution have been haunted by the question of whether their conceptions are or are not 'Darwinian'. While it may not be unique, this persistent positioning of new developments in relation to a single, pioneering figure is quite exceptional in the history of modern natural science. Physicists currently working in the domains of relativity or quantum theory may refer sometimes to Einstein or Bohr; but their debates are not massively structured by this reference as evolutionary theory has been and remains structured by reference to Darwin. A proximate cause of Darwin's enduring presence is that evolutionary biologists have never stopped reading him. The remarkably numerous editions and translations of Darwin's books have in themselves helped to make this possible. But the availability of key texts only takes us so far in understanding why evolutionary biologists go on reading Darwin, referring to him, feeling the necessity of labelling their theories as 'Darwinian' or 'non-Darwinian' or 'anti-Darwinian'.

Indeed, on the face of it, there are compelling reasons for modern biologists to avoid affiliating their work with Darwin's. Darwinism does not belong only to the history of science; it also belongs to cultural and political history.[1] Among other things, neo-liberal economics, social Darwinism, racial anthropology, Nazi ideology and the materialistic monism of Darwin's German supporter Ernst Haeckel had strong interactions with Darwinism in the first century of its history. Likewise, in more recent times, sociobiology (in its more ideological forms), American liberalism and the European right-wing have been more thoroughly committed to Darwinism than their opponents.[2] All these aspects of cultural and political modern history could have made overt reference to Darwin and Darwinism unattractive. Indeed, as evolutionary biology emerged as a professional scientific discipline, it became routine to distance the subject from suspect elements in its past. As Michael Ruse has shown, professionalisation after the Second World War had the effect of excluding 'amateurish' topics from the field – notably, Ruse argues, in connection with evolutionary progress, a traditional topic in the evolutionary literature, but little mentioned in the professional periodicals and books after 1945.[3]

Nevertheless, from Theodosius Dobzhansky and Ernst Mayr to Richard Lewontin, Motoo Kimura, Stephen Jay Gould and Stuart Kauffman, the question of whether evolutionary biology should or should not be Darwinian has been explicit. More generally, the constant and overwhelming interest of working evolutionary biologists in Darwin since 1859 – rather than, say, in Lamarck or Geoffroy Saint-Hilaire or Chambers – indicates a strong relation, such as that between a model (Darwin) and a copy (Darwinism as a scientific tradition). The Darwin–Darwinism relation is in certain respects a causal relation, in the sense that Darwin influenced the debates that followed him. But there is also something more: a kind of isomorphism between Darwin's Darwinism and historical Darwinism. It is as though Darwin's own contribution has constrained the conceptual and empirical development of evolutionary biology ever after.

To bring the nature of this constraint into focus, this chapter undertakes a broad survey of the history and present state of evolutionary biology from the viewpoint of its relation to Darwin or presumed Darwinian schemes. We will have to characterise as clearly as possible both the continuity between Darwin and various changes in evolutionary biology, and the major kinds of theoretical dissents that have accompanied evolutionary biology from 1859 to the present day. Those dissents will include dissents *from* the dominant Darwinian tradition and dissents *within* Darwinism. Another distinction we will need is that between Darwin's idea of 'descent with modification', or the tree of life, and his idea of natural selection as the main cause of the modification of species. In the rest of the chapter, I make use of this distinction as follows. First, I examine whether descent with modification has been challenged after Darwin.

Secondly, I show that a good deal of past and present controversy over the triumph versus the decline of Darwinism can be understood from within two perspectives on natural selection that Darwin himself developed: natural selection as an existing natural process; and natural selection as a unifying and explanatory principle for the entirety of phenomena that constitute the history of life.[4]

II THE TREE OF LIFE AS THE PATTERN OF EVOLUTION

It is now often said that, since Darwin, the 'fact of evolution' has been established beyond dispute. Yet Darwin himself did not often use the word 'evolution'. Although the last sentence of the *Origin of Species* says (in all editions) that 'endless forms most beautiful and wonderful have been, and are being, evolved', Darwin did not like his theory about the branching transmutation of species to be called a 'theory of evolution'. Nowhere in the first edition of the *Origin* can the phrases 'theory of evolution' or 'principle of evolution' be found, nor even the word 'evolution'. For Darwin, and many other English naturalists of his era, 'evolution' was an ambiguous word. It evoked various theories that closely associated the history of species with both individual development and an overall progressionist interpretation of the history of nature. Clustered around 'evolution' were, among others, the old theory of embryogenesis as the expansion of a preformed organism (this being the primary meaning of 'evolution' in the seventeenth and eighteenth centuries); the associated theory of the pre-existence of germs, in connection with which the Swiss naturalist Charles Bonnet first applied 'evolution' not only to individual generation, but to the history of the successive appearance of species;[5] the transcendental morphology of the nineteenth century, with its emphasis on parallelisms between embryogenesis and the graduated complexity of species; and the British philosopher Herbert Spencer's 'evolutionist' philosophy, postulating the existence of a universal principle of 'evolution' or 'development' in nature (a progressive tendency towards increased complexity).[6] Darwin was especially familiar with this latter sense of 'evolution', and did not want his scientific theory to be confused with Spencer's philosophical speculation.

These various connotations throw light on why 'evolution' does not appear in Darwin's manuscripts and publications up to the

1870s.[7] The public, however, was quick to associate Spencer's philosophy of nature and Darwin's theory of the transmutation of species. Darwin resisted such assimilation, and went on avoiding the word 'evolution' for some time. But he finally adopted it in the final, sixth edition of the *Origin* (1872). There he used the word seven times, with unequivocal reference to his own theory. The first occurrence is: 'At the present day almost all naturalists admit evolution under some form.' A few lines later, Darwin writes that the kind of evolution he favours is 'slow and gradual evolution', not sudden changes. A few more lines, and we have Darwin's full formulation: his was a 'theory of gradual evolution, through the preservation of a large number of individuals, which varied more or less in any favourable direction, and of the destruction of a large number which varied in an opposite manner'.[8]

The context of these sentences is worth noting. Darwin was responding in detail to St George Jackson Mivart, a Catholic zoologist who admitted the evolution of organic forms and the existence of natural selection, but opposed Darwin on two points: first, Mivart believed that evolution occurred by sudden changes; second, he thought that the major evolutionary factor was an internal tendency to vary in a given direction, rather than natural selection alone.[9] Mivart – whose objections were taken very seriously by Darwin – was typical of a new generation of biologists for whom the issue was not the modification versus the independent creation of species, but the tempo of modification and its explanation. In such a context, it made sense for Darwin to admit that he was an 'evolutionist'. One may recall here a passage in a letter Darwin wrote to Asa Gray in 1863: 'Personally, of course, I care much about Natural Selection, but that seems to me utterly unimportant compared to the question of *Creation* **or** *Modification*.'[10] If a majority of biological thinkers preferred to say 'evolution' rather than 'descent with modification', and if they accepted this idea, then Darwin had little reason to object.

His final linguistic compromise is well revealed by another passage of the 1872 edition of the *Origin*. In the first edition, Darwin had written: 'If numerous species, belonging to the same genera of families, have really started into life all at once, the fact would be fatal to the theory of descent with slow modification through natural selection.'[11] In the last edition, the first part of this sentence does not change. But the second part becomes: 'the fact would be fatal to the theory of evolution through natural selection'.[12] This change makes perfectly clear that Darwin admitted the word 'evolution'. provided that it meant 'descent with slow modification'. Whence his famous often-quoted declaration in the last version of the conclusive chapter:

> I formerly spoke to very many naturalists on the subject of evolution, and never once met with any sympathetic agreement. It is probable that some did then believe in evolution, but they were either silent, or expressed themselves so ambiguously that it was not easy to understand their meaning. Now, things are wholly changed, and almost every naturalist admits the great principle of evolution.[13]

These sentences are written as if Darwin had always spoken of 'evolution'.

Has scientific consensus about the fact of evolution, thus construed as branching descent, been significantly threatened after Darwin? The classical answer to this question is 'no'. After a few years of turmoil caused by the publication of the *Origin* – so goes the story – biologists stopped disputing over the question of the transmutability of species. Organic evolution became so widely accepted that biologists began to see it as a general fact rather than a theoretical principle. Consequently, controversies concentrated upon the causal explanation of this general fact. Was natural selection the main cause, or should one explore alternative factors of evolution, such as an inner tendency of species to evolve in a given direction (orthogenesis); adaptation through the inheritance of acquired characters (neo-Lamarckianism); or sudden changes of species (mutationism)? Peter Bowler has well described these various modes of post-Darwinian evolutionism during the 'eclipse' of Darwinism in the decades around 1900.[14] But Bowler has no parallel story to tell about post-Darwinian controversies over the very existence of organic evolution. A similar observation could be made about most historical studies on the subject of organic evolution after Darwin.

On the whole, this consensus picture is certainly right. After Darwin's death in 1882, and even more so after 1900, it is almost impossible to find significant biologists who plainly and explicitly denied the *existence* of evolution in the sense that species modify and are physically related with previous species through uninterrupted generations. Denials of this idea can be found on the borderlines of the sciences, in the history, for example, of American creationism, or of similar religious reactions to biological evolution; and these are of course non-negligible parts of the cultural history of modern science.[15] But such denials are not a significant feature of the history of post-Darwinian biology as a professional discipline.

More than anything else, it is Darwin's tree-of-life diagram that summarised his proposal that the entire history of life can be represented as a general phenomenon of gradual modification, splitting, divergence and extinction of species. This diagram – the sole illustration in the *Origin* – was tremendously important for Darwin, who, in the first edition, devoted ten pages of comments to it in the fourth chapter and twenty-five pages in the thirteenth. It had an almost immediate effect upon the entirety of the biological community. Within a remarkably short period of time, it became the paradigmatic representation of organic evolution and its status as an established fact. Thomas Kuhn's concepts of scientific revolution and paradigm shift are exactly appropriate here.[16] Some historians have claimed that Darwin's theory did not first function as a paradigm in the history of science, but rather the reverse: it opened a long period of crisis.[17] Certainly that is true of natural selection. But the same does not apply to descent with modification. Retrospectively, the sudden and dramatic effect of the famous tree-of-life diagram constitutes one of the most spectacular examples of a shift of paradigm.

The kind of theory embodied in Darwin's diagram is not a causal theory, in the sense of an assembly of hypotheses about the mechanisms that govern given processes. Rather, it is a theory that postulates the general existence in nature of several classes of phenomena, such as the gradual modification of species, splitting and so forth. Such a theory looks like a descriptive generalisation, but it is not: it is a heuristic device, a plausible bet about the general form and pace of the big classes of phenomena that constitute organic evolution. Of course, the more scientists accumulate data within such a framework, the more they tend to consider this framework as a literal description of the contents of the world. This is exactly what happened to Darwin's diagram. Along with the key concepts embedded within it, the diagram quickly became a consensual representation of the general fact of evolution.

It is difficult to imagine a more successful aspect of Darwinism than the idea of the tree of life. The whole industry of evolutionary biology has been based upon it for almost a century and a half. Soon after 1859, biologists and palaeontologists began constructing specific phylogenetic trees, and this is still today one of the major dimensions of evolutionary biology.[18] Systematists may disagree on the appropriate method for the reconstruction and interpretation of phylogenies; but they hardly disagree on the extreme importance of this enterprise.[19] Strictly speaking, of course, Darwin was not the inventor of this mode of practice. But he was the one who gave it a systematic basis, understood its tremendous heuristic power, and found the appropriate words and images for its diffusion.

III CRITICAL PERSPECTIVES ON THE TREE-OF-LIFE IDEA

Nevertheless, for all the strength and longevity of consensus surrounding the fact of species branching, there have been at least three serious challenges to certain aspects of Darwin's tree-of-life picture. Each of these challenges, or classes of criticism, relates to the form or the shape of the tree.

A first class of criticism emphasises that evolution is something that does not happen only at the level of the species, but also at other levels. Criticism along these lines has its basis in a rather common observation in palaeontology: that the higher taxa in animals and plants – for example, the various orders of mammals – tend to appear and diversify suddenly, giving rise to morphological types with general characteristics that remain approximately stable ever after. The inference is that the pattern of life is less of a tree than a bush, with more or less parallel twigs arising from a given level. For any particular taxonomic group, the branching pattern will look like a candelabra. A further variant of this 'bush of life' idea, quite popular among biologists in the period from 1880 to 1930, supposes that the lineages composing the higher taxonomic groups evolve in a similar direction. The general emphasis on bushiness often goes along with a weakening of the ideas of gradual modification and indefinite divergence of species. On this view, species or genera or even families may change, split and diverge; but, at a higher level, something different happens, something which is not just a mass effect of what happens at the level of species.

Such a view has occasionally been put forward by palaeontologists and morphologists, especially those advocating a theory of evolution based upon a combination of orthogenesis and mutationism. Significant examples of this trend of thinking can be found in the works of palaeontologists such as Karl von Zittel, Charles Dépéret, Otto Schindewolf and the French zoologist Louis Vialleton.[20] The latter used to say that 'transformism' – the common Lamarckian–Darwinian representation of the history of life – should not be equated with 'evolution'. For 'there exists an absolute difference between the diversification or multiplication of species, and the evolution or formation of types or organisation'.[21] Such language, of course, is incompatible with any form of Darwinism. But twentieth-century evolutionary biologists do admit that the modification and diversification of species may have very different tempos. The American palaeontologist G. G. Simpson's notion of quantum evolution and the common acceptance of such 'big bang' events as the Precambrian 'explosion' belong to this tradition.[22]

A second, related class of criticism has been raised by all those biologists who have advocated a non-gradual, or saltationist, representation of the origin of species. Since Thomas Huxley, Francis Galton and the majority of the early Mendelians (including William Bateson, Hugo De Vries, Lucien Cuénot, Wilhelm Johannsen and, somewhat later, Richard Goldschmidt), saltationists have been extremely numerous. Today, this major alternative view of descent with modification is represented by Niles Eldredge and Stephen Jay Gould's 'theory of punctuated equilibrium', postulating that the preponderant amount of evolutionary change is concentrated during the events of speciation or 'cladogenesis'.[23] Eldredge and Gould do not claim that the change leading to a new species is so sudden that it occurs in a single generation (as some geneticists believed at the beginning of the twentieth century). On the basis of palaeontological data, they argue instead that, at a geological scale, species evolve much more rapidly when they emerge from splitting than they do thereafter. Saltationist views of evolution entail an obvious modification of the general pattern of the genealogical tree. Instead of branches that progressively diverge, the tree will have the shape of successive small candelabras with two branches.

Saltationist conceptions are most often encompassed from the point of view of causal processes rather than patterns. Indeed, if we do not take account of the detail of the multiplication of particular species, the genealogical tree of a given group on the Eldredge–Gould model will have an overall appearance roughly similar to the Darwinian diagram. The relation between pattern and process here is this: if, as saltationists maintain, divergence of species is mainly accomplished through splitting, rather than through gradual modification subsequent to splitting, then the causal theory of evolution should primarily focus on splitting rather than modification.[24]

The two previous classes of criticism cover a wide spectrum of authors since 1859. The third is recent. It bears upon the postulate that the history of biological diversity is adequately (or sufficiently) represented by a tree of irreversible divergence of *species*. The worry here is that evolution at a large timescale might well involve several processes that contradict this postulate. One such process is the lateral transfer of genes in microorganisms. For, say, a group of modern bacteria, a fraction of the genome can be isolated while another fraction recombines with the genomes of other groups of bacteria. This phenomenon renders the notion of independent species lineages problematic. To a certain extent, lineages of genes seem to be as important as lineages of organisms and of species. Divergence between species in bacteria does exist; but it is only one side of their evolutionary story. Species that have diverged for a long time can go on exchanging important fractions of their genomes (such as factors of resistance to antibiotics). Moreover, microbiologists suspect that lateral gene transfer was much more common in the past than it is now. Carl Woese, the molecular biologist who established the existence of the group *Archaea*, has been a major protagonist in this debate on the phylogeny of the entire living world.[25] Woese has provided a vivid formulation of the problem:

> Lateral gene transfer was part and parcel of the universal ancestor. That ancestor was a communal entity, a community that survived and evolved as a whole, as an aggregate, not as individual lineages... In my view, the highest level taxa, the domains [i.e. *Archaea, Bacteria, Eucarya*] need not reflect the evolutionary course that split the universal ancestor into the individual ancestors of the three primary lines of descent. This is not a matter of cataloging extant organisms. Nor is it even a matter of representing genealogical relationships. Modern phenotypes did not exist and organismal genealogies probably had no meaning at the time when the domains formed... Evolution at this early stage was probably a symphony of lateral gene flow.[26]

Considering that 90 per cent of present terrestrial biomass is microbial, and that the first three billion years of organic evolution were exclusively microbial, Woese's proposal is a major challenge indeed to the classical Darwinian view of the genealogy of living beings. At the most inclusive level of description, Darwin's diagram shows its limits: organismal and species genealogies encapsulate only one fraction of the entire graph of descent with modification.

Another process likely to have a profound impact on the common arborescent representation of genealogical relationships between organisms is symbiosis, which has certainly been a major evolutionary process, especially in cell evolution.[27] It is still probably an important phenomenon. Although the process itself is well understood, its consequences for phylogenetic patterns are not. But symbiosis will almost certainly be a major topic for future evolutionary-biological enquiry. Symbiosis does not challenge the notion of irreversible divergence. Separate organisms that fuse initiate new species that diverge as do others. But, by enabling the possibility of major fusion events between evolutionarily remote groups, symbiosis introduces complications that cannot be easily assimilated into a simple tree-like pattern of phylogeny.

Darwin's principle of branching descent turns out to be a theoretical principle after all. It involves a series of heuristic postulates about what the general pattern of the history of life could look like.[28] Darwin's heuristic postulates about the general shape of the events constituting the history of life have proved to be immensely fertile. They fostered the discovery of the evolutionary relationships between innumerable organisms. They also paved the way for a number of valuable descriptive generalisations about many groups of organisms. This is why so many biologists came to believe that the postulates behind Darwin's tree amounted to a general fact of nature. But, like all other such postulates, the branching tree of life may be subject to revision in the light of new theoretical and empirical knowledge.

IV NATURAL SELECTION AS THE MAIN EVOLUTIONARY PROCESS

In the *Origin*, Darwin had a double strategy for justifying belief in natural selection. The first strategy was to provide inductive arguments in favour of the existence and adequacy of natural selection as a causal process. The second strategy was hypothetico-deductive: it consisted in showing that natural selection explains and unifies various classes of independent facts.[29] Since 1859, challenges to natural selection have been mounted against both parts of this general argument.

What went into eclipse during the so-called 'eclipse of Darwinism' was the idea that natural selection is a cause of adaptive evolutionary change. Most attacks between 1859 and the 1930s indeed targeted the very existence of natural selection. There were a number of impressive difficulties. One was the absence in the *Origin* of a theory of hereditary transmission of characters. Darwin postulated that variation was heritable, but he did not prove it, nor did he indicate the mechanism of inheritance. Did parental characters blend in the progeny, or were they transmitted as discrete entities? And how did the mechanism of inheritance affect the efficiency of natural selection?[30]

Another difficulty resulted from the apparent rarity of adaptive change and the smallness of the advantage accruing from such change, especially in comparison with the considerable rate of elimination of individuals in most species. For instance, if a given variation increases the chances of survival by one in fifty and occurs in one individual in a million, in a species where one individual per hundred survives to reproduce, then the probability is high that the advantageous variation will be lost by chance. The Scottish engineer Fleeming Jenkin raised the issue with outstanding perspicacity in his 1867 review of the *Origin*.[31] Jenkin's review made it clear to a number of people that the demonstration of the existence of natural selection as an efficient cause for the modification of species required not only clarification of the problem of heredity, but the development of a quantitative approach to phenomena such as variation, advantage, rate of survival, rate of reproduction and the role of chance. The complexities proved to be greater than anything Darwin could have anticipated. It took approximately seventy years for biologists and mathematicians to develop the appropriate tools. Inspired by Galton's populational studies of inheritance, 'biometricians' such as Karl Pearson and W. F. R. Weldon played a prominent role in reformulating natural selection in statistical terms. When this statistical approach was in turn enriched by the new Mendelian genetics in the early years of the twentieth century, there emerged a theory of hereditary transmission capable of underwriting a predictive theory of the evolution of populations. This new genetics of populations provided the first firm basis upon which the questions of the possibility, existence and limits of natural selection as a cause of evolution could be properly assessed.[32]

Initially, in the years after the rediscovery in 1900 of Gregor Mendel's seminal 1865 paper on some laws governing hybridisation, Darwinism and 'Mendelism' were often thought opposed; for Mendelism, in a number of ways, seemed to support saltationist mutationism rather than gradual selectionism. By the 1920s this opposition was resolved, thanks mainly to the *Drosophila* fly experimentalists working under Thomas Hunt Morgan at Columbia University and another group under William Castle at Harvard. Along with a new interpretation of genes as linearly arranged on chromosomes, a view now emerged that mutations of Mendelian genes were non-Lamarckian and, generally, quite inadequate to produce adaptive and progressive evolutionary change on their own, without natural selection. First of all, mutations arose at very low rates and were mostly recessive and disadvantageous. In those rare cases where mutations chanced to be advantageous, natural selection was the only process that could guarantee their diffusion through the population. Furthermore, it became clear that continuous variation in a trait could be explained as a macroscopic effect of the influence of a large number of separately acting genes (polygenic determinism). The upshot was the rehabilitation of the Darwinian concept of natural selection as a process that acts on *infinitesimally small differences*, producing a *gradual* transformation of species. In this way, a new understanding of hereditary variation saved selection from the old Jenkinian objection. It also vindicated selection as a necessary and, indeed, sufficient cause of adaptive evolution.[33]

Building on these vindications of selection, the mathematical population genetics of R. A. Fisher, J. B. S. Haldane and Sewall Wright, who wrote in the late 1920s and early 1930s, constituted the major intellectual event in the history of theorising about natural selection after Darwin, for at least three reasons.[34] First, this science provided a clarification of the role of natural selection in evolution. In theoretical population genetics, natural selection does not automatically modify a population. Rather, selection is a force that acts more or less efficiently depending on a balance of various parameters. The main parameters are mutation rate, selection pressure, random genetic drift and migration.[35] These can oppose each other or co-operate. In other words, all evolutionary modification in a population is not presumptively due to natural selection. It is but one factor among other factors in a sort of 'mechanics of evolution' (Haldane's expression). Whether natural selection is, as Darwin once put it, a 'paramount power', is an empirical matter, depending on circumstances.[36]

The second contribution of population genetics was to catalyse both the widespread acceptance of natural selection and the search for direct proof of its operation in a particular case. Not that acceptance waited upon proof. The first conclusive evidence for evolutionary change caused by natural selection came only in the 1950s – almost one century after the *Origin* – with H. B. D. Kettlewell's famous work on industrial melanism in the peppered moth.[37] Population genetics made Kettlewell's achievement possible. But natural selection by this time was already a mainstream biological belief. It had become a working paradigm for the various disciplines that together formed the 'Modern Synthesis' in the 1930s and 1940s: experimental genetics, the genetics of natural or experimental populations, animal and plant systematics, and palaeontology. In this spectacular triumph of Darwinism, theoretical population genetics, as built up by Fisher, Wright and Haldane, played a major role. It provided compelling theoretical reasons for thinking that natural selection was a major cause in evolution. It provided efficient tools for detecting natural selection in nature (as distinct from other causes). And it defined the methodological conditions under which an exhaustive direct demonstration of a particular case of natural selection could be accomplished.

Finally, population genetics brought about an important reformulation of natural selection itself. As Fisher showed, the Malthusian principle is not a necessary condition of the existence of natural selection.[38] Natural selection can be efficient in a population with no 'check to increase'. It follows that the rate of reproduction of a given species is not a precondition of natural selection, but is itself the result of evolution by natural selection. For natural selection to happen, only three conditions are required: heritable variation, differential fitness and correlation between these two phenomena. Today, this generalised concept of natural selection has been extended beyond the domain of population genetics; but population geneticists were the first to appreciate the conceptual shift fully.[39]

This revival of natural selection by the new genetics was pursued most comprehensively in Theodosius Dobzhansky's influential book *Genetics and the Origin of Species*, first published in 1937. Here Dobzhansky brought together three kinds of genetics: the new mathematical population genetics, especially as he had learned it in personal collaborations with Wright; the cytological genetics of the Morgan school, which Dobzhansky had joined in 1927 (on arriving in the United States from the Soviet Union); and the pioneering Russian work on the experimental genetics of wild populations, especially Drosophilid flies – work meshing closely with his own earliest researches on the taxonomy and biogeography of lady beetles. The book self-consiously brought the whole of genetics to a reaffirmation of Darwin's legacy. (Indeed, Dobzhansky once slipped in a speech and talked of 'Darwin's great book, *Genetics and the Origin of Species*'.[40])

Within a few more years, Julian Huxley, the grandson of Darwin's defender T. H. Huxley, had published an even more wide-ranging text, *Evolution: The Modern Synthesis* (1942). Claiming that evolution was 'the most central and the most important of the problems of biology', Huxley announced 'the re-animation of Darwinism', on the basis of 'facts and methods from every branch of the science – ecology, genetics, palaeontology, geographical distribution, embryology, systematics, comparative anatomy'.[41] Huxley's confidence recalls the second aspect of Darwin's justification of the principle of natural selection: the explanatory power of the principle. Indeed, a number of the *Origin*'s chapters try to show that natural selection 'explains several large and independent classes of facts': not only morphological adaptations, but also instincts, divergence, extinction, geographic distribution of present and past species, and so on.[42] This explanatory ambition of Darwinism became a major commitment of the Modern Synthesis. The biologists and palaeontologists who participated in this movement tried hard to show that, in its modernised genetical version, natural selection was a major principle in the explanation of such phenomena as geographical variation, speciation, extinction, the tempo of evolution and phylogenetic trends. These were characteristic subjects of the founders of the synthesis: Dobzhansky (genetics), Huxley and Mayr (zoology), Simpson (palaeontology) and G. Ledyard Stebbins (plant biology). After 1950, the Synthesis favoured the expansion of Darwinian modes of explanation into still other fields, such as ethology (Konrad Lorenz, Nikolaas Tinbergen), ecology (David Lack, Robert MacArthur and E. O. Wilson), evolutionary embryology (C. H. Waddington) and morphology (notably allometry – the study of differential growth rates for different parts of an organism).[43]

In 1959, the year of the centenary of the publication of the *Origin*, the triumph of natural selection as an explanatory principle seemed to have no limit.[44] In the subsequent forty years or so, however, evolutionary biologists have become more circumspect. Their concerns basically fall into two categories: those dealing with micro-evolution (that is, evolutionary changes at the level of species) and those concerned with macro-evolution (that is, evolutionary changes on a larger scale).

V THE MICRO-EVOLUTIONARY CRITIQUE OF NATURAL SELECTION

At the level of micro-evolution, natural selection traditionally explains adaptations.[45] Contesting the explanatory power of natural selection at this level has taken several forms. One strategy is to reveal apparently adaptive features as non-adaptive and thus beyond the realm of natural selection. Another strategy is to show that there are genuinely adaptive features that are nonetheless out of natural selection's explanatory reach. A third and more radical strategy is to show that, in certain circumstances, natural selection can fail to accomplish what it is widely supposed to do, namely increase fitness. Since the Modern Synthesis, evolutionary biologists have debated anti-adaptation challenges of all three sorts.

The discovery of a large amount of polymorphism at the level of proteins and DNA clearly constituted a challenge of the first sort: something previously taken for granted as adaptive now appeared to be non-adaptive. The question was whether such polymorphism is explicable by natural selection or requires some other explanation.[46] This latter possibility was explored most famously by the Japanese geneticist Motoo Kimura in his neutral-mutation / random-drift theory of molecular evolution, later called his theory of 'non-Darwinian evolution'.[47] Following Kimura, 'neutralists' propose that a large amount of variation at the molecular level is neutral with respect to natural selection. They do *not* say that evolutionary change is mostly neutral. Rather, they make an important distinction between change at the organismic level and change at the molecular level. On their view, at the organismic level, natural selection is indeed the paramount power and virtually controls the majority of evolutionary change. At the molecular level, however, there exists a huge amount of variation which is invisible to natural selection. According to Kimura, most mutations at the level of nucleotides disappear or get fixed through the action of stochastic factors such as genetic drift. What natural selection controls at the genetic level is the limited fraction of mutations that affect organismic characters. The neutralist claim that natural selection does not make use of a huge amount of variation at the genetic level was difficult for many Darwinian biologists to accept when it first appeared. That the claim is now widely accepted is a good sign of contemporary biologists' subtler attitude regarding the explanatory power of natural selection.

The challenge represented by the theory of group selection is the most important example of a challenge based on the apparent impossibility of natural selection, traditionally construed, to account for certain adaptive natural features.[48] At issue is whether natural selection in its classical form – selection of traits among individuals – can explain the origin of attributes that are advantageous to a group. The debate goes back to Darwin, who almost completely rejected the notion of group selection. He had a famous private controversy on the subject with Wallace. There is only one case where Darwin plainly admitted the existence of 'tribal selection', when he tried to explain the origin of the moral sense in the human species.[49] Later, when population genetics emerged in the first half of the twentieth century, group selection was either explicitly rejected (as by Fisher) or largely ignored.[50] Although it superficially resembles group selection, Wright's theory of 'inter-demic' selection was in fact quite different. Wright's idea was that, once groups have acquired fitter genotypes in a given environment, they tend to diffuse those genotypes among other groups with which they come in contact. This is not the same as the group-selectional idea that traits might be selected because they benefit the group as such.

When group selection became a talking point in the 1960s, it was often in conjunction with concerns about evolutionary altruism.[51]

Altruistic traits are traits detrimental to the individual's fitness but advantageous for the group. Evolutionary altruism should not be confounded with moral altruism in humans (although moral altruism can possibly be interpreted as a special case of evolutionary altruism); most 'altruistic' traits discussed by contemporary evolutionary biologists refer to insects, worms, bacteria and even viruses. Group selection requires special models, which involve the partial isolation and periodic fusion of groups. Groups with altruists grow faster than those with no altruists. But altruists tend to disappear within the group because of their lower fitness. The only way, it seems, for group selection to occur is through the extinction of selfish groups or submersion by the altruistic groups.[52]

Claims about the existence and extent of group selection in nature have generated intense controversies among population geneticists. Since the Modern Synthesis, when Darwin's 'individualistic' concept of selection was adopted and even reinforced, group selection has been perceived as a major departure from the traditional understanding of natural selection. On that understanding, explanations of altruistic traits ought to rely upon various modes of genic selection, in combination with concepts such as kin selection or more generally the theory of games. Nevertheless, the perception of group selection as a threat to Darwinism reflects too narrow a conception of Darwinism. Group selection, if it exists, broadens the application of the concept of natural selection rather than contradicts it. Group selection is probably an important process involved in phenomena such as the origin and maintenance of sex and the evolution of virulence in micro-organisms. If it comes to be regarded as a major mode of natural selection, the historian will justifiably be able to characterise group selection as both anti-Darwinian (since Darwin and his major followers for more than a century regarded it that way) and an interesting expansion of the content of Darwin's central theory. Moreover, the historian should, as noted, also add that group selection was already in place when the theory of natural selection was born. Wallace and Darwin debated the matter over and over again in letters, never coming to an agreement. The modern controversy is, in this sense, an exploration of a theoretical possibility that was part of the initial schema.

The most dramatic objection that could be made to natural selection is that this process can just fail to accomplish what it is widely supposed to do, that is increase fitness, or adaptation in the Darwinian sense of competitive highness. Some theoretical biologists claim that the emerging theory of complexity imposes limits of this sort. Stuart Kauffman in particular has defended the thesis that complexity imposes serious limits to the adaptive power of natural selection.[53] Through genetic regulation, the genomes of organisms are typically complex systems, with lots of connectivity. Kauffman argues that a number of properties of these systems arise as a function of their degree of intrinsic complexity, whatever the selective pressures applied to them. These 'generic properties', as he calls them, cannot be viewed as the specific results of selection. They emerge not by natural selection but by 'self-organisation'. Furthermore, there may be a sense in which complexity restricts the field of possible adaptive solutions. Kauffman and other contemporary theoretical population geneticists argue that, beyond a certain degree of complexity, there are serious limits to the ability of organic systems to evolve towards higher fitness or even to maintain themselves at a given level of fitness. Various kinds of 'complexity catastrophes' arise as a function of the organisational constraints imposed on the system.

This kind of criticism is impressive, because it challenges the most intuitive aspect of natural selection as a causal process: natural selection should at least increase fitness. ('Can we doubt', asked Darwin, '... that individuals having any advantage, however slight, over others, would have the best chance of surviving and of procreating their kind?'.[54]) Nevertheless, it is far from the first result of twentieth-century theoretical biology to challenge the intuitive notion of natural selection. After all, genetic drift and selfish behaviour are classical examples of factors that limit the capacity of natural selection to increase the fitness of a population. Complexity must now be added to the long and long-standing list of factors that restrict the adaptive power of natural selection 'from the inside'.

VI THE MACRO-EVOLUTIONARY CRITIQUE OF NATURAL SELECTION

These criticisms of natural selection do not really threaten Darwinism as a scientific paradigm. After all, none of them suggests that adaptations, when they exist, can be explained by anything other than natural selection. As we have seen, neutral mutations are not adaptations; altruistic traits can be explained by an enlarged concept of selection; and self-organisation, while it can generate order or oppose natural selection, does not of itself produce adaptation. In the past forty years, it is not the micro-evolutionary phenomena of adaptation, but several macro-evolutionary phenomena which have produced the most serious cracks in the Darwinian edifice.

Darwin himself thought that extinction, divergence, the distribution of organisms in space, the general shape of classification and the genealogy of life were genuinely explained and unified by the theory of natural selection. In Darwin's terms, this explanatory capacity of natural selection was the real 'test' of its acceptability as 'a well-grounded theory'. Seventy-eight years later, Dobzhansky wrote something in the same vein in his *Genetics and the Origin of Species*: 'Experience seems to show . . . that there is no way towards an understanding of the mechanisms of macro-evolutionary changes, which require time on a geological scale, other than through a full comprehension of the micro-evolutionary processes observable within the span of a human lifetime and often controlled by man's will.'[55] For Dobzhansky, if natural selection is the main force that orients micro-evolutionary change – a thesis that finally prevailed among all the founders of the Modern Synthesis – then it follows that natural selection is the cornerstone of macro-evolutionary theory.

But such reasoning has been vigorously contested within modern evolutionary biology. Palaeobiology as a discipline emerged out of a conviction that macro-evolution requires specific causal theories and modes of explanation which, while compatible with micro-evolutionary processes, cannot be reduced to them. The most convincing example of this way of thinking has been David Raup's work on extinction. In a book recalling a lifetime of investigation into extinction, Raup explains with precision why the classical Darwinian account of extinction is unsatisfying.[56] In the classical view, perfectly explicit in Darwin's *Origin*, extinction is a consequence of natural selection. As natural selection transforms species, some of them happen to be fitter in the competition with other species. The less favoured forms decrease in number and finally go extinct.[57]

Raup does not deny that species go extinct in this way. He recognises, moreover, that Darwin's intuition has generated a great deal of interesting research in the ecology of extinction. But he says that this is not the whole story. In Raup's view, mass extinction events have been rather frequent in the history of the earth, even if most of them have not been as spectacular as the mass extinctions at the end of the Permian and the Cretaceous periods. So much mass extinction can hardly be explained only on the basis of biotic factors, and even less on the basis of interspecific competition alone. Major physical changes seem to be involved, with complex ecological consequences. In episodes of mass extinction, species go extinct not because of their relative success in the ecological theatre, but because they are ill equipped to face brutal perturbation of their physical environment. An especially interesting aspect of Raup's position is his attitude towards natural selection. He insists that his interpretation of extinction does not refute natural selection, which remains the only possible explanation for adaptations. But he adds that natural selection alone could not have produced mass extinction events, or the explosive diversification that most often follows such events.

In such cases, natural selection is merely a local agent, not the fundamental cause accounting for the general pattern of events. Although Raup claims to be a Darwinian, this kind of argument is an excellent example of a departure from Darwinism in the sense of what Darwin named the 'well-grounded theory' of natural selection. For Raup, the theory is neither a necessary nor a sufficient explanation for the patterns of extinction and diversification observed by the palaeobiologist.

Other, similar challenges to Darwin's grand theory can be easily identified in macro-evolutionary studies. The proponents of punctuated equilibria have contested the traditional Darwinian account of divergence. For them, morphological divergence is not primarily the result of continued selection, but a consequence of speciation. As we have seen, on this account, most of the morphological change is concentrated in the period when cladogenesis is accomplished. Natural selection may and must surely play a role in this process. But it is the pace of speciation (and extinction) events, not the intrinsic mechanics of natural selection, that determines the genealogical and macro-ecological patterns observed at a large geological scale.[58]

It is unclear what kind of causal theories could explain and unify patterns interpreted in this way. Perhaps there are no such theories to be had, but only ever more complete catalogues of the unique sequences of causes and effects which, together, constitute the history of life. Present knowledge about mass extinction and explosive diversification seems to indicate that these kinds of historical events indeed cannot be subsumed under a single causal theory. If this is so, then there is no point in looking for a theory to replace Darwin's explanation of macro-evolution through natural selection. The aim must instead be the more modest one of reconstructing particular chains of causes and effects, responsible for this or that pattern or aspect of a pattern. Limited generalisations may be possible, but probably no more that that. Natural selection will always be useful for such reconstructive purposes, because natural selection is likely to operate constantly. But, on this sceptical view, this constant action does not justify the claim that natural selection 'explains' macro-evolutionary phenomena.

This epistemically bleak prospect explains why contemporary evolutionary biologists working on macro-evolution, in particular palaeobiologists and biologists working on phylogenies, are now more interested in patterns than in processes. In spite of its tremendously increased theoretical and experimental basis, evolutionary biology remains today a largely descriptive and historical science.

VII CONCLUSION

Has Darwin's theory of evolution withstood the test of time? Earlier we noted the strange singularity of a modern scientific discipline that has never ceased to structure its debates by reference to the work of one figure. The reason for the continued vitality of Darwinism is not that Darwin 'was right'. Actually, in comparison with modern standards, he was wrong on many points, or, more precisely, partially wrong. As we have seen in this chapter, Darwin's thinking about evolution has constantly been rectified rather than refuted. What explains the vitality of Darwinism is the heuristic power of the concepts that Darwin left to his followers: variation, competition, inheritance, chances of survival and reproduction, descent and genealogical arrangement. These replaced or marginalised the much less fecund concepts of organisation, type, metamorphosis, species and taxonomic rank. The former, Darwinian categories, it now seems, pick out real properties; while the latter, pre-Darwinian categories are a matter of mere convenience.[59]

So how did Darwin do it? How can we explain his success at developing concepts with such a firm grip on the science and phenomena of evolutionary biology? Here, perhaps, is part of the answer. Recall that Darwin had an exceptionally thorough acquaintance with the philosophical debates in his time over the nature and structure of scientific theories. Michael Ruse has even spoken of 'Darwin's debt' to the philosophers, especially John Herschel. Ruse is right. Darwin may well not have read much philosophy; but the model of scientific theorising that he found in Herschel in the early 1830s was certainly of the utmost importance for his own creativity in the field of philosophical natural history.[60] Darwin's framing ideas are almost always in a zone intermediate between 'general facts' of nature and theoretical 'hypotheses' justifiable through their consequences. His special talent was to understand that this methodological approximation was crucial to the success of causal theories in natural history. Descent with modification, while more of a 'general fact' than a 'hypothesis', is nevertheless both. Natural selection, while more of a 'hypothesis' than a 'general fact', is nevertheless both. This curious feature of what the French philosopher of science Gaston Bachelard might have called Darwin's 'spontaneous epistemology' opened the route to an indefinite number of rectifications, on the side of both theory and empirical data.

NOTES

I would like to thank Jon Hodge and Greg Radick for their useful comments and suggestions on the content of this chapter. I am especially indebted to Greg Radick for his linguistic help in the final revision.

1. On the history of the term 'Darwinism', see J. R. Moore 1991 and Ruse 1992.
2. On the social and political consequences of Darwinism, see Paul, this volume.
3. Ruse 1996.
4. This double strategy of justification of the principle of natural selection is made explicit in the introduction to *The Variation of Animals and Plants Under Domestication* (C. Darwin 1868). For more details, see Gayon 1997. See also Hodge, Waters and Hull, this volume.
5. In his *Palingénésie philosophique* (1769), Bonnet argued that God had prearranged the occurrence of new species in the germs of the first

organisms he had created. For this reason, Bonnet extended the use of the word 'evolution' (literally 'unfolding') to the genesis of species.

6. Spencer [1864–7] 1884.
7. Cf. R. J. Richards 1992 on possible affinities between Darwin's theorising about evolution and the tradition of embryological progressionism.
8. C. Darwin 1959, 264–5.
9. Mivart 1871.
10. Darwin to A. Gray, 11 May 1863, in F. Burkhardt *et al.* 1985–2001, *Correspondence* XI, 403.
11. C. Darwin [1859] 1964, 302.
12. C. Darwin 1959, 507.
13. C. Darwin 1959, 751.
14. Bowler 1983.
15. On American creationism, see Numbers 1992. On its latest variant, the 'intelligent design' movement, see Ruse, this volume.
16. Kuhn 1970.
17. Bowler 1983; Gayon 1998.
18. Haeckel coined the word in 1866, and provided many hypothetical examples (Haeckel 1866). In the same year, the first phylogenetic tree for a real group of fossil organisms, with clear reference to specific geological epochs, was proposed by Gaudry for fossil elephants (Gaudry 1866). On post-Darwinian species genealogies, see Bowler 1996.
19. For these debates, see Hull 1987. On the conceptual problems involved in generating and testing genealogical hypotheses, see Sober, this volume.
20. Zittel 1895; Dépéret 1907; Schindewolf 1936; Vialleton 1929.
21. Vialleton 1929.
22. Simpson 1944.
23. Eldredge and Gould 1972. On the history of saltationist theorising in evolutionary biology, see Schwartz 1999.
24. Extinction may also be expected to play an important role in saltationist theories of evolution.
25. Woese *et al.*, 1990.
26. Woese 1998, 11044–5.
27. Margulis 1981. On the history of symbiosis in evolutionary thinking, see Sapp 1994.
28. I use the word 'pattern' here in the modern sense of 'a class of historical events', as opposed to a causative process. See Eldredge and Cracraft 1980.
29. See note 4.
30. On Darwin's views on inheritance, see Endersby, this volume. Even those who accepted the existence of natural selection sometimes had doubts about its ability to cause all of evolution in the time made

available by the physicists' estimates of the age of the earth. On these debates, and especially, the contributions of Lord Kelvin (William Thomson), see Burchfield 1975.

31. Jenkin [1867] 1973.
32. For further discussion of this complex story, see Provine 1971 and Gayon 1998.
33. Gayon 1998.
34. On the founders of evolutionary genetics, see the papers collected in Sarkar 1992.
35. Gayon 1998. For a recent account of the controversies surrounding Kettlewell's claims, see Hooper 2002.
36. Quote from, C. Darwin 1868, chs. 21 and 28.
37. Kettlewell 1955. On Kettlewell's experiments, see Rudge 1999 and Hagen 1999. Weldon's work on crabs in the 1890s did not constitute exhaustive proof for natural selection. As he himself recognised, he was not able to establish the heritability of the characters he considered (Gayon 1998).
38. Fisher 1930. For discussion, see Radick, this volume.
39. Lewontin 1970.
40. Dobzhansky 1937. On Dobzhansky, see Adams 1994.
41. J. Huxley 1942, ch. 1, sect. 1.
42. See Waters, this volume.
43. On the Modern Synthesis, see Mayr and Provine 1980 and Depew and Weber 1995, chs. 10–12.
44. On the centennial celebrations in the United States, see Tax 1960 and Smocovitis 1999.
45. On the history of the Darwinian concept of adaptation, see Radick, this volume. On some of the conceptual problems involved in generating and testing adaptive hypotheses, see Sober, this volume.
46. Lewontin 1974.
47. Kimura 1968; King and Jukes 1969.
48. For a general review, see Sober and Wilson 1998.
49. C. Darwin [1871] 1981. See Richards, this volume. Although it might appear that Darwin appeals to group selection at several points, such as in his explanation of the origins of neuter worker ants, Darwin in the end almost always appeals to family selection, a process compatible with individual selection. For discussion, see Gayon 1998, esp. 70–3.
50. Important exceptions are the Oxford zoologists of the 1910s and 1920s, who did appeal to group selection in their ecological work. See Morrell 1997, ch. 7.
51. V. C. Wynne-Edwards, trained at Oxford, wrote the classic defence of group selection. See Wynne-Edwards 1962.
52. For further discussion, see Rosenberg, this volume.

53. Kauffman 1993.
54. C. Darwin [1859] 1964, 80–1.
55. Dobzhansky 1937, 12.
56. Raup 1991.
57. C. Darwin [1859] 1964, 109–11.
58. Eldredge and Gould 1972; Eldredge 1989; Gould 2002.
59. For instance, Darwin denied that species as a category could be defined, or that taxonomic ranks had an independent objective existence. What mattered to Darwin was the evolutionary significance of species and higher (or lower) taxa. Whether a given group of organisms had this or that taxonomic rank was for him a pragmatic issue. On Darwin's concept of species, see e.g. Stamos 1996 and 1999.
60. Ruse 1975. See also Sloan and Hull, this volume.

Part III
Philosophical themes

ELLIOTT SOBER

11 Metaphysical and epistemological issues in modern Darwinian theory

I A TWO-PART THEORY

Like Darwin's own theory of evolution, the modern Darwinian theory of evolution has two main elements:

> The Tree of Life: All organisms now alive on earth trace back to a common ancestor.
>
> Natural Selection: Natural selection has been an important cause of the similarities and differences that exist in the earth's biota.

The first of these propositions says that any two contemporary organisms have a common ancestor. Human beings are genealogically related to each other, but each human being also has a common ancestor with chimps, dogs, clams, daffodils, bacteria and yeast.[1] The second proposition, as I have formulated it, does not say that natural selection is the *only* cause of evolution. Indeed, it should be understood to leave open the possibility that there are traits for which natural selection is entirely irrelevant. This is the big picture, and evolutionary biology is devoted to filling in the details.

Although Darwinism is easy to describe, this simple theory gives rise to a rich range of metaphysical and epistemological questions. It is the purpose of this chapter to discuss some of them. In conformity with the structure of Darwinian theory, I have chosen one metaphysical and one epistemological problem from each of the two big ideas. I begin with a problem in the metaphysics of natural selection – the role of chance – followed by a problem in the metaphysics of the tree of life – the nature of a biological species. Turning from metaphysics to epistemology, the later sections of the chapter examine the testing of hypotheses about genealogical relatedness (the tree of life) and the testing of adaptive hypotheses (natural selection).

II THE LOGICAL CHARACTER OF DARWINIAN THEORY

Before moving on to these four topics, it is useful to contemplate the logical character of the two propositions that comprise the Darwinian theory. Each is a historical claim, not a law of nature. Laws of nature are conventionally understood to be empirical generalisations that do not refer to any place, time or individual. In addition, they cannot be true accidentally; they are supposed to possess a kind of necessity (*nomological*, not *logical*). In contrast, the two propositions we are considering are expressed in singular statements about the organisms that happen to exist on earth.

In the days when philosophy of science was dominated by philosophy of physics, this feature of Darwinian theory was a matter of concern, if not embarrassment. With Newtonian mechanics, relativity theory and quantum mechanics as their paradigms of what a scientific theory should be like, the logical empiricists often equated science with the search for law. Since the Darwinian propositions are not laws, in what sense do they constitute a scientific theory at all? Now, in these post-positivist times, the impulse to make biology fit this physical ideal is less compelling. It now seems natural to recognise that sciences are of two types – *nomothetic* and *historical*. Nomothetic sciences aim at the discovery of laws; they use historical information about specific objects as a means to that end. Historical sciences aim to discover facts about the histories of specific objects; they use information about laws as a means to that end.[2]

This broader picture of what counts as science allows us to recognise that physics contains disciplines of both types, and so does evolutionary biology. The physical theories cited above belong to nomothetic disciplines. But physicists are also interested in the histories of stars and galaxies; as such, astronomy is an historical science. Indeed, the division of nomothetic from historical sciences need not be strict. Astronomers are interested in the histories of specific stars and also try to describe the laws that govern the development of stars. In the same way, biologists seek to understand the evolution of specific groups of organisms and also to describe the laws that govern evolutionary change. A student of the social insects might also develop general models of sex ratio evolution.

Although theoreticians in evolutionary biology seek to formulate generalisations that are not true simply by accident (as is the case for many statements about 'evolutionary trends' – for example, that size increase has been more common than size reduction in the earth's evolving lineages), there is a feature of these generalisations that fails to conform to the logical empiricist concept of law. Whereas the logical empiricists held laws to be empirical rather than mathematical, models in evolutionary biology are 'if... then' statements that are mathematical truths. Consider, for example, elementary models in evolutionary genetics. They assign fitnesses to the various genotypes in a population, and assert that *if* those fitnesses have these values, *then* the population will evolve to certain future states. The 'if... then' statement that summarises such models is true *a priori*. No observations are needed to see that it is true; checking the algebra suffices. Of course, it is an empirical matter whether this or that natural population satisfies the conditional's antecedent. However, this empirical question concerns a *singular* statement – that *this population* exhibits certain properties.[3]

III CHANCE

The concept of chance features in evolutionary theory in two contexts. First, the variation on which natural selection operates is said to arise 'by chance'. Second, probabilities appear twice over in the characterisation of a selection process – the concept of fitness is defined probabilistically and finiteness of population size introduces a stochastic element into evolutionary trajectories.

Beginning with the first of these usages, we can discern one of its meanings in a remark of Darwin's: 'I have hitherto sometimes spoken as if the variations... had been due to chance. This, of course, is a wholly incorrect expression, but it serves to acknowledge plainly our ignorance of the cause of each particular variation.'[4] Here Darwin echoes the French astronomer Pierre-Simon Laplace, who claimed that a demon with complete knowledge of the relevant laws and initial conditions, and who had limitless computational powers, would never need to talk about what would *probably* occur. Rather, for such a being, 'nothing would be uncertain, and the future, and the past, would be present to its eyes'.[5]

A second meaning that modern biologists attach to the idea that variation arises by chance came to the fore only after Darwin's time. This is the doctrine, due to the German biologist August Weismann, that beneficial variations do not arise *because* they would be beneficial.[6] This doctrine amounts to a rejection of the Lamarckian idea that there is inheritance of acquired characteristics. Applied to the distinction between genotype and phenotype, Lamarckism requires that a phenotype acquired by parents should change the genes that parents transmit to their offspring. Whereas the blacksmith gets big muscles because and only because he works at the forge, his son develops big muscles whether he exercises them or not – an acquired character is transformed into one that is 'innate'. When modern biologists say that mutations occur 'by chance', one thing they mean is that this Lamarckian causal pathway does not exist.

I now turn to the question of whether there is a 'chance element' in the process of natural selection itself. Modern biologists define natural selection in terms of the concept of fitness – a selection process occurs precisely when there is variation in fitness. An organism's fitness is its 'ability' to survive and reproduce. This ability is represented probabilistically, in terms of a fertilised egg's probability of reaching adulthood and the adult organism's expected number of offspring.

We may begin with the point that fitness is a theoretically interesting property because it is a property of *traits*. It is traits that evolve through multi-generational selection processes, whereas individual organisms are here today and gone tomorrow. Biologists care about the fitness of dorsal fins, not about the fitness of individual tunas. That said, evolutionary theory does not *reify* traits; the fitness of a trait does not float free of the fitnesses of the individuals that have the trait. The two are linked by a simple formula – the fitness of a trait is just the average fitness of the individual organisms that possess the trait.[7]

Let us apply this framework to a concrete example. Suppose that running speed is evolving in a population of zebras. Some zebras run fast while others run slowly. If the frequencies of these traits are changing because there is natural selection, the two traits *running fast* and *running slowly* must differ in fitness. This means that fast zebras, on average, have a different fitness value from slow ones. Let us suppose that this is because fast zebras, on average, are better able to avoid being killed by predators.

Fast zebras differ among themselves in countless ways, so it is a mistake to think that there is a single fitness value that they have in common. Perhaps fast zebras have a thousand different probabilities of surviving to adulthood. Or maybe the lifetime of each zebra is a deterministic process wherein the organism is fated to die before reaching adulthood, or fated not to do so. This choice does not matter, because whether we average a thousand different probabilities, or average a thousand different 1's and 0's, the upshot is the same – we represent the fitness of the trait *running fast* as being between 0 and 1.

Once fitness values are assigned to the two traits, the fundamental question concerning what natural selection can be expected to produce depends on a simple comparative question – which trait is fitter? The absolute values of the fitnesses do not matter. If *running fast* is fitter than *running slowly*, then it is more probable than not that *running fast* will increase in frequency (assuming that the traits are heritable). But *how* probable is this outcome?

This is where the size of the population becomes relevant. The larger the population, the more certain it is that the fitter trait will increase in frequency. Consider an analogy – two coins that differ in their biases. The first has a probability of landing heads when tossed of 0.8, while the second has a probability of landing heads of 0.6. If I toss each coin a number of times, I expect the first to land heads more often than the second. However, the strength of this expectation depends on how many times the coins are tossed. If each is tossed twice, there is a considerable probability that the first coin will *not* yield the larger number of heads. But if I toss the coins a thousand times, this probability shrinks. The Law of Large Numbers says that as sample size increases, the probability increases that the frequency of heads produced by a coin will be close to its probability of landing heads. In the limit, the probability approaches unity (that is, certainty) that the first coin will land heads $80\% \pm \varepsilon$ of the time and the second will land heads with a frequency of $60\% \pm \varepsilon$, no matter how small ε is.

In coin tossing, small sample size gives 'chance' an enhanced opportunity to show itself. In evolution, it is small population size that has this effect. This is the idea that Motoo Kimura exploited in his 'neutral theory of molecular evolution'.[8] If traits differ only a little in fitness, and if population size is small enough, then traits will evolve by random walk. Modern Darwinians either reject the neutral theory or restrict their Darwinism to changes at higher levels of organisation; random walk is not evolution by natural selection.

I hope this brief discussion gives the reader a feeling for the fact that modern evolutionary theory is saturated with probability concepts. Probabilities are used to describe mutations, they are used to characterise the fitness values of traits, and they are used in models that allow one to calculate the outcomes of specified initial conditions. Some of these models are said to be 'deterministic'; they apply only to populations that are infinitely large. Such models may be suitable idealisations when the finite populations under study are big enough, but these deterministic models are a special case. The body of theory, taken as a whole, is probabilistic to its core.

What do these probability concepts mean? To begin with, they do not entail that determinism is false. This is not a problem on which biology has any purchase. When a biological model assigns a probability to a given event, there may be factors influencing the process leading up to that event that are not acknowledged in the biological model. These *hidden variables* may be biological in character (and so a more complex biological model can be constructed to capture them), or they may involve events that cannot be described in biological language. Either way, the theory is said to be causally incomplete. It is at this point that physics may have to take over – the buck has been passed. It is interesting that the buck never gets passed in the opposite direction – when physicists think that a physical model is incomplete, they do not turn to biologists for help. This asymmetry arises because there is no reason to think that biology is causally complete, but the idea that physics is causally complete is taken very seriously indeed.[9]

In order to investigate how the probability concepts used in evolutionary biology should be interpreted, let us assume that determinism is true. The Laplacean interpretation (with which the quotation from Darwin agrees) is that probability concepts must therefore be placeholders for ignorance; either determinism is false or probabilities must describe subjective degrees of belief.

There is a third possibility. Consider, first, the fact that the mathematical formalism of the probability axioms can be interpreted in terms of *actual frequencies*. Under this interpretation, 'the probability is 1/2 that the next toss of this coin will land heads' means that the coin's history of tosses (past, present and future) yields 50 per cent heads. I do not claim that this interpretation does justice to much of what we want to say in probability language – after all, a fair coin can be tossed an odd number of times – but it does bring out the possibility that probability statements can describe objective features of the world even if determinism is true.

The question of whether probability statements can be objectively true in a deterministic world needs to be separated from the pragmatic question of which statements we should use in making a prediction. If we toss a coin and determinism is true, full information will allow us to predict with certainty whether the coin will land heads. If we had this full information, we would not use the fact that the coin landed heads half the time in past tosses to infer that the probability of heads on the next toss is $^1/_2$. However, this is a pragmatic point, not a semantic one. The fact that we would not *use* the probability statement to make our prediction does not mean that it is not objectively *true*.

Scientists introduce probability models to describe repeatable processes that exhibit different outcomes with different frequencies. The probability of an outcome is not the same as the observed frequency, but rather is a theoretical quantity introduced to explain and predict that observed frequency. Like all theories, probabilistic theories are inferentially connected to observations. Values for probabilities are estimated from observed frequencies, and postulated probabilities make predictions about which observations will (probably) occur. When we ask whether nonprobabilistic theoretical postulates are objectively true, all we can do is point to the confirmation that those theories have received. This is why we are entitled to think that electrons objectively exist – they are not figments of our imagination. Precisely the same standard should be applied to the question of whether various probability concepts are objective. We know that uranium has a given half-life; this is an objective feature of that substance. The same holds true of the mutation probabilities and fitness values discussed in evolutionary biology.[10]

This point about the interpretation of probability concepts in a deterministic world has implications for how probabilities should be understood if determinism is false. Suppose that a complete physical theory were to assign a probability of x to a given event (where $0 < x < 1$). What does this imply about the probability that some other (perhaps biological) theory must assign to that event? Must the other theory also assign a value of x, on pain of being dismissed as 'merely subjective' (or just outright false)? The answer is *no*. The physical theory assigns a value of x by conditionalising on a set of (true) propositions P. A different theory can conditionalise on a different set of (true) propositions Q, and thereby assign a value of y. The probability statements do not conflict, since they conditionalise on different propositions. Laplace assumed that determinism is true, and concluded that all probability statements are mere confessions of ignorance. But the deeper position he defended goes beyond the assumption of determinism – this is the idea that the only objective probabilities are the ones provided by a theory that is causally complete. Here is a reductionist thesis that we should reject.[11]

IV ESSENTIALISM AND THE SPECIES CONCEPT

Species have long been a favourite example that philosophers cite when they discuss *natural kinds*.[12] For example, John Stuart Mill claims that *human being* is a natural kind, but the class of *snub-nosed individuals* is not, on the grounds that 'Socrates is a human being' allows one to predict many of the other characteristics that Socrates has, but 'Socrates is snub-nosed' does not.[13] Aristotelian essentialism endows the concept of natural kind with a more burdensome characterisation. Natural kinds not only have predictive richness; in addition, they have *essences*. The essence of a natural kind is the necessary and sufficient condition that all and only the members of the kind satisfy. Indeed, it is a necessary truth that the members of the kind, and they alone, have this essential property. Further, the essence is explanatory; the fact that an individual has this species-typical essence explains many other features that the individual possesses.

Besides citing biological species as examples, philosophers often point to the chemical elements as paradigm natural kinds. Gold is a kind of substance; its essence is said to be the atomic number 79.

This atomic number is what makes a lump of matter an instance of gold. And atomic number explains many other properties that gold things have. According to Saul Kripke and Hilary Putnam, science is in the business of empirically discovering the essences of natural kinds.[14] Formulated in this way, essentialism is not established by the existence of trivial necessary truths. It is a necessary truth that all human beings are human beings, but this does not entail that there is an essence that human beings have. It also is important to separate the claim that kinds have essences from the claim that individuals in the kind have essential properties.[15] The fact that different elements have different atomic numbers leaves open the possibility that an individual may persist through time as it changes from being made of one element to being made of another. Essentialism does not rule out the possibility of radioactive decay (nor of more mundane replacements, as in the constantly rebuilt ship of Theseus).

The example of the chemical elements illustrates a further feature that kind essences are supposed to have. Notice that 'atomic number 79' does not refer to any place, time or individual. What makes two things members of the same natural kind is that they are similar in the requisite respect. There is no requirement that they be causally connected to each other. The essence is intrinsic, not relational.

Although philosophers who accept this essentialist picture of the chemical elements usually think that chemistry has already discovered the essences that various chemical kinds possess, they must concede that biology so far has not done this for biological species. Is this simply because biology's work is not yet done? No – there are strong reasons to think that Darwinian theory undermines this essentialist picture of biological species.[16] Species are not natural kinds, at least not on the usual essentialist construal of what a natural kind is.

The reasons for this conclusion need to be stated carefully. The fact that species evolve is, *per se*, not a conclusive argument against essentialism. Just as essentialists can agree that chemical elements undergo transmutation, so essentialists can agree that lineages undergo evolution, with ancestor and descendant belonging to different species. And the fact that there are vague boundaries between species is not, in itself, a refutation of essentialism, either. When an atom of uranium-235 gives rise to atoms of bromine and lanthanum, there may be intermediate stages of the process in which it is indeterminate what the natural kinds are to which the matter belongs.[17]

Unfortunately, there still is disagreement in evolutionary biology about how the species category should be understood. The most popular definition is Ernst Mayr's[18] *biological species concept.*[19] Its anti-essentialist consequences are to a large extent also the consequences that other species concepts have, so we may examine it as an illustrative example. Mayr's idea is that a biological species is an ensemble of local populations that are knit together by gene flow. The individuals within local populations reproduce with each other. And migration among local populations means that there is reproduction between individuals in different populations as well. This system of populations is reproductively isolated from other such systems. Reproductive isolation can be a simple consequence of geographical barriers, or it can mean that the organisms have behavioural or physiological features that prevent them from producing viable fertile offspring even when they are brought together. Reproductive isolation allows two species to evolve different characteristics in response to the selection pressures imposed by their different environments. However, the different phenotypes that evolve are not what make the two species two; it is reproductive isolation, not physical dissimilarity, that is definitive.

Mayr initially allowed two populations to belong to the same species if there is *actual or potential* interbreeding between them, but he later changed the definition so that *actual* interbreeding is required. This raises the question of what the time scale is on which interbreeding must take place. How often must individuals in different local populations reproduce with each other for the two populations to belong to the same species? Indeed, the same question can be posed about individuals living in the same local population. Another detail that needs to be addressed concerns individuals that exist at different times. Human beings who are alive now are not having babies with human beings who lived thousands of years ago. What makes past and present human beings members of the same species? One necessary condition is that human beings now and human beings then are genealogically related. But this is clearly not sufficient; otherwise, we could not make the distinctions we do between a present-day species and a distinct ancestral species. Finally, I should note that

Mayr's definition excludes the possibility of asexual species; this is another feature that has made it controversial.

The important point about Mayr's definition is that similarity is neither necessary nor sufficient for conspecificity. Members of the same species may have very different characteristics. And if creatures just like tigers evolved independently in another galaxy, they would not belong to the species to which earthly tigers belong. Conspecificity is defined by the causal-historical connections that arise from reproductive interactions. Biological species and chemical elements are very different in this regard.

Evolutionary biologists talk about species in the same way they discuss individual organisms. Just as individual organisms bear genealogical relationships to each other, so species are genealogically related. Just as organisms are born, develop and die, so species come into existence, evolve and go extinct. These considerations led Michael Ghiselin and David Hull to maintain that *species are individuals, not natural kinds*.[20] There is room to doubt, however, that species are as functionally integrated as individual organisms often are. The parts of a tiger depend on each other for survival; excise an arbitrary 30 per cent of a tiger, and the tiger dies. However, the extinction of 30 per cent of a species rarely causes the rest of the species to go extinct. This suggests that individuality (in the sense of functional interdependence of parts) comes in degrees, and that species are often less individualistic than organisms often are. Still, Hull and Ghiselin's main thesis remains; perhaps it should be stated by saying that species are *historical entities*.[21]

Similar points apply to broader classificatory groupings, that is, higher taxa. Although ordinary language may suggest that carnivores all eat meat, this is not how biologists understand *Carnivora*. Taxa are understood genealogically; they are *monophyletic groups*, meaning that they are composed of an ancestral species and all of its descendants. Pandas belong to *Carnivora* because they are descended from other species in *Carnivora*; the fact that pandas are vegetarians does not matter. Superspecific taxa, like species themselves, are conceptualised as big physical objects; they are chunks of the genealogical nexus. And just as species are often not very individualistic, superspecific taxa are even less so.[22]

The chemical kinds do not comprise an *ad hoc* list. Rather, there is a theory, codified in the periodic table of elements, that tells us how to enumerate these chemical kinds and how they are systematically related to each other. To say what the chemical kinds are, we can simply consult this theory; we do not, in addition, have to do fieldwork. No such theory exists in biology for species and higher taxa; fieldwork is the only method that biology has for assembling its list of taxa. The terms 'botanising' and 'beetle collecting' both allude to this feature of systematic biology. Species and higher taxa are things that happen to come into existence owing to the vagaries of what transpires in the branching tree of life.

It does not follow that there are no natural kinds in evolutionary biology. Perhaps sexual reproduction is a kind; perhaps being a predator is another.[23] What makes it true that two organisms each reproduce sexually, or that both are predators, is that they are similar in some respect; it is not required that they be historically connected to each other. The sexual species do not form a monophyletic group, and neither do the predators. These kind terms appear in models of different evolutionary processes; there are models that explain why sex might evolve and models that describe the dynamics of predator/prey interactions. Although Darwin's theory of evolution undermines essentialist interpretations of species and higher taxa, it is another matter whether essentialism is the right way to understand these other, nontaxonomic, theoretical categories.

V TESTING HYPOTHESES ABOUT COMMON ANCESTRY

Although a great deal of work in evolutionary biology is devoted to inferring phylogenetic relationships, almost none of it provides a test of the tree-of-life hypothesis. When biologists attempt to reconstruct the phylogenetic relationships that link a set of species, they usually *assume* that all the taxa under study are genealogically related. Whatever method one uses – cladistic parsimony, distance measures, or maximum likelihood methods – the typical question is *which* tree is the best one, not *whether* there is a tree in the first place.[24]

This is not to say that biologists have totally ignored the issue of how the tree-of-life hypothesis might be tested. For example, Francis Crick, co-discoverer of the double helical structure of the genetic molecule DNA, argued that the genetic code is a 'frozen accident', meaning that the pattern by which nucleotide triplets code for amino acids is functionally arbitrary.[25] Given Crick's thesis, the (near) universality of the genetic code among the earth's organisms provides strong evidence that all trace back to a common ancestor. If the tree-of-life hypothesis were true, we would expect the code to be universal; however, if lineages arose separately, we would not expect them to exhibit the same code. This argument is often repeated as if it constitutes a conclusive case for the tree-of-life hypothesis, but, in fact, the claim that all codes are equally fit raises subtle and ongoing questions. For example, it has been argued that the code we now observe is optimal.[26] If this turns out to be correct, the argument for the tree-of-life hypothesis that appeals to the universality of the genetic code must be rethought. If there is a selective advantage to the code we observe, the question of whether the tree-of-life hypothesis or the hypothesis of multiple start-ups is better supported will depend on quantitative considerations – how much of a selective advantage did the code we observe possess, how much time would there have been for selection to make over a lineage that initially exhibited an alternative, and how deep and wide is the 'valley' that separates a code on one adaptive peak from a code on another?

I now turn to the methods that biologists use to evaluate competing phylogenetic hypotheses that all assert that the taxa under study have a common ancestor. Parsimony is the method most often used. The basic idea can be understood by considering the two trees depicted in Figure 11.1. Suppose we observe that Sparrows and Robins both have wings, but that Crocodiles do not. On the assumption that winglessness is the ancestral condition (that it is the character state

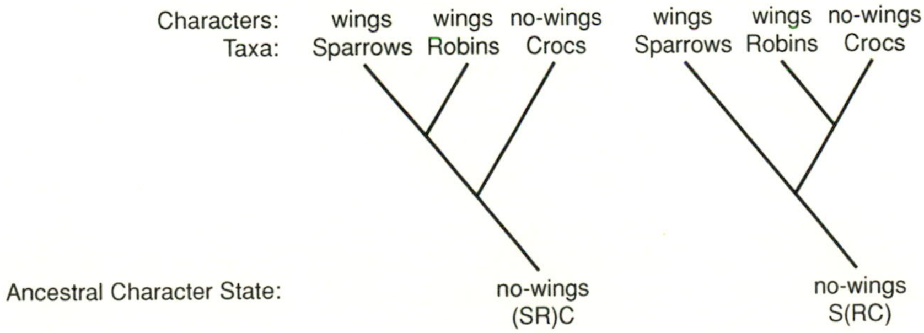

Figure 11.1. Parsimony favours the (SR) C tree on the left.

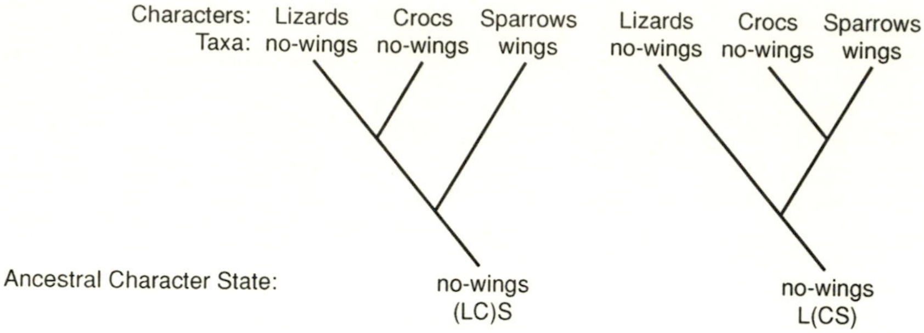

Figure 11.2. Parsimony does not discriminate between these trees.

of the common ancestor at the root of the tree),[27] the (SR)C tree can explain the observations by postulating a single change in character state (from no wings to wings) in the tree's interior; the S(RC) tree, on the other hand, requires two such changes. Thus, the (SR)C tree provides the more parsimonious explanation of the data.

Now consider the problem represented in figure 11.2, which also involves evaluating two trees. We observe that Lizards and Crocodiles lack wings, but that Sparrows have them. If winglessness is the ancestral condition, the (LC)S tree and the L(CS) tree each can explain the observations by postulating a single change in character state. If parsimony is our guide, we will conclude that this character distribution does not discriminate between the two phylogenetic hypotheses.

As this pair of examples illustrates, parsimony treats some similarities, but not others, as evidence of common ancestry. Notice that the similarity considered in figure 11.1 is derived, while that in figure 11.2 is ancestral. The principle of cladistic parsimony regards only the former as evidentially significant. Parsimony therefore is a different methodology from that of phenetic clustering, which counts *all* similarities (ancestral as well as derived) as evidence of relatedness.

In addition to parsimony and phenetic clustering, there is a third approach to phylogenetic inference, which is explicitly statistical. The maximum likelihood approach is to find the phylogenetic tree that maximises the probability of the observations.[28] In terms of the problem depicted in figure 11.1, the question will be whether the (SR)C hypothesis makes the observations more probable than the S(RC) hypothesis does. This question cannot be answered until a probabilistic model of character evolution is provided.

Unfortunately, biologists who do not already know the genealogy of a set of taxa will often also be in the dark as to the rules of character evolution that those taxa obeyed. And if one simply *assumes* that a given process model is correct, maximum-likelihood inference of phylogenetic trees can lead one seriously astray, if that model is mistaken.

Although biologists usually use parsimony and phenetic clustering without stating an explicit process model, this does not mean that these methods perform well regardless of how the evolutionary process proceeds. For example, a tree of the form (XY)Z can follow rules of character evolution that lead X and Z to exhibit far more similarities (both ancestral and derived) than X and Y. When this happens, parsimony and phenetic clustering will both mislead; each will converge on the wrong tree as more and more data are gathered.[29]

The problem of evaluating competing methods of phylogenetic inference is an active area of current investigation. The debate is by no means over. One central line of enquiry is the investigation of what parsimony and phenetic clustering presuppose about the evolutionary process. Another is the development of more realistic process models that can be used in maximum-likelihood inference.

VI TESTING ADAPTIVE HYPOTHESES

How can hypotheses about the effects of natural selection be tested? If you catch natural selection in the act, you can observe the process of replacement unfold, and empirically determine whether the trait that is increasing in frequency allows its bearers to survive better and reproduce.[30] If the zebras in the herd you are observing differ in running speed, you can check whether fast zebras are killed by lions less often than slow ones. But suppose you come on the scene too late; the variation has disappeared, and so you cannot directly compare the fitness values of different traits. If all the zebras in the population you observe run fast, how are you to test the hypothesis that fast zebras replaced slow ones, and that this happened because slow zebras were more vulnerable to lion attack?

In fact, comparison still is possible, but you must conceive it on a wider scale. Rather than compare one zebra with another, you should compare one population to another. If running speed is an adaptive response of prey organisms to predator attack, then you should find that the running speeds of prey species differ in the same direction as the running speeds of their predators. If species A preys on species X, and species B preys on species Y, then if A runs faster than B, X should run faster than Y.[31] This is a modest deployment of what biologists call 'the comparative method'.[32] The comparison, of course, is *across* species, not within them.

Suppose the running speeds of A and X are 35 and 33 miles per hour respectively, and that the running speeds of B and Y are 22 and 19 miles per hour. This is evidence that running speed in predators and running speed in prey are not independent. It does not tell you whether predators evolved to catch their prey, or prey evolved to evade their predators, or both. Still less do these data tell you that the running speeds of the four species are *optimal*. After all, your verdict would have been the same if you had observed that the four running speeds are 50, 45, 10 and 7. The observations you made do not settle whether the observed running speeds are the best ones that the different species could deploy.

The attentive reader will have detected a change in subject in the preceding three paragraphs. I began by asking whether zebras run fast in order to avoid lions. I then shifted to the more general question of whether prey species run fast in order to avoid predators. These questions are not the same, and it is conceivable that the zebra–lion relationship differs from the relationship that obtains between most prey organisms and their predators. Though the questions are different, the shift is forced on us if all zebras run fast and we want to test adaptive hypotheses empirically. Adaptive hypotheses assert that natural selection played a specified *causal role*. And causal claims assert that one factor *makes a difference* in the expression of another. For example, the hypothesis that smoking causes lung cancer predicts that smokers should get cancer more often than nonsmokers, once one has controlled for other causal influences. If everyone smokes, the hypothesis cannot be tested.

Although these remarks may sound humdrum, they in fact have implications about a controversy that has stirred strong feelings in biology. This is the debate about *adaptationism*. Stephen Jay Gould and Richard Lewontin criticised biologists for uncritically espousing 'just-so' stories about natural selection.[33] They even went so far as to claim that adaptationism is unfalsifiable; since the defeat of one adaptive hypothesis allows you to invent another, there is no way to refute adaptationism as a claim about nature. Gould and Lewontin also defended a 'pluralistic' view of the evolutionary process, according to which natural selection is one, but not the only, important influence on trait evolution. John Maynard Smith responded by defending adaptationism – although he conceded that observations never test the claim that a trait is an adaptation.[34] This appeared to confirm the worst fears that critics of adaptationism harboured: adaptationism seems to be an undefended and indefensible assumption.

One clarification that this debate sorely needs concerns what adaptationism asserts as a claim about nature. Here it is useful to distinguish the following two propositions:

(I) Natural selection has been an important cause of the evolution of most phenotypic traits in most populations.
(O) Natural selection has been the only important cause of the evolution of most phenotypic traits in most population.

Gould and Lewontin say that they agree with Darwin that (I) is true. What they deny is that nonselective influences on trait evolution can be ignored. In this light, it does no good to point out that natural selection is the only resource that evolutionary theory has for explaining complex features like the vertebrate eye.[35] This is not at issue. The question is whether the features of the eye are optimal – whether natural selection has sifted through a rich array of variation and provided organisms with the best of the available phenotypes. The debate concerns the *hegemony* of natural selection, not whether selection is *important*; (O) is the heart of the matter.

To understand the debate about adaptationism, it is important to distinguish methodological claims from claims about nature. Gould and Lewontin advanced both – they criticised the inferential practices of their colleagues, and they advanced a pluralistic conception of how traits evolve. These points are separate. Their critics sometimes responded by claiming that the concept of adaptation is an indispensable tool in investigating nature.[36] The point is correct and important; both adaptationists and anti-adaptationists need optimality models if they are to determine empirically the degree to which an organism's traits are optimal. However, this observation does not establish that adaptationism is correct as a claim about nature, nor does it show that adaptationists have tested their hypotheses with sufficient rigour.

At the same time, it needs to be recognised that Gould and Lewontin overstated their contention that adaptationism is untestable. They are right that if one adaptationist explanation of a trait is refuted by observations, another can be constructed. However, the same can be said of a pluralistic model. Adaptationism and pluralism are both *isms*. Each describes the *kind* of explanation that most traits have without saying anything very specific about why any given trait evolved. It is *specific* optimality models and *specific* pluralistic models that, in the first instance, can be brought into contact with data. This does not mean that the *isms* are untestable, but just that they can be evaluated only in the long run.[37] Each embodies a large-scale generalisation about trait evolution; case studies of individual traits are the vehicles by which these larger generalisations can be judged.[38]

The controversy about adaptationism has been heated, but nowhere more so than in discussions of human evolution. Gould and Lewontin criticised adaptationism because they saw it as the deep problem afflicting E. O. Wilson's sociobiology.[39] For Gould and Lewontin, sociobiology was the symptom, naive adaptationism the disease. I began this section by discussing the methodological problems that need to be addressed if all zebras run fast. The very same problems arise in sociobiology when one considers a trait that all human beings share. Why are human beings able to speak a language? Why do human societies have religious practices and ethical norms? If a trait is a human universal, how can an adaptive explanation of the trait be tested? When we reach for the comparative method to answer this question, we run into a problem. The nice feature of running speed is that it is a quantitative characteristic; there is no difficulty in comparing the running speeds found in different species. But how can 'speaking a language' and 'having a religion' be redescribed, so that they become quantitative characters that render cross-species comparisons intelligible? This is the challenge that faces those who want human evolution to be part of the larger story.

VII CONCLUDING COMMENTS

It is remarkable that philosophical questions about meaning and methodology engage the attention of evolutionary biologists. Like Molière's Monsieur Jordan, who spoke prose without realising it, biologists will not always describe their research as philosophical in character, but the fact remains that this is part of what they are doing. Here is a case in which philosophy is continuous with the science it studies. However, it would be a mistake to conclude from the fact that philosophical questions are live issues in this science that something is amiss. Enquiry does not proceed with clear concepts and well-justified methods all laid out at the outset. Rather, the methods of science and the results of science both develop, with each informing the other.

In the previous sections on the testing of genealogical and adaptive hypotheses, I outlined some of the methodological questions that this two-part theory raises. Indeed, a good deal of current scientific work seeks to bring these two components – the tree of life and natural selection – into more intimate contact with each other. Hypotheses about phylogenetic relationships cannot be tested in isolation from models of the processes governing trait evolution. And adaptive hypotheses about trait evolution are increasingly being examined against the background of our knowledge of phylogenetic relatedness. Darwinism is a two-part theory, but the two parts are methodologically connected. The metaphysical picture is that life-on-earth is a large physical object, extended through space and time. Biological taxa are pieces of this branching tree, with characters evolving on branches according to rules that need to be described in the language of probabilities. So novel is this framework for describing nature that science is still developing methods for testing hypotheses concerning the details of the evolutionary world picture.

NOTES

My thanks to James Crow, Anthony Edwards, Ellery Eells, Chris Lang, Michael Steel, Christopher Stephens and the editors of this volume for useful comments on earlier drafts.

1. The tree-of-life hypothesis, thus stated, does not assert that life forms a phylogenetic tree in the strict sense of that term. As one goes from root to tips in a tree, lineages split but never join. Plant species formed by hybridisation do not form a tree, and the same is true when there is pervasive horizontal transfer, as is the case in some bacteria. See also Gayon, this volume.
2. See Sober 1993.
3. See also Beatty 1987; Lloyd 1988; and Thompson 1988.

4. In C. Darwin [1859] 1964, 131.
5. See Schweber 1983.
6. Mutation gives rise to novel *alleles*, but recombination is another source of variation, in that it generates novel *combinations* of already existing alleles.
7. See Mills and Beatty 1978 and Sober 1984.
8. Kimura 1983. See also Gayon, this volume.
9. See Sober 1999.
10. This brief discussion is not intended as a defence of scientific realism; the point is just that the standards we use for deciding whether electrons are objective should be the same as the standards we use for deciding whether probabilities are objective.
11. For a different interpretation, compare Brandon and Carson 1996.
12. This section is drawn from Sober 2002.
13. Mill 1872.
14. Kripke 1980 and Putnam 1975.
15. Enç 1986.
16. Hull 1965 and E. Mayr 1976.
17. See Sober 1994b.
18. See E. Mayr 1963, 1970.
19. For other species concepts, see Ereshefsky 1992.
20. Ghiselin 1974 and Hull 1978, 1987.
21. See Wiley 1981.
22. See Ereshefsky 1991.
23. On adaptations as forming a natural kind, see Radick, this volume.
24. It is widely held that if a given tree-selection method (e.g., parsimony) singles out the same tree as best when different data sets are considered, this is evidence that the taxa considered have a common ancestor. Penny *et al.* 1982 have made this argument rigorous. I suggest that the test is flawed – a tree can generate characters that are incongruent with each other, and a set of unrelated species can generate characters that all lead parsimony to the same (erroneous) tree.
25. Crick 1968.
26. In Freeland *et al.*, 2000.
27. Why think that winglessness is the ancestral condition? Characters are usually polarised by the method of outgroup comparison. See Sober 1988 for discussion.
28. See Lewis 1998.
29. Felsenstein 1978.
30. Endler 1986.
31. See Burt 1989 and Orzack and Sober 2001.
32. See Harvey and Pagel 1991.

33. In Gould and Lewontin 1979.
34. In Maynard Smith 1978.
35. See Dawkins 1983.
36. See Dennett 1995.
37. See Sober 1993 and also Orzack and Sober 1994.
38. In just the same way, the generalisation 'most speciation is allopatric' can be tested, but only indirectly, by looking at a range of case studies.
39. E. O. Wilson 1975.

KIM STERELNY

12 Darwinian concepts in the philosophy of mind

I A CLASH OF PERSPECTIVES?

Human beings are part of nature. We are primates, mammals, animals. Animals, in turn, are nothing but very complex biochemical systems. So humans are biochemical machines, though extraordinarily complex ones. That complexity ensures that it will rarely be practically possible to predict future human behaviour, or explain past human behaviour, through a fine-grained molecular understanding of human bodies. But, in principle, a detailed enough understanding of the physical and chemical processes internal to an agent would suffice to predict and explain all of that agent's behaviour. A full list of the complete physical, natural facts about an agent is all the facts there are. The natural story is the whole story. So, at least, the sciences of physiology, morphology, neuropsychology and the like suppose.

But humans are also conscious agents. We are aware of ourselves and our world. In Thomas Nagel's famous phrase, there is 'something that it is like' to be a person. What is more, we are *rational* agents. We are not, of course, perfectly rational. We make errors of reason and judgement. Most of the time, however, our beliefs about our immediate environment are sound, and our actions are rational in the light of those beliefs and our goals. My belief that good coffee is available in the student union may be false, perhaps even unreasonable. But given that I have that belief, and that I aim to have an espresso, my taking myself off to the union is rational. My colleagues, knowing these facts about me, can use that knowledge to predict my future actions and to explain my past ones. Such explanations are intentional explanations, and agents whose acts can be explained via their beliefs and preferences are intentional agents. In short, humans are conscious, deliberative, rational agents. So says 'folk psychology', the set of concepts for thinking about other people that we acquire in infancy and use through our lives.

Can the scientific and the folk perspectives both be right? For much of philosophy's modern history it has been supposed that the two perspectives are incompatible, and so one must be wrong. One response to the apparent clash between these perspectives has been to argue that the scientific perspective is incomplete. Notoriously, Descartes thought the human mind was not part of physical nature, and he continues to have intellectual descendants to this day.[1] More recently, an alternative incompatibilist position has been articulated. Eliminativists agree with Descartes' descendants that the folk and scientific perspectives cannot both be true. But they think that it is the folk perspective that must be rejected.[2]

Many philosophers nowadays, however, do not assume the folk and scientific perspectives are incompatible. Rather, they think both perspectives are right, and turn to a standard model, known as functionalism, to reconcile the two. On the functionalist view, folk psychology is a theory of human cognitive organisation that implicitly defines the nature of human cognitive states such as belief, preference, emotion and the like. These states, according to the theory, are functional states. In general, functional kinds are defined not by their physical constitution, but by their causal role. Something is a cat-door if it serves to let cats in and out of a house without human assistance or a permanently opened window, whatever its physical structure. Likewise, a kind of cognitive state – recognising a friend's face, say – is defined by the role it plays in mediating between sensory stimuli and behaviour, rather than by its physical structure. Just as every cat-door is a physical structure of some kind (but not always the same kind), so too every cognitive state is a physical structure of some kind (but not always the same kind). Hence humans can be both biochemical machines and intentional agents, just as a physical structure can be both a hinged plywood oval and a cat-door. A specific version of this idea is now very influential: the so-called 'computational theory of mind'. On this version of functionalism, the role a mental state plays in mediating between stimuli and behaviour is analysed in computational terms. A chain of thought from stimulus to response is a sequence of computations.[3] These days functionalism in one of its forms is the theory of choice for *compatibilist naturalists*: those who accept the scientific view of our place in the world, and take that to be compatible with folk psychology.

This compatibilist, functionalist, computational perspective is decidedly controversial. Some critics, influenced by the eliminativist perspective, argue that cognition is more deeply connected to the physical nature of the brain than functionalism suggests.[4] Other critics, impressed by the problem of incorporating subjective phenomena into our theory of mind, think that there is more to a mental state than its having a certain causal role in the organisation of behaviour.[5] I shall not give a comprehensive review of the debate here. Nor shall I do more than allude to the difficult problem of understanding the relationship between our cognitive capacities and the conscious, subjective aspects of our minds. Rather, I will concentrate on the relevance of Darwinism to compatibilist approaches to the mind. The issues are not straightforward. In some ways, as might be expected, a Darwinian perspective strengthens the compatibilist position. But in other ways, Darwinism threatens to undercut compatibilism.

II DARWINISM AS A MIXED BLESSING FOR THE COMPATIBILIST NATURALIST

The mechanism that Charles Darwin and his successors exploited to explain complex biological structures can be exported to new domains. Daniel Dennett has called Darwin's insight 'universal acid' because Darwin's conception of how complexity can arise is domain neutral. Random variation, stable selection and heritability will generate local adaptive change whatever the nature of the entities: genes, organisms, ideas.[6] Trial-and-error learning, for example, is now often interpreted as an essentially Darwinian process, one involving an undirected generation of a pool of behaviours, followed by selective retention of more successful ones. Experience fine-tunes our minds by processes analogous to those that built them over evolutionary time. A number of thinkers have attempted to apply the same ideas to change in human culture over time.[7]

Darwinism is of particular importance in the solution of one of compatibilist naturalism's most difficult problems: how does thought fit into the physical world? A folk explanation of behaviour depends on taking actions to flow from a combination of beliefs and preferences. My trip to the union is explained by my desperate desire for coffee, and my belief that the union is a coffee provider. Beliefs and preferences are representations of the world. But what in the physical world is a representation? I believe tigers to be the most handsome members of the cat family. But what makes my tiger thoughts *about* tigers? What makes certain neural structures within my brain a *symbol* of tigers?

This has turned out to be an exceptionally difficult question for the naturalist, for none of the obvious answers seem to work. Concepts are not images: the relation between a symbol and its target certainly does not depend on any physical resemblance between a structure in my brain and (say) real tigers. There are no tiny model tigers in my head. Nor is my concept of a tiger an ability to recognise or describe tigers. For I can have a concept without that ability. As it happens I can recognise tigers with fair accuracy. But I could make mistakes. With other concepts, I make more. My lesser-sand-plover thoughts are about lesser sand plovers, but I certainly would not undertake to pick one out of a crowd of greater sand plovers. The suggestion to be explored in the next section is that my tiger thought is about tigers because of the natural history of that thought. On this view, my tiger concept is an adaptation, one with the function of directing my behaviour with respect to tigers. The tiger concept exists in me because similar concepts in my ancestors helped them become ancestors, by making their interactions with tigers more successful (or rarer).

Darwinism thus promises to help the compatibilist naturalist account for the 'aboutness' of certain thoughts. But a Darwinian perspective brings problems as well as solutions. For one thing, it can lead to a picture of cognitive architecture that is directly in conflict with folk psychology. Paul Griffiths, for example, has recently used an evolutionary perspective to argue that the folk category of the emotions should be eliminated. He argues that certain core emotions – fear, anger, disgust and a few others – are integrated systems of arousal and response ('affect programs') built into us by evolution. Other so-called emotions – depression, romantic love – have very different evolutionary histories, developmental trajectories and physiological foundations. They are not the same kind of psychological state at all.[8] One slightly provocative way of expressing Griffiths' thesis is: there is no such thing as 'the emotions'.

The threat is not just to the folk view of the emotions but also to the folk view of agency. According to our folk conception, we are rational agents. Our actions are typically rational in the light of our beliefs and utilities. We act to maximise our expected utilities. Moreover those expectations themselves are in general rational. They are responsive to evidence. Many animals, by contrast, seem to have island intelligences – they are extraordinarily adept at some cognitive tasks, but hopeless at others. It is part of the folk image that we humans do not have island minds. We have domain-general intellectual capacities, supported by a capacity to learn about our social and physical environment, whatever that environment turns out to be like.

One important version of evolutionary psychology undermines this view of agency. According to proponents of this view, since humans are evolved organisms, we should not expect them to have general purpose, domain-independent reasoning and learning powers. Rather, evolutionary theory predicts that humans have particular cognitive talents with respect to particular problems posed in ancestral environments. On the plausible assumption that social exchange was a very important part of hominid ecology and society, humans will have well-developed cognitive skills for detecting would-be cheats and shysters. Since language is a very important part of human life, we have cognitive specialisations that mediate the learning and use of language. Since predicting the behaviour of members of our social group will often be a matter of life or death, we have cognitive specialisations for keeping tabs on our fellows. That is where folk psychology itself comes from. But Pleistocene hominids would not have evolved general purpose cognitive mechanisms that could be applied with success to any type of problem. In any given domain, the specialist in the domain would have beaten a generalist. And since the problems humans faced have been predictable over long periods, human minds are probably ensembles of special purpose devices.[9] I explore these claims more fully in the fourth section.

A second problem that Darwinism brings for the compatibilist naturalist is an increased explanatory burden. Sometimes, of course, it is obvious that cognitive capacities are adaptive. It is easy to see that being good at recognising the faces of other humans, for example, would have helped our ancestors to survive and reproduce. In less straightforward cases, we can sometimes at least make a plausible conjecture about the way a feature of our mental life adds to our fitness – for example, the fact that we enjoy some experiences and dislike others may enable us better to calculate costs and benefits.[10] But some characteristic human mental states seem not to add to their possessor's fitness at all. Modern evolutionary theory has developed several strategies for explaining how apparently altruistic actions have evolved in a world where selection typically rewards only those individuals whose watchword is 'look out for number one'.[11] But these are of limited use to the compatibilist, since they are widely interpreted as revealing psychological altruism to be a myth. An evolutionary perspective on altruism thus tends to exacerbate the tension between the scientific and the folk images of the mind.

There are still further explanatory difficulties. If a mental mechanism is an adaptation, it must not only boost its possessor's fitness, but also be evolvable. Complex adaptations are constructed one step at the time, with each step being an improvement over its predecessor. Once we begin thinking about complex human mental capacities in an evolutionary framework, we are faced with having to specify evolutionary pathways capable of building those capacities. The task is to show how gradual, adaptive changes in an initially simple capacity ultimately led to the emergence of the present complex capacity. That is no mean feat. After all, though all organisms need to sense and respond to some aspects of their environment, the vast majority manage to do so without anything remotely comparable to human, or even primate, cognitive complexity.

There are interesting conjectures on the general issue here.[12] But they are not worked out in detail, and the evidence needed to test them is difficult to gather. The problem of explaining how intentional psychology evolved from simpler cognitive organisations – the trajectory problem – is a serious one. Should a compatibilist naturalist be particularly worried by this fact? One reason to think not is that the problem appears to confront all who believe that human cognitive capacities have evolved by natural selection. The compatibilist-Darwinian does not seem to be in a worse situation than, say, the eliminativist-Darwinian when it comes to solving the trajectory problem.

An important dissent here is due to Patricia Churchland. In her view, evolvability considerations count against compatibilism and for eliminativism. She argues that in folk psychology the human mind is understood as something that could not possibly have evolved through a Darwinian process; hence no Darwinian should embrace folk psychology, much less seek to reconcile it with scientific psychology. According to Churchland, folk psychology characterises our beliefs and preferences as inner sentences. If folk psychology is the right view of human cognition, then human minds are qualitatively, not just quantitatively, different from the minds of any other living animals. So the trajectory from animal thought to human thought would involve a qualitative jump of some kind – something Churchland takes to be out of Darwinian bounds. By contrast, on the eliminativist view, human cognition is just a more complex version of animal cognition. For the eliminativist, the challenge is thus to explain how neural networks became more complex, powerful and flexible. That is tough. But it is not impossible.[13]

Churchland's argument can be resisted, however. First, there *are* qualitative changes in evolutionary trajectories. In the evolution of flight, for example, there must have been a transition from animals that could not fly to those that could. Second, it is far from certain that folk psychology is committed to a sentential view of thinking.[14] Third, no Darwinian thinks every feature of an organism is an adaptation – and that goes for mental features too. In thinking about cognitive adaptation, we must distinguish between a cognitive system and the states it produces. My ability to recognise faces is almost certainly an adaptation to human social life. My recognition of an old photo as a picture of Charles Darwin is not an adaptation. It is a product of an adaptive mechanism rather than being itself an adaptation. Only one person boosted her reproductive prospects by recognising Charles Darwin, and she was no ancestor of mine.

So some particular mental states are produced by adapted mental mechanisms, but they are not themselves adaptations – just as the colour of blood is not an adaptation, but merely a chemical side-effect of blood's adaptation for oxygen transport. It may be that the size and complexity of the mind generate cognitive by-products. Our ability to enjoy music, for example, might be a side-effect of communicative adaptations. However, the more complex and co-adapted a mental subsystem, the less it is likely to be a side-effect of some other evolutionary process. A compatibilist naturalist cannot think a mental mechanism is complexly structured and take it to be a mere side-effect of evolution. In the fifth section, I look in some detail at recent attempts to solve the trajectory problem for one particular complex human mental capacity: the capacity for articulate language.

III DARWINIAN SYMBOLS

What natural relationship exists between a mental symbol and the external target of that symbol? What is the natural connection between thought and the world in virtue of which a mental symbol is *about* its referent? In other words, what gives representations their meaning? One idea is that my tiger thoughts are about tigers in the way that lightning signifies rain. Lightning is a reliable sign of rain, just as a fresh dog-dropping is a reliable sign of a dog in the immediate neighbourhood. In the 1980s, Fred Dretske and Jerry Fodor attempted to use the lightning/rain relation as a model of the symbol/referent relationship. Lightning covaries with rain, and perhaps mental symbols covary with what they mean.[15] But the problems facing this view are desperately difficult.

For one thing, my tiger thoughts are not a reliable sign of tigers in the immediate neighbourhood; I rarely walk with tigers, but quite often think about them. Moreover, I can have thoughts about dinosaurs – animals which I have never seen. Arguably, I can have thoughts about dragons, and they have never existed at all. For example, I can think that it would be great if genetic engineers designed and built dragons. So the covariational analysis of meaning has to take perceptual representation as its central case. My thoughts about tigers do not in general covary with tigers. But perhaps some of my tiger thoughts, namely the thoughts I have in the presence of tigers – my *perceptual* tiger thoughts – do. Perhaps my ability to think about tigers in general depends, in some way, on my ability to perceive tigers when they are present.

But the problems do not end here. Consider a very simple case: a chicken that takes cover when it sees a hawk-shaped silhouette passing overhead. Intuitively, we want to say that the chicken's perceptual state is a symbol of a raptor, though doubtless a crude one. In other words, we think the chicken took cover *because it feared being attacked by a hawk*. But this particular kind of mental structure in the chicken will certainly not covary perfectly with a hawk being nearby. A chicken will take cover in response to various harmless birds and even to dummies and cutouts of various kinds. So if the meaning of the chickenish thought is settled just by what the chicken responds to, its 'hawk' thoughts will not mean 'hawk nearby'. They will mean 'hawk, or raven, or other biggish short-necked bird, or hawk-like cut-out nearby'. An absurd consequence follows: that the chicken never suffers from false alarms. When it nervously takes cover because a duck flies over head, we would have to say that there really was a hawk, or raven, or other biggish short-necked bird or hawk-like cut-out nearby. The chicken was not wrong.

This is known as the 'disjunction' problem. The logic of the covariational view of meaning presses the theory into replacing a covariation which is not perfect but which does intuitively capture the meaning of a symbol – the chicken alarm/hawk covariation – with a perfect symbol/world covariation. But the state of the world with which the symbol perfectly covaries is not a plausible candidate for its meaning. So this view of meaning re-interprets the chicken as a being that believes only truths, albeit very uninteresting ones. Chickens turn out to be very restrained in their judgements about their environment. Furthermore, sometimes meaning does not seem to line up even with an imperfect covariation. When false negatives are more to be avoided that false positives, a symbol may not even approximately covary with its target. Chickens in a state of nature are likely to be very cautious: their 'hawk' thoughts might be occasioned by real hawks in only a minority, perhaps a small minority, of cases.[16]

David Papineau and Ruth Millikan have suggested an alternative based on biological function.[17] The biological function of, say, the pattern on oystercatcher eggs is concealment. Those eggs are *camouflaged*. Eggs that were difficult for predators to spot against typical backgrounds of sand and debris were more likely to hatch than those easier to find. This selective history is what makes it true to say that the biological function of the pattern is camouflage. On any particular egg, the pattern has that biofunction even if it does not have that effect. The pattern is *supposed* to conceal the egg even if the egg is seen anyway; even if the egg is very easily seen, because the parent has laid it on white sand against which it stands out. Indeed, Millikan has pointed out that some structures almost never carry out their biological function. Sperm is her favourite example. The shape of human sperm has the function of driving the sperm to an egg to fertilise it. And yet almost no sperm scores. Similarly, thoughts have biological functions. Their function is to direct behaviour that adapts an organism to a specific feature of its environment. The chicken's thought is *about* hawks because its function is to adapt the chicken's behaviour to the presence of hawks in its environment. The blotchy pattern exists on contemporary oystercatcher eggs because of past selection. So too chickens take cover at hawk-caused shadows, because previous chickens with that tendency were more likely to live than those without it.

This view of meaning, of the symbol/world relationship, has some very attractive features. It explains why we want to say of the chicken that it is afraid of hawks, rather than being afraid of {hawks, ravens, vultures, other biggish short-necked birds, and hawk-like cutouts} even though the chicken takes cover when confronted with any member of the latter, larger group. For it is hawk avoidance, not {hawk, raven, vulture, other biggish short-necked bird, and hawk-like cut-out avoidance} that made its ancestors into ancestors. Now we can explain how it is possible to misrepresent. Misrepresentation is failure of function. When the chicken flees the duck overhead, the chicken has misrepresented its environment – that is, the chicken's internal state is not performing its selected role of hawk avoidance.

As the sperm example makes vivid, failure of function is common. This last point is very important. For many in this field have thought misrepresentation to be a fatal stumbling block for naturalised views of thought. The claim is that error, or misrepresentation, is a *normative* notion.[18] And normative claims cannot be defined in factual terms; this is an instance of the infamous 'fact/value' distinction. A teleosemantic theory of meaning promises to finesse this problem. Facts about what an organ, including a mental organ, is supposed to do are facts about the selective history of that organ. Those are natural facts.

The teleosemantic theory does, however, face very considerable problems of its own, and debate continues on the viability of this approach to the symbol/world relationship. The most difficult problem is that of scaling up. If chickens really have thoughts at all, the range of topics on which they cogitate is surely very limited. So for chickens it is quite plausible to suppose that each concept they can deploy has a selective history in its own right. If so, each chicken thought does have a biological function. That is manifestly not true of humans. We have concepts for a multitude of phenomena – coffee-pots, kiwis, x-rays, machine guns, lawyers, cafés – that as a species we have experienced only recently. Far too recently for selection to have built into our minds concepts for these kinds. Most of our concepts are not innate. So how can a biofunctional theory be extended to cover such concepts as these?

Millikan has argued that new human concepts inherit a biological function, second-hand, from the function of those cognitive devices we use to form and apply new concepts. Some chunks of our cognitive machinery have direct selective histories, and the other chunks inherit a function from them. Her example is the chameleons, which can adjust their skin colour pattern to match their background. She suggests that a chameleon in an unusual environment might have a genuinely novel pattern on its skin, a pattern never before generated in the history of the group. Nevertheless, Millikan argues, that pattern would have the function of rendering the beast invisible. For that is the direct function of the chameleon's pattern-building mechanisms. Papineau takes a different route, looking to an analogy between learning and selection to argue that even learned concepts can have biological functions. The adequacy of these strategies, however, is very much in question.[19]

Moreover, it is arguable that these teleosemantic theories have indeterminacy problems of their own. The problem is that there are many different ways of specifying both the dangers and the opportunities to which animals are adapted. Return to our chicken. Is its fear directed to a particular species of hawk? A few particularly dangerous and salient species? Raptors in general? Danger from the air, in whatever form? Danger, period? What facts, were we to know them, about the evolution of chickenry would settle this question? Human thoughts, do not forget, can be more or less specific. We are certainly able to think about (say) the swamp harrier, rather than raptors in general.

Finally, the teleosemantic approach has the apparent consequence that only evolved organisms have thoughts. Some have found this consequence deeply counter-intuitive. In a striking example of philosophers' predilections for thought experiments, we are asked to imagine 'swampman' – a human replica assembled by an extraordinary quantum accident. Such a replica, by hypothesis, has no evolutionary history at all, and, also by hypothesis, swampman exactly resembles an ordinary person. When swampman asks for a beer in a bar, the argument goes, surely swampman wants a beer. He has a beer-directed thought. But since his internal states have no evolutionary history, they have no biological function. There are no Darwinian symbols in his brain. The teleosemantic programme is committed to the view that when swampman utters the phonemes 'Beer, please', he does not want anything, beer included.

IV EVOLUTIONARY PSYCHOLOGY MEETS FOLK PSYCHOLOGY

Evolutionary psychologists typically defend a modular theory of mind. On that view, the mind is a cluster of *evolved information-processing mechanisms*.[20] Here the ideas of Noam Chomsky on language serve as a template for thinking about other cognitive skills. If Chomsky is right about language, the differences between languages are not profound, for variation between them is quite tightly constrained by an innate language-acquisition device. Moreover, that device contains conditional elements whose different settings explain many of the differences between languages. So language illustrates two themes of evolutionary psychology. Diversity is less profound than it appears, and it can be explained by a single mechanism operating in different circumstances. In following up this model, David Buss and Donald Symons argue that there are Darwinian algorithms of sexual attraction. These result in the tendency of human males to find those females attractive who bear the cultural marks of youth, and of females to find attractive those males that bear the cultural marks of high status. Simon Baron-Cohen and Dan Sperber have argued that we have a specific mental mechanism, a 'mind-reading' device, designed to enable us to anticipate others' behaviour.[21] This general picture of the mind, as comprising specific mental mechanisms or modules, is sometimes known as the 'Swiss army knife' model of the mind.

Suppose this hypothesis of evolutionary psychology is right. Human minds are ensembles of adapted modules. What follows for folk psychology? It is compatible with a partially modular theory of mind. For example, Fodor develops a hybrid architecture. He predates evolutionary psychology in defending the idea that much of human cognitive life rests on special purpose modules. But he also argues that we come equipped with a central processor with the critical role of maintaining an overall model of the agent's environment, and using that model to guide rational action.[22] But if there is no general purpose device – if there is nothing like a central processor – it is hard to see what the integrated, cohesive unity of a person's mental life could consist in. And it is hard to see how a rational actor model could accurately describe the pattern of human action. When humans respond to problems that were important in the environments in which our cognitive mechanisms evolved, and when they do so in environments relevantly like those ancestral environments, and when fitness consequences correlate well with individual welfare, then of course human behaviour may maximise expected utility. But much human behaviour is not directed to problems that were critical to our ancestors, and humans often act in environments very different from those in which humans evolved. So when we humans act outside the domains our minds are adapted for, we ought to expect frequent failure.

The evolutionary psychologists Leda Cosmides and John Tooby claim that is just what we find. We solve certain problems when they are about social exchange, but flounder hopelessly on logically equivalent problems in different domains. Sperber realises, though, that often our actions are successful even in evolutionarily novel circumstances, and he tries to explain this fact. He defends the view that the mind is wholly an ensemble of modules. But one of these modules, the metarepresentation module, can act as a surrogate general-purpose device. The function of the metarepresentation module is to guide our behaviour with respect to other humans. For we can estimate their actions best by estimating their representation of the world. Since the proper function of the metarepresentation module is to represent representations, we have a derived, second-hand capacity to represent anything, or at least anything that anyone else can represent.[23] But Sperber's explanation of religion and other human irrationalities depends on the fact that we can represent representations – other people's thoughts – without really understanding them or integrating them fully into our own mental world. Moreover, since Sperber's focus is on the transmission of religious and other culturally mediated myths, he has no explanation of how humans can effectively respond to novel aspects of our physical environment.

It appears that we have to choose between a wholly modular theory of the mind and folk psychology. If this choice were forced, it would not be insane to choose folk psychology. For folk psychology is confirmed by its great utility in guiding our daily interactions with one another. Moreover, evolutionary psychology remains very speculative. Evolutionary psychologists make claims about the adapted structure of the mind, using very little direct evidence about human evolutionary history. Instead, they suggest the following discovery procedure. Consider, first, the problems our ancestors would have needed to solve, given their way of life and their environment. Then develop a theory of the cognitive mechanisms needed to solve those problems. Specify the ways such mechanisms would be manifest in development and behaviour, and then deploy the experimental techniques of developmental, cognitive and social psychology to test for those mechanisms' presence. If they are discovered, that confirms the adaptive hypothesis that led to the tests.[24]

We have here a version of inference to the best explanation. The best explanation of the mechanism discovered experimentally is the evolutionary scenario that led to its discovery. Such inferences are sometimes sound. There are cases where we can infer from a given structure or mechanism to the evolutionary cause. But we can do so for a cognitive mechanism only when (a) a system is complex and integrated; (b) it powers a very distinctive type of behaviour; (c) that behaviour is central to the life history of the animals in question; (d) it supports only that type of behaviour. The first condition, adaptive complexity, is the mark of an adaptation; the others allow us to identify that adaptation more-or-less unequivocally. The hypotheses of evolutionary psychology may sometimes satisfy these criteria, but often they do not. For example, there is no evidence that mate choice depends on a complex and integrated system.

On closer inspection, however, the choice is not forced. Evolutionary psychologists should probably retreat from their commitment to a wholly modular theory of mental organisation. One problem is control. If the mind is a Swiss army knife, what system determines which blade is in use? What mechanisms 'decide' that the current circumstances pose a mate-choice problem rather than a social-exchange problem, and assign control to the relevant specialist? The metaphor of the army knife conceals a coordination problem. Furthermore, language, the central example of domain-specific cognition, is in one critical respect very unusual. It poses no problem of exploitation or conflict of interest. However their ultimate interests conflict, both parties in a conversational exchange share an interest in having each utterance decoded by the other. Neither will succeed unless their utterances are understood. So game-theoretic models of the evolution of language have a strong cooperative element; they are close to one end of a mathematical spectrum from games of pure cooperation to games of pure conflict.[25] Hence evolution can tune language decoding to a set of stable, invariant features of the human linguistic environment, just as our visual depth-from-motion systems can be tuned to stable features of the physical world. There is no arms race between speakers and hearers to block interpretation of what is said.

This cooperative, and hence stable, context may not exist for other posited modules. Typically, social exchange, mate selection and intentional interpretation lack this cooperative feature. So there is no reason to suppose that there will be a stable set of cues to which modules can be tuned. The psychology of emotion reinforces this point. A number of emotions have modular aspects. Frank points out that emotions are not under intentional control, and he argues that this is critical to their biological role in human life, namely to commit us to future courses of action, even when those actions at the time would not be in our prudential interests. Similarly, Griffiths points out that fear, disgust, anger and other core emotions are modular with respect to their effects – of arousal, of facial expression, of posture and of the behaviours they prime. But they are not at all modular with respect to the information that triggers them.[26]

The fact that fear, anger, trust or suspicion are not switched on by a specific, trans-cultural set of cues is no cause for surprise. Many important problems cannot be solved by modular mechanisms. Fodor has convincingly argued that the pragmatics of language cannot be handled by a specialist device.[27] It is one thing to know what a sentence means; it's another to know the intentions that lie behind its utterance. The latter problem is not solvable by shortcuts from a restricted data base. Everything the hearer knows is potentially relevant and potentially used in decoding the speaker's intent. The same problem seems to arise for many domains of interest to evolutionary psychology. Could a specialised mechanism deliver reliable judgements about the probability of a prospective partner's cheating? It is not at all obvious that there are cues that are *reliable* and are *stable across generations*. Both conditions must be met, if selection is to build a specialist mechanism to solve such problems. So the most plausible version of evolutionary psychology might be somewhat closer to a hybrid architecture: a complex of domain-general and domain-specific devices. If so we are not forced by evolutionary considerations into some version of eliminativism.

V LANGUAGE AND EVOLUTION

One important version of naturalism trades on the computational theory of mind to link folk psychology with the scientific perspective. On that hypothesis, distinctively human cognitive capacities are realised by algorithms that process symbols. Thinking is computing, and thoughts are data structures. Folk psychology, on this view, becomes a prototype of cognitive psychology: it is a first approximation to a theory of the cognitive operations of the central processor.[28] This is an important idea in the defence of naturalism. But, the argument continues, this computational view of human cognitive capacities is biologically implausible.

This charge is levelled, in particular, at Chomsky's conception of language. The Chomskians argue (a) that language is a distinctively human cognitive specialisation; (b) that when we learn a particular language, what we have learned is an abstract system of rules – that is, when we produce or understand an utterance, our linguistic performance depends in some way on our mastery of those rules; (c) that our knowledge of those rules is physically encoded in neural tissue, probably in specific locations; and (d) that we are innately equipped with quite rich information about the general form of language. This information is encoded in human genomes. This theory of language is a central exemplar of the computational-naturalist theory of mind. Yet if this is right, the argument goes, language could not be an adaptation. For it would be unevolvable. If Chomsky is right about the nature of language, language is a complex structure. So it must be an adaptation. But if it is an adaptation, it must evolve through a sequence of simpler systems. But there are no good theories on offer about intermediate forms of language. So this picture of language must be mistaken.

To this challenge, three reactions are possible. Steven Pinker argues that the Chomskian conception of language is right, but that it does meet the Darwinian constraint on the evolution of complex structures. Derek Bickerton (and perhaps also Chomsky) has rejected the constraint. Bickerton used to argue that language evolved from a much simpler system in a single step. Terrence Deacon argues that this constraint on evolution undermines Chomsky's view of language, and we need an alternative compatible with that constraint.[29]

I agree that the evolution of language is deeply puzzling. But I do not think that the mystery is an artefact of Chomsky's view of language. Rather, language evolution poses a problem for every view of the mind. No other living species manifests homologous behaviour, so it is very hard to reconstruct language's evolutionary history. Even the gross chronology of language evolution is subject to major dispute. Philip Lieberman, in particular, has argued on the basis of the architecture of the skull and vocal track that only anatomically modern humans have full speech. In his view, not even Neanderthals had the full range of our articulatory competence. Their speech sounded nasalised, and it lacked a few, but particularly distinctive, vowels: [i] and [u].[30] So Neanderthal speech would have been more equivocal: it would have been harder to interpret, and/or more in need of contextual cues. Lieberman's view of the speech capacities of other hominids is highly controversial, as is his interpretation of the significance of their limitations. Michael Corballis, in particular, has argued that we cannot identify *linguistic competence* with *speech competence*. In his view, language began with gesture, not speech.[31] That view has some prima facie plausibility. Speech requires extraordinarily complex motor control systems. Moreover, hand movement, in contrast to vocalisation, is primitively voluntary. Chimps have much more control over hand position and movement than they do over their vocalisations.

In Corballis' view, the evolution of language does not have to be routed through the voluntary control of vocalisation and the elaboration of its fine motor control. Moreover, if language began as speech, it makes it even harder to account for the initial take-off of language. As Deacon points out, initially speech would have been either slow and laborious, or error prone.[32] Fewer phonetic differences were available to mark word differences, and the available phonemes would have been less distinctive (with no or few vowel contrasts). Moreover, the specialised peripheral systems that we have now evolved for both the production and the comprehension of language were not then in place. So if language began as speech, the adaptive advantage these early versions of language offered, whatever they were, would have had to be highly error tolerant. Furthermore, Corballis' view makes sense of the ease and naturalness with which the deaf acquire signing. The point is not that signing is a reversion. Rather, a gestural origin of language would explain why the cognitive and motor aspects of language can be decoupled; it explains why language is medium independent. Articulatory phonology, on Corballis' hypothesis, was grafted onto a competence that was already present.

However, if we accept Corballis' idea that language had an origin close to the base of the hominid clade, but as gesture, we are left with a problem. Why do we not find other animals that use a simple, cut-down language? Why is language unique to our clade? If early hominid minds could run a simple language, there is no obvious reason why we fail to find simple languages in use by the great apes, elephants and dolphins.[33]

Bickerton and Lieberman, in contrast to Corballis, think that language is a recent human adaptation. Only humans use language because its cognitive demands are so intense that they can be met only by a large-brained, cognitively sophisticated animal. Indeed, Bickerton and Lieberman tie full human language to a remarkable event in human prehistory: a cultural explosion of 40,000 or so years ago. Around then, there was a marked change in the diversity and the rate of change of human material culture. Since one aspect of that explosion was the great expansion of symbolic artefacts, seen in cave paintings, carved ivory and bone, it is very tempting to follow Bickerton and Lieberman in supposing that this explosion is a consequence of the final invention of fully human language. But that view is inconsistent with seeing human language as a biological adaptation. For *Homo sapiens* came into existence, *and dispersed*, well before this explosion. The explosion, if it is real, is out of step with any species-wide change in human biology.

Even if we could construct the chronology of the evolution of language, we would still be left with the problem of intermediate forms.

There is one reasonably good model of an intermediate, so-called 'protolanguage' – a model based on pidgins. Pidgins come into existence as a means of communication when people who have no language in common are bought into enduring contact. Pidgins are characterised by a simplified syntax and a corresponding absence of determiners, articles, tense and aspect markers, and the like. That is, they lack lexical items that have only a structural role within a sentence, rather than pointing to something outside it. Consequently, pidgin-mediated communication relies heavily on context for interpretation. But a pidgin-like protolanguage is far too sophisticated to be close to the first step on the trajectory to full human language. Pidgins can be quite lexically rich, and pidgin speakers have full human language and the full apparatus of speech production and comprehension. Yet, as Bickerton in particular has emphasised, the structural complexity and expressive power of protolanguage is a long way short of any natural language.

Protolanguage might be a fair estimate of one intermediate form on the evolutionary trajectory to human language. But it will be one of a number of systems, and we have not much sense of what earlier, proto-protolanguages would have been like, nor any good models of protolanguage-plus, the protolanguage/language intermediates. What is more, there is no well-articulated model of the selective advantage of protolanguage-plus. That is hardly surprising. Given that we have little idea of the character of these rudimentary forms of language, it follows that there are no good theories about what their advantage would have been. Pinker argues that we get a huge advantage from the recursive properties of language. But speakers of pidgins, which lack most of the recursive apparatus of language, can talk about people's property and describe their movements, even if they do not use expressions with recursively embedded structures like 'the man's hat' or 'I think he left'.[34]

In sum, it is very hard to give even a modestly convincing scenario of language evolution. But that is not the result of a specifically computational view of language. It is hard to understand the evolution of language because it is unique to humans (hence our theories lack empirical constraints) and because it is an adaptation for phenotypically plastic cooperation, and evolutionary theory lacks good models of the evolution of plastic behaviours, of general-purpose rather than special-purpose adaptations.

VI CONCLUSION

Naturalist philosophy of mind has been slow to take up both the opportunity and the challenge of Darwinism. In part, this has been due to the fact that, for most of this century, psychology has developed largely independently of evolutionary considerations.[35] Neither behaviourist not cognitive psychology had strong links to evolutionary biology. So, to the extent that naturalistically inclined philosophers looked to psychology, philosophy of mind would not take a Darwinian turn until psychology did. But there were reasons internal to philosophy itself. Naturalism was blocked by a perceived division of intellectual labour between conceptual truths (the province of philosophy and the formal sciences) and empirical truths (the province of the natural sciences). Folk psychology was seen as a theory only after confidence in this dichotomy was eroded. Folk psychology's adequacy was questioned only after it was seen as a theory. So eliminativism was not explicitly formulated until the 1960s.[36]

As we have seen, the injection of evolutionary considerations into the naturalistic debate has mixed consequences for naturalists. It has provided the naturalist with an important set of tools, especially in giving an account of the symbol/world relationship. Moreover, evolvability considerations offer the naturalist another way of filtering theories of human cognitive competence. But the challenge posed by evolutionary psychology is serious. As I have noted, some versions of evolutionary psychology have been too quick to adopt an extremely modular view of the mind, a view which would be bad news for folk psychology. But though less modular models may be compatible with folk psychology, they are hardly guaranteed to be.

In his landmark defence of eliminativism, Paul Churchland argued that we should expect scientific psychology to displace folk psychology on the grounds that this was the normal pattern, displayed in, for example, folk medicine and folk physics.[37] Churchland overstates the case, especially when we note that elimination is a matter of degree. The ancients certainly misunderstood the nature of the solar system. But they correctly identified some of the planets, the sun and the moon and they distinguished these from the stars. Moreover, folk psychology might be better than folk astronomy. We may well have been under intense selection to develop an accurate theory of other people. Indeed, our interactions with them provide us with a good deal of evidence against which to test such theories. Furthermore, to some extent we can use ourselves as a model of other agents. Even so, Churchland's general point is well taken. It will be a surprise if evolutionary psychology does not lead to some important revisions of our folk conception of what we are.

NOTES

1. See Chalmers 1996.
2. See P. M. Churchland 1996.
3. For classic expositions of the functionalist strategy, see Armstrong 1968 and Smart 1959. For versions of the computational theory of the mind, see Fodor 1987; Dennett 1987; and Pinker 1997.
4. See A. Clark 1997.
5. See Searle 1994.
6. Dennett 1995.
7. Boyd and Richerson 1985.
8. See Griffiths 1997.
9. On the general programme of evolutionary psychology, see Tooby and Cosmides 1992; Cosmides and Tooby 1994, 1995; Pinker 1997. For a sceptical response, see Fodor 2000. On social exchange, see Cosmides and Tooby 1989. On language, see Pinker 1994. On folk psychology as itself an adaptive specialisation, see Sperber 1996.
10. Dickinson and Balleine 2000.
11. See Rosenberg, this volume.
12. See Godfrey-Smith 1996; Sterelny 2000; and Whiten and Byrne 1997.
13. Patricia Churchland 1986.
14. See Dennett 1987; Braddon-Mitchell and Jackson 1996.
15. For the development of this programme, see Dretske 1981; Fodor 1987; Fodor 1990.
16. Godfrey-Smith was the first to press this point vigorously: see Godfrey-Smith 1991, 1992.
17. See Millikan 1984, 1993; Papineau 1984, 1987.
18. See Kripke 1992.
19. See Sterelny 1990; Godfrey-Smith 1994a.
20. For a lucid discussion of modular versions of evolutionary psychology, see Samuels 1998.
21. For mate selection, see Symons 1979 and Buss 1994. For a sceptical response from an evolutionary perspective, see Hrdy 1999. On mind-reading, see Baron-Cohen 1995 and Sperber 1996. For a somewhat

sceptical response to a wholly modular view of mind reading, see Currie and Sterelny 2000.

22. See Fodor 1983, 2000.
23. On abilities specific to social exchange see Cosmides and Tooby 1992. Sperber's views are developed in Sperber 1996.
24. See Tooby and Cosmides 1992. For a critical response see Griffiths 1996; Sterelny and Griffiths 1999; and Lloyd 1999.
25. See Skyrms 1996.
26. See Frank 1988 and Griffiths 1997.
27. See Fodor 1983.
28. See especially Fodor 1975, 1990. There is some debate as to how specific a computational architecture the naturalist has to posit in order to develop this conception of the relationship between folk psychology and cognitive psychology. See A. Clark 1997 for a view that contrasts sharply with that of Fodor.
29. For Pinker's view that language is built through orthodox incremental selection, see Pinker 1994. For Bickerton's one-step view, see Bickerton 1990, 1995. For Deacon's use of the constraint against a computational view of language, see Deacon 1997.
30. Lieberman 1998, 94.
31. Corballis 1991.
32. Deacon 1997, 363.
33. Perhaps these animals do not lack the cognitive competence for a simple language. Rather, their failure to sign is part of their general lack of cooperative behaviour. Humans are an extraordinarily cooperative and social species, and speech – exchanging information – is a special case of cooperation. Perhaps chimps and elephants do not cooperate enough to talk.
34. Pinker 1994, 368.
35. Not for all of it. There was an early surge of interest in psychology on evolution, well described in R. J. Richards 1987.
36. Though an implicit eliminativism existed earlier under the banner of 'hard determinism'. For hard determinists thought that agency was a myth, disproved by the natural fact that humans are part of a closed causal order
37. P. M. Churchland 1981.

ALEX ROSENBERG

13 Darwinism in moral philosophy and social theory

I DARWINISM, NATURALISM AND HUMAN AFFAIRS

Among philosophers, naturalism is the view that contemporary scientific theory is the source of solutions to philosophical problems. Naturalists look to the theory of natural selection as a primary resource in coming to solve philosophical problems raised by human affairs in particular. For the theory combines relevance to human affairs and scientific warrant more strongly than does any other theory. Theories in physics and chemistry may be more strongly confirmed, especially because their more precise predictions can be tested in real time. But these theories have little to tell us about human conduct and institutions. On the other hand, actual and possible theories in the social and behavioural sciences may in the future have more to tell us about humanity than Darwinian theory; but these theories do not as yet have anything like the degree of confirmation of Darwin's theory.

This chapter surveys contemporary strategies for providing a Darwinian understanding and vindication of morality, ethical norms, our conception of justice, and the cooperative human institutions which those norms and conceptions underlie. We will see that while the prospects for a Darwinian vindication of moral claims – as true or well founded – remain clouded, the prospects for explaining the normative dimension of human affairs by appeal to Darwinism appear to be improving. Indeed, the emerging evolutionary understanding of why human beings have been selected to be moral agents may come as close to a vindication of morality in human affairs as naturalism will allow.

II TWO TASKS FOR DARWINISM IN ETHICS

Taken together, the ubiquitous human practices of making judgements of right and wrong, declaring moral goodness and badness, imposing standards of fairness and justice, attributing moral duties and responsibility, and according autonomy to other humans constitute one of the most difficult challenges to naturalism. The problem is that the truth or falsehood of statements expressing these judgements, standards and assumptions does not appear to depend on facts accessible to scientific discovery. These statements appear to report non-natural facts, which are not amenable to evidential support by the employment of scientific methods, and cannot be accommodated within a naturalistic metaphysics. In an attempt to reconcile the human commitment to norms with a purely scientific worldview, naturalists have turned increasingly to Darwin's theory of natural selection.

There are broadly two programmes for bringing together normativity and natural selection. One seeks to underwrite received moral judgements or some successors to them as true or correct in the light, not of special kinds of facts (this option being ruled out by naturalism), but of the history of those judgements, where this history is understood as a Darwinian selection process of sorts. This programme belongs to substantive normative ethics, identifying what is morally right and wrong, good and bad, just and unjust. Let us call this project 'Darwinian morality'. The other programme seeks to explain, or explain away, the human capacity for moral judgements as due to nothing more than the operation of natural selection on hereditary variation among ancestral hominids. This programme, naturalists will argue, is a new twist on the enterprise that philosophers call 'metaethics', devoted to analysing the meaning of ethical claims. It is a new twist on traditional metaethics because it expresses naturalistic doubts about separating claims about the *meanings* of ethical concepts from claims about the *causes* of the ethical commitments expressed in those concepts. Thus, if naturalism can give an explanation of why we make the normative claims we do, it will claim to have provided as much of an account of their meaning as can be provided. Let us call this second project 'Darwinian metaethics'.

Both Darwinian morality and Darwinian metaethics must take seriously a peculiar feature of moral judgements: that they are supposed to enjoin and condemn certain actions not just as prudentially advisable or inadvisable, in the light of our interests, but as right or wrong in themselves. This is a feature of normative claims which philosophers have dubbed 'ethical internalism'. If we accept that moral claims have this feature, then they cannot, for instance, be merely injunctions of prudence, of merely instrumental ends-means rationality. We accept that at least some moral judgements seem to make claims on us that are not instrumental, but categorical; not 'If thou wish to avoid some bad end, or to attain some good one, thou should not commit adultery', but 'Thou shalt not commit adultery.' Darwinian metaethics may explain away the internalism of some moral judgements as an illusion, though perhaps an adaptive illusion. For Darwinian morality the bar is higher. Darwinian morality must ground the internalism of moral judgements evolutionarily. It will have to identify quasi-Darwinian ends or objectives, such as species perpetuation or ecological preservation, in virtue of which some moral judgements are internally motivating.

According to most philosophers the trouble with Darwinian morality has been well known for almost a century. As a philosophical programme, it allegedly rests on a mistake: the so-called 'naturalistic fallacy'. In his *Principia Ethica*, G. E. Moore offered the so-called 'open question' argument against any identification of a normative property, such as goodness, with a non-normative or 'natural' property, such as pleasure, or happiness, or, for that matter, the survival of the individual or species or even planet.[1] Of any property that a person can exemplify – an emotion such as love, say, or a virtue such as heroism, or a generalised feeling of pleasure – it may sensibly be asked whether that virtue or emotion or feeling is good. In other words, it is *always* an open question whether the property is a good one. Accordingly, argued Moore, the identification of any such property with goodness cannot be correct. For if it were correct, the question 'Is Jones' love for Smith, or for that matter for humankind as a whole, good?' would not be what it is, namely, an open question, to which a negative answer might be given. Rather, it would be a question like 'Is Jones' mother a woman?' This question is not open to a negative answer. On the basis of this argument, Moore claimed that all attempts to naturalise the normative are fallacious. His open-question argument defines the 'naturalistic fallacy'. The argument's acceptance by philosophers has made Darwinian morality an unattractive option to most naturalists.[2]

III DARWINIAN MORALITY

The objection lodged against Darwinian morality may be illustrated by considering a recent, philosophically sophisticated version of this programme. It takes the name 'moral realism' to echo the epistemological programme of scientific realism, which argues that scientific theories about unobservable properties and entities should be treated as literally true descriptions of reality, and that the properties and entities to which these theories refer must exist notwithstanding the absence of direct empirical evidence for them. Similarly, latter-day moral realism holds that some moral properties, such as goodness, really do exist, that some social arrangements really do exhibit these moral properties more than others, and that we know this to be true on the basis of scientific theory – in particular, a theory of the Darwinian selection of moral norms. Peter Railton provides an excellent example of this Darwinian moral realism. Railton aims to provide 'descriptions and explanations of certain prominent features of the evolution of moral norms' that will establish their naturalistic foundations.[3] If Darwin's name does not figure in his account, it is because Railton recognises that, when it comes to the emergence of normatively right social institutions in the absence of ruling intentions to establish them, the only explanation can be Darwinian.[4]

According to Railton, the morally good reflects what it is rational to want, not from an individual point of view, but from 'the social point of view'.[5] What is rational from the social point of view is what would be rationally approved of were the objective interests of all potentially affected individuals counted equally. Railton holds that social arrangements depart from rationality when they significantly discount the interests of particular groups. When this happens, there is 'potential for dissatisfaction and unrest', which reduces the viability – that is, the fitness – of these social arrangements, and of the whole society so arranged. In Railton's view, reduced viability of an arrangement, whether a norm, an institution, or whatever, is reflected in 'alienation, loss of morale, decline in the effectiveness of authority...potential for unrest,...a tendency towards religious or ideological doctrines, or towards certain forms of repressive apparatus...' and so on.[6]

On the other hand, social arrangements tending to be more fully in the interests of all individuals in the society counted equally – in other words, more rational social arrangements – will be selected for. Societies bearing such arrangements will be more viable, presumably because these arrangements, by promoting equality of treatment, better adapt these societies to the environments in which they find themselves. The environment of a given society is not just its physical, geographical surroundings. It includes other societies with which it is in competition for scarce resources, and also the individuals composing that society, who have been selected for fitness- (and thus utility-) maximisation by natural selection. In the long run, just as biological natural selection winnows for those available traits that best 'match' organisms' local environments, so the struggle for survival among societies with varying moral traits will eventually winnow for those moral traits – principles, norms, institutions – that best match societies' environments. These selected traits, according to Railton, will invariably be ones that foster equality of various kinds, since egalitarian arrangements most nearly fulfil the objective, scientifically determinable interests of individuals.

One objection to this approach is its commitment to the natural selection of groups, whole societies, as opposed to individuals. What if, in a society more viable than others because of its more extensively egalitarian norms, individuals arise who free-ride upon and flout these norms when they can? In this case, intragroup selection for immorality (inequality in treatment of others) may be stronger than intergroup selection for morality. In such a case, evolution will not proceed in the direction of greater egalitarianism. Of this more below. Another objection is that Railton's account requires the truth of substantive claims that social arrangements which treat society's members in more nearly equal ways will be more adaptive, under any conditions, than those arrangements which entrain, enhance or preserve inequalities. Even if this claim were correct, Railton's moral realism would still fall foul of Moore's argument. There is no reason to think that the survival of any particular social group, individual, or *Homo sapiens* in general for that matter, is intrinsically good or morally required. There is in a naturalistic worldview no scope for grounding such claims of intrinsic value.

Suppose it is retorted that Railton's thesis is an analysis of what moral goodness consists in, not a justificatory endorsement of it. But if we accept this interpretation, moral realism does not accomplish what it has set out to do for Darwinian morality. So understood, moral realism fails to motivate any commitment to the moral principles it singles out as true. Indeed, it appears to deny or ignore the internal normativity of moral judgements, treating them as implicit claims about instrumental rationality, as rules justified by the success of those individuals or groups that employ them in attaining their non-normative objectives.[7] Railton may well view his normative claims as merely instrumentally useful, and without internal moral force. He describes them as part of 'the skeleton of an explanatory theory that uses the notion of what is ... rational from a social point of view ... that parallels in an obvious way ... assessments of [instrumental] rationality ... in explanations of individual behaviors'. In fact, Railton recommends we surrender 'the idea that moral evaluations must have categorical force'.[8] This denial of the internal normativity of moral judgements has the prospect of reducing Darwinian morality into some versions of Darwinian metaethics. For now it turns out that moral judgements are really just disguised claims about means-ends instrumental rationality to which we attribute some purely prudential normative force.

Note that non-naturalistic forms of moral realism are not similarly threatened with such reduction to metaethics. For they claim that the normativity of moral judgement reflects some factual condition in the world which our moral detection apparatus enables us to identify. It has sometimes been claimed, for example, that we have direct intuition of the moral qualities of an act, and these intuited qualities motivate our approval or disapproval of the act in question. Needless to say, naturalists of all stripes declare such putative qualities either non-existent or unintelligible. Certainly there is no room for them in a naturalistic metaphysics.

The naturalists' denial that a range of distinctive moral facts exists and makes moral judgements true, together with the force of Moore's diagnosis of a naturalistic fallacy, makes Darwinian metaethics a far more attractive programme for naturalists than Darwinian morality. Indeed, once we deny the existence of a separate range of moral facts to be learned by some sort of interaction, either with the natural world or with an abstract Platonic realm of values, metaethics becomes a matter of urgency. Metaethics is in large part the study of the nature and meaning of moral judgements. Without truth-makers for moral judgements – that is, without facts in virtue of which moral judgements are true or false – ethical claims may be threatened with meaninglessness. There are four options. If ethical claims are meaningless, we need at least an explanation of why all *Homo sapiens* make these apparent 'judgements'. If they are not meaningless, but, say, all false, we need an explanation of why the error should persist from time out of mind. If moral judgements are neither true nor false, but expressions of our emotions, we need an account of why these expressions take the form they do, and why they are coordinated in the way they are. And if moral judgements express the norms of conduct we embrace, we again need a theory to explain why we embrace these norms and not other ones. In each of the four cases, an account needs to be provided of why we humans feel the commitment to an objective morality, reflecting facts that exist independently of us, and which motivate our conduct. It seems the only naturalistic metaethical theory that can do any of these things is a Darwinian one.

IV DARWINIAN METAETHICS

Most of the metaethical theories incorporating Darwinian considerations belong to a species of metaethical theories collectively called 'non-cognitivist', because they hold that moral judgements are neither true nor false reports about the world, and as such have no propositional or 'cognitive' content. Among the earliest non-cognitivist theories was the 'emotivist' doctrine advanced by A. J. Ayer and C. L. Stevenson and associated with logical positivism.[9] This doctrine held that moral judgements express the emotional states and attitudes of the utterer. This otherwise implausible theory has two virtues. One is its ability to explain intransigent moral disagreement, as the upshot of incompatible emotions. The other is its account of the apparent internalism of moral judgements, as deriving from the emotional attitudes they express. But non-cognitivism will not account for the complex character of ethical reasoning characteristic of human life. Nor does it do well with the fact that, when people issue moral judgements on events distant in space or time, they often do so in such a cool and bloodless way that they seem not to express emotions at all. Few latter-day naturalists have been attracted by emotivism.

A more sophisticated version of non-cognitivist metaethics has been developed within a Darwinian framework by Alan Gibbard.[10] For Gibbard, the emergence of morality can be linked to coordinated strategies which were adaptive for the individuals who employed them; and this has consequences for our understanding of the nature of moral judgements. Although Gibbard's metaethical theory is only one of several actual and possible Darwinian metaethics, it is well worth examining closely. Widely discussed, it has provided a philosophical foundation for the developments in evolutionary game theory and Darwinian political philosophy to be explored later in this chapter. Moreover, it avoids many of the traditional objections to non-cognitivism, while making as strong a positive case for moral objectivity as naturalism will allow. The details of any such theory will be important to philosophers anxious about the meaning of moral judgements; while biologists and others interested in the more general question of how moral judgements are possible within the Darwinian perspective will be interested in how Gibbard develops the general strategy of a Darwinian metaethics. Before proceeding, however, we should note that the crucial difference between the Darwinian moralist Railton and the Darwinian metaethicist Gibbard is that, where Railton sets out to vindicate the norms which have in fact evolved as the morally right ones, Gibbard sets out to show merely that the evolved norms are the most adaptive ones.

In Gibbard's view, the 'key to human moral nature lies in coordination broadly considered'.[11] He points out that past members of *Homo sapiens* needed to coordinate their actions in order successfully to compete with megafauna, to sustain cooperative enterprises of proto-agriculture and generally to survive and flourish. The design problem nature thus set for *Homo sapiens*, of establishing and securing this coordination, was, he argues, accomplished in large measure by coordinated emotions (here his non-cognitivism shows its hand). Gibbard's objective is less to establish how institutions of morality or particular moral judgements emerged or might have emerged, as a result of random variation and natural selection, than to give an analysis of the meaning of moral judgements which, *inter alia*, makes such a derivation possible.

According to Gibbard, a moral judgement is not the expression of an emotion, but a judgement of what sort of emotion or feeling it is rational to have. An emotion is rational if it is permissible in light of the norms one accepts. The capacity to accept norms depends on language, because language is required to coordinate several agents' norms in ways that are mutually fitness enhancing. From these premises, Gibbard argues that the environment of early humankind selected for emotional propensities which enhanced coordination, and for linguistic potential that enabled norms governing the display of these emotions to emerge and spread. Gibbard identifies resentment, anger, guilt and shame as central moral emotions. In his view, norms prescribing when it is appropriate to feel these emotions have been coordinated with one another via natural selection so as to encourage or reestablish cooperative conduct among moral agents. The metaethical upshot is that an action is morally wrong if, in the light of norms that the actor accepts, it makes sense for the actor to feel guilty, say, and for others to feel resentment about the action in the light of the norms they accept. Note the coordination of emotions here: A's guilt meshes with B's anger; C's shame with D's disdain. If uncoordinated, such emotions can lead to escalating conflict. Coordinated, however, they make possible the acknowledgement of wrong-doing and reconciliation.

In brief, what it makes sense to do, or to feel, in the light of norms a person accepts is what Gibbard defines as 'rational'. He rejects a purely instrumental account of rationality, both because of classical puzzle cases in decision theory, and, more importantly, because 'rational' has an appraising or approving connotation (a reflection of the internalism of moral judgements) that rational choice theory cannot capture. But, for Gibbard, to call an act or feeling 'rational' is not to state a fact about it. Rather, it is to express one's acceptance of norms that permit the act or feeling.

How strong are the naturalistic credentials of Gibbard's metaethics, and what, precisely, is the role of Darwinism within it? The metaethics is naturalistic because it requires no distinct range of independent moral facts to make moral judgements true or false. In Gibbard's view, our moral psychologies do not enable us to recognise and represent independently existing moral facts. Rather, they are systems that coordinate what is in one agent's head with what is in other agents' heads. What is coordinated is the acceptance of norms in the light of which people's actions and emotions mesh to mutual advantage. For Gibbard, then, our moral psychologies are biologically *functional*. That is where the Darwinism comes in, since biological functions, on a widely accepted view, are just what emerge from causal histories of natural selection upon genetic variation.[12] Furthermore, according to Gibbard, the evolutionary pressures that selected for coordination-enhancing emotions among humans must also have selected for enhanced language abilities, because the capacity to be guided by words, in one's actions and emotions, is indispensable to the formulation and acceptance of the norms which produce cooperation. Without an advanced language, there can be none of that discussion which, over time, tends towards consensus, consistency and similarity of motives.

If moral judgement is not a matter of discerning truths but of expressing one's acceptance of norms that make sense of anger, resentment, guilt and shame, whence their apparent feeling of objectivity, of existence independent of us? Again, Gibbard insists that this feeling does not derive from the existence of any Platonic range of moral facts or truths. Rather, norms appear objective to us depending on how strongly we accept them. For Gibbard, a norm is felt to be objective if it would be rational even for those who do not accept the norm themselves. Furthermore, the norms that moral agents accept are not felt to be equally objective. Instead, they form a hierarchy, with those at the top appearing more objective than those at the bottom. Gibbard is tempted by a parallel to the doctrine of secondary qualities. Colour, it has long been argued by some empiricists, is a secondary property – that is, a property of our experience, in our heads, and not in the objects we see as coloured. We mistakenly project this property on to objects. Neverthless, colour attributions have considerable 'objectivity'. A thing is red if and only if normal observers in normal conditions have red sensations when looking at it. Similarly, in Gibbard's view, the objectivity of moral judgements is a matter of normal agents in normal circumstances accepting the same set of norms of anger, guilt, disdain and resentment.

In sum, for Gibbard, norms, emotions and language arose together through natural selection. A moral judgement is rational if it accords with widely accepted norms. These norms were selected for because they solve problems of cooperation. The emotions that give these norms their internal motivational force were selected for because they coordinate and convey commitment to action in accordance with the norms. Language and other higher cognitive functions were selected for to facilitate such social coordination. Language in particular enables agents to express, discuss and accept norms, enhancing mutual influence and consistency while at the same time moving people to act in a coordinated fashion (whence the felt objectivity of the norms).

Gibbard's Darwinian metaethics, for all its speculative character, thus turns out to give empirical promissory notes about the origins of cooperation, cognition and language that only biological anthropology and evolutionary psychology can cash in. Indeed, independent of Gibbard, developments in biological anthropology were in fact substantiating several factual presuppositions of his theory. Only a sketch of these considerations can be given here. To begin with, there is evidence that our hominid ancestors were originally solitary and highly competitive, not members of extended family troops with strong kinship relations. Cooperation can be expected to emerge among kin groups through the maximisation of inclusive fitness (that is, fitness calculated as a function, not of an individual's offspring, but of the total number of copies of its genes that make it into the next generation). But cooperation among originally solitary unrelated hominids requires communication of strategies. Independently, the shift from forest to savannah environments may have selected for the shift of control of vocalisation from limbic to neocortical brain centres. (Uncontrolled reflex vocalisation in the vicinity of predators – of the sort arboreal apes display – is maladaptive on the savannah, where there are no trees to climb.) In other words, whatever selected for the hominid shift to the savannah also selected for the neocortical control of vocalisation that is necessary for language.[13] Evidence from evolutionary psychology suggests that the need for cooperation among unrelated individuals put a further adaptive premium on language, as well as on the cognitive equipment required for recognising cooperative strategies and distinguishing them from non-cooperative ones.[14] Finally, recent work on the theory of emotions provides further evidence that an adaptational account of anger, especially as an irrational precommitment to cooperative outcomes, seems correct.[15]

V CAN COOPERATION EVOLVE?

Most of all, what Gibbard's account of moral judgement requires is a great deal of detailed explanation of how natural selection could have brought about norms of cooperation. Without the detail, his Darwinian metaethics is little more than what Stephen Jay Gould has stigmatised as a 'just so' story. Recent developments in evolutionary biology, game theory and political philosophy go a long way to filling out the picture.

The emergence of cooperation is one of the classic topics of Darwinian theory. On the one hand, there appears to be a great deal of selfless cooperation in nature – individuals putting themselves at risk to aid others (for example, by giving alarm cries). On the other hand, we expect natural selection to penalise such risk-taking, since risk-takers lower their prospects of survival and reproduction. At first glance, in short, altruism looks like an evolutionary impossibility. More precisely, natural selection relentlessly shapes organisms for individual fitness maximisation. An act is deemed altruistic if it results in an increase in the fitness of another organism and a decrease in the fitness of the actor. For persistent cooperation among organisms to emerge, therefore, there need to be acts of reciprocated altruism, such that the net pay-offs to mutual cooperators are greater than the rewards of mutual non-cooperation. Other things being equal, however, natural selection will block the building up of altruism among randomly chosen organisms, because altruistic acts offer opportunities to 'free-ride' – to decline to reciprocate – and being a free-rider maximises individual fitness. Yet, undeniably, altruism and cooperation characterise several infrahuman species, and all *Homo sapiens* societies. It thus appears that evolutionary theory has little to tell us about this central aspect of human conduct. Reflections along these lines led Edward O. Wilson in the mid-1970s to hold that altruism posed the gravest challenge to the fledgling science of sociobiology.[16]

Wrestling with this problem earlier in the twentieth century, some theorists concluded that individual altruism can be selected for because of the contribution it makes to the fitness of the group in which the individual finds itself. Group selection as an account of the evolution of altruism fell into great disfavour, however, when it was shown that groups of altruists would be evolutionarily unstable, since the effects of individual fitness maximisation would almost inevitably swamp the effects of group selection. To see this, suppose all members of a group are predisposed to cooperate, that is, to engage in altruistic acts because their genes programme them to do so. Suppose further that through mutation, recombination or immigration, a new organism, lacking the gene for the propensity to cooperate, becomes part of the group. Instead, this organism is genetically programmed to free-ride, cheat, slack off, shirk and take more than its share, whenever it can do so undetected. This free-rider has to get away with free-riding only some of the time in order to to have a higher fitness level than the rest of the group. Moreover, the offspring of the free-rider will in turn bear the free-riding gene, and will take advantage of the altruists in the group as ruthlessly as did their immediate ancestor. And so on, generation after generation, until, ultimately, genetically encoded reciprocal altruism has been extirpated from this group – which now of course has lower average fitness than it had when composed of altruists. Hence, in John Maynard Smith's terms, genetically programmed altruism in a group is not an 'evolutionarily stable strategy'.[17] The problem of reconciling the ubiquity of cooperation with natural selection remained.

The key theoretical insight was to see that, when fitness is measured in terms of the number of copies of itself a gene leaves, selection for genetic selfishness can lead to organismal altruism. For instance, if an organism behaves altruistically towards its offspring, enhancing their survival and reproductive opportunities, the result may be a decline in the altruistic parent's viability, but not a decline in its inclusive fitness – the fitness of its genes. This is called 'kin selection'. But, of course, cooperation is far more widespread among *Homo sapiens* than selection for altruism towards kin can explain. Sociobiology still faced the problem that Wilson posed. Without some further account, moreover, Darwinian metaethical claims – that moral judgements arose through selection for behaviour that coordinated individuals into cooperative exchanges – remained ungrounded.

It was by exploring the economists' puzzle of *the Prisoner's Dilemma* that evolutionary theorists were able to develop this further account of what is now called 'reciprocal altruism'. The general scenario is as follows. Two agents, A and B, are faced with mirror-image choices of whether to cooperate with one another or to decline to do so (that is, to defect). Pay-offs to mutual defection are lower than pay-offs to mutual cooperation, but defecting when the other party cooperates gives the highest pay-off. The prisoner's dilemma is a dilemma because the rational strategy for each player – defection – leads to an outcome neither prefers.

Something very much like this scenario occurs frequently in everyday life. Every exchange of money for goods represents what looks like such a problem. The customer would be best off if she grabbed the merchandise and left without paying. The salesperson would be best off if she could grab the money out of the customer's hands and withhold the goods. The third best outcome for both is that the customer keeps the money while the salesperson keeps the goods. Almost always, of course, both attain the second most preferred outcome for both, of exchanging goods for money. The parties to this exchange are not irrational; so we need to explain why they attained the cooperative outcome – why the scenario does not end as badly as it might have.

The reason is that the store-exchange game is part of a larger game. It is an iterated or repeated prisoner's dilemma, in which the two agents play again and again, whenever the customer comes to the store. What is the best strategy in an iterated prisoner's dilemma? In computer simulations famously carried out by Robert Axelrod, the optimal strategy in most iterated prisoner's dilemma games of interest is one called 'tit-for-tat': cooperate in the first game, and then in each subsequent round do what the other player did in the previous round. In iterated prisoner's dilemmas among humans, tit-for-tat is an effective strategy for several reasons. First, it is clear – opponents do not need a great deal of cognitive skill to tell what strategy a player is using. Second, it is nice – it starts out cooperatively. Third, it is forgiving – for each attempt to free-ride there is only one act of retaliation.[18]

When a group of players play tit-for-tat among themselves, the group and their strategy are not vulnerable to invasion by players using an always-free-ride-and-never-cooperate strategy. Players who do not cooperate will do better on the first round with each of the tit-for-tat-ers, but will do worse on each subsequent round. In the long run, the free-riders will be eliminated. Tit-for-tat is thus an evolutionarily stable strategy: if it gets enough of a foothold in a group, it will spread until it is the dominant strategy, and will not be overwhelmed by another strategy.

We can expect that nature's relentless exploration of the space of adaptive strategies in cooperative situations will have uncovered tit-for-tat, and that, long before the appearance of *Homo sapiens*, this strategy will have been written into the genes, and with it the genetic predispositions that make potential cooperation actual. By the time human beings emerged, these dispositions will have included the cognitive ability to discern which strategies others are using, the linguistic ability to coordinate different strategies, and emotions that meshed sufficiently to reinforce cooperative behaviour. In other words, Darwinian selection for fitness maximisers will have provided the biological details that a Darwinian metaethics such as Gibbard's requires.

It may even do more. Once there is recognition of partners, and memory about how they played in previous iterations, there may even be sufficient cognitive resources to enable a cooperative solution to the one-shot prisoner's dilemma. This, at any rate, appears to be the conclusion of Elliott Sober and David Wilson's revisionist argument that group selection for cooperation is possible after all, and that the conditions under which it can occur may well have obtained in hominid and human evolution.[19] Their argument is disarmingly simple. Everyone grants that there has been much kin selection in the history of life. It is also clear that one parent acting altruistically towards one offspring provides adaptative advantages to the two-membered 'group' which together they compose. In a one-shot prisoner's dilemma involving kin, therefore, both may be advantaged by cooperation regardless of the other's action, if the pay-off they are 'designed' to maximise (reproductive fitness) satisfies the inequality $r > b/c$, where r is the coefficient of relatedness (1/2 in the case of offspring and siblings, 1 in the case of identical twins, 1/4 in the case of cousins and nephews), b is the pay-off to mutual cooperation, and c is the cost of cooperation in the face of selfishness. If the group's fitness is a function of individual fitnesses, then groups of kin-related agents playing the cooperative (or 'sucker's') strategy in a one-shot prisoner's dilemma will be fitter than groups composed of pairs of mutual free-riders playing the defector strategy, and also fitter than mixed groups of pairs of free-riders and suckers. The result generalises to larger groups than pairs. Indeed, once players can recognise their degrees of relatedness, or for that matter what strategies they are genetically programmed to play in prisoner's dilemmas, they can preferentially aggregate into such fitter groups. Furthermore, when players seek out one another on the basis of what strategy they play, the long-term result will be a 'correlated equilibrium' of groups of cooperators only, the non-cooperating groups having been driven to extinction.

But recall the problem of invasion. Once started, these groups of cooperators will nevertheless be vulnerable to invasion or mutation that subverts from within, producing free-riders that take all other players in the group for suckers and increase in proportion from generation to generation, until eventually selfishness becomes fixed in every erstwhile altruistic group. Sober and Wilson suggest that cooperating groups preserve themselves by means of secondary enforcement behaviours. Norms of cooperation are policed by norms of enforcement, and enforcement – shaming, reporting, confiscating – is far less costly to the enforcing individuals than the breakdown of the norms of cooperation would be. Sober and Wilson argue that unrelated human cooperative groups attain stable equilibria (ones that cannot be invaded) through the enforcement of social norms that lower the costs of cooperating and raise the costs of defecting.

VI IS JUSTICE SELECTED FOR?

Evolutionary game theory seems capable of rendering human cooperation compatible with natural selection, and thus helps to explain the emergence of the norms and emotions that underwrite Gibbard's Darwinian metaethical programme. Evolutionary game theory may be able to go still further and identify the content of some of these norms. Brian Skyrms has shown how a Darwinian process can result in the fixation among humans of the norm of justice-as-fair-division. The key to this demonstration is, again, the evolution of a correlated equilibrium among like strategies through a mechanism of random variation and natural selection.

Consider the problem of 'divide the cake'. Two players bid independently on the size of the piece of the cake they want. If the bids add up to more than the whole cake, neither gets any cake. Otherwise, they get what they bid. Most people, of course, bid 1/2. This outcome is an equilibrium such that neither can do better, no matter what strategy the other employs. There are indefinitely many other such so-called 'Nash' equilibria (after the economist John Nash): for example, I bid 90 per cent, you bid 10 per cent. But none of them is evolutionarily stable. A population whose members demand more than 1/2 or less than 1/2 of the cake will be invaded and swamped by pairs who demand 1/2. Consider a bidding game in which random proportions of three strategies – bid 1/3, bid 2/3, and bid 1/2 – are represented at the outset. Skyrms has shown that, in a computer simulation in which strategies of lowest fitness are regularly removed, the fair-division strategy (bid 1/2) is the sole remaining strategy after 10,000 rounds in 62 per cent of the trials. Moreover, when strategies correlate so that the fair-division strategy plays against itself more frequently, or with increasing frequency as the game proceeds, it almost always swamps any other strategy. Skyrms concludes that in 'a finite population, in a finite time, where there is some random element in evolution, some reasonable amount of divisibility of the good and some correlation, we can say that it is likely that something close to share and share alike should evolve in dividing-the-cake situations. This is, perhaps, a beginning of an explanation of the origin of our concept of justice.'[20]

Skyrms has derived a number of other intriguing results. When divide-the-cake is played serially instead of simultaneously, so that one player can demand more than 1/2 and thus force the other player to choose between less than a fair share and nothing at all, correlation among strategies enables selection to give rise to fair-shares cooperation. Strategy correlation in the defence of territories can lead to the emergence of private property as a cooperative, adaptive solution. Finally, as we shall see, strategy correlation can give rise to meaning. One of Skyrms' larger aims is to show that these happy outcomes are attainable only when the choice of individual strategies is governed by natural selection. None are attainable when the choice of individual strategies is governed by considerations of maximal pay-off, of economic rational choice.

But how can we be confident that the degree of strategy correlation required for the evolution of cooperation arose in our own evolutionary past? Here is the problem, illustrated by one of Skyrms' results. In groups of related individuals, for example troops of vervet monkeys, signals that indicate the presence of various threats – for vervets, snakes, leopards and eagles – can develop from correlated conventions as to what noises consistently to make in the presence of different stimuli. Natural selection will prefer systems in which senders and receivers treat noises as bearing the same 'news'. It will also select for altruistic employment of signals to warn kin, even at the signaller's expense. Note that this is a result which both Gibbard and Sober–Wilson require, since it is language that makes norms of cooperation and enforcement possible. Indeed, language is so important to the evolution of cooperation that one might even argue that language emerged because of its impact on cooperation.

Skyrms' model for the evolution of language presupposes a high degree of strategy correlation. In the case of vervets, their population structure makes that presupposition reasonable. An individual vervet is more likely than not to encounter vervets playing the same genetically fixed strategy. Hominid evolution, however, most probably proceeded in the absence of this sort of population structure. It seems likely that our ancestors were solitary individuals, dispersed from their kin and roaming the savannas alone.[21] The cooperation they needed to establish in order to survive could not have arisen on the back of kin-based correlation. Nor does there seem to be an alternative to population structure as a source of a high degree of correlation. Hence there is no basis in evolutionary game theory to be confident that cooperation, or its semantic prerequisites, would have arisen among ancestral humans. There is more work to do in developing plausible models of the evolution of cooperation among humans and our ancestors.

But what has been done in evolutionary game theory certainly has begun to provide the empirical foundations that a Darwinian metaethics requires for its claims about meaning and the foundations of moral judgement. In some attenuated sense, the result may even satisfy the hopes for a Darwinian morality. Without vindicating the internalism of moral judgements as reflecting objective demands on our conduct, Darwinian metaethics approaches the goals that one tradition in ethics since Hobbes has set for itself: the task of showing that it is rational to be moral. Cooperation makes us each better off than we would be in a state of nature. But this outcome is not attainable as a bargain among rational agents; rather, it is the result of natural selection operating over random variation. This is almost, but not quite, Darwinian morality.

VII BROADER IMPLICATIONS OF DARWINISM FOR SOCIAL THEORY

Well before the developments surveyed above, Darwinism was guiding a research programme in the empirical social sciences – sociobiology. Latterly, some sociobiologists have substituted the name 'evolutionary psychology' for their science, in part to avoid the controversies that vexed sociobiology, in part to reflect a much stricter commitment than in the past to selection on genes or individuals (rather than groups) as the force shaping human behaviour and social institutions. Some critics charge that sociobiology, in its newer as well as its older versions, adopts a 'Panglossian', adaptationist methodology that effectively and perniciously legitimates the human social *status quo* as inevitable and unchangeable.[22] According to these critics, if lamentable social institutions – such as the division of labour, both sexual and industrial; economic and racial inequality; vast power asymmetries; and coercive violence – are claimed to be the results of long-term selection processes, these institutions will wrongly be deemed no more subject to amelioration or change than, say, eye colour. Such conclusions, especially if based merely on stories about variation and selection rather than hard-won empirical data, should be regarded with suspicion and evaluated with the greatest scepticism.[23]

Some work carried on under the banner of Darwinian sociobiology may certainly warrant such hostility.[24] But not all of it can be so criticised. Reviewing this work would take us too far afield; but at least some of the criticism of the sociobiological research programme can be deflected by the developments in moral and political philosophy reviewed here. For if, as we have seen, individual fitness maximisation can result in the morality most of us share, and in institutions of cooperation and justice, then Darwinian social thinking is not guilty simply of underwriting an unjust, non-egalitarian, sexist, racist *status quo*. Whatever the explanation of the social present, natural selection will feature at most as one among a large array of causal factors. Moreover, there are environments, perhaps even attainable ones, in which natural selection will not inevitably lead to nefarious social outcomes.

Darwinian metaethics and evolutionary game theory have succeeded, perhaps beyond the naturalist's hopes, in providing an account of how cooperative institutions can emerge despite the absence of designing intentions among their participants. This success has in turn strongly encouraged other non-normative explanatory programmes in the social sciences. What unites these programmes is a search for stable equilibria that optimise some function without any participant intending or acting to attain such an outcome. Darwinism may thus in part vindicate the 'invisible' or 'hidden' hand strategy of Adam Smith and his market-oriented followers in economics.

Smith's laissez-faire economic theory implies that self-seeking in free markets will lead, as if by an invisible hand, to outcomes advantageous for all. It is now well known, of course, that this is not the case. Rational-choice behaviour among economic agents leads to non-optimum outcomes in many different circumstances: in the provision of public goods, or when large companies can make things more cheaply than small ones (what economists call 'positive returns to scale'), or when there are a small numbers of traders, or asymmetries of information, or high transaction costs, or a difference in the interests of principals and agents. These 'market failures' have led critics of the market to deny both that market economic arrangements reflect the operation of an optimising invisible hand and that social institutions are the result of what F. A. Hayek called 'spontaneous order'.[25]

What evolutionary approaches have shown is that, when behaviour is the result of natural selection for outcomes that enhance fitness, instead of the rational choice of outcomes that enhance individual welfare, market failures can be avoided and optimal outcomes may after all be attainable. These approaches have shown in addition that these outcomes result from the aggregation of individual behaviours, not the selection of some properties of the group (beyond those correlated pairs that Sober and Wilson's group selection countenances). Of course, if the maximisation of welfare is among the ways in which fitness is often maximised, then natural selection for individual fitness maximisation will bring individual welfare maximisation along with it, thus substantiating Smith's laissez-faire conclusions if not his reasoning. In short, successful Darwinian explanations in the social sciences will substantiate both methodological individualism and invisible or hidden-hand perspectives.

There is another, potentially more promising adaptation of Darwinism in the social sciences. If genes and packages of genes can replicate and be selected for in virtue of their effects on organisms, why cannot beliefs, desires and other cognitive states be selected for as a consequence of their effects on cognitive agents? Richard Dawkins has called these cognitive states 'memes' (mental 'genes'). Individual memes vary in their effects on human behaviour.[26] As a result, they are differentially copied (reproduced) into the cognitive systems of other agents. Here again, the attractions of memetic selection are its freedom from assumptions about the conscious rational choices of individuals to adopt particular ideas, values, fashions and so on, as well as the availability of an invisible-hand mechanism that explains how they spread, become fixed in a population, and often become less widespread as environmental change (or even frequency-dependent selection) makes them less adaptative.

Nevertheless, it would be wrong to suppose that Darwinism vindicates the notion, sometimes attributed to Smith and his followers, that human social and economic interactions are inevitably and beneficially competitive. As we have already seen, under certain conditions, cooperation is a more adaptive Darwinian strategy than competition. That this is a possibility is something one might have inferred from Darwinian biology directly. The mistaken inference from Darwinism directly to a view of nature or society as 'red in tooth and claw' is due in part to the neglect of the role of the environment, which, perhaps more often than not, does select for competitive rather than cooperative behaviour. However, Darwinian social thinkers cannot deny the charge that, on Darwinian principles, cooperation is in the end a strategy only locally adaptive, and adaptive for fundamentally 'selfish genes', whose own fitness-maximising strategies are what organismal cooperation ultimately fosters.

VIII CONCLUSION

Darwinian morality has been a recurrent goal among naturalists. If present thinking among philosophers holds, however, it will remain an unattainable goal. Darwinian metaethics, by contrast, is flourishing, carried forward on a rising tide of research into human affairs from the perspectives of game theory, biological anthropology and evolutionary psychology. Building on insights from these disciplines, several philosophers have recently advanced our understanding of the nature and significance of morality. They have shown how morality may be expected to have emerged among fitness-maximising animals, and how nature may have selected both for cooperative norms and for the emotions that express our commitment to those norms. The specificity and detail that these accounts have already acquired are impressive. Whatever the long-term limits of a Darwinian understanding of human affairs, the short term promises further progress in attempts to bring Darwinian thinking to bear on moral philosophy and social theory.

NOTES

1. G. E. Moore [1903] 1988, ch. 1.
2. For further discussion see Rosenberg 1990.
3. Railton 1986, 203.
4. Railton 1986, sections 3 and 4, and especially footnote 21.
5. Railton 1986, 180.
6. Railton 1986, 192.
7. Railton 1986, 200.
8. Railton 1986, 204.
9. Ayer 1936 and Stevenson 1944.
10. Gibbard 1990.
11. Gibbard 1990, 26.
12. L. Wright 1976.
13. Maryanski and Turner 1992.
14. Barkow, Cosmides and Tooby 1992.
15. Griffiths 1997.
16. E. O. Wilson 1975. On the evolution of altruism and traditional theistic views of human morality, see Ruse, this volume.
17. Maynard Smith 1974.
18. It is important to bear in mind that tit-for-tat is an optimal strategy for maximising the individual's pay-off (evolutionary or otherwise) only under certain conditions. See Axelrod 1984.
19. Sober and Wilson 1998.
20. Skyrms 1996, 21.
21. Maryanski and Turner 1992.
22. On adaptationism, see Sober, this volume.

23. A sustained argument for this conclusion about Darwinism's baleful influence in the social sciences is offered in Lewontin, Rose and Kamin 1984, esp. ch. 9.
24. See Philip Kitcher 1985a.
25. Hayek 1982. For further discussion of 'invisible hand' arguments, see Rosenberg 1995, ch. 6 and Hull 2001, ch. 6.
26. Dawkins 1976, ch. 11. For further discussion of memes, see Dennett and Kitcher, this volume.

MICHAEL RUSE

14 Belief in God in a Darwinian age

I SIGNS OF THE TIMES

Darwinism has long been in the thick of science–religion debates, and never more so than today.[1] Among the latest of a series of American states to legislate in a manner unfriendly to Darwinism is Oklahoma, insisting that science textbooks carry an explicit statement that 'human life was created by one God of the Universe'.[2] Not all religious believers feel so threatened by evolutionary ideas, of course. Pope John Paul II – hardly a man to take doctrine lightly – has sent out a letter endorsing not just evolution *per se*, but modern theories of organic change.[3] In the same spirit, Keith Ward, Regius Professor of Divinity at Oxford, speaks of natural selection as a 'simple and extremely fruitful theory', and goes on to say that there is 'every reason to think that a scientific evolutionary account and a religious belief in a guiding creative force are not just compatible, but mutually reinforcing'.[4] Nevertheless, even liberal Christians often feel the need to supplement the theory of evolution through natural selection with other special mechanisms.

For their part, many of those on the science side of these debates think that Darwinism sounds the death knell for Christianity and other theistic systems. Writing with the passion of Savonarola, the well-known Darwinian Richard Dawkins (author of *The Selfish Gene*) regrets that a 'cowardly flabbiness of the intellect afflicts otherwise rational people confronted with long-established religions'. As a Darwinian, he wants no compromise or mutual embrace. 'Given a choice between honest to goodness fundamentalism on the one hand, and the obscurantist, disingenuous doublethink of the Roman Catholic Church on the other, I know which I prefer.'[5]

In this chapter, I consider the present relationship and interaction between Darwinism and religion. Confining my discussion to the cutting-edge issues, I avoid the visible but sterile discussion between evolutionists of all kinds and the American evangelical Protestants who would have us read the Bible absolutely literally. At least since the time of Augustine, a mere four centuries after Christ, it has been accepted that one may legitimately interpret Scripture metaphorically or allegorically if need be.[6] Here I assume, in addition, that the theory of evolution by natural selection is sufficiently well established that no more debate is needed on this matter. Throughout I am concerned especially with Christianity, for it is from this one, particular religion that Darwinism grew and reacted. But the main points apply to the other great theistic faiths, Judaism and Islam, as well.

A central issue in these faiths is the relationship between God and His favoured creation, humans; and this issue structures the discussion that follows. First I examine the consequences of Darwinism for arguments for and against the existence of God. I look at three arguments in particular: the argument from design (that God brought designed organisms into being directly); the argument from progress (that God guided the evolutionary process from simple beginnings to ensure that humans eventually emerged); and the argument from evil (that so wasteful and cruel a process cannot be God's handiwork, therefore God does not exist). Moving to the other side of the relationship, I explore the impact of Darwinism upon traditional theistic views of the unique status of humans: as bearers of immortal souls; as beings capable of moral choice; and as witnesses to God's mystery.

II DESIGN

The argument from design, also known as the teleological argument, starts from the belief that the world – the organic world particularly – is not just thrown together randomly, but works or functions in a harmonious way towards certain ends. Taking a famous example, the eye seems as if it is designed for the purpose of enabling sight. Just as other objects designed to enable sight (such as the telescope) have designers, so, by analogy, the eye must have a designer, adequate to the task. The argument concludes that only the all-powerful and all-loving being that Christians call 'God' could have designed the eye. Therefore God exists.

Following Darwin himself, the defining mark of Darwinism today is the commitment to explain apparent design as the product of natural law operating blindly.[7] If you are a Darwinian, then above all you believe that the abundant design-like features of the world are due to natural selection.[8] For some scientists, this commitment is the ultimate issue. Dawkins declaims (with some relief) that Darwinism at last makes it possible to be 'an intellectually fulfilled atheist'.[9] He argues that, although David Hume in the eighteenth century made the argument logically implausible, in the absence of an alternative explanation of apparent design, Hume's contemporaries really had no option but to continue to accept the argument. After Darwin, however, and the theory of natural selection, the argument is completely pushed aside, and the way is open to fulfilling non-belief.

Other scientists are less confident. A number of physicists today are drawn to some version of the so-called 'anthropic principle', the belief that, had the laws of nature not been exactly as they are, then life could never have evolved, and that, since the exact form of nature's laws could have been any one of an infinite range, the only plausible conclusion is that there was design in some sense.[10] Of course, as critics point out, the problem with this argument is the assumption that there is an infinite range, and that the actual universe contingently fits only one point on this range. Nor is it obvious that the conclusion of design follows even if the laws of nature could only have been what they are. Is there design behind the fact that Pythagoras' theorem holds only of right-angled triangles? Alternatively, consider the possibility that the infinite range *is* fully satisfied, and there are multiple universes. That our universe is what it is, perhaps uniquely with living beings, is then no more evidence of design than the fact that one particular person wins the lottery rather than another, or that the winner is richer than the losers.[11]

There are other strategies for refloating the argument from design. One vocal group of biologists are enthusiasts for so-called 'intelligent design'. They argue that the organic world is just too tightly functioning to be a product of blind laws, natural selection in particular. The biochemist Michael Behe claims that, at the micro-level, we find that organisms exhibit 'irreducible complexity': they are just too smoothly integrated and well functioning to be the product of nature unaided.[12] In support of his case, Behe instances a number of processes which he believes are irreducibly complex, among them the mammalian blood-clotting system, which works in a sequential way (as a 'cascade') with every stage absolutely essential. In Behe's view, such a mechanism cannot have been produced through selection, since gradual transitions from one functioning precursor of the system to another would simply have been impossible. At some point in the process, Behe argues, there must have been an absolute break – a jump or 'saltation' from one precursor to another. Only a designing intelligence, Behe concludes, could have engineered such a change.

In the opinion of his critics, however, this claim of discontinuity is precisely the point at which his argument is vulnerable.[13] There are few, if any, complex processes which show no traces of their evolutionary past. Furthermore, to assume that something is essential now is not to say that it was always essential or that there was no other, now eliminated, precursor process which performed some other task in the past. From the Darwinian point of view, blood clotting appears to offer exemplary testimony to selection's power. Almost every stage seems to have been made from some other process, which evolved for a different function.[14] The same is true for other, similar biochemical processes. Recently, for instance, the Krebs cycle, the biochemical process which captures energy for the functioning cell, has been shown in detail to be jerry-built from other already existing parts.[15] In any case, critics argue, a position such as Behe's leaves itself open to major theological problems. If God (or an intelligent designer) is needed to produce the very complex, why then did God not prevent the dreadfully bad but very simple? Some horrendous ailments start with a small change in one molecule. Why was this not prevented – surely a task within the range of a being who created the blood-clotting cascade?

Here William Dembski has stepped in, supplying theological support for Behe's science-based argument.[16] Dembski proposes an 'explanatory filter'. He argues that there is a three-tier level to the world and to its explanations. Some things happen just as a matter of expectation, with regularity. One thinks for instance of a blue-eyed child from blue-eyed parents. At this level, a scientific explanation referring to law is adequate. Then there are things which happen occasionally, by chance. A random new feature, caused by a mutation. Here no explanation is needed, other than to say it happened by chance. Finally some things are so improbable, so unlikely, we think that law and chance are excluded. Here, as with blood clotting, a designer is needed.[17]

A neat solution, but problematic. It works only if law, chance and design are mutually exclusive. But are the options exclusive? Why should one not say – following the evolutionary geneticist R. A. Fisher – that new variations, caused by mutation, arise by chance with respect to our knowledge of the appearance of any individual instance, but are certainly caused lawfully? Why should one not say – again following Fisher, who was a practising Anglican – that God stands behind everything, whether we ourselves see the working of law or not?[18]

Dembski is silent on these points. Not so others. Can the Designer, the Christian God, work through law rather than miracle? Alvin Plantinga – arguably North America's leading philosopher of religion – rather doubts this possibility. For Plantinga, to push God back to a remote law-governed past is to slide from theism (an immanent God) to some form of deism (God as unmoved mover). Plantinga writes: 'according to serious theism, God is constantly, immediately, intimately, and directly active in his creation: he constantly upholds it in existence and providentially governs it. He is immediately and directly active in everything from the Big Bang to the sparrow's fall. Literally nothing happens without his upholding hand.' As a theist, therefore, one would expect God to intervene in the creation. Plantinga continues: 'There is nothing in the least untoward in the thought that on some occasions God might do something in a way different from his usual way – e.g., raise someone from the dead or change water into wine.'[19] To argue otherwise, as the Darwinian would have us do, is to thrust us away from true belief.

Not all theists would agree with Plantinga on this point. The Catholic priest Ernan McMullin replies that the real issue 'is not whether God *could* have intervened in the natural order', for it is surely within God's power to do so. Rather, the question is whether it is at all likely that God would have done so. 'In the absence of the Genesis narrative', writes McMullin, 'would it appear likely that the God of the salvation story would also act in a special way to bring the ancestral living kinds into existence? It hardly seems to be the case.'[20] McMullin himself stills finds virtue in the teleological argument, although he accepts that the argument is no longer compelling but more something after the fact (of having committed oneself to God on other grounds). It is less a proof and more an illustration of the glory of what God has wrought. McMullin points out that there is a venerable strain of Christian thought which regards creation less as a miraculous one-shot affair and much more of an unfurling that will take considerable time. Augustine in particular saw God, who Himself stands outside time, as having created everything in an instant but in the form of 'seeds' of potentiality, which will then develop through time. This is not evolutionism; it is not even evolutionism by another name or in anticipation; but it *is* a theological position which finds law-bound evolution a congenial world picture.[21]

III PROGRESS

If one looks at the whole sweep of evolutionary history, from the emergence of primitive bacteria onward, one sees a sequence marked by a slow but gradual rise in complexity and sophistication.[22] It is overly simplistic to think of a straight progression from sea to land to air to consciousness and culture; but, that said, something much like this seems to have happened. Furthermore, on the Darwinian view, this has been a selection-driven process. With humankind as its highest point and apparently inevitable product, Darwinian evolution seems not merely something compatible with Christianity, but positively supportive.

Certainly there have been those who have backed such a view. Famously (or notoriously) in the last century, the French Jesuit palaeontologist Pierre Teilhard de Chardin claimed that there is an upward progression to life, ending at something called the 'Omega Point', which he identified with Jesus Christ.[23] More recently, the Anglican palaeontologist Simon Conway Morris has suggested that life is bound to move upwards towards the human form. 'Although there may be a billion potential pathways for evolution to follow from the Cambrian explosion', he has argued, 'in fact the real range of possibilities and hence the expected end results appear to be much more restricted.'[24] Consequently, 'within certain limits the outcome of evolutionary processes might be rather predictable'. It is important, however, to note the extent to which both Teilhard and Conway Morris do not belong to the mainstream of evolutionary thinking. Teilhard was much influenced by the vitalist philosopher Henri Bergson, who in turn took much of his evolutionism from Herbert Spencer. Teilhard's science was strongly criticised by biologists, especially Peter Medawar.[25] Conway Morris' thinking is more in line with non-Darwinian sentiments about non-adaptive constraints, and also very controversial.

Interestingly, today there is much support amongst unimpeachably orthodox Darwinians (including those with little sympathy for religion) for a progressivist reading of evolutionary history, with selection playing a key role. The sociobiologist Edward O. Wilson writes that: 'the overall average across the history of life has moved from the simple and few to the more complex and numerous. During the past billion years, animals as a whole evolved upward in body size, feeding and defensive techniques, brain and behavioral complexity, social organization, and precision of environmental control – in each case farther from the nonliving state than their simpler antecedents did.' He adds: 'Progress, then, is a property of the evolution of life as a whole by almost any conceivable intuitive standard, including the acquisition of goals and intentions in the behavior of animals.'[26] Dawkins likewise has been at the forefront of those arguing that upward progress is more than mere contingency. In a tradition going back to Darwin himself, Dawkins and like-minded biologists argue that evolving lineages get caught up in 'arms races', where they compete against each other, thus improving adaptations.[27] The prey gets faster and in response the predator gets faster, and then in counter-response the prey gets yet faster. Dawkins argues that the ultimate result of the arms race is the emergence, with humankind, of creatures with the most powerful mental equipment on earth. The fact that we humans seem to be twenty-three times more intelligent than the hippopotamus does not make our species 'higher', in his view; but it does reveal something fundamental about evolution.[28] In recent years, Dawkins has come increasingly to describe human intelligence as the non-contingent apotheosis of the selection-driven course of biological history.[29]

There are long-standing criticisms of this whole line of argumentation. For a start, modern evolutionary ideas are in part the offspring of Enlightenment hopes and beliefs in social and cultural progress, so it is not surprising that evolutionists, even today, should find that their theories support progress. For all of the appeal to natural selection, the progressivism may still be no more than a cultural gloss on the science.[30] Moreover, the relationship between theism and progressivism is far from straightforward. Traditionally, the philosophy of progress has been considered deeply antithetical to Christian beliefs, for progress is the alternative to the Christian's belief that we are in the hands of Providence, that we ourselves can improve nothing, and it is only through God's grace that we can have hope of salvation.[31] Teilhard ran into trouble with his authorities and was forbidden to publish in his lifetime. On the side of science, there are those – the palaeontologist Stephen Jay Gould particularly, eloquently and adamantly in recent years – who have argued that evolutionary progress is an illusion, and that we are going nowhere, slowly.[32] Drawing attention to the asteroid that wiped out the dinosaurs some 65 million years ago, Gould concluded that, since there is no evidence that the dinosaurs were evolving in the direction of larger brain size, 'we must assume that consciousness would not have evolved on our planet if a cosmic catastrophe had not claimed the dinosaurs as victims. In an entirely literal sense, we owe our existence, as large and reasoning mammals, to our lucky stars.'[33]

None of these arguments is irresistible. One can argue that the fact that social progress was the spur to evolutionism does not mean that, scientifically, one must reject the notion. Many Christians have made an accommodation with progress.[34] As for the non-directedness of evolution, one can point out that, however defined and however caused, Gould seems to allow some kind of rise of complexity. Moreover, many, including palaeontologists, think his worries are overblown.[35] Perhaps easiest for the Christian is to sidestep the whole debate by taking the neo-Augustinian position endorsed by McMullin – that the laws of nature are God's laws, and He could create humans however He wished. Progress or not, direction or contingency: for both options, 'the outcome is of God's making, and from the biblical standpoint could properly be said to be part of God's plan'.[36] The point here is that God is outside time and hence for Him, the thought, the creation and the product are all one. God is not simply forecasting on the basis of what will happen. 'For God to plan is for the outcome to occur. There is no interval between the decision and completion.'[37]

IV THE PROBLEM OF PHYSICAL EVIL

There is a special problem inherent in the idea that God might have chosen to create humans, and all other species, through natural selection. On the face of it, natural selection is egregiously wasteful and cruel. Consider those arms races, which produce adaptive traits in predator and prey species at the cost of the destruction of generations of individual creatures. What sort of God enacts a law that imposes such suffering on the sentient world? At the very least, God comes across as a sadist who has set up a kind of ongoing, gladiatorial contest as a condition of survival here on earth. Better, some suggest, to infer that there is no God, and no larger meaning to the suffering. According to Dawkins, the 'universe we observe has precisely the properties we should expect if there is, at bottom, no design, no purpose, no evil and no good, nothing but blind, pitiless indifference'.[38]

This problem is a special, Darwinian case of a more ancient theological problem, the problem of evil. If God is (as the theist insists) all loving and all powerful, then why does evil exist? If God were all powerful God could stop it, and if God were all loving God would stop it. Traditionally this problem is divided into two parts, that of human-caused evil (Auschwitz) and that of physical evil (an earthquake). For the moment, let us concentrate on physical evil, in its Darwinian dimensions, recognising immediately that, although the problem of physical evil is not a problem raised exclusively by Darwinism, the problem is one Darwinism exacerbates.

No theist can (or does) take lightly the challenge of reconciling God's putative beneficence with the undeniable existence of physical evil. A traditional countermove is to argue that being all powerful does not imply the ability to do the impossible. On this argument, God cannot make $2 + 2 = 5$, and no more can God, having decided to create through law, make physical evil disappear. It is as if, once God had elected for a law-governed universe, physical evil simply came as part of the package. Along these lines, the philosopher B. R. Reichenbach has asked, 'what would it entail to alter the natural laws regarding digestion, so that arsenic or other poisons would not negatively affect my constitution? Would not either arsenic or my own physiological composition or both have to be altered such that they would, in effect, be different from the present objects which we now call arsenic or human digestive organs?'[39] Paradoxically, perhaps, Dawkins himself aids this line of argument. He has long maintained that the only way in which complex adaptation could have been produced by law is through natural selection. He argues that alternative mechanisms for producing adaptation (notably Lamarckism) do not in fact work, while alternative mechanisms for producing non-adaptive change (notably evolution by jumps, or saltationism) are inadequate. For Dawkins, if 'a life-form displays adaptive complexity', anywhere in the universe, then 'it will always be recognizable as Darwinian life'.[40] In short, if God was to create through law, then it had to be through Darwinian law. There was no other choice. (This of course is not to say that, knowing the subsequent pain, God was right to create at all, but that is another matter, and none of Darwinism's business.)

There are other, perhaps more theological responses to the problem of evil. For some, the problem has meant a radical rethinking of their conception of God. Particularly influential here has been the process philosophy of Alfred North Whitehead, who argued that we see in the world God's own struggle to impose His will on matter and to bring things to a triumphant conclusion.[41] Clearly this whole position is deeply evolutionary, for it has at its heart a God who is not fixed and beyond improvement, once and for all, but rather changing and itself striving towards greater perfection. For this reason alone, more traditional Christians find this theology unacceptable – it is to compromise God's omnipotence. Remember that, for Augustine, God stands outside time and hence beyond change.

Many of the traditionalists prefer rather a position on evil which makes it essential, in some way, for moral improvement. This earth of ours is the vale of 'soul making', as we are burnished and tempered by strife and suffering. The philosopher John Hick argues that, without physical evil, we would feel no inclination to better ourselves in any way. 'The systematic elimination of unjust suffering, and the consequent apportioning of suffering to desert, would entail that there would be no doing of the right simply because it is right and without any expectation of reward.'[42] Without random pain and suffering, so the argument goes, we would always and only do good on the assured expectation of reward. There would never be the possibility or inclination to do good simply because it is good: to exercise what Kant called the 'good will', acting virtuously purely for virtue's sake. Of course, whether or not well taken, none of this line of argument has much to do with evolution *per se*. However, it is often bound up with an appeal to mystery – ultimately physical evil is mysterious and inexplicable – and this does have something to do with evolution, and with Darwinism in particular. I return to the point below.

V THE SOUL

The time has come to move from God's side of the relationship between God and humankind, and to consider issues of special relevance to the theistic view of what it is to be human. Christian doctrine proclaims that we humans have immortal souls. These souls are not to be identified directly with mind and consciousness, but there is a close link. For Aquinas, souls are the possession of all living things. Humans alone have 'intellectual souls'.[43] Obviously, the Darwinian position impinges here. But what is the Darwinian position? There is no standard view, but all would insist that the mind is in some sense connected to the brain, emergent in some way, and that the mind/brain evolved for adaptive reasons. Presumably, brains grew larger and more complex, minds started to come into being, and then perhaps proved their own adaptive worth by dragging brains along after them. Wilson proposes something he calls a theory of 'autocatalytic' evolution: at points or thresholds one gets positive feedback and evolution goes very rapidly.[44] In human evolution this could have happened twice. First, when ancestral humans began walking upright, it paid either to be on all fours, or to be on two legs, but not to be in-between. There was thus strong selection pressure not to delay the transition from one to the other. Second, when ancestral humans developed large brains. These are so expensive to produce and maintain that they need to be really big or their benefits do not outweigh their costs.

As soon as one gets into details, of course, one gets into speculation. The evolution of the brain and of consciousness is a massive problem and no one could pretend that Darwinians now have a full and canonical answer. But one thing should be emphasised: although Darwinians are seeking a natural explanation, this is not at the expense of denying or downgrading consciousness. No one is claiming that it does not exist or is not important. The very opposite in fact.

'Saying that we have no scientific explanation of sentience is not the same as saying that sentience does not exist at all', writes the linguist and evolutionary psychologist Steven Pinker. 'I am as certain that I am sentient as I am certain of *anything*, and I bet you feel the same. Though I concede that my curiosity about sentience may never be satisfied, I refuse to believe that I am just confused when I think I am sentient at all!'[45]

For present purposes, we can short-circuit most of this debate. Even if the full explanation of consciousness remains hidden from scientific eyes, there is reason to think that the way the Darwinian approaches the problem is one which resonates very much with Christian thinking, especially with the official position of modern-day Catholicism. Few Darwinians today would think that the conscious mind involves a distinct substance, as was supposed by Plato in antiquity and Descartes in modern times. Rather, they would think that consciousness is rooted in the material world, and comes about because of the distinctive organisation of the brain. Order the neurons one way and you get Shakespeare. Order them another way and you get Hitler, or an idiot, or nothing at all. It is much the same with Christianity, particularly with Thomism. The tradition of Thomas Aquinas, reflecting the ideas of Aristotle in *De Anima*, sees the soul as embodied in organisation rather than being a separate substance. For Aristotle and Aquinas, the human soul is less a material thing, and more a principle of ordering, or what, in Aristotelian terms, is called the 'form'.[46] It exists and can function causally – Aquinas speaks of 'actuating' – but it is not a substance. Rather, 'the soul is the ultimate principle', enabling all vital actions; it is the motive factor behind nutrition, sensation, locomotion and acts of understanding. For Aquinas, 'this prime factor in intellectual activity, whether we call it mind or intellectual soul, is the formative principle of the body'.[47]

This is not to say that all tensions between the Darwinian view of consciousness and the Christian view of the soul are now gone. Even if you agree that there are interesting and fruitful parallels between the Aristotle/Aquinas approach to souls and consciousness and the Darwinian approach to that aspect of intellect and consciousness which makes humans special, there are still problems remaining. These are highlighted by the population geneticist (and sometime Dominican priest) Francisco J. Ayala.[48] There is the question of the introduction of the soul, and then there are subsequent questions about such matters as original sin. If one identifies the soul fairly closely with the mind, then one is (as just above) rather suggesting a natural and (for the Darwinian) gradual evolution. This goes against Christian theology, as stressed by the Pope in his recent papal letter. He would take the whole issue out of the range of science. 'The sciences of observation describe and measure the multiple manifestations of life with increasing precision and correlate them with the time line. The moment of transition to the spiritual cannot be the object of this kind of observation.'[49] Rather, 'the experience of metaphysical knowledge, of self-awareness and self-reflection, of moral conscience, freedom, or again, of aesthetic and religious experience, falls within the competence of philosophical analysis and reflection, while theology brings out its ultimate meaning according to the Creator's plans'. For John Paul, the soul is something introduced at one point in time, miraculously. 'With man, then, we find ourselves in the presence of an ontological difference, an ontological leap, one could say.'[50]

Once we stop treating the soul and the mind as equivalent, the rapprochement sketched above begins to look less likely. Evolutionary biologists believe that a group of proto-humans evolved into early humans. There was no bottleneck down to just two people, a male and a female, an Adam and an Eve. Are Darwinian Christians to believe that one generation had no souls and the next did, even though, intellectually, they were virtually identical? Are we to believe that one pair had souls and no others? Popular recently has been the 'Eve hypothesis', arguing (on the basis of mitochondrial evidence) that all humans are descended from one woman. But as Ayala points out, this does not mean that we had no other contemporaneous female ancestors – we all share at least one ancestor but we had many others.[51]

Logically one can certainly insist that souls were inserted at one specific point, but in spirit this goes against Darwinism. Or one can suggest that (intellectual) souls are not necessarily something possessed only by humans, although this would be contested by traditional Christians. The point is that there are questions here – some would say tensions – that have to be answered and resolved. Darwinism throws up major questions for the Christian which cannot be ignored.

VI THE MORAL LIFE

The question of human origins and of our immortal souls leads straight to another important point of contact between Darwinism and Christianity. Being made in the image of God entails that we are beings with freedom and choice, with the ability to do right and wrong. For the Christian, we humans are fallen beings, tainted with original sin. We are free to choose the good but we have a tendency to fall away, to do that which we should not. Hence the existence of moral evil. How does the Christian moral perspective on human nature fit with the theory of evolution through natural selection? Let us begin with the question of morality and then move to the question of freedom.

Moral codes and directives are an essential part of theism.[52] Judaism has its ten commandments, Christianity its additional love commandment, and Islam likewise its directives, for instance about obligations to orphans and to widows. Popular lore has it that here is a point of major conflict with Darwinism, for the science promotes a very different set of ethical norms.[53] Supposedly, evolution gives rise (under the name of 'social Darwinism') to extreme laissez-faire economics, to a creed of selfishness, and at worst to a bloody lust for battle and extermination.[54] Struggle for existence in nature; struggle for existence in human affairs. But this is a simplistic reading of matters, particularly with respect to modern thinkers. Notoriously, E. O. Wilson is ardent in his Darwinian ethicising, and yet his moral directives translate into an enthusiasm for biodiversity and an urge to preserve the vanishing Brazilian rain forests.[55] In true dispensationalist fashion, he warns of an ecological Armageddon to come and begs us to repent our profligate ways before it is too late.[56] Sounding much like the theist who interprets God's charge to Adam as one of stewardship, Wilson tells us that we are to rule nature and not to destroy it. Now, alas, we are destroying species at an unprecented rate, and, most tragically, among the worst affected places are the rain forests and jungles of the tropics. We must do something before it is too late. We must respond. The challenge lies before us.

Recent Darwinian theorising has taken a somewhat different tack to the question of morality. With the development of 'sociobiology', it is now argued that much animal social behaviour – and this includes human social behaviour – was shaped by selective forces in the past.[57] Success in life's struggles can depend as much on cooperation as on conflict, and this gives rise to 'altruism', where this is understood as behaviour which benefits others on the expectation (not necessarily conscious) of benefits given in return.[58] For obvious reasons, sociobiology has attracted the attention of those interested in moral questions.[59] An increasing number of philosophers, theologians and others feel that there is here truly a link between biology and these most central of human activities and feelings. Needless to say, acts of biological altruism are not necessarily moral acts; simply going blindly through the motions is not the same as deliberately doing things because they are right and refraining from other things because they are wrong. But perhaps, it is suggested, in order to get us humans to be good biological altruists – something of great importance for animals like us, who can succeed only if we work together – selection has put into place sentiments which inspire us to moral action. In other words, our sense of right and wrong is an adaptation put into place by natural selection to make us good cooperators.[60]

Such a Darwinian picture of human nature obviously meshes well with the central moral tenets of Christianity, as well as those of other great world religions. The central love commandment – 'love your neighbour as yourself' – is a perfect exemplification of Darwinian, enlightened self-interest. If I help you when you need it, then I can expect you to help me when I need it. It costs me little to pull you out of the well, but it means much to me when you pull me out of the well. Perhaps some tension arises because the Darwinian is committed to a differential morality – aid to close relatives first, and only later to others in one's group, and finally (if at all) to outsiders. This does not harmonise with Jesus' parable of the Good Samaritan. But religions themselves have always wrestled with this issue – 'Do I have an equal obligation to all or should I put family and friends first?' Moreover, religions are by no means as inevitably universalistic as certain themes and sayings in the Gospels might suggest. Judaism has often seemed an inwardly looking religion, concerned first and most significantly with the good of the tribe. Likewise, the followers of Jesus spent much time justifying special attitudes to relatives and to those in one's group.[61] In the New Testament, one reads that if 'anyone does not provide for his relatives, and especially for his own family, he has disowned the faith and is worse than an unbeliever'.[62]

What about freedom? It is central to theism that we humans, though fallen, are free to choose between good and ill. But does not a causal theory like Darwinism cast doubt on both our fallenness and our freedom? Is not Darwinism particularly egregious in this respect? After all, as we have seen, the Darwinian reading of Adam and Eve as at best mythological and symbolic does not seem to leave much scope for the reality of original sin. As for free will, it is often said that sociobiology implies 'genetic determinism', with humans being mere marionettes dancing to the tune of their DNA.[63] If a commitment to Darwinism has any such implication, that does not bode well for science–religion harmony on the issue of free will.

On closer inspection, however, matters are less straightforward. For one thing, it is far from clear that we should accept the age-old opposition of 'determinism' and 'freedom'. Yes, Darwinian theory is causal, and in that sense deterministic. But, on one view, determinism is not the opposite of genuine freedom; rather, it is a precondition for its existence. Consider that, in a completely random world, the results of one's own freely chosen actions would not result in the outcomes that one had intended.[64] Genuine freedom may exist only in a deterministic world. Moreover, while it is true that Darwinian sociobiology is genetically deterministic, we should note the level of determinism being imposed. It is claimed that our moral sentiments and attitudes derive from our genes (in the context of culture, of course). In other words, biology determines what we regard as right and wrong. But no one, other than the existentialists at their most extreme, ever claimed that we have freedom about the content of right and wrong. For sociobiologists as for most other thinkers, the freedom comes in the choice to be good or not. The Darwinian allows – insists on – a dimension of autonomy for humans.[65] Ants are hardwired to do what they do, without choice. But humans, thanks to their large brains and subsequent intelligence, have the choice to follow the dictates of conscience or to be selfish.

Indeed, biological studies of behaviour have if anything made us appreciate far more vividly than before how unlike hardwired insects we humans are. If something goes wrong, the insects have no recourse, no way of escaping their problems. Daniel Dennett tells of a wasp which brings food to its nest to provision its young:

> The wasp's routine is to bring the paralyzed cricket to the burrow, leave it on the threshold, go inside to see that all is well, emerge, and then drag the cricket in. If the cricket is moved a few inches away while the wasp is inside making her preliminary inspection, the wasp, on emerging from the burrow, will bring the cricket back to the threshold, but not inside, and will then repeat the preparatory procedure of entering the burrow to see that everything is all right.

This can go on and on indefinitely. 'The wasp never thinks of pulling the cricket straight in. On one occasion this procedure was repeated forty times, always with the same result.'[66] We humans, who live socially, who invest so much effort in raising but a few offspring, cannot afford to be waspish. Fortunately, we do have ways – put in place by selection because of the kind of animals that we are – which enable us to think about our problems and challenges and respond to obstacles. Although we are causally bound in this Darwinian world, we thus have a dimension of the freedom demanded by the Christian, the freedom to do good or ill.

And here, perhaps, we edge towards a Darwinian gloss on original sin. If the sociobiologists are right, then it is part of our biological heritage to be torn by conflicting emotions. In part, what one wants to do is what is in one's own direct interest. In part, what one wants to do is what is in the interests of others. We are pulled in two directions at once. The New Testament well describes our divided predicament. 'I see in my members another law at war with the law of my mind and making me captive to the law of sin which dwells in my members.'[67] We have freedom, but we also have conflicting desires. So sometimes we do what we should – we follow the dictates of morality – and sometimes we do not. What the Christians described, the Darwinians have explained.

VII MYSTERY

Central to theism is the notion of mystery: that we can approach God but a short way, and that ultimately His nature must lie beyond the veil. We are finite, and He is infinite. Thomists stress that one can in some sense speak of God analogically – it makes sense to speak of God as a parent, whereas it makes little or no sense to speak of God as (say) the Empire State Building – but truly God is beyond our ken. Making a virtue from this limitation, theologians have seen another response to the problem of physical evil. Although stressing the significance of physical evil for human soul making, the philosopher John Hick returns, in the end, to our blindness beside the true Creator of all. He writes: 'The only appeal left is to mystery. This is not, however, merely an appeal to the negative fact that we cannot discern any rationale of human suffering. It may be that the very mysteriousness of this life is an important aspect of its character as a sphere of soul making.'[68]

It is the very fact that suffering makes no sense that makes it significant for the Christian. True spiritual development demands that one overcome the apparent irrationality through an appeal to faith. Mystery therefore is something positive. Referring to a tradition which includes both Kierkegaard and Karl Barth – the latter one of the greatest theologians of the twentieth century – John Haught writes: 'The Bible... proclaims the paradoxical possibility of faith and hope in God in spite of all evil and suffering. Some of us would even argue that faith has no intensity or depth unless it is a leap into the unknown in the face of such absurdity. Faith is always faith "in spite of" all the difficulties that defy reason and science.'[69]

Many Darwinians find this attitude quite incompatible with their commitment to that rationality and evidence exemplified by Darwinian theory. Dennett complains to the mysterians: 'You must not expect me to go along with your defense of faith as a path to truth if at any point you appeal to the very dispensation you are supposedly trying to justify. Before you appeal to faith when reason has you backed into a corner, think about whether you really want to abandon reason when reason is on your side.'[70] Dennett points out that we all use reasoning and evidence when it suits us. On what grounds, then, do we abandon them when we come to the biggest questions of all? Bluntly, he presses the point that, however much discomfort we save ourselves by letting faith do the work that reason should do, the intellectual justification is nil. 'If you think that this common but unspoken understanding about faith is anything better than socially useful obfuscation to avoid mutual embarrassment and loss of face, you have either seen much more deeply into this issue than any philosopher ever has (for none has ever come up with a good defense of this) or you are kidding yourself.'[71]

Nevertheless, there is a line of ultra-Darwinian thought that might calm Dennett's worry. Natural selection cares little about truth and knowledge in their own right. It cares only about survival and reproduction. For this reason, selection did not design humans to peer into the ultimate mysteries of the universe. Rather, from what we know of human evolution, we were designed to come down from the trees, move onto the plains, and to become scavengers – picking up the pieces after the big predators had had their fill. In the light of this evolutionary heritage, we should perhaps not expect that we are capable of finding the truth about everything. Answers to some question, even some of the most important questions – such as why a good God would permit evil in the world – could be forever hidden from us. To quote the great twentieth-century evolutionist J. B. S. Haldane: '[M]y own suspicion is that the universe is not only queerer than we suppose, but queerer than we *can* suppose.'[72]

An argument along these lines obviously does not vindicate Christianity as reasonable, nor does it count as a solution to the problem of evil. The point, rather, is that if one wishes to emphasise the mystery of life – and such an emphasis has always been central to Christian faith – then there is warrant in Darwinism for just such an emphasis. The Darwinian agrees with the Christian that it is not necessarily within the reach of humankind to know everything.

VIII DARWINISM AND RELIGION

There is still much debate about the proper relationship between Darwinism and religion, and between science and religion more generally.[73] Some, including Richard Dawkins in our day and Thomas Henry Huxley before him, think science and religion are necessarily in conflict. Others, including Stephen Jay Gould and neo-orthodox theologians such as Karl Barth, think that science and religion do not speak to the same things. A third group, including the Pope, think that science and religion touch and overlap but are essentially separate. Yet another party, prominently the followers of Whitehead, would integrate science and religion. We have seen all of these different positions exhibited in the above discussion. Most people tend to be somewhat ecumenical on these issues. When the science seems to be reasonably favourable, they do not mind a certain degree of interaction. When the science threatens religious belief, the two are kept fairly separate.

It is no surprise that Darwinism should remain so central to the science–religion debate. In major respects an outgrowth of religion, the Darwinian theory of natural selection offers answers to questions that are of interest and concern to the religious believer, especially to the Western theist.[74] There are as yet no definitive answers to all of the questions. Indeed there is probably more debate and discussion and controversy on these matters now than at any time since the *Origin*. My own opinion is that there is no absolute barrier to a committed Darwinian being a Christian, or indeed to adhering to any other of the major religions of the West.[75] Clearly it will not always be easy, but no one ever thought that it would be. What is encouraging is that even within – especially within – the most orthodox and committed of Darwinian positions, there is much that is congenial to a believer of a fairly conservative nature. Design, pain, souls, freedom, sin, mystery: all of these and more are illuminated from a Darwinian perspective. One cannot ask for much more that this. Darwinism is one of the most important and stimulating ideas known to humankind. It is always challenging; it is not necessarily always threatening.

NOTES

1. Ruse 2000a.
2. Holden 2000, 431.
3. John Paul II 1997.
4. Ward 1996, 63.
5. Dawkins 1997b, 399.
6. Ruse 2000a, ch. 3.
7. Ruse 1999a.
8. Williams 1966.
9. Dawkins 1986, 5.
10. Barrow and Tipler 1986.
11. Weinberg 2001.
12. Behe 1996.
13. Pennock 1998.
14. Doolittle 1997.
15. K. Miller 1999.
16. Dembski 1998a, b.
17. Dembski 1998a, 98.
18. Fisher 1930, 1947.

19. Plantinga 1997, 149.
20. McMullin 1991, in Hull and Ruse 1998, 712.
21. McMullin 1993.
22. Ruse 1993a.
23. Teilhard de Chardin 1955.
24. Conway Morris 1998, 202.
25. Medawar 1967.
26. E. O. Wilson 1992, 187.
27. Dawkins and Krebs 1979.
28. Dawkins 1986.
29. Dawkins 1997a.
30. Ruse 1996, 1999b.
31. Bury 1920.
32. Gould 1989, 1996.
33. Gould 1989, 318.
34. Wagar 1972.
35. Vermeij 1987; Conway Morris 1998.
36. McMullin 1996, 156–7.
37. McMullin 1996, 157.
38. Dawkins 1995, 133.
39. Reichenbach 1976, 185.
40. Dawkins 1983, 423.
41. Haught 1995.
42. Hick 1978, 333.
43. Aquinas 1970, 43; *Summa Theologiae* (hereafter *ST*) 1a, 76, 1.
44. E. O. Wilson 1975.
45. Pinker 1997, 148.
46. Frede 1992.
47. Aquinas 1970, 43; *ST* 1a, 76, 1.
48. Ayala 1967.
49. John Paul II 1997, 383.
50. John Paul II 1997, 383.
51. Ayala 1998.
52. Ruse 2000a.
53. Ruse 2000a.
54. Paul, this volume.
55. E. O. Wilson 1992.
56. E. O. Wilson 1975.
57. Ruse 1985.
58. E. O. Wilson 1975.
59. Ruse 1994; Murphy 1982; Skyrms 1996.
60. Ruse and Wilson 1985, 1986; Rosenberg, this volume.

61. Wallwork 1982.
62. 1 Timothy 5.8.
63. Ruse 1985.
64. Ayer 1954.
65. Ruse 1987; Dennett 1984.
66. Dennett 1984, 11, quoting Wooldridge 1963, 82.
67. Romans 7.23.
68. Hick 1978, 333–4.
69. Haught 1995, 59.
70. Dennett 1995, 154.
71. Dennett 1995, 154–5.
72. Haldane 1927, 208–9; Pinker 1997 makes a similar point.
73. Barbour 1988; Gould 1999.
74. Brooke, this volume.
75. Ruse 2000a, b.

Part IV
Ways forward

DANIEL C. DENNETT

15 In Darwin's wake, where am I?

Parfois je pense; et parfois, je suis.
Paul Valéry[1]

Valéry's 'Variation sur Descartes' excellently evokes the vanishing act that has haunted philosophy ever since Darwin overturned the Cartesian tradition. If *my body* is composed of nothing but a team of a few trillion robotic cells, mindlessly interacting to produce all the large-scale patterns that tradition would attribute to the non-mechanical workings of my mind, there seems to be nothing left over to be *me*. Lurking in Darwin's shadow there is a bugbear: the incredible Disappearing Self.[2] One of Darwin's earliest critics, Robert MacKenzie, saw what was coming and could scarcely contain his outrage:

> In the theory with which we have to deal, Absolute Ignorance is the artificer; so that we may enunciate as the fundamental principle of the whole system, that, IN ORDER TO MAKE A PERFECT AND BEAUTIFUL MACHINE, IT IS NOT REQUISITE TO KNOW HOW TO MAKE IT. This proposition will be found, on careful examination, to express, in condensed form, the essential purport of the Theory, and to express in a few words all Mr. Darwin's meaning; who, by a strange inversion of reasoning, seems to think Absolute Ignorance fully qualified to take the place of Absolute Wisdom in all the achievements of creative skill.[3]

This 'strange inversion of reasoning' promises – or threatens – to dissolve the Cartesian *res cogitans* as the wellspring of creativity, and then where will we be? Nowhere, it seems. It *seems* that if creativity gets 'reduced' to 'mere mechanism' *we* will be shown not to exist at all. Or, we will exist, but we won't be thinkers, we won't manifest genuine 'Wisdom in all the achievements of creative skill'. The individual as Author of works and deeds will be demoted: a person, it seems, is a barely salient nexus, a mere slub in the fabric of causation.

Whenever we zoom in on the act of creation, it seems we lose sight of it. The genius we thought we could see from a distance gets replaced at the last instant by stupid machinery, an echo of Darwin's shocking substitution of Absolute Ignorance for Absolute Wisdom in the creation of the biosphere. Many people dislike Darwinism in their guts, and of all the ill-lit, murky reasons for antipathy to Darwinism, this one has always struck me as the deepest, but only in the sense of being the most entrenched, the least accessible to rational criticism. There are thoughtful people who scoff at creationism, dismiss dualism out of hand, pledge allegiance to academic humanism – and then get quite squirrelly when somebody proposes a Darwinian theory of creative intelligence. The very idea that all the works of human genius can be understood *in the end* to be mechanistically generated products of a cascade of generate-and-test algorithms arouses deep revulsion in many otherwise quite insightful, open-minded people.

Absolute Ignorance? Fie on anybody who would thus put 'A' and 'I' together! Serendipity is the wellspring of evolution, so it is fitting that an evolutionist such as I should adapt MacKenzie's happy capitalisation for a purpose he could hardly have imagined. His outraged scoffing at the powers of Absolute Ignorance has an uncannily similar echo more than a century later in the equally outraged scoffing at those who believe in what John Searle[4] has called 'strong AI', the thesis that *real* intelligence can be made by artifice, that the difference between a mindless mechanism and a mindful one is a difference of design (or *programme* – since whatever you can design in hardware you can implement in a virtual machine that has the same competence).[5]

Darwin's 'strange inversion of reasoning' turns an ancient idea upside-down. The 'top-down' perspective on creative intelligence supposes that it always takes a big, fancy, smart thing to create a lesser thing. No horseshoe has ever made a blacksmith; no pot has fashioned a potter. Hence we – and all the other fancy things we see around us – must have been created by something still fancier, something like us only more so. To many – perhaps most – people, this idea is *just obvious*. Consider this page from a creationist propaganda mailing:

> 1. Do you know of any building that didn't have a builder? YES/NO
> 2. Do you know of any painting that didn't have a painter? YES/NO
> 3. Do you know of any car that didn't have a maker? YES/NO
>
> If you answered 'YES' for any of the above give details: ________

But however strongly the idea appeals to common sense, Darwin shows us how it can be, in a word, false. Darwin shows us that a bottom-up theory of creation is, indeed, not only imaginable but empirically demonstrable. Absolute Ignorance *is* fully qualified to take the place of Absolute Wisdom in all the achievements of creative skill – *all* of them.

John Searle's Chinese Room thought experiment is a variation on the desperate joke of the creationists:

> Do you know of any machine that can understand Chinese? YES/NO
>
> If you answered 'YES' give details!________

While the creationists' rhetorical questions merely gesture towards the presumed embarrassments facing anybody who tries to 'give details' of an instance of bottom-up creation, Searle's challenge offers a survey of possible avenues the believers in strong AI might take in their attempts to 'give details' and purports to rebut them one and all. The believers in strong AI have been remarkably unmoved by Searle's attempts at refutation, and the comparison of Searle's position with creationism shows why. Biologists who cannot *yet* explain some particular puzzle about the non-miraculous path that led to one marvel of nature or another, who cannot *yet* 'give details' to satisfy the particular critic, nevertheless have such a fine track record of success in giving the details, and such a stable and fecund background theory to use in generating and confirming new details, that they simply dismiss the rhetorical implication: 'You'll never succeed!' They calmly acknowledge that they may need to develop a few new wrinkles before they can declare victory. Believers in strong AI are similarly content to concede that all AI models to date have been deficient in many respects, orders of magnitude too simple, many of them pursuing particular visions of AI that are simply mistaken. They go on to note that Searle isn't challenging particular details of the attempts to date; he purports to be offering an argument for the *in principle* impossibility of strong AI, a conclusion that he insists is meant to cover all *imaginable* complications of the underlying theoretical framework. They know that their underlying theoretical framework is nothing other than the straightforward extension, into the human brain and all its peripheral devices and interfaces, of the Darwinian programme of mindless mechanism doing, in the end, all the work. If Darwinian mechanisms can explain the existence of a skylark, in all its glory, they can surely explain the existence of an ode to a nightingale, too.[6] A poem is a wonderful thing, but not clearly more wonderful than a living, singing skylark.

Unsupportable antipathies often survive thanks to protective colouration: they blend into the background of legitimate objections to overstatements of the view under attack. Since the reach of Darwinian enthusiasm has always exceeded its grasp, there are always good criticisms of Darwinian excesses to hide amongst. Likewise, of course, for the excesses of the ideologues of AI. And so the battle rages, generating as much suspicion as insight. Darwinians who are sure that a properly nuanced, sophisticated Darwinism is proof against all the objections and misgivings – I am one such – should nevertheless recall the fate of the Freudian nags of the 1950s and 1960s, who insisted on seeing everything through the perspective of their hero's categories, only to discover that by the time you've attenuated your Freudianism to accommodate *everything*, it is Pickwickian Freudianism most of the way. Sometimes a cigar is just a cigar, and sometimes an idea is just an idea – not a meme – and sometimes a bit of mental machinery is not usefully interpreted as an adaptation dating back to our ancestral hunter-gatherer days or long before, even though it is, obviously, descended (with modifications) from some combination or other of such adaptations. We Darwinians will try to remind ourselves of this, hoping our doughty opponents will come to recognise that a Darwinian theory of creativity is not just a promising solution but the only solution in sight to a problem that is everybody's problem: *how can an arrangement of a hundred billion mindless neurons compose a creative mind, an I?*

William Poundstone has put the inescapable challenge succinctly in terms of 'the old fantasy of a monkey typing *Hamlet* by accident'. He calculates that the chances of this happening are '1 in 50 multiplied by itself 150,000 times'.

In view of this, it may seem remarkable that anything as complex as a text of *Hamlet* exists. The observation that *Hamlet* was written by Shakespeare and not some random agency only transfers the problem. Shakespeare, like everything else in the world, must have arisen (ultimately) from a homogeneous early universe. Any way you look at it *Hamlet* is a product of that primeval chaos.[7]

Where does all that design come from? What processes could conceivably yield such improbable 'achievements of creative skill'? What Darwin saw is that design is always both valuable and costly. It does not fall like manna from heaven, but must be accumulated the hard way, by time-consuming, energy-consuming processes of mindless search through 'primeval chaos', automatically preserving happy accidents when they occur. This broadband process of Research and Development is breathtakingly inefficient, but – this is Darwin's great insight – if the costly fruits of R and D can be thriftily conserved, copied and re-used, they can be accumulated over time to yield 'the achievements of creative skill'. 'This principle of preservation', Darwin says, 'I have called, for the sake of brevity, Natural Selection.'[8]

There is no requirement in Darwin's vision that these R and D processes run everywhere and always at the same tempo, with the same (in-)efficiency. Consider the unimaginably huge multi-dimensional space of all *possible* designed things – both natural and artificial. Every imaginable whale and unicorn, every automobile and spaceship and robot, every poem and mathematical proof and symphony finds its place somewhere in this Design Space. If we think of design work or R and D as a sort of *lifting* in Design Space,[9] then we can see that the gradualistic, frequently back-sliding, maximally inefficient basic search process can on important occasions yield new conditions that speed up the process, permitting faster, more effective local lifting.[10] Call any such product of earlier R and D a *crane*, and distinguish it from what Darwinism says does not happen: *skyhooks*.[11] Skyhooks, like manna from heaven, would be miracles, and if we posit a skyhook anywhere in our 'explanation' of creativity, we have in fact conceded defeat – 'Then a miracle occurs.'[12]

What, then, is a mind? The Darwinian answer is straightforward. A mind is a crane, a mechanism of not quite unimaginable complexity that can clamber through Design Space at a giddy – but not miraculously giddy – pace, thanks to all the earlier R and D, from all sources, that it exploits. What is the anti-Darwinian answer? It is perfectly expressed by one of the twentieth century's great creative geniuses (though, like MacKenzie, he probably didn't mean by his words what I intend to mean by them):

> Je ne cherche pas; je trouve.
>
> Pablo Picasso

Picasso purports to be a genius indeed, someone who does not need to engage in the menial work of trial and error, generate-and-test, R and D; he claims to be able to *leap* to the summits of the peaks – the excellent designs – in the vast reaches of Design Space without having to guide his trajectory (he searches not) by sidelong testing at any waystations. As an inspired bit of bragging, this is *nonpareil*, but I don't believe it for a minute. And anyone who has strolled through an exhibit of Picasso drawings (as I recently did in Valencia) looking at literally dozens of variations on a single theme, all signed – and sold – by the artist, will appreciate that whatever Picasso may have meant by his *bon mot*, he could not truly claim that he didn't engage in a time-consuming, energy-consuming exploration of neighbourhoods in Design Space. At best he could claim that his own searches were so advanced, so efficient, that it didn't seem – to himself – to be design *work* at all. But then what did he have within him that made him such a great designer? A skyhook, or a superb collection of cranes?[13]

We can now characterise a mutual suspicion between Darwinians and anti-Darwinians which distorts the empirical investigation of creativity. Darwinians suspect their opponents of hankering after a skyhook, a miraculous gift of genius whose powers have no decomposition into mechanical operations, however complex and informed by earlier processes of R and D. Anti-Darwinians suspect their opponents of hankering after an account of creative processes that so diminishes the Finder, the Author, the Creator, that it disappears, at best a mere temporary locus of mindless differential replication. We can make a little progress, I think, by building on Poundstone's example of the *creation of the creator of Hamlet*. Consider, then, a little thought experiment.

Suppose Dr Frankenstein designs and constructs a monster, Spakesheare, that thereupon sits up and writes out a play, *Spamlet*. My question is not about the author of *Waverley* but about the author of *Spamlet*.

Who is the author of *Spamlet*?

First, let's take note of what I claim to be irrelevant in this thought experiment. I haven't said whether Spakesheare is a robot, constructed out of metal and silicon chips, or, like the original Frankenstein's monster, constructed out of human tissues – or cells, or proteins, or amino acids, or carbon atoms. As long as the design work and the construction were carried out by Dr Frankenstein, it makes no difference to the example what the materials are. It might well turn out that the only way to build a robot small enough and fast enough and energy-efficient enough to sit on a stool and type out a play is to construct it from artificial cells filled with beautifully crafted motor proteins and other carbon-based nanorobots. That is an interesting technical and scientific question, but not of concern here. For exactly the same reason, if Spakesheare is a metal-and-silicon robot, it may be allowed to be larger than a galaxy, if that's what it takes to get the requisite complication into its programme – and we'll just have to repeal the speed limit for light for the sake of our thought experiment. These technical constraints are commonly declared to be off-limits in these thought experiments, so so be it. If Dr Frankenstein chooses to make his AI robot out of proteins and the like, that's his business. If his robot is cross-fertile with normal human beings and hence capable of creating what is arguably a new species by giving birth to a child, that is fascinating, but what we will be concerned with is Spakesheare's purported brainchild, *Spamlet*. Back to our question:

Who is the author of *Spamlet*?

In order to get a grip on this question, we have to look inside and see what happens in Spakesheare.[14] At one extreme, we find inside a file (if Spakesheare is a robot with a computer memory) or a basically *memorised* version of *Spamlet*, all loaded and ready to run. In such an extreme case, Dr Frankenstein is surely the author of *Spamlet*,[15] using his intermediate creation, Spakesheare, as a mere storage-and-delivery device, a particularly fancy word processor. *All* the R and D work was done earlier, and copied to Spakesheare by one means or another.

We can visualise this more clearly by imagining a sub-space of Design Space, which I call the Library of Babel, after Jorge Luis Borges' classic short story by that name.[16] Borges invites us to imagine a warehouse filled with books which appears to its inhabitants to be infinite; they eventually decide that it is not, but it might as well be, for it seems that on its shelves – in no order, alas – lie all the *possible* books.

Suppose that each book is 500 pages long, and each page consists of 40 lines of 50 spaces, so there are 2,000 character-spaces per page. Each space is either blank, or has a character printed on it, chosen from a set of 100 (the upper- and lower-case letters of English and other European languages, plus the blank and punctuation marks).[17] Somewhere in the Library of Babel is a volume consisting entirely of blank pages, and another volume is all question marks, but the vast majority consist of typographical gibberish; no rules of spelling or grammar, to say nothing of sense, prohibit the inclusion of a volume. Five hundred pages times two thousand characters per page gives a million character-spaces per book, so there are $100^{1,000,000}$ books in the Library of Babel. Since it is estimated that there are only 100^{40} (give or take a few) *particles* (protons, neutrons and electrons) in the region of the universe we can observe,[18] the Library of Babel is not remotely a physically possible object, but thanks to the strict rules with which Borges constructed it in his imagination, we can think about it clearly.

We need some terms for the quantities involved. The Library of Babel is not infinite, so the chance of finding anything interesting in it is not literally infinitesimal.[19] These words exaggerate in a familiar way, but we should avoid them. Unfortunately, all the standard metaphors – astronomically large, a needle in a haystack, a drop in the ocean – fall comically short. No *actual* astronomical quantity (such as the number of elementary particles in the universe, or the time since the Big Bang measured in nanoseconds) is even visible against the backdrop of these huge-but-finite numbers. If a readable volume in the Library were as easy to find as a particular drop in the ocean, we'd be in business! Dropped at random into the Library, your chance of ever encountering a volume with so much as a grammatical sentence in it is so vanishingly small that we might do well to capitalise the term – *Vanishingly* small – and give it a mate, *Vastly*, short for Very-much-more-than-astronomically.[20]

It is amusing to reflect on just how large this finite set of possible books is, compared with any actual library. Most of the books are pure gibberish, as noted, so consider the Vanishing subset of books composed entirely of English words, without a single misspelling. It is itself a Vast set, of course, and contained within it, but Vanishingly hard to find, is the Vast subset whose English words are lined up in grammatical sentences. A Vast but Vanishing subset of this subset in turn is the subset of books composed of English sentences that actually make sense. A Vast but Vanishing subset of these are about somebody named John, and a Vast but Vanishing subset of these are about the death of John F. Kennedy. A Vast but Vanishing subset of these are true... and a Vast but Vanishing subset of the possible true books about the death of JFK are written entirely in limericks. There are many orders of magnitude more possible true books in limerick form about the death of JFK than there are books in the Library of Congress.

Now we are ready to return to that needle-in-a-haystack, *Spamlet*, and consider how the trajectory to this particular place in the Library of Babel was traversed in actual history. If we find that the whole journey was already completed by the time Spakesheare's memory was constructed and filled with information, we know that Spakesheare played no role at all in the search. Working backwards, if we find that Spakesheare's only role was running the stored text through a spell-checker before using it to guide its typing motions, we will be unimpressed by claims of Spakeshearian authorship. This is a measurable, but Vanishing, part of the total R and D. There is a sizeable galaxy of near-twin texts of *Spamlet* – roughly a hundred million different minor mutants have but a single uncorrected typo in them, and if we expand our horizon to include one typo per page, we have begun to enter the land of Vast numbers of variations on the theme. Working back a little further, once we graduate from typos to *thinkos*,[21] those arguably mistaken, or sub-optimally chosen, words, we have begun to enter the land of serious authorship, as contrasted with mere copy-editing. The relative triviality of copy-editing, and yet its unignorable importance in shaping the final product, gets well represented in terms of our metaphor of Design Space, where every little bit of lifting counts for something, and sometimes a little bit of lifting moves you onto a whole new trajectory. As usual, we may quote Ludwig Mies van der Rohe at this juncture: 'God is in the details.'

Now let's turn the knobs on our thought experiment, as Douglas Hofstadter has recommended,[22] and look at the other extreme, in which Dr Frankenstein leaves most of the work to Spakesheare. The most realistic scenario would surely be that Spakesheare has been equipped by Dr Frankenstein with a virtual past, a lifetime stock of pseudo-memories of experiences on which to draw while responding to its Frankenstein-installed obsessive desire to write a play. Among those pseudo-memories, we may suppose, are many evenings at the theatre, or reading books, but also some unrequited loves, some shocking close calls, some shameful betrayals and the like. Now what happens? Perhaps some scrap of a 'human interest' story on the network news will be the catalyst that spurs Spakesheare into a frenzy of generate-and-test, ransacking its memory for useful titbits and themes, transforming – transposing, morphing – what it finds, jiggling the pieces into temporary, hopeful structures that compete for completion, most of them dismantled by the corrosive processes of criticism that nevertheless expose useful bits now and then, and so forth, and all of this multi-levelled search would be somewhat guided by multi-level, internally generated evaluations, including evaluation of the evaluation . . . of the evaluation functions as a response to evaluation of . . . the products of the ongoing searches.[23]

Now if the amazing Dr Frankenstein had actually anticipated all this activity down to its finest grain at the most turbulent and chaotic level, and had hand-designed Spakesheare's virtual past, and all its search machinery, to yield just this product, *Spamlet*, then Dr Frankenstein would be, once again, the author of *Spamlet*, but also, in a word, God. Such Vast foreknowledge would be simply miraculous. Restoring a smidgen of realism to our fantasy, we can set the knobs at a rather less extreme position and assume that Dr. Frankenstein was unable to foresee all this in detail, but rather delegated to Spakesheare most of the hard work of completing the trajectory in Design Space to *one literary work or another*, something to be determined by later R and D occurring within Spakesheare itself. We have now arrived, by this simple turn of the knob, in the neighbourhood of reality itself, for we already have actual examples of impressive artificial Authors who Vastly outstrip the foresight of their own creators. Nobody has yet created an artificial playwright worth serious attention, but an artificial chess player – IBM's Deep Blue – and an artificial composer – David Cope's EMI – have both achieved results that are, *in some respects*, equal to the best that human creative genius can muster.

Who beat Garry Kasparov, the reigning World Chess Champion? Not Murray Campbell or any of his IBM team. Deep Blue beat

Kasparov. Deep Blue designs better chess games than any of them can design. None of them can author a winning game against Kasparov. Deep Blue can. Yes, but. Yes, but. I am sure many of you are tempted to insist at this point that when Deep Blue beats Kasparov at chess, its brute force search methods are *entirely* unlike the exploratory processes that Kasparov uses when he conjures up his chess moves. But that is simply not so – or at least it is not so in the only way that could make a difference to the context of this debate about the universality of the Darwinian perspective on creativity. Kasparov's brain is made of organic materials, and has an architecture importantly unlike that of Deep Blue, but it is still, so far as we know, a massively parallel search engine which has built up, over time, an outstanding array of heuristic pruning techniques that keep it from wasting time on unlikely branches. There is no doubt that the investment in R and D has a different profile in the two cases; Kasparov has methods of extracting good design principles from past games, so that he can recognise, and know enough to ignore, huge portions of the game space that Deep Blue must still patiently canvass *seriatim*. Kasparov's 'insight' dramatically changes the shape of the search he engages in, but it does not constitute 'an *entirely* different' means of creation. Whenever Deep Blue's exhaustive searches close off a *type* of avenue that it has some means of recognising (a difficult, but not impossible task), it can re-use that R and D whenever it is appropriate, just as Kasparov does. Much of this analytical work has been done for Deep Blue by its designers, and given as an innate endowment, but Kasparov has likewise benefited from hundreds of thousands of person-years of chess exploration transmitted to him by players, coaches and books. It is interesting in this regard to contemplate the suggestion recently made by Bobby Fischer, who proposes to restore the game of chess to its intended rational purity by requiring that the major pieces be *randomly* placed in the back row at the start of each game (random, but mirror image for black and white). This would instantly render the mountain of memorised openings almost entirely obsolete, for humans and machines alike, since only rarely would any of this lore come into play. One would be thrown back onto a reliance on fundamental principles; one would have to do more of the hard design work in real time – with the clock running. It is far from clear whether this change in rules would benefit human beings more than computers. It all depends on which type of chess player is relying most heavily on what is, in effect, rote memory – reliance *with minimal comprehension* on the R and D of earlier explorers.

The fact is that the search space for chess is too big for even Deep Blue to explore exhaustively in real time, so, like Kasparov, it prunes its search trees by taking calculated risks, and, like Kasparov, it often gets these risks pre-calculated. Both presumably do massive amounts of 'brute force' computation on their very different architectures. After all, what do neurons know about chess? Any work *they* do must be brute force work of one sort or another.

It may seem that I am begging the question in favour of a computational, AI approach by describing the work done by Kasparov's brain in this way, but the work has to be done somehow, and no *other* way of getting the work done has ever been articulated. It won't do to say that Kasparov uses 'insight' or 'intuition' since that just means that Kasparov himself has no privileged access, no insight, into how the good results come to him. So, since nobody knows how Kasparov's brain does it – least of all Kasparov – there is not yet any evidence at all to support the claim that Kasparov's means are 'entirely unlike' the means exploited by Deep Blue. One should remember this when tempted to insist that 'of course' Kasparov's methods are hugely different. What on earth could provoke one to go out on a limb like that? Wishful thinking? Fear?

But that's just chess, you say, not art. Chess is *trivial* compared to art (now that the world champion chess player is a computer). This is where David Cope's EMI comes into play.[24] Cope set out to create a mere efficiency-enhancer, a composer's aid to help him over the blockades of composition any creator confronts, a high-tech extension of the traditional search vehicles (the piano, stave paper, the tape recorder and so on). As EMI grew in competence, it promoted itself into a whole composer, incorporating more and more of the generate-and-test process. When EMI is fed music by Bach, it responds by generating musical compositions in the style of Bach. When given Mozart, or Schubert, or Puccini, or Scott Joplin, it readily analyses their styles and composes new music in their styles, better pastiches than Cope himself – or almost any human composer – can compose. When fed music by two composers, it can promptly compose pieces that eerily unite their styles, and when fed, all at once (with no clearing of the palate, you might say) all these styles at once, it proceeds to write music based on the totality of its musical experience. The compositions that result can then also be fed back into it, over and over again, along with whatever other music comes along in MIDI format, and the result is EMI's own 'personal' musical style, a style that candidly reveals its debts to the masters, while being an unquestionably idiosyncratic integration of all this 'experience'. EMI can now compose not just two-part inventions and art songs but whole symphonies – and has composed over a thousand, when last I heard. They are good enough to fool experts (composers and professors of music) and I can personally attest to the fact that an EMI-Puccini aria brought a lump to my throat – but then, I'm on a hair trigger when it comes to Puccini, and this was a good enough imitation to fool me. David Cope can no more claim to be the composer of EMI's symphonies and motets and art songs than Murray Campbell can claim to have beaten Kasparov in chess.

To a Darwinian, this new element in the cascade of cranes is simply the latest in a long history, and we should recognise that the boundary between authors and their artefacts should be just as penetrable as all the other boundaries in the cascade. When Richard Dawkins notes that the beaver's dam is as much a part of the beaver phenotype – its *extended phenotype* – as its teeth and its fur, he sets the stage for the further observation that the boundaries of a human author are exactly as amenable to extension.[25] In fact, of course, we've known this for centuries, and have carpentered various semi-stable conventions for dealing with the products of Rubens, of Rubens' *studio*, of Rubens' various students. Wherever there can be a helping hand, we can raise the question of just who is helping whom, what is creator and what is creation. How should we deal with such questions? To the extent that anti-Darwinians simply want us to preserve some tradition of authorship, to have some *rules of thumb* for determining who or what shall receive the honour (or blame) that attends authorship, their desires can be acknowledged and met, one way or another (which doesn't necessarily mean we should meet them). To the extent that this is not enough for the anti-Darwinians, to the extent that they want to hold out for authors as an objective, metaphysically grounded, 'natural kind' (oh, the irony in those essentialist wolf-words in naturalist sheep's clothing!), they are looking for a skyhook.

The renunciation of skyhooks is, I think, the deepest and most important legacy of Darwin in philosophy, and it has a huge domain of influence, extending far beyond the skirmishes of evolutionary epistemology and evolutionary ethics. If we commit ourselves to Darwin's 'strange inversion of reasoning', we turn our backs on compelling ideas that have been central to the philosophical tradition for centuries, not just Aristotle's essentialism and irreducible *telos*, but also Descartes's *res cogitans* as a causer outside the mechanistic world, to name the three that had been most irresistible until Darwin came along. The siren songs of these compelling traditions still move many philosophers who have not yet seen fit to execute the inversion, sad to say. Clinging to their pre-Darwinian assumptions, they create problems for themselves that will no doubt occupy many philosophers for years to come.[26] The themes all converge when the topic is creativity and authorship, where the urge is to hunt for an 'essence' of creativity, an 'intrinsic' source of meaning and purpose, a locus of responsibility somehow insulated from the causal fabric in which it is embedded, so that within its boundaries it can generate, from its *own* genius, its *irreducible* genius, the meaningful words and deeds that distinguish us so sharply from mere mechanisms.[27]

Plato called for us to carve nature at its joints, a wonderful biological image, and Darwin showed us that the salient boundaries in the biosphere are not the crisp set-theoretic boundaries of essentialism, but the emergent effects of historical processes. As one species turns into two, the narrow isthmus of intermediates disappears as time passes, leaving islands, concentrations sharing family resemblances, surrounded by empty space. As Darwin noted (in somewhat different terms), there are feedback processes that enhance separation, actively depopulating this middle ground. We might expect the same sort of effects in the sphere of human mind and culture, cultural habits or practices that favour the isolation of the processes of artistic creation in a single mind. 'Are you the author of this?' 'Is this all your own work?' The mere fact that these are familiar questions shows that there are cultural pressures encouraging people to *make* the favoured answers come true. A small child, crayon in hand, huddled over her drawing, slaps away the helping hand of parent or sibling, because she wants this to be *her* drawing. She already appreciates the norm of pride of authorship, a culturally imbued bias built on the palimpsest of territoriality and biological ownership. The very idea of being an artist shapes her consideration of opportunities on offer, shapes her evaluation of features she discovers in herself. And this in turn will strongly influence the way she conducts her own searches through Design Space, in her largely unconscious emulation of Picasso's ideal, or, if she is of a contrarian spirit, defying it, like Marcel Duchamp:

> Cabanne: What determined your choice of readymades?
>
> Duchamp: That depended on the object. In general, I had to beware of its 'look'. It's very difficult to choose an object, because, at the end of fifteen days, you begin to like it or to hate it. You have to approach something with an indifference, as if you had no aesthetic emotion. The choice of readymades is always based on visual indifference and, at the same time, on the total absence of good or bad taste . . .[28]

There is a persistent problem of imagination management in the debates surrounding this issue: people on both sides have a tendency to underestimate the resources of Darwinism, imagining simplistic alternatives that do not exhaust the space of possibilities. Darwinians are notoriously quick to find (or invent) differences in *genetic fitness* to go with every difference they observe, for instance. Meanwhile, anti-Darwinians, noting the huge distance between a beehive and the *St Matthew Passion* as created objects, are apt to suppose that anybody who proposes to explain both creative processes with a single set of principles must be guilty of one reductionist fantasy or another: 'Bach had a gene for writing baroque counterpoint just like the bees' gene for forming wax hexagons' or 'Bach was just a mindless trial-and-error mutator and selector of the musical memes that already flourished in his cultural environment.' Both of these alternatives are nonsense, of course, but pointing out their flaws does nothing to support the idea that ('therefore') there must be irreducibly *non-Darwinian* principles at work in any account of Bach's creativity. In place of this dimly imagined chasm, with 'Darwinian phenomena' on one side and 'non-Darwinian phenomena' on the other side, we need to learn to see the space between bee and Bach as populated with all manner of mixed cases, differing from their nearest neighbours in barely perceptible ways, replacing the chasm with a traversable gradient of non-minds, protominds, hemi-demi-semi minds, magpie minds, copycat minds, aping minds, clever-pastiche minds, 'path-finding' minds, 'ground-breaking' minds, and eventually, genius minds. And the individual minds, of each calibre, will themselves be composed of different sorts of parts, including, surely, some special-purpose 'modules' adapted to various new tricks and tasks, as well as a cascade of higher-order reflection devices, capable of generating ever more rarefied and delimited searches through pre-selected regions of the Vast space of possible designs.

It is important to recognise that genius is itself a product of natural selection and involves generate-and-test procedures all the way down. Once you have such a product, it is often no longer particularly perspicuous to view it solely as a cascade of generate-and-test processes. It often makes good sense to leap ahead on a *narrative* course, thinking of the agent as a self, with a variety of projects, goals, presuppositions, hopes... In short, it often makes good sense to adopt the intentional stance towards the whole complex product of evolutionary processes. This effectively brackets the largely unknown and unknowable mechanical microprocesses as well as the history that set them up, and puts them out of focus while highlighting the patterns of rational activity that those mechanical microprocesses track so closely. This tactic makes especially good sense to the creator himself or herself, who must learn not to be oppressed by the revelation that on close inspection, even on close *intro*spection, a genius dissolves into a pack rat, which dissolves in turn into a collection of trial-and-error processes over which nobody has ultimate control.

Does this realisation amount to a loss – an elimination – of selfhood, of genius, of creativity? Those who are closest to the issue – the artistic and scientific geniuses who have reflected on it – often confront this discovery with equanimity. Mozart is reputed to have said of his best musical ideas: 'Whence and how do they come? I don't know and I have nothing to do with it.'[29] The painter Philip Guston is equally unperturbed by this evaporation of visible self when the creative juices start flowing:

> When I first come into the studio to work, there is this noisy crowd which follows me there; it includes all of the important painters in history, all of my contemporaries, all the art critics, etc. As I become involved in the work, one by one, they all leave. If I'm lucky, every one of them will disappear. If I'm really lucky, I will too.[30]

In closing, I would like to acknowledge a few of my co-authors:

Anonymous
Jorge Luis Borges
David Cope
Charles Darwin
Richard Dawkins
Susan Dennett
René Descartes
Marcel Duchamp
Thomas Edison
Bobby Fischer
Philip Guston
Douglas Hofstadter
Nicholas Humphrey
Robert MacKenzie
Tony Marcel
Victoria McGeer
Ludwig Mies van der Rohe
Pablo Picasso
William Poundstone
John Searle
William Shakespeare
Mary Shelley
Paul Valéry

NOTES

This essay appeared in *Proceedings and Addresses of the American Philosophical Association* vol.75, no. 2 (November 2001), and is reprinted by permission of the Association.

1. Valéry 1973–4, II, 1388.
2. Dennett 1984, 13.
3. MacKenzie 1868.
4. Searle 1980.
5. This is obviously true of all competences of information-processing or control, but not of productive or transformative processes, such as lactation, which requires the transport and assembly of particular materials. Since Searle purports to distinguish the brain's 'control powers' from

its 'bottom-up causal powers' that 'produce intentionality', some have thought Searle imagines intentionality to be a special sort of substance secreted by the brain. Since he denies this, he owes us some other way to distinguish these mysterious causal powers from the control powers that software can implement and an explanation of why they are not implementable in a virtual machine.

6. This perspective helps to explain the visceral appeal to many onlookers of the various *apparent* alternatives to Darwinian mechanism that have flourished over the years. The most prominent recently have been the appeal to 'self-organization' 'on the edge of chaos' (Stuart Kauffman, Per Bak, and others), and 'dynamical systems theory' in both evolution and cognition (Esther Thelen, Walter Freeman, Timothy van Gelder and others), and, of course, Stephen Jay Gould's insistence that evolution is not, as I have claimed (building on the work of theorists from Darwin to Fisher and Haldane to Williams and Maynard Smith), fundamentally an algorithmic process. After the smoke of battle clears, these ideas can be readily seen to be, at best, interesting complications of the basic Darwinian mechanisms, just as connectionist architectures and embodied cognition models are interesting complications of the basic ideas of AI. These controversies are, at best, constructive disagreements over how to 'give the details', not challenges to the basic Darwinian vision. See Gayon, this volume, for further discussion.
7. Poundstone 1985, 23.
8. C. Darwin [1859] 1964, 127 – ch. 4 summary.
9. This tactic of mapping evolutionary processes and results onto space is a natural and oft-used metaphor, exploited in models of hill-climbing and peaks in adaptive landscapes, to name the most obvious and popular applications. Its naturalness does not guarantee its soundness, of course, and may even mask its limitations, but since the basic mapping strategy has proved to be particularly useful in expressing *criticisms* of over-simple evolutionary ideas (e.g., Kauffman's 'rugged landscape', Eigen's 'quasi-species'), it is not obviously biased in favour of simplistic visions of Darwinism.
10. Maynard Smith and Szathmary 1995 identify eight occasions (major transitions) when the evolutionary process became more efficient, creating cranes.
11. Dennett 1995, 73–80.
12. See the famous cartoon by Sydney Harris, in which the physicist's blackboard is covered with impressive formulae, except for this bracketed phrase in the middle, which leads the onlooker scientist to say 'I think you should be more explicit here in step two' (reprinted in Dennett 1991, 38).

13. I have been unable to discover the source of Picasso's claim, which is nicely balanced by a better-known remark by a more down-to-earth creative genius, Thomas Edison: 'Genius is one per cent. inspiration and ninety-nine per cent. perspiration' (in a newspaper interview in 1932, according to the *Oxford Dictionary of Quotations*).
14. Yes, I intend the homage to an old favourite of mine, *What Happens in Hamlet*, by J. Dover Wilson (1951).
15. Unless we find there is a Ms Shelley who is the author of Dr Frankenstein!
16. In Borges 1962.
17. Borges chose slightly different figures: books 410 pages long, with 40 lines of 80 characters. The total number of characters per book is close enough to mine (1,312,000 versus 1,000,000) to make no difference. I chose my rounder numbers for ease of handling. Borges chose a character set with only 25 members, which is enough for upper-case Spanish (with a blank, a comma and a period as the only punctuation), but not for English. I chose the more commodious 100 to make room without any doubt for the upper- and lower-case letters and punctuation of all the Roman alphabet languages.
18. Stephen Hawking insists on putting it this way: 'There are something like ten million million million million million million million million million million million million million (1 with eighty zeroes after it) particles in the region of the universe that we can observe.' Hawking 1988, 129. Michael Denton (1985) provides the estimate of 10^{70} atoms in the observable universe. Manfred Eigen (1992, 10) calculates the volume of the universe as 10^{84} cubic centimetres.
19. The Library of Babel is finite, but, curiously enough, it contains all the grammatical sentences of English within its walls. But that's an infinite set, and the library is finite! Still, any sentence of English, of whatever length, can be broken down into 500-page chunks, each of which is somewhere in the library! How is this possible? Some books may get used more than once. The most profligate case is the easiest to understand: since there are volumes which each contain a single character and are otherwise blank, repeated use of these one hundred volumes will create any text of any length. As Quine (1987) points out, in his informative and amusing essay, 'Universal Library', if you avail yourself of this strategy of re-using volumes, and translate everything into the ASCII code your word-processor uses, you can store the whole Library of Babel in two extremely slender volumes, in one of which is printed a 0 and in the other of which appears a 1! (Quine also points out that Theodor Fechner, the psychologist, propounded the fantasy of the universal library long before Borges.)

20. Quine coins the term 'hyperastronomic' for the same purpose. See Quine 1987. The previous two paragraphs are drawn, with minor changes, from Dennett 1995, 108–9.
21. For more on this concept, see Dennett (forthcoming).
22. Hofstadter's 'Reflections [on Searle]', in Hofstadter and Dennett 1981.
23. Shakespeare himself was, of course, a tireless exploiter of the design work of others, and may well have been poking fun at his own reputation, quoting a critic, when he had Autolycus describe himself as 'a snapper-up of unconsidered trifles' in *The Winter's Tale* (Act IV, scene iii). Thanks to Tony Marcel for drawing this passage to my attention.
24. For the details, see Cope and Hofstadter 2001, including my commentary, 'Collision Detection, Muselot, and Scribble: Some Reflections on Creativity'.
25. Dawkins 1982.
26. Three examples: Jerry Fodor's series of flawed theories of psychosemantics; John Searle's inability to account for how 'intrinsic intentionality' could evolve when it has no 'control power' consequences visible to selective pressure; John McDowell's quest for a non-Darwinian alternative to what he calls 'bald naturalism', a struggle to secure a variety of normativity that is not the mere *as-if* normativity he finds discernible in evolution. See Dennett 1995, 1996 and 1993 for my analyses of Fodor's and Searle's difficulties. My discussion of McDowell must be deferred to another occasion.
27. See Dennett 1998 for my analysis of this theme in Fred Dretske's search for a privileged place where the understanding happens.
28. Cabanne 1971, 48. Thanks to Nicholas Humphrey and Victoria McGeer for ideas expressed in the previous paragraph.
29. In an oft-quoted but possibly spurious passage – see Dennett 1995, 346–7.
30. I have been unable to locate the source of Guston's quote, but I have found much the same remark attributed to the composer John Cage, a close friend and contemporary of Guston's, who (is said to have) said this about painting:

    > When you are working, everybody is in your studio – the past, your friends, the art world, and above all, your own ideas – all are there. But as you continue painting, they start leaving, one by one, and you are left completely alone. Then, if you are lucky, even you leave.

    Like all other creators, Guston and I like to re-use what we find, adding a few touches from time to time.

OWEN FLANAGAN

16 Ethical expressions: why moralists scowl, frown and smile

I DARWINISM AND THE MANIFEST IMAGE OF HUMANKIND

A major task for philosophy is to adjudicate conflicts between our ordinary way of understanding persons and the world – what Wilfrid Sellars called the 'manifest image' – and scientific accounts of persons and the world – the 'scientific image'. Sometimes, of course, it is possible to blend the two images so as to produce a genuinely stereoscopic or synthetic picture. But this is not always possible. In the case of Darwin's theory of natural selection, we seem to have a scientific theory that cannot be comfortably assimilated into the extant manifest image by adding, in Sellars' phrase, a 'needle point of detail' to that image.[1]

As traditionally understood, we humans are made in God's image and sit beneath God and the angels and above the animals on the 'Great Chain of Being'.[2] There is a tripartite ontology of Pure Spirit(s) (God and angels), pure matter (rocks, plants and animals), and dualistic beings who, while on earth, partake of both the immaterial realm and the material realm (us). We humans know the material realm through our senses and reason, and the immaterial realm – theological and moral truths in particular – through illumination, grace or other non-empirical and nonrational or arational means. God sets out the moral law, and if we obey it, thereby using our free will properly, we will gain eternal salvation.

Nothing in this metaphysics, epistemology and ethics seems to square with the theory of natural selection. On this theory, no divine, intelligent designer is needed to explain the existence of humans or any other type of organic life. Moreover, as animals, descended from other animals, we humans possess no mysterious epistemic powers to detect what is true or what is good. The idea that morality has a divine origin and justification loses its force. The prospects for personal immortality seem nil. The manifest image of humankind thus takes a major hit at the hands of Darwin's theory, and it is not clear how to maintain sensibly the central components of that image.

Daniel Dennett in particular has pressed home this point, telling us that Darwin's theory is akin to a 'universal acid', eating through everything it touches – and, for Dennett, it touches virtually everything human. But Dennett should not be misunderstood here. He does not mean that everything human can be explained by the theory of natural selection. He is no pan-adaptationist, believing all human traits to be fitness-enhancing adaptations. Rather, Dennett sometimes uses Darwin's theory in a strict way, to explain how certain human traits arose through the natural selection of genetically based variation, and othertimes is engaged in analogical extension of the theory, treating it as a paradigm case of how natural phenomena can be explained by appeal to causal processes having a selection-like form. This distinction between strict Darwinism and Darwinism by analogy, often overlooked, is crucial to understanding what Darwinism can offer to philosophy, and especially to ethics – the subject of this chapter. A closer look at this distinction will help clarify what is at stake in attempts to Darwinise ethics.

II STRICT DARWINISM AND DARWINISM BY ANALOGY

Strictly speaking, natural selection operates (we now know) when genetic variation is the major causal contributor to variation in certain traits, and when variation in these traits enhances or detracts from fitness in a particular environment. Traits rise in frequency if they are heritable and if they enable organisms to be more reproductively successful than average. Most such traits are adaptations. The primary aim of modern Darwinian theory is to explain adaptations by reference to population genetics. This is important, and sets a strong standard for when an explanation is strictly Darwinian.[3]

Many traits that are modified over time and reach a certain frequency or stability in human populations – literacy, religious commitments, proficiency at physics or the tango – are the results of largely non-biological causes. Furthermore, the fact that some non-biological causal processes have structural similarities to natural selection does not mean that their effects fall in the explanatory domain of Darwin's theory. There are many processes that are analogous to natural selection in that there is what the psychologist B. F. Skinner called 'selection by consequences'. Becoming a good chess, bridge, soccer or tennis player has no interesting relation to Darwinian fitness. But becoming good at a game does involve gradual modification over time in a test-retest situation. As alternate strategies are developed and tested, those with negative consequences (losing) are dispensed with, while those with positive consequences (winning) are retained and built upon. The phenomenon of selection by consequences is ubiquitous, but needn't be Darwinian in the strict sense.[4] The simple reason is that the consequences that affect the development, modification, transmission and spread of traits thus established are not necessarily reproductive success or increased inclusive genetic fitness.

Philip Kitcher has rightly been a consistent critic of what he calls 'hyper-Darwinism', the view that Darwin's theory can resolve virtually all scientific and philosophical questions about human life and mind. The range of Darwin's theory extends only as far as traits whose evolution is governed by forces of natural selection. In cases where forces of cultural selection are involved, its explanatory power wanes. Thus when Kitcher cites Donald Campbell's evolutionary epistemology and Richard Dawkins' theory of memetic selection governing social learning, he indicates, but I think not forcefully enough, that these theories are Darwinian in virtue of emphasising certain structural analogies of individual and social learning with the way natural selection operates. They are mere analogues of natural selection, because they show how ideas can be learned, modified or fixed in a population independently of the effects they have on fitness enhancement. Nor are the traits in question heritable – a *sine qua non* of strict Darwinian explanation.[5]

If the proponents of 'evolutionary ethics' were resolutely careful about distinguishing (a) claims about how moral norms or practices promote Darwinian fitness, from (b) claims about norms or practices changing over time – 'evolving' in the popular and misleading sense – in a selection-like manner, my hunch is that Kitcher would be less sceptical about the contribution evolutionary thinking might make to metaethics and, to some extent, to the justification of certain normative ethical judgements. So far as norms or practices selected in virtue of their consequences are 'adaptive', they are adaptive in a sense unconnected with number of offspring or changing gene frequencies.[6]

Such fastidiousness about what counts as a genuinely Darwinian phenomenon and as a genuinely Darwinian process is useful in reading Rosenberg's and Dennett's contributions to this volume. Rosenberg insists that true Darwinians will be committed to a form of naturalism according to which they 'look to the theory of natural selection as a primary resource in coming to solve philosophical problems raised by human affairs'. Then he tells us that 'the social and behavioural sciences may in the future have more to tell us about humanity than Darwinian theory, but these theories do not as yet have anything like the degree of confirmation of Darwin's theory'. The first claim sounds as if it insists that we should seek explanations of human nature and social life in terms of the fitness-enhancing features of the traits we display. But the second claim is that features other than fitness-enhancement may be shown to be crucial causal contributors to 'human affairs' once the other human sciences mature and weigh in. I don't share Rosenberg's assessment of the immaturity of the other human sciences, so I think we already know that the most likely explanations of certain widespread human traits do not turn primarily – or at least not exclusively – on their fitness-enhancing role.

Armed with this distinction between strict Darwinian explanation and Darwinism by analogy, as well as with a thoroughgoing commitment to philosophical naturalism, we can now address some of the questions traditionally asked in ethics. What is the genealogy of morals, of our basic dispositions to live cooperatively and conform our behaviour to norms? Are the aims of morals best explained as fitness-enhancing strategies, or is there more to morality than the aim of fitness enhancement? Are moral judgements best understood cognitively, as expressing moral truths, or noncognitively, as expressing emotions and preferences? On the latter view, moral judgements are akin to hurrahing and booing at a sporting match. Such verbal ejaculations are neither true nor false. The apparent conflict between cognitivism and noncognitivism has long afflicted modern moral philosophy. One of my aims here is to show how a strict Darwinian perspective can create some leverage to break this impasse. Our Darwinian history has bequeathed to us moral natures partaking as much of reason as of the emotions.[7]

III ETHICS AS HUMAN ECOLOGY

Rosenberg urges that the prospects for Darwinian metaethics generally are much rosier than the prospects for Darwinian morality. He recommends, in other words, that philosophers use Darwinian resources to understand the nature of moral judgements, rather than to justify them, as right or true or good. Another of my purposes is to suggest that this dichotomy cannot be sustained. Darwinian metaethics and Darwinian morality are inextricable.

As I conceive it, normative ethics is part of the science of ecology.[8] Ecology is the discipline that tells us what conditions lead to the flourishing of various natural systems (wetlands, orchids, beavers) in certain environments. Ethics is ecology for humans and other sentient beings. Ethics, so conceived, is both empirical and normative. It asks: what are the conditions that lead to fitness and flourishing for humans and other sentient beings?[9] To answer, we need to look and see what sorts of environments lead to flourishing and what sorts don't. There will be tough calls when what conduces to fitness and flourishing compete, as well as when goods internal to our conception of flourishing – loyalty and honesty, say – conflict. Nevertheless, there are facts of the matter to be discovered about what is good and desirable.

Ethics thus construed is Darwinian in spirit, in two ways. It is thoroughly naturalistic in its judgements of the worth of certain traits, virtues, social practices and norms. And it appeals to selection by consequences in order to explain the development and modification of our moral systems. Ethics-as-human-ecology is not strictly Darwinian, however, since it concerns itself with more than Darwinian fitness. It is concerned with a wider aim which, following Aristotle, I simply call 'flourishing'.[10] Flourishing may – indeed typically does – involve surviving long enough to be reproductively successful. But it involves more than this. Flourishing includes, in the human case, being happy, contented and virtuous. Nevertheless, Darwinian fitness is arguably a necessary condition for the achievement of most moral aims, under most circumstances. Furthermore, nature did, I believe, select for traits, in the strict Darwinian sense, that provide certain basic moral or, better, proto-moral dispositions.

If fitness is judged normally to be a necessary condition of achieving the other ends that morality recommends or suits us for, then the fact that some trait or norm is conducive to survival may serve as part of its rationale, part of its justification. Moreover, so far as certain dispositions, selected for fitness-enhancing reasons, underpin our moral sense, these dispositions are legitimately judged as good for this reason. Getting almost anywhere with this line of thinking should give pause to those sceptical about whether Darwin's theory can make a contribution to normative ethics. Along these lines, I will argue here that some of our basic proto-moral dispositions, fixed in us by natural selection, may be judged good – that is, worthy of refinement and development in ways suited to profitable interpersonal relations in particular environments. These proto-moral dispositions provide a foundation for the institution of morality.

IV HUMAN NATURE

With reason, emotions and the origins of morality in our sights, it is instructive to compare Darwin's own contribution to ethical thinking with that of another great moralist, Thomas Hobbes. Dennett calls Hobbes 'the first sociobiologist' because 'he saw that there *had* to be a story to be told about how the state came to be created, and how it brought with it something altogether new on the face of the earth: morality'.[11] According to Hobbes' 'just so' story there was a time – or at least there would have been such a time had it not been utterly imprudent for *Homo sapiens* to reveal their true colours – when pure self-interest reigned. Every ego for itself. Reason, however, quickly surmised that going with the flow of natural impulses would impede, if not outright defeat, individual self-interest. Morality was invented. The Hobbesian story thus makes quick work of the transition from a world of psychological egoists to a world of prudential moralists.

Darwin's story of the origin of morality differs from Hobbes' in two important respects.[12] First, Darwin is more of a Humean than a Hobbesian. If we are egoists, then, for Hume as for Darwin, we are egoists with fellow-feeling. We care about the weal and woe of, at least, some others. Second – and this follows from the first point – morality was not 'something altogether new on the face of the earth' at some moment in human history. According to Darwin, *Homo sapiens*, presumably like their extinct social ancestors, as well as certain closely related species, such as chimps and bonobos, possess instincts and emotions that are proto-moral; that is, these creatures possess the germs, at least, of such virtues as sympathy, fidelity and courage. In Dennett's terms, there is no 'skyhook' being invoked here. The relevant instincts and emotions did not emerge in a miraculous instant. They emerged through natural selection, gradually. We are endowed with these instincts and feelings thanks to a 'craning operation' that began with unicellular organisms.

What sort of cranes did nature equip us with such that morality could be hoisted from below? Here is Darwin's own answer, from the *Descent of Man* (1871):

> In order that primeval men, or the ape-like progenitors of man, should have become social, they must have acquired the same instinctive feelings.... They would have felt uneasy when separated from their comrades, for whom they would have felt some degree of love; they would have warned each other of danger, and have given mutual aid in attack or defence. All this implies some degree of sympathy, fidelity, and courage.... The love of approbation and the dread of infamy, as well as the bestowal of praise or blame, are primarily due... to the instinct of sympathy; and this instinct no doubt was originally acquired, like all the other social instincts, through natural selection.... With increased experience and reason, man perceives the more remote consequences of his actions, and the self-regarding virtues, such as temperance, chastity, &c., which during earlier times are... utterly disregarded, come to be highly esteemed or even held sacred.... Ultimately a highly complex sentiment, having its first origin in the social instincts, largely guided by the approbation of our fellow-men, ruled by reason, self-interest, and in later times by deep religious feelings, confirmed by instruction and habit, all combined, constitute our moral sense or conscience.[13]

Most philosophers prefer the Humean–Darwinian picture of human nature to Hobbes' 'red in tooth and claw' picture. One might think this is because the Humean–Darwinian picture is more flattering than the Hobbesian one. But even if this partly explains the attraction, the Humean–Darwinian picture nevertheless has science on its side. Non-human primates do, in fact, seem to display a social side, a convivial side, quite naturally. Furthermore, we can explain this sociality in terms of the theory of natural selection. Individuals possessed of at least a modicum of fellow-feeling will do better at dating, mating and child-rearing – the key ingredients of reproductive success – than individuals who ignore their conspecifics or see them only as means to their own ends. An additional advantage of the Humean–Darwinian view is that it ties morality to something more than mere prudence.[14] Our social instincts and proto-moral emotions are there from the start, and thus morality has on its agenda, from the very beginning, concern for the welfare of (some) others, as well as for oneself. Hobbes' story really does involve the invention of morality as something totally new on the face of the earth. *Homo sapiens* moves within the lifetime of the species from a state of amorality to one of morality. But Darwin's story, as one might expect, is gradualist. Humans, thanks largely to the possession of a cognitive-conative economy that was passed on from ancestors, have moral or, at least, proto-moral dispositions from the start. Furthermore, these dispositions are adjustable during one's lifetime. Social insects, not being conscious, organise social life without feeling or thought. Most mammals seem to organise their social lives with and through feelings, selfish-feelings and fellow-feelings. In the case of primates, the role of emotions in social organisation is especially conspicuous.

But the Humean–Darwinian story apparently has a serious downside; namely, it ties morality too closely to the emotions. Many of the same philosophers who prefer the cheerier Humean–Darwinian picture of human nature to the Hobbesian picture will say that, even if Hobbes was wrong about what we are like deep down, at least he saw that morality has to do with reason. Darwin, in the quotation above, appears to agree: sympathy, experience, reason, instruction, and habit are all involved in the development of our moral sense. Hume, of course, thought the same. But what Hume and Darwin share in addition to a similar take on human nature is the view that the emotions are essential to morality even when experience, habit, and reason enter the picture. For Hume, and possibly for Darwin as well, moral reason works with and through the emotions.

V BASIC EMOTIONS AND THE REACTIVE ATTITUDES

The quotation from Darwin in the previous section contains all the germs of a sensible theory. We humans are social animals concerned in the first instance with our own fitness and that of our conspecifics. We are equipped with some rudimentary proto-virtues – instincts of sympathy, fidelity and courage – which can be shaped by experience and reason, and which regulated social life long before *Homo sapiens* got around to articulating moral codes, rules and principles. More precisely, our ancestors used their emotions, as expressed physically, though gestures, grimaces and groans, to communicate desires that certain norms be observed, and to elicit conformity to these norms. The universality of the expression of certain emotions in certain commonly and repetitively occurring kinds of social situations – especially (but not necessarily, even at the start, exclusively) in situations where fitness was at stake – explains why, when modern humans express desires for normative conformity, the appeal is universal, or at least more universal than emotive expression in rooting for favourite sports teams.

What is a norm? Nothing queer or mysterious. Roughly, norms – moral ones, at any rate – express evaluations and make appeals that certain practices creating, protecting or maintaining what is valuable be observed. When I display anger, I express a desire that you back off. If you get the message you will do so, and if you are smart you will continue to do so in relevantly similar situations. Supposing you do so, you now govern your behaviour by a norm, consciously or unconsciously.[15] So ethical expression – even as it might be imagined to have occurred before we added language to our expressive arsenal – involves emotional expression. But it is not simply a matter of my hurrahing and booing, and thereby getting things off my chest. I am communicating with you about our interaction. I am asking for more, less or something different. My expressions have an epistemic dimension. My reactions reveal that I like or don't like something you are doing, or appear disposed to do, and I am attempting to convey information about how I'd prefer things to go.

In the light of Darwin's own arguments in *The Expression of the Emotions in Man and Animals* (1872), together with the important work of Paul Ekman a century later, it is well established that certain human emotions and their expressions are universal.[16] Which ones?

According to Ekman, fear, anger, surprise, happiness, sadness, disgust and contempt, for sure.[17] Let us accept that these emotions and their expressions are evolved traits of *Homo sapiens*. They are part of our original equipment, just as eyes, ears, noses and hearts are. However, unlike eyes and ears, used in the first instance to pick up information, scowls and smiles are used to express how we feel and to convey information to others about how we would like them to behave. Paul Griffiths calls Ekman's basic emotions 'affect programs', which is Griffiths' way of marking their complexity. Each of the basic emotions involves environmental triggers, which activate perception, which give rise to inner emotional states and prompt expressions of approval or disapproval.[18]

The Darwinian genealogy of morals I am sketching ties the origin of morality very closely to Darwinian fitness. A basic emotional expression communicates the wish that others behave in certain ways, ways that will promote the survival and reproductive success of the expressor. It doesn't matter whether fitness is a conscious aim. It is enough that fitness enhancement is the selected-for outcome. Note, too, that this account, while emphasising emotions, does not amount to noncognitivism. Expressions of emotions at the same time express judgements about better and worse ways of behaving. This much provides a start to the project of making room for the truth in both noncognitivist and cognitivist metaethics.

Even if ethics began with fitness enhancement, there is nothing in the Darwinian picture stipulating that, as social life developed and evolved, according to its own rules, fitness remained the sole aim of human moral life. Darwin himself was quite clear that certain emotions or attitudes required psychosocial development. Thus temperance and chastity were not, in his view, adaptations. Rather, they were discovered to be good as humans gained experience of social life and became aware of the 'remoter consequences' of their actions.

In a famous 1962 paper, P. F. Strawson proposed an account of what he called the 'reactive attitudes'. His analysis helps reveal how emotional expression provides just the right sort of crane to hoist morality up from below. The reactive attitudes comprise the set of human responses that include indignation, resentment, gratitude, approbation, guilt, shame, pride, hurt feelings, feelings of affection and love, and forgiveness. Strawson claimed that the reactive attitudes are part of the normal and original conative repertoire of members of the species *Homo sapiens*; that the reactive attitudes express normal human reactions to acts, traits, dispositions or to whole persons; that the normal expression of the reactive attitudes involves interpersonal relations where benevolence or malevolence is displayed or, at least, where they are at stake; and that the reactive attitudes are not only other-regarding, but can be self-regarding – guilt, say, is a form of anger – as well as experienced vicariously when others suffer harm.

Strawson emphasised that the reactive attitudes appear in some form across all cultures, and their ubiquity has something to do with our nature as social creatures. Needless to say, Strawson's reactive attitudes are not the same as Ekman's basic emotions. Strawson's list depicts a range of familiar attitudes that bear a good deal of cultural colouration from Enlightenment thinking and, as such, have a rich and idiosyncratic cultural character, structured and honed by the moral history of Western European civilisation. It is hard to imagine our ancestors at the end of the Pleistocene experiencing affronts to their dignity or experiencing our kinds of love, indignation, regret and so on. That said, Strawson's reactive attitudes are excellent examples of attitudes built on the basic emotions, themselves considered as the original reactive attitudes.

VI JUSTIFYING THE REACTIVE ATTITUDES

In a telling footnote, Strawson countered an important criticism of his analysis. Even if he were right about the reactive attitudes, didn't there remain a need to establish whether the reactive attitudes were rationally justified? Strawson answered: 'Compare the question of the *justification* of induction. The human commitment to inductive belief-formation is original, natural, and non-rational (not *ir*rational), in no way something we choose or could give up.' The idea, I take it, is that what goes for induction also goes for the reactive attitudes – they are original, natural, non-rational and not something we ever could give up. It is not much of a stretch to add a pragmatist, Darwinian rider. Given that the reactive attitudes are a basic feature of our kind of animal, the way inductive thinking is, the justification of the reactive attitudes and induction lies with their fitness-enhancing properties.

Again, it will be insisted: causal explanations don't justify anything, they only explain why it exists. Yes, mothers whose feelings of affection lead them to care for their offspring were more fit than uncaring mothers were, and being quick at picking up on regularities in nature led to reproductive success for creatures with the right equipment. But these facts do not amount to justification. To follow Strawson's lead is to allow, on the contrary, that these facts are all there is to justification. Parental care makes for happy, fit offspring, as well as happy-making interactions between parents and offspring. Using induction has so far produced knowledge, and knowledge is good, better than the alternative. These are good things, and we have reason to behave accordingly.

Offering justifications such as these, and saying we have reason to utilise the relevant dispositions, even where this requires some effort, and thus doing more than just what comes naturally, is not to claim that parental care and induction are guaranteed to produce in perpetuity the goods they have yielded so far. If future environments are wildly different from past or present ones, they may not do so. Nor do the justifications rest on any particular features of the causal accounts of why we have the relevant traits. Suppose that our parental instincts and inductive abilities were caused last week by exposure to a passing radioactive asteroid, rather than by Darwinian gradualism. We might still credibly judge the relevant traits good. They help us pick up knowledge faster than before, and our new caring ways lead to longer survival, warm cuddly feelings and so on. These things are good. They do jobs we want done.

If the reactive attitudes can be plausibly understood as cultural sophistications of Ekman's basic emotions, then the basic emotions are moral attitudes to some degree, or at least proto-moral ones. Their expressions appear to have been designed to communicate positive or negative feelings, typically where such feelings are elicited by interactions with others, in circumstances relevant to survival and reproductive success. Note that allowing this much blocks the extreme moral relativism often associated with noncognitivism. Murder or stealing are bad not solely because we don't like these things, but because we don't like these things and want the murderers and robbers to cease and desist. Our emotions have an underrated epistemic dimension. The basic emotions are reliable detectors of modes of interaction that interfere or have the potential of interfering with fitness.

Are the proto-moral emotions therefore adaptations? It is easy to imagine emotions such as anger and fear as having credible links to fitness. Closely related species with these emotions commonly display them when they are in physical danger. Moreover, emotions such as happiness and sadness might well subserve various types of social interaction that promote fitness. If I find sex pleasant I will mate, and I will convey my pleasure, my happiness, possibly my gratitude, to whomever it is I find it pleasant to mate with. If I find playing or being with others pleasant, I will be concerned (not necessarily consciously) that they fare well. Dispositions to express reactive attitudes vicariously might naturally extend to my offspring or my mate, as well as to any others whose company I find pleasant, who do me good, or who I detect are in a position to do me good. Likewise, assuming I have come to care about others, even if for totally selfish reasons, I will be disposed to experience anger towards those who harm them, or seem likely to harm them. Possibly I will act on this anger. Primatologists often speak of 'moralistic aggression' among primates, where aggressive display can arise when a chimp or bonobo is directly threatened or when another chimp cared about is threatened. Indeed, an early warning system, with emotions being displayed facially and bodily before being acted upon, seems like a good design strategy for creatures who should, all else being equal, wish to make their feelings and desires known without being maimed or killed. These and other considerations support the idea that the proto-moral emotions are adaptations in the strict Darwinian sense.

VII ADJUSTABLE ADAPTATIONS

Even if we take it for granted that the proto-moral emotions or reactive attitudes can be plausibly described as adaptations, according to the criterion that weights most heavily the causal contribution of a trait to fitness in the original evolutionary situation in which the trait evolved and proliferated, it does not follow that the trait is *now* adaptive. Any adaptation can cease to be fitness enhancing if the environment changes enough. Our basic reactive attitudes may well have evolved as adaptations in close ancestors or in us. But assessing whether they continue to function as such requires us to understand, better than we now do, relevant differences between the environments these attitudes arose in and the environments we now live in.

There are also questions concerning the degree of modifiability of the basic reactive attitudes and, assuming they are to some extent modifiable, whether there are reasons to modify them. Some moral philosophers regard Darwinism warily precisely because they believe that traits delivered by natural selection are unmodifiable. The worry is unfounded, however, so long as creatures can learn and so long as the natural traits in question are socially and/or cognitively penetrable. Following Strawson's arguments, there are grounds for cautious optimism about how modifiable the reactive attitudes are. On the one hand, as we have seen, they are not something we could choose to give up. On the other hand, like our inductive strategies, our reactive attitudes can perhaps be refined and modified through rational criticism and reflection.[19]

We cannot disentangle emotions from morality, nor should we want to. But we can moderate, modify and adjust our emotions, making them more 'apt' to different situations, different social environments, different moral conceptions. The analogy with induction is instructive. Suppose there was selection in the past for the straight rule of induction: if it has been observed that regularity R occurs m times out of n, infer that it will continue to do so in the future. It is a familiar fact that this rule works fairly well in elementary situations. But it leads in more complex situations to flawed reasoning. Living at a time when social groups were relatively small, conspecifics were all well known, and hunting and foraging ranged over relatively close ranges, ancestral humans might not have often confronted such complex situations. It was only after the rule's deployment over many centuries that we humans came to discover ways in which the application of the rule needed to be constrained and modified. There is no interesting sense in which the canons of inductive logic, statistics and probability were naturally, as opposed to culturally, selected for. Nevertheless, if one aims to accrue firmly grounded knowledge, one had better apply the relevant canons. In this non-Darwinian sense, the canons are as adaptive as literacy. But neither excellent reasoning nor high literacy is interestingly fitness enhancing. Indeed, the best predictor in the modern world for low birth-rate is the average level of education attained, the two having an inverse relation.

The point is that a trait can be adaptive in the sense that possessing the trait contributes to knowledge, flourishing, happiness and the like, but not adaptive in the sense that it promotes inclusive genetic fitness. The same applies in the moral case. Some of the reactive attitudes, especially those on Strawson's list, require development, discovery and canonisation over some segment of world-historical time. Feelings of pride, dignity, and respect fit this description, as do Darwin's own examples of temperance and chastity. They require, at least as we now understand these concepts, development of a certain conception of a person, of norms governing behaviour, do's and don'ts, oughts, institutions governing moral praise and blame, and methods for punishment of those who stray too far from the right path. Analogously, induction is made sophisticated through cumulative, communal discussions of past inductive practices. Induction is not a ladder we climb and then push away, and neither are the moral emotions. Our moral emotions are inextricable from our values and our allegiances. At no point in moral development do the moral emotions ebb away.

But doesn't morality involve knowing that one ought to do one's duty even when one doesn't feel like it? Well, yes. The right way to think about such cases, however, is by understanding them as cases where we have learned to value, to care about certain things that are not altogether easy to care about or follow through on. The fact remains that caring about doing our duty amounts to being emotionally engaged and invested in doing our duty. And, for morality's sake, it had better be; otherwise we won't do the right thing.

VIII HOW FLOURISHING 'FITS' IN

To say that the basic reactive attitudes are original and natural – and adaptations to boot – is not to say that they evolved in *Homo sapiens*. It is possible that these attitudes, much in the form we are naturally disposed to display them, were delivered by gene sequences that belonged to and evolved in earlier groups of hominids or even in some non-hominid ancestors. This prospect raises the possibility that, as our brains, bodies and social structures differ so much from those of our evolutionary ancestors, it might not be optimal to have inherited emotional equipment much the same as theirs. Like the tinkering with the panda's wrist bone that produced the panda's sub-optimal thumb, direct transmission of the reactive attitudes of early hominids may have been the best natural selection could do under the circumstances that brought *Homo sapiens* on the scene, without being optimal in either the original evolutionary situation or in the changed circumstances of later, especially cultured, environments which humans would create and inhabit.[20]

This possibility, based on knowing the twin facts that an adaptation can cease to be fitness enhancing if and when an environment changes enough and that Mother Nature often satisfices even when it comes to adaptive designs, makes me hesitant to assert wholeheartedly that our original and natural reactive attitudes are still adaptive, even if we restrict the meaning of 'adaptive' to fitness enhancing. To speak with confidence on this matter, we need to know about the standard intensity, if there is such a thing, of the basic reactive attitudes. How strong or weak were they in the original settings? We will also want to know what sorts of situations generally elicited these attitudes. Saying that they were elicited by benevolence and malevolence amounts to little until we know what sorts of things were perceived as benevolent or malevolent. We can make some plausible educated guesses here. But much information is missing, crucially about the influence of culture, for we know that different cultures conceive of benevolence and malevolence somewhat differently.

Despite these gaps in our knowledge, there are nevertheless grounds for supposing that, in current environments, especially with certain technologies at our disposal, we need to be wary of certain of the original and natural reactive attitudes. Expressions of anger in an environment filled with guns are, all else being equal, more dangerous than in a world in which the standard expressions can only go as far as fists and sticks. Many people worry, rightly, that willingness to fight a mutually catastrophic nuclear war is caused in part by the facelessness of the enemy. Due to our evolutionary legacies, it seems we are attuned to feel emotions, of compassion as well as of anger, in response to faces, but not in response to large chunks of land on maps. Conversely, mass communication gives face to suffering. We see starving children half way across the globe and are, at least sometimes, moved to help. So the verdict is mixed as to whether, in the world as we know it, our reactive attitudes are well suited, however well suited they may have been in the original evolutionary context, for doing the job they were designed to do.

We can answer with more confidence the question of whether the basic reactive attitudes are modifiable. The evidence for their modifiability abounds. Contemporary moral educational practices aim at and sometimes succeed in moderating what are judged to be excessively angry displays. Benevolent dispositions can be developed and enhanced, although it is a variable matter how hard we try to do so. Different cultures, different moral communities work in different ways to increase or decrease guilt, and so on.

The aims of morality go beyond setting down norms that enhance or protect fitness, however. We also aim to live happy, high-quality lives, to flourish in ways that have virtually nothing (at least directly) to do with fitness. This is where elaborate moral systems come into their own. All over the world, ideas about what it is to be a good person and to live a moral life have been developed and articulated. Every wisdom literature I am familiar with – whether the Torah, the Old and New Testaments, Confucius' *Analects*, the *Puranas* and the *Bhagavad Gita*, the Koran, Buddhist texts, or secular moral writings from the likes of Aristotle, Mill and Kant – offers all sorts of advice about how we ought to structure our cognitive-conative economies, how best to live a life, what virtues are the best expressions of our common humanity and which feelings and vices we need to be most watchful of and ready to fight off. It seems to me that each of these literatures, despite sometimes displaying parochial, xenophobic, sexist and racist attitudes, does identify problems with living our lives solely according to our biological natures, and provides considerable wisdom, each in its own way, for being better that we are naturally prone to be. There is absolutely nothing in Darwinism that says that humans, as evolved rational-emotional beings, can't or don't acquire aims that go beyond fitness. What I call 'flourishing' is one such aim.

Homo sapiens evolved as creatures with fellow-feeling as well as with a strong selfish streak. Long before we spoke, much less engaged in explicit ethical reflection or wrote ethical treatises, our basic emotions, our reactive attitudes used the vehicle of our faces (as well as other forms of body language) to express and communicate our normative preferences. In the first instance, these normative preferences revolved almost exclusively around issues pertinent to fitness. With culture, experience, learning and reason, humans came to understand the 'more remote consequences' of their actions and to see the merits of abiding by more complex norms. Those norms involved delayed gratification. They inculcated complex virtues, promoting the development of stable traits of character. We can speak here, perhaps, of an extended moral phenotype, enhancing Darwinian fitness but not just Darwinian fitness; for by this time, humans saw certain prospects for flourishing – for living well even if not for long.[21] For all this, there has never been a virtue proposed or a moral principle espoused that did not appeal to our emotions or utilise our nature as emotional beings. The picture of a morality that transcends or overcomes the emotions is not Darwin's. We are not built in a way that allows such transcendence or overcoming.

We can, of course, through culture, reason and experience learn to moderate, modify, adjust and amplify our basic reactive attitudes in ways that enhance both fitness and flourishing. Furthermore, we can often give reasons as to why such adjustments are desirable. But – and this is the main point – we don't, in moral development, either phylogenetically or ontogenetically, climb out of the basic emotions, as if they were a cave or cocoon, from which we then escape or drop off. We are thinking-feeling creatures all the way up. If in doubt, just look at people's faces when the categorical imperative or the principle of utility is violated.

IX TOWARDS A DARWINIAN UNDERSTANDING OF THE GOOD LIFE

The traditional picture of the nature and function of morality as contained in the manifest image, as endorsed and refined by perennial philosophy, needs to be replaced. Darwin's theory of natural selection holds promise as part of the replacement view, so far as natural selection provided us humans with some basic equipment for negotiating social environments. Some mechanisms for social cooperation and coordination might be part of the original equipment. One place to look for the relevant traits or dispositions is in our proto-moral emotions, our primitive reactive attitudes. And, indeed, recent scientific work supports the view that there are certain universal basic emotions and expressions. The basic emotions are complex mechanisms that involve feelings (this is their noncognitive component), but that also, as expressed facially, bodily and, eventually, in words and complex moral codes, communicate judgements about how humans perceive certain behaviours, motives and states of affairs. When I glare at you for contemplating stealing my stash of roots, I am conveying (a) that I don't want you to do so – and thus I am trying to bring your behaviour under normative control – and (b) I am conveying a judgement that if you proceed either or both of us will be worse off. If (b) is true, then my communiqué is true, if not it is false. On the view sketched here, even as the ice melted at the end of the Pleistocene, humans were engaging in communication about the value or disvalue of certain states of affairs relative to certain ends. These statements, judgements, expressions – call them what you will – either described things truly or falsely.

Whether we judge some innate or learned disposition to be good depends on how we judge the way it typically functions in the complex ecology of human life. It is a commonplace of most moral codes that compassion and anger are apt feelings depending on the situation. We work hard to enhance and expand compassion, largely because we see few ways in which it can cause anything but good. With anger, however, we work hard to rein it in. Why? Because we see dangers abounding if we don't, especially if we create environments in which it is encouraged and grows. So, right from the start, we are positioned to make judgements about which natural traits to grow and enrich and which ones to moderate and, possibly, to suppress. Such judgements are made from the increasingly sophisticated perspectives of life in worlds, in ecological niches, where we aim to achieve multiple, heterogeneous ends. There is nothing illegitimate in saying of some proto-moral trait that it is good because it is an adaptation, promoting fitness, rarely causing harm, and almost always greasing the gears on which happy and healthy communal life turns. Such a judgement does not involve making the mistake of saying that the trait is good simply because it is an adaptation, simply because it is fitness enhancing. Judgements of goodness are normally all-things-considered judgements. Fellow-feeling is, by my lights, a basic reactive attitude that deserves this sort of verdict. It is an unmitigated good.

NOTES

1. Sellars 1963, 1. For an in-depth analysis of the conflict between the manifest and scientific images, see Flanagan 2002.
2. See Lovejoy 1936.
3. Certain fitness-enhancing traits or practices are not Darwinian adaptations – not, that is, the results of natural selection. Giving insulin to diabetics who would otherwise die young is an example.
4. Skinner 1966.
5. Robert Brandon puts heritability first on his five-component list for giving what he calls an 'ideally complete adaptive explanation'. See Brandon 1990. More generally, see the chapter by Hull, Langman and Glenn in Hull 2001, 49–93.
6. The term 'adaptive' is a troublemaker. Sometimes it is used as a synonym for 'adaptation'; sometimes to refer to any trait that increases reproductive success regardless of its historical origins, that is, even if it is a cultural invention; and sometimes to refer to any trait that is well suited to achieve certain ends or goals in a certain environment. The first use is a mistake. In discussing humans, I use 'adaptive' primarily in the third way, although the second sometimes has its uses. For further discussion, see Flanagan, Hardcastle and Nahmias 2001.
7. On Darwinism and ethics generally, see Rosenberg, this volume.
8. I develop this conception of ethics as human ecology in Flanagan 1996 and 2002, ch. 7.
9. In Flanagan 2000a, I argue that sleeping is an adaptation whereas dreaming is an evolutionary epiphenomenon, a free rider that comes with having a conscious mind that doesn't turn off while we sleep. Dreams therefore serve no proper Darwinian function themselves.
10. See the *Nicomachean Ethics* especially.
11. Dennett 1995, 453–4.
12. On Darwin's view of morality, see also Richards and Paul, this volume.
13. C. Darwin [1871] 1981, 1, 161–6.
14. For some philosophers, morality must be more than a prudential theory because, well, that is what morality is. Rosenberg (this volume) gives voice to this widespread view even if he does not endorse it himself. I don't see that we could complain if the truth was that morality was in fact a subset of a general theory of prudence. The advantage in thinking of our nature as involving pro-social and not merely prudential attitudes comes not from this sort of conceptual demand, originating with what 'morality' means, but from the fact that imputing dispositions of fellow-feeling best explains the way(s) that the members of many related species interact with their conspecifics. We care about certain others for their own sake.

15. See Gibbard 1990 and Blackburn 1998. Gibbard and Blackburn are 'expressivists', and emphasise the role of the emotions in moral theory. They describe their positions as noncognitivist. But they are good examples, as I read them, of philosophers who work through the cognitivist–noncognitivist impasse in a way that allows us to understand ethical judgements as incorporating both cognitive and noncognitive components.
16. Darwin had two data sources for his claim that certain human emotions are universal: (1) he showed photographs of people making different facial expressions to British subjects and noted remarkable consistency in judgements of what emotional state these people were in; and (2) he asked missionaries and others abroad to respond to a series of questions about emotional expression in the races they observed. Even if one argues that Darwin's conclusions about the universality of certain emotional expressions were tainted by using only British subjects and leading his witnesses in the field, there is now utterly convincing independent confirmation of Darwin's view thanks to the work of Paul Ekman and his colleagues. See Ekman 1972, 1992 and 1998. There are several reasons for saying that basic emotions exist and evolved via natural selection. First, homologues appear in other animals – canines, as well as in close ancestors – of the emotions we experience and express (whether or to what extent canines feel emotions as opposed to simply making expressions that will produce normative conformity is an issue about which I remain agnostic). Second, in social mammalian species there are characteristic movements of the facial musculature that are recognised for what they are (that is, for the behavioural dispositions they display) by conspecifics who then seem to respond appropriately to the particular display. Third, for the basic emotions of fear, anger, surprise, happiness, sadness, disgust and contempt (the search continues for reliable evidence for certain other likely suspects – embarrassment, jealousy, puzzlement, defiance or obstinacy) we have or are well on our way to locating ever better physiological markers that distinguish among the different emotional expressions. Fourth, the emotions, or at least the relevant facial expressions, alleged to be universal, are in fact recognised across human societies – among pre-literate New Guineans as well as native New Yorkers – for what they are.
17. It is important to point out that the search for basic emotions depends upon the isolation of distinctive behavioural expressions, especially facial expressions. There may be emotions that are basic but which cannot be detected this way. Finding someone sexually attractive can (I am told) be detected by widening pupils. This may be basic, but notice that it involves almost no movement of the facial musculature. Agreeing or disagreeing with someone could also, I suppose, be thought to fall on

the side of the emotions. Darwin among others suspected that nodding universally indicated agreement, whereas shaking the head from side to side indicated disagreement. This turns out not to be the case. Furthermore, there are, according to Ekman, culturally specific display rules that make emotions harder to detect from facial expressions in certain cultures.

18. Griffiths 1997, 77ff.
19. Strawson 1962. In Flanagan 2000b, I examine Buddhist views on the modifiability of the basic emotions.
20. The classic discussion of the Panda's thumb is Gould 1980.
21. On the notion of an extended phenotype, see Dawkins 1982. I am using the phrase in a less-than-strict sense here.

PHILIP KITCHER

17 Giving Darwin his due

I POLAR PERSPECTIVES

Twentieth-century attempts to evaluate the philosophical significance of Darwinism have been dominated by a pair of polar perspectives. At one extreme stand those who insist on the autonomy of philosophy and who conclude, with the early Wittgenstein, that 'Darwin's theory has no more to do with philosophy than any other hypothesis in natural science.'[1] At the other extreme are naturalists who maintain that 'now that we know' this or that other fact about the cosmos, the human brain, or (most pertinently for present purposes) the role of natural selection in hominid evolution, traditional philosophical problems are easily solved. Each opponent lives off the excesses of the other. Both also overlook the possibility that scientific ideas, including Darwin's, might play a useful, but partial, role in a variety of philosophical discussions. It has proved remarkably difficult to give Darwin his due.

Philosophers drawn to the Wittgensteinian pole typically assume that there are concepts and methods whose application to philosophical questions is unaffected by the deliverances of any science, even a science that might transform ideas about life and mind. Their discussions of questions in metaphysics, epistemology and ethics take over the idioms in which traditional philosophy has posed them, often without appreciating the fact that the language they employ was developed in response to a scientific picture that has long been superseded. Consider, for example, the group of philosophers most influenced by the younger Wittgenstein, the Vienna Circle. Their attempts to reformulate parts of classical epistemology as issues about the logical relations among statements took for granted a psychological picture that emerged in the early modern period. Far from freeing themselves from the psychological assumptions of Locke and Hume, the logical positivists and their logical empiricist successors simply buried those assumptions in their framing of problems about 'basic sentences' and the 'observational vocabulary'.[2]

No more plausible is the view that instant 'scientisation' of old philosophical problems leads immediately to their solution or dissolution. In a famous passage, E. O. Wilson claimed that the time might have come for 'ethics to be removed temporarily from the hands of the philosophers and biologicized'.[3] His subsequent discussions of the topic, with their inadequate response to the difficulties of deriving normative conclusions from factual premises, only showed that Wilson had not appreciated the depth and recalcitrance of the problems of moral philosophy. Philosophers have sometimes been tempted by similar grand visions of conquest in the name of their favourite science – particularly when the area to be conquered is the philosophy of mind and the science is some combination of fragments from the neurosciences; although their ventures are sometimes more sophisticated than Wilson's, they fail for parallel reasons.

We should treasure whatever resources we have, wherever they come from. I want to resist both the anti-naturalism that celebrates the purity of philosophy and the hyper-naturalism that denies the possibility that genuine insights might be captured in language infected by outmoded science, thus ignoring the subtleties of the problems at which it flourishes its brave new findings. Philosophers should find it worthwhile to read Hume and Darwin, Kant and Einstein, Descartes and Chomsky. In what follows, I want to make a particular case for bringing Darwin on to the philosophical team, not as the star player who wins the day all by himself, but as a contributor to a much larger effort.

II MODEST IMPLICATIONS

Darwin's significance for philosophy is clouded not only by the polarisation I've just sketched but also by the fact that there are at least three Darwinian doctrines that may be applied to philosophical questions. First is his insistence on the extent of variation within natural populations.[4] Second is his claim that all living things are related by descent with modification and his use of this claim to explain a wide variety of biological phenomena. Third, and surely most well known, is the thesis that 'natural selection has been the main but not exclusive means of modification'.[5] As we shall see, much philosophical discussion has been provoked by this last idea, both by those who maintain that important aspects of our cognitive and emotional lives can be fathomed by viewing our minds as targets of natural selection, and by those who think that the theory of natural selection provides a model for building explanations in other, philosophical, domains.

Now these three doctrines inspire a range of philosophical investigations and conclusions, some of which seem to me far more well grounded than others. The most visible ventures are those that make use of 'Darwin's dangerous idea', the notion of natural selection, attempting to show how conceiving of our species as a product of natural selection will illuminate old philosophical issues.[6] But we should not overlook projects that apply more basic Darwinian insights. Consider, for example, Darwin's emphasis on intra-specific variation (what Ernst Mayr has called Darwin's replacement of 'typological thinking' by 'population thinking').[7] Darwin's point about variation often goes unappreciated today in philosophical discussions, even though it has been uncontroversial for well over a century. Recent discussions of natural kinds, prompted by the seminal ideas of Saul Kripke and Hilary Putnam, often assume that one can revive essentialism.[8] Yet if species are natural kinds no such revival is in prospect. Kripke and Putnam largely restricted their discussions to the cases of elements and compounds, and with good reason. For, given the insights of neo-Darwinism, it's clear that the search for some analogue of the microstructural essences can't be found. No genetic or karyotypic property will play for species the role that atomic number does for the elements.

Darwin's anti-essentialist message is important for other philosophical discussions, for example, attempts to provide a value-free analysis of human nature or human functioning. Faced with the difficulty of understanding what makes human lives go well, some philosophers have been attracted to objectivist accounts of the human good: lives go well, they say, if the lives exemplify particular properties, independently of the subject's desires or plans. Articulating an account of this type requires some way of motivating the specific choice of properties that is made, and it's at this point that essentialism offers inspiration. For one might take the properties to be exactly those that develop 'the human essence'.[9] Neo-Aristotelian efforts founder, however, on Darwin's critique of essentialism. The Aristotelian revival declares that some properties of ourselves – our capacity for rational deliberation, for example – are part of the human essence, and that the development of these is especially valuable. Unfortunately, not all members of our species share that capacity, and the essentialist claim must come to terms with sad variations.[10] As we scrutinise the ways in which the moral theorising proceeds, it becomes increasingly evident that some variants are being dismissed beyond the pale of humanity by the tacit invocation of value judgements. Biology won't support the claims that these properties truly develop the human essence, and, in effect, the theory of the good simply recapitulates moral judgements that were made at the beginning.[11]

It's important not to overinterpret this debate, and to conclude that Darwin's undermining of essentialism refutes objectivism about the human good. What collapses is a particular strategy for articulating objectivism, one which responds directly to the reductionist challenge to provide a characterisation of the objectively good in a language that refers only to biological properties (or to biological and psychological properties). If the objectivist denies that the reductivist challenge needs to be met, then the focus of debate shifts to complex questions in moral epistemology on which, at least *prima facie*, Darwinism has little to say. We see here, in miniature, a situation that often obtains in the relation between Darwinism and philosophical discussion: Darwinian considerations reveal that an option we might have taken to be available or a strategy that we might have pursued is closed off; philosophical debate is advanced, but not ended.

I've begun in this relatively small and apparently unexciting place because we ought to be aware of such partial successes as we attend to the ambitions of those who would build evolutionary epistemologies or found ethics on the deliverances of Darwinism. Too often, the views derived from Darwin are wild extrapolations from the core tenets of contemporary evolutionary theory. This is most evident when the philosophical project to be advanced requires a claim about the form of complex human capacities and the candidate claim rests on allegations about the history of natural selection in hominid evolution.

III SOCIOBIOLOGY'S SIREN SONG

Since the controversy about human sociobiology, it's been evident that the attempt to attribute faculties, dispositions and forms of behaviour to natural selection is fraught with pitfalls.[12] Serious theorising about natural selection requires assumptions about the range of genetic variation, views about which phenotypic traits are genetically or developmentally tied together, understanding of the complexities of the environment, detailed investigations of the possibilities of building rival models, and, in the case of human beings and other primate species, recognition of the possible roles played by cultural transmission. In some subfields of sociobiology – I think particularly of the study of insect behaviour – meticulous field-work and sophisticated mathematical modelling have gone hand-in-hand, yielding enhanced understanding.[13] By contrast, in studies of human dispositions to behaviour, grand conclusions have often been launched on the sketchiest evidence and have deployed qualitative arguments whose shortcomings were revealed at the first efforts in formalisation.

Chastened by criticisms of early human sociobiology, many who are attracted to a Darwinian programme of studying human behaviour, whether they come to it from philosophy, from anthropology, or from psychology, have decided to change the name of the enterprise and to declare, very loudly, that they have acknowledged the errors of their predecessors.[14] Yet recent literature in evolutionary psychology, some of which quickens philosophical pulses, has changed remarkably little. The fundamental strategy is to characterise human psychological nature by exposing the ways in which particular 'modules' have been individually fashioned by natural selection. So we are informed that there are modules for women's being attracted to men with resources, for men's being attracted to women with a waist–hip ratio of around 0.7, and for both sexes to detect social cheats.[15] Some of these conclusions have little bearing on philosophical discussions, others are taken to have import for epistemology and for ethics. I want to offer some brief reasons for scepticism about the ways in which this strategy has been undertaken so far.

The first point to note is that one can adopt Darwinism, including the claim about the importance of natural selection in evolutionary change, without endorsing any such particular conclusions about how selection has acted on our species. There's no forced choice between accepting the evolutionary psychologist's favourite collection of stories and reverting to Creationism. Second, one should note that the programme of evolutionary psychology, with its commitment to a single human psychological nature, is at odds with the modest Darwinian theme of anti-essentialism – indeed, evolutionary psychology is dominated by a tendency to write as if frequency-dependent selection and polymorphism didn't exist. Third, the claims about the operation of natural selection may rest on more systematic evidence than those made in the heyday of human sociobiology, but they still share the old defects both of failing to develop careful mathematical models and of ignoring the possible impact of cultural transmission. Fourth, and to my mind most important, the conclusions typically presuppose guesswork both about the character of the (lightly sketched) savannah environment and about the ways in which phenotypic traits are linked together.

Rather than venturing into the slough of evolutionary psychology's depiction of human sexual relations, I'll express my doubts by reference to the study that's usually (and with justice) viewed as emblematic of evolutionary psychology, the hypothesis, advanced by Leda Cosmides and John Tooby: that human beings have evolved not to have a general-purpose logical faculty but a collection of specialised mechanisms, including one that detects violations of social rules.[16]

The essentials are as follows. There is a well-known psychological experiment (the Wason card-selection test) on which subjects do very badly when the problem is posed in abstract form, and much better when it is related to familiar social situations. The test requires identifying the conditions under which a general statement would be shown false. Cosmides and Tooby document the ability of subjects to do much better when the task can be understood as a matter of detecting violations in social rules. They hypothesise that this signals the existence of a special-purpose module that evolved under pressure to identify cheats in the ancestral savannah environment.

There are three reasons to be sceptical. First, the ability to identify cheating would appear to be favoured by natural selection long before our ancestors, or their primate relatives, reached the stage of being able to formulate linguistic rules and wonder about their violation. As I'll suggest below, the standard ways of conceiving the early scenarios of cooperation on the savannah (or in the forests) may be quite inadequate – our ignorance of the types of cooperation and of the details of the environments is, as Darwin would say, 'profound'. But insofar as we have any grasp of the kinds of interactions that were important in the genesis of social relations among primates, it seems that it must have been important for animals to survey their conspecifics and judge whether others were continuing to participate in a joint venture.[17] *Speculatively*, we can entertain the idea of an advantage obtained by those animals whose abilities to process or retain information were superior, and such differences *might* result from differences in genotypes expressed in the forms of neurotransmitters.

The speculation introduces my second point. It's extraordinarily implausible to suppose that natural selection could have produced a device that *just* promoted the detection of social cheating. Evolutionary psychologists may not like to talk about genes, but, as soon as they start to discuss natural selection, they are up to their eyebrows in genetic hypotheses. If there was natural selection for social-cheat detection then there must have been genetic variation in some ancestral population; this genetic variation must either have been expressed at the phenotypic level *only* in the ability to detect cheats, or else in that ability and in other characteristics whose selective importance is trivial by comparison; otherwise there's not selection for cheat-detection, but for a *suite of traits* in which detecting cheats is one component. When we recall that genetic variation usually produces differences in proteins, we recognise that the entire story rests on the not-very-compelling idea that some protein difference is localised in one of the two ways just mentioned.

We might be inclined to swallow the genetic hypothesis and to disregard my first point about the evolution of social-cheat-detection on the grounds that Cosmides and Tooby have the best psychological explanation of the data. But this would be a mistake. Despite their considerable ingenuity in constructing experiments, Cosmides and Tooby fail to consider an important (but banal) rival hypothesis. That hypothesis claims that we have a general-purpose logical ability but that our logical reasoning works best on the types of problems with which we're most familiar. Now Cosmides and Tooby do spend a great deal of time and trouble in contrasting their own proposal with what they term the 'familiarity hypothesis'. But there are two importantly different versions of the familiarity hypothesis, only *one* of which has been addressed in the experiments that Cosmides and Tooby so painstakingly devise. A test may be familiar or unfamiliar because the subject is, or is not, at home with the *content of the propositions* in terms of which it's couched. Alternatively, a test may be familiar or unfamiliar because subjects have, or have not, done *problems with that logical structure* before.[18] The version of the familiarity hypothesis which I propose focuses on this second type of familiarity. *Pace* Popper, the falsification of generalisations isn't something in which people much engage outside of academic disputes and one very special context, to wit our everyday checking of breaches of rules. Thus I propose that we have a generalised ability to do logic, that it is expressed in terms of our ability to solve problems with structures that recur frequently in our lives (or on which we've been trained), and that the effects that Cosmides and Tooby see result from a commonplace fact that falsification problems only arise for many people in social contexts. Given the Darwinian difficulties of their preferred hypothesis, the balance of evidence should favour my suggestion, mundane and boring though it undoubtedly is.

I have gone into a little detail because I want to contrast two strategies for generating Darwinian insights in philosophy. One, that I commend, remains close to the core doctrines of Darwinism, the three claims about variation, descent with modification and the importance of natural selection as a cause of evolutionary change. The other, which needs to be undertaken with caution by enthusiasts and scrutinised closely by those to whom they announce their findings, attempts to advance specific claims about the ways in which natural selection has moulded human propensities, and, on this basis, to resolve traditional philosophical problems. *In principle*, there is no bar to illuminating human behaviour and psychological propensities by employing the perspective of natural selection, but it's important to recognise just how onerous are the demands of doing this in a responsible fashion.[19]

IV DARWINIAN EPISTEMOLOGY

So what can we glean from Darwin? In the next sections, I'll look at ways in which central tenets of Darwinism might offer insights for epistemology and for ethics. Let's start with the theory of knowledge, assuming that the Darwinian epistemologist avoids the trap (described in the last section) of trying to generate an account of our cognitive propensities from some fanciful adaptationist story.

Many philosophers have been inspired by the thought that human knowledge might conform to abstract versions of the principles that govern the history of life. The idea can take a stronger or a weaker form. In the weaker version no more is supposed than the *evolution* of human knowledge – we are to think of knowledge as historical process and historical product, and invited to think of ways of characterising the states of knowledge at various times, the kinds of transitions among such states, and the causal factors that promote or retard transitions of specific types.[20] The stronger form, 'evolutionary epistemology' as it's usually known, insists on a much closer analogy between Darwin's account of the history of life and the growth of knowledge either in the individual or in the species. I'll consider two versions. On one of these, prominent in the writings of Donald Campbell, the individual's knowledge is conceived as something like a Darwinian process.[21] Ideas are randomly generated and tested by experience. Those that are retained are those that survive the process of selection. A second approach, originally presented by Richard Dawkins, supposes that there are analogues of the entities whose transmission measures the course of evolution. Just as there are genes, and just as evolution is recorded in changes in the frequency of alleles, so too there are memes, and the growth of knowledge in the species is understood in terms of the spread of memes.[22]

Insofar as either of these proposals is likely to illuminate epistemological questions, it will be because the theorist is able to understand those parts of the growth of knowledge that are either non-Darwinian or else fall outside the scope of the analogy. Consider first the use of evolutionary epistemology to understand an individual's cognitive accomplishments. We may concede that there are occasions in which novel concepts and propositions are randomly generated, and that there is a sense in which the testing of ideas is like a process of natural selection. Yet it's also pertinent to note that there are other procedures through which people develop new notions and theses. We reason from our prior beliefs, generalising and using analogies (indeed, this is evident in the process of generating evolutionary epistemology itself!). Hence the process of generation isn't much like random mutation in the Darwinian story about life. Further, if the evolutionary epistemologist proposes that the processes to which I've alluded are analogues of recombination, we should point out that those processes don't consist in the swapping of bits and pieces of antecedent propositions. To make the analogy work, one would need a detailed account of just what the forms of the 'recombination' are, and this requires engaging all the serious epistemological problems of understanding methods of discovery.

Nor can we gain much insight into individual knowledge by likening the testing of ideas to a selection regime. To suppose that propositions augment their fitness when they occur in complexes that predict claims we discover to be true, and lose fitness when they are found in clusters that generate expectations that are unsatisfied, only substitutes a biological vocabulary for more familiar idioms in confirmation theory. The problems of understanding the gains and losses in 'fitness' with any precision remain just as they were when we posed them in terms of confirmation and falsification. All that has been added is a misleading suggestion about the link between success in a regime of tests and the proliferation of 'copies' or 'descendants' of beliefs, which seems to make little sense within the context of individual epistemology.

Matters are somewhat better, I think, when we try to apply Darwinian ideas to problems in social epistemology. Although we should be cautious in supposing that the transmission of culture across the generations can be conceived in terms of 'cultural atoms', analogues of the genes, there are instances in which the Dawkinsian notion of a meme is suggestive. Consider, for example, the spread of Christianity across the Roman Empire. Insofar as we can estimate the numbers of believers in major cities at various times in the first three centuries, the growth curve takes the sigmoidal shape familiar from population ecology. Conceivably, one could investigate this process from the perspective of evolutionary epidemiology, using the kinds of models that are available for studying the invasion of populations by pathogens. Although the work has not yet been done, success in this venture would obviously inspire efforts to find analogues of the parameters that appear in the models. We might thus discover something about the flexibility of Christian doctrine by comparison with its religious rivals by using analogies with mutation or with virulence.[23]

In indicating possibilities of this kind, I emphatically don't want to claim more than that Darwinian thinking about the spread of ideas can offer us a perspective on historical processes that may or may not prove applicable to studies of change of belief. The ultimate test will be whether we can do justice to the phenomena in their full complexity. Darwin supplies us with some tools. There's no reason to insist, in advance, that they must be applicable or that they exhaust the arsenal we need.

My pragmatic opportunism about using Darwinian ideas in epistemology can be illustrated by a cluster of projects I've commended elsewhere. Scientific enquiry is a social phenomenon. Hence we should not simply focus on the ways in which individual beliefs are justified, but also enquire about the ways in which individual efforts are organised so as to promote the knowledge of the community. Given a particular type of epistemic predicament, we can consider which distribution(s) of group endeavours would yield the best chances of success and we can then investigate whether specified social institutions and individual motivations would lead the community towards or away from the optimum(a). To cite an example I've discussed in detail, if there are several methods for pursuing a particular enquiry then, under some circumstances, the best community policy is to explore more than one approach, even though one method would stand out as preferable if just one person were to be assigned the problem; moreover, it can be shown that motivations and social arrangements that might have seemed antithetical to the pursuit of truth bring the community quite close to the preferred division of labour.[24] Problems of this type are similar in some respects to those arising in evolutionary ecology, and the mathematical formalisms developed there prove useful in the epistemological context. Thus the epistemologist can borrow tools forged by evolutionary biologists, but, as I've emphasised, this brings with it no commitment to a more global vision of the growth of knowledge as a Darwinian process.

The chief Darwinian moral for epistemology is, I think, connected with a more basic evolutionary theme. As numerous commentators have noted, Darwin's commitment to the idea of descent with modification resonates with the broad class of nineteenth-century proposals to understand facets of the contemporary world as products of history.[25] Historicism in epistemology doesn't need to rest on Darwinian grounds, but an evolutionary perspective offers a healthy antidote to the disease of synchronism that often besets philosophical efforts to explain human knowledge. From Descartes to the present, generations of epistemologists have written as though the central problem is to uncover a structure of justification in an individual's beliefs that identifies special warranting relations only among the beliefs themselves or between particular beliefs and the individual's experiences. A far more realistic picture would identify the individual as part of a community, from which much is absorbed, most of it never to be seriously queried, and to view that community as one stage in a historical lineage.[26] Perplexities about particular types of knowledge thus give way to attempts to understand how the pertinent propositions came to be incorporated within the set passed on by the tradition. Further, we can look to Darwin and to the theorists who have succeeded him for clues about how to represent the states of community knowledge at particular times and the transitions among them.

Consider, for example, our knowledge of mathematics. Epistemologists who are wedded to the project of synchronic reconstruction of an individual's beliefs have explored many possible sources for the ways in which our fundamental mathematical beliefs are justified (and, of course, they have differed in their choices about which are the fundamental beliefs). Appeals to knowledge grounded in grasp of concepts and to processes of intuition have been perennially popular. Given the well-known difficulties with both sorts of explanation, they appear as counsels of despair, especially when viewed from a Darwinian, or more generally, from a historicist perspective. Why not say the obvious things?[27] Our knowledge of mathematics rests on the testimony of those who taught us. Collectively, mathematical knowledge evolves as successive communities of mathematicians respond to the mathematics they have inherited and to the problems bequeathed to them by natural scientists. The ultimate roots of the tradition lie in relatively primitive manipulations of the environment, carried out by our remote predecessors in India, Babylon, Egypt and perhaps in sites of which we are ignorant. In the course of the subsequent history, mathematicians have been given a very special role, licensed to devise new languages that relate in ways they find interesting and illuminating to the corpus they have inherited. The demarcation of that role itself represents a discovery about community enquiry, to wit that it is good for other investigations that the role be filled.

Historicism, to repeat, is not specifically Darwinian. But Darwin provided one of the most successful and elaborate schemes of historical explanation, and is both inspiration and resource for historicist programmes. Since epistemology can benefit from historicism, it can learn from Darwin.

V DARWINIAN ETHICS?

I turn now to the area in which the significance of Darwinian ideas has been most hotly debated. Does Darwinism reveal how human societies ought to be constructed, or how human beings ought to behave? Does it finally debunk morality? Or is it simply irrelevant to our understanding of morality? Eminent scholars can be recruited in support of all the obvious responses. So what exactly is the relationship between evolutionary theory and ethics?

Let's start with a simple answer.[28] There are many different projects relating evolutionary biology to ethics, some of which are perfectly sensible, others flawed. The hyper-Darwinian ambition is to show how our understanding of the history of life yields new basic moral principles. Somewhat less ambitiously, one might contend that Darwinism supports some distinctive metaethical view, that it shows, for example, that moral judgements cannot have truth-values or that moral knowledge is impossible. Much more modestly, we can see the evolutionary understanding of our species as relevant to the tracing of all aspects of human history, including the history of our morality and social systems. Finally, one might suppose that recognition of the kinship of life, coupled with moral principles we already hold, enables us to arrive at new derivative moral judgements – perhaps we come to understand ourselves as having obligations not to treat other animals in particular ways. The simple answer proposes that the first two of these ventures are illegitimate, while the latter two are well grounded.

This seems at least three-quarters right. Although proposals to derive substantive new ethical principles as corollaries of Darwinism sometimes acknowledge the familiar difficulty of inferring normative statements from factual statements, they fail to show how such inferences work. Whether the would-be evolutionary ethicist adverts to (speculations about) 'evolved human nature' or to 'the fundamental character of life', it's always legitimate to ask whether we ought to acquiesce in the propensities attributed to us or to aspire to the ends that are singled out. On the other hand, the project of using what we know about hominid evolution to inform our account of the history of human morality (or of human societies) seems perfectly justified, and, in similar fashion, there is no bar against using empirical information, in conjunction with normative principles, to justify further normative claims. So the first, third and fourth parts of the response withstand scrutiny. What is more problematic – and more interesting – is the claim about the irrelevance of Darwin for metaethics.

Towards the end of *Principia Ethica* G. E. Moore declares that the only two things that are of fundamental value are personal relations and beautiful things.[29] Sceptics might wonder how Moore could know that this is so, and their qualms wouldn't be assuaged by his murky references to 'non-natural properties' and 'intuitions'. Mindful of the epistemological points made in the last section, we might recall that Moore's judgement is the response of an exceptional thinker to very particular circumstances: Moore, brought up in late Victorian England, considers the nature of goodness from his rooms in a beautiful city, doubtless recalling his own experiences of friendship. Appeals to 'intuition' are the last resort of those who deny the relevance of Moore's personal history. We understand his judgement better if we see it as a reaction to the views he acquired in childhood, tempered by his experiences and his reflections upon them. Like the creative mathematician, Moore extends and modifies the practice that his predecessors bequeathed to him, but, if we are to make clear the status of his moral judgements, we have to recognise both the rationale for his own amendments and the historical process that formed the backdrop to his own education. If Moore is justified, then we won't find the justification in a synchronic reconstruction of his beliefs, but in a genealogy of morals that leads to him.

This example is intended to reveal that the connection between the second enterprise (Darwinian reforms in metaethics) and the third (tracing the history of our moral attitudes) is more intimate than we might have thought.[30] We can't simply assume that a historical investigation will leave everything in place. For it might turn out that our reconstructed genealogy was difficult, even impossible, to square with the view that shifts in moral attitudes embodied discoveries. The details of the story might make us unable to see how successive transformations could be gains in moral knowledge.

In response to hyper-Darwinism's claim to draw normative moral conclusions from evolutionary premises, it's easy to swing to the Wittgensteinian pole and contend that the central questions of normative ethics and metaethics must be tackled in purely philosophical terms. Not only do those 'purely philosophical terms' typically fail to acknowledge the importance of historicism in epistemology, but they also are laden with psychological assumptions that we've inherited from the eighteenth century. Without denying the genuine insights of contemporary moral philosophy, it's possible to envisage that the idiom in which they are couched might need reform in the light of better views about our psychological capacities, and that the result might enable us to adopt different positions from those that comprise the current menu of options.

The rest of this section will explore, speculatively, the possibilities at which I've gestured. Suppose we try to tell a story about the emergence of human morality. What might it look like?

I'll begin from one of the most celebrated problems in the evolutionary study of behavior, the problem of altruism. Biologists, of course, take altruistic behaviour to consist in activities that benefit another organism at cost to the agent, where both cost and benefit are measured in the Darwinian currency of reproduction. Models of kin selection and of reciprocal altruism, usually understood in the last twenty years in terms of evolutionary game theory applied to iterated Prisoner's Dilemma, have demonstrated possibilities for sustaining, and in some instances, originating altruism in this bare biological sense.[31] Far more important to moral philosophy, however, is a richer conception of altruism that involves recognition of the needs of others and responses directed at fulfilling those needs.

In previous work, both Elliott Sober and I have argued, on different grounds, that natural selection permits the evolution of this richer sort of altruism.[32]

Unfortunately, as primatologists have provided richer descriptions of the behaviour of our evolutionarily closest relatives, it's become evident that the models constructed to understand the evolution of psychological altruism are quite unrealistic.[33] Common chimpanzees and bonobos act very differently from the strategies that theorists attribute to altruists; in particular, they are frequently much less concerned to punish defections than they 'ought' to be. I propose that our evolutionary theorising about altruism has substituted mathematically tractable games for the complex many-agent interactions that are omnipresent in the social lives of higher primates. The central problem for a young social primate is to be accepted as part of a stable coalition, and there is good reason to believe that the selection pressure arising from this problem favours a blind and relatively non-punitive disposition to aid particular 'friends'. Natural selection, then, *may* have fostered the development of capacities for sympathy.

Yet it's clear from studies of chimpanzee social behaviour that those capacities are far from limitless. In situations where large evolutionary rewards are at stake, propensities to ally with another animal can be overridden by selfish aspirations.[34] *One* possible view of chimpanzee (and bonobo) social life is that it's a battleground of conflicting tendencies, some of them altruistic (in the interesting psychological sense) and some of them self-interested. The conflict produces frequent ruptures in the social fabric, and the constant breaking-up makes way for constant making-up. Because the work of social repair is so costly and the sympathetic dispositions so limited, our evolutionary relatives can only manage societies of a limited size.

Extend these speculations one step further. Somewhere in hominid evolution we acquired the ability to live in larger social groups. How did we do it? One *possibility* is that, with the acquisition of language came also an ability to prescribe rules for ourselves and to obey them. Instead of the melée of competing tendencies that make chimpanzee/bonobo sociality so fragile, we evolved a rudimentary psychological faculty of normative guidance. Perhaps the primitive rules by which our ancestors governed themselves were the kinds of kinship regulations still recorded by anthropologists who visit the contemporary humans whose environments most resemble those of the distant past. Proto-morality might have begun from the injunction to act with the clan, and the evolutionary advantage of guiding behaviour by proto-morality might have consisted in its yielding a more efficient taming of socially disruptive tendencies than that achieved by our evolutionary relatives.

How do we trace a route from proto-morality to Moore's refined reflections? If anything is clear, it's surely that any such historical process would be largely subject to non-Darwinian forces. Cultural transmission and cultural selection will have been the prominent shapers of the modifications. The historical challenge of extending the story requires us to do justice to the great transformations that have obviously occurred in the construction of systems of moral rules, as our ancestors came to terms with other groups, fashioned societies in which individuals were assigned distinct roles, recognised the equal capacities of human beings with different phenotypes, and so forth. In outline, we can view morality as a human phenomenon that enters our history as a device for regulating the conflict between our sympathetic and selfish dispositions (where regulation plays a key role in the maintenance of our societies) and is further articulated through interactions among different social groups and members' reflections on those interactions. What status this assigns to our moral claims depends, I suggest, on the details of the story, and the details require much more research in evolutionary biology, anthropology, psychology and history than anyone has yet attempted. Nonetheless, it ought to be evident that this kind of history is potentially relevant to metaethical questions, and that we cannot neatly separate projects in the manner that my original simple answer proposed.

Everything I have said about the evolution and history of morality is admittedly conjectural. My sentences are peppered with 'might' and 'possibility', sometimes italicised, to draw attention to the fact that this is a story awaiting evidence. Any attempt to go further and to explore the intricacies of the history should be held to the same standards as those I proposed in the third section, in the case of evolutionary psychology. As I pointed out there, using arguments about the action of natural selection to arrive at claims about psychological faculties and propensities is always vulnerable to alternative explanations. Thus, even if the account I have sketched were elaborated more fully, it would be appropriate to begin from the claim that this is an explanation of how human morality *might* have evolved. Of course, the more phenomena that can be assembled within the purview of the explanation, the more constraints are generated for potential rivals – this, after all, was Darwin's argumentative achievement in the *Origin*.[35]

VI DARWINIAN EUGENICS?

So far, I have paid little attention to the possibility that Darwinian ideas might help us in dealing with issues of applied ethics. Here it is useful to consider an example that is becoming as salient for us as it was for Darwin's younger contemporaries. Darwin's cousin, Francis Galton, was only one of many who saw their new awareness of human history as offering new moral imperatives. The eugenics movement was born of the idea that actual cultural practices may shift the regime of human selection in ways that detract from the human good. Eugenicists may disagree in their visions of what constitutes the human good, but, within their moral systems, they could – and can – adapt Darwinian ideas to draw moral conclusions.

However reluctant we are to use the name, we stand at the beginning of new ventures in eugenics. Once we have the opportunity to identify the probabilities that people yet unborn will have particular traits, then we are forced to make eugenic decisions: for even the decision not to act on the basis of such information reflects a preference for certain types of lives.[36] Eugenic practices differ in the quality of the information they use, in the target population and the target characteristics, and, most importantly, in the freedom with which couples (or individuals) can make reproductive decisions. The Human Genome Project will offer thousands of pre-natal tests within the next decade or so; provided equal access to tests is guaranteed, it appears to lead naturally to a *utopian* eugenics, in which couples will be free to use genetic information in deciding whether to continue or to terminate a nascent life. Prospective parents will have (we assume) first-class information, and, far from being coerced into pursuing some socially dictated programme, they will be able to take steps to avoid bringing into the world a child with characteristics that they would regard as unfortunate.

Utopian eugenics is surely benign in the most dramatic cases. The incidence of Tay-Sachs disease has been reduced, world-wide, to about 1 per cent of its former value, thanks to a humane programme of pre-natal testing. At the same time, the creation of facilities for pre-natal testing has enabled people in some Asian countries to discover the sex of a foetus and to terminate unwanted female pregnancies. Whether or not there are strong causal relations between particular alleles and forms of behaviour, the coming years will surely bring all sorts of correlational claims: those interested in marketing tests will be able to offer probabilistic predictions about such things as sexual orientation, body-build, temperament and academic performance in children reared in common environments.[37] Should genetic tests that bear on these traits be used in our coming eugenic practices?

A natural response to the question is to declare that using some kinds of pre-natal tests is morally justified, but that using others is not: we are right to try to avoid the dreadful degeneration of the Tay-Sachs child, but we are quite wrong to narrow the vision of humanity to a small range of 'acceptable' phenotypes. Some may even think that there is a sound Darwinian argument behind this response. After all, we know that species that deplete the stock of genetic variation are more vulnerable to extinction. A good evolutionary strategy for us would therefore be to maintain the (limited) genetic variability of *Homo sapiens*. This line of reasoning, like other ambitious Darwinising that has erupted in previous sections, is flawed. However we conceive of the good for human beings, none of us is simply an instrument for the survival of the species, a genotype to be kept around in the interests of preserving some exotic genetic variant. Individual lives matter, and the character of those individual lives ought to be the focus of our reproductive decisions.

A more serious application of Darwinian ideas in the present context is to reveal, once again, the problems of superficially attractive ways of reacting to our predicament. Consider the simple proposal that eugenic interventions are justified in cases in which the child-to-be would be at high risk for some disease or disability. That proposal evidently requires a prior understanding of the concept of disease (for, as the history of medicine reminds us, all kinds of socially unwelcome traits have been viewed as diseases). Those who hope to short-circuit discussions of values may try, at this point, to articulate a 'value-free' conception of disease, suggesting that diseases occur when some organ or system fails to discharge its proper function.

Their efforts will succeed only to the extent that they can analyse the notion of function without appealing to judgements of value, and it is here that Darwin enters the picture. For, according to a widely accepted account, the function of an entity is to be identified with the effect for which it was selected.[38] Functions are tactics used against Darwin's hostile forces.[39]

We can now see, I think, why the simple proposal will not do. The objective notion of disease is founded on the Darwinian concept of function, but that notion of disease cannot do the moral work the proposal demands of it. What matters to us in assessing human lives, including those currently in prospect, are the possibilities for the people whose lives they are, and those possibilities may bear little relation to the challenges and responses of ancient environments. Even if human reproductive systems were shaped by natural selection to produce many more offspring than people actually do, we should not regard questions about our goals in life as somehow settled by reminding us of such functions. An objective, Darwinian, account of disease is of no help, precisely because it grounds our eugenic discussions in facts about our evolutionary history that are external to our goals for ourselves.

Plainly, I have not tried to settle the hard questions about the coming eugenics. My aim has been, rather, to illustrate the ways in which our Darwinian understanding of ourselves can enter discussions in applied ethics. I have tried both to expose the unambitious ways in which such understanding can promote clarity, and also to reveal the dangers of overreaching.

VII DARWIN'S DUE

In a famous, and, to my mind, accurate description of the discipline, Wilfrid Sellars proposed that 'philosophy is the study of how things, in the broadest sense of the term, hang together, in the broadest sense of the term'.[40] Philosophers work in the interstices of other people's lines of business. Their task, and their opportunity, is to fit together pieces of the enormous fabric of human achievement. Because Darwin's account of the history of life is so large and important a part of that fabric, it must be relevant to philosophical ventures. Yet, for reasons at which I've gestured throughout this essay, there are major difficulties in applying Darwinian ideas in all the domains that excite his epigones. Moreover, as I've insisted, Darwin's great achievement doesn't make all other considerations and disciplines irrelevant, and, in particular, it shouldn't lead us to dismiss the potential insights of pre-Darwinian philosophising.

The history of enquiry, including the history of what we call 'Philosophy', bequeaths to us a large number of hard problems. How are we to understand what, if anything, is distinctively human? What is the place of mind in physical nature? What is the extent, and what are the limits of human knowledge? What is our basis for making the moral claims that we do? Our ability to pose these larger questions in sharp and fruitful ways evolves as we learn more from the investigations of natural scientists, and, sometimes, scientific enquiry allows us to resolve a smaller conundrum that troubled our predecessors (recall the way in which studies of continuity and convergence have helped us respond to Zeno's paradoxes). With the hardest questions, however, what the sciences seem to offer us is partial clarification, not complete solution. The polar perspectives with which I began expect either everything or nothing, and, in their different ways, they overlook what great scientific advances, like Darwin's, can genuinely offer.

My recommendations for applying evolutionary ideas within philosophy are, I trust, obvious from my illustrative examples, and their prevailing character is one of cautious exploration. I hope to recapture a philosophical middle-ground that seems in constant danger of vanishing. Darwin deserves his due, neither more nor less.

NOTES

I am very grateful to Dan Dennett, Owen Flanagan and especially the editors for their constructive advice about earlier versions of this chapter.

1. Wittgenstein [1922] 1961, 4.1122.
2. Philip Kitcher 1993a, 61–3.
3. E. O. Wilson 1975, 562.
4. E. Mayr 1976, 1991.
5. C. Darwin [1859] 1964, 6.
6. Dennett 1995.
7. E. Mayr 1976.
8. Kripke 1980 and Putnam 1975; see also Dupré 1981 and Sober, this volume.
9. Hurka 1993.

10. Hull 1986.
11. Philip Kitcher 1999.
12. Lewontin, Rose and Kamin 1984; Philip Kitcher 1985a.
13. Philip Kitcher 1985a, ch. 5.
14. R. Wright 1994, 150.
15. Barkow, Cosmides and Tooby 1992 and Buss 1994.
16. Barkow, Cosmides and Tooby 1992, 163–228; for cogent criticism, see Lloyd 1999.
17. Philip Kitcher 1993b.
18. Kuhn 1970, 189–90.
19. Philip Kitcher 1990.
20. Kuhn 1970; Lakatos 1970; L. Laudan 1977; Philip Kitcher 1993a.
21. D. Campbell 1974.
22. Dawkins 1976, ch. 11.
23. Stark 1996; Philip Kitcher 2001.
24. Philip Kitcher 1993a, ch. 8.
25. Patricia Kitcher 1992.
26. Philip Kitcher 1993c.
27. Philip Kitcher 1983, 2000.
28. Philip Kitcher 1994.
29. G. E. Moore [1903] 1988, section 113.
30. See also Flanagan, this volume
31. Hamilton 1995, 31–82; Axelrod 1984; Sober and Wilson 1998; Rosenberg, this volume.
32. Philip Kitcher 1993d; Sober 1994c.
33. Philip Kitcher 1998.
34. De Waal 1984, 1989.
35. Hodge 1977; Philip Kitcher 1985b.
36. Philip Kitcher 1996, 196–7.
37. See Philip Kitcher 1996, ch. 11.
38. L. Wright 1976; Millikan 1989; Godfrey-Smith 1994b.
39. Philip Kitcher 1993b.
40. Sellars 1963, 1.

GUIDE TO FURTHER READING

DARWIN'S PUBLISHED WORK

Darwin's major books are available in a wide range of formats, from free online editions to inexpensive paperback facsimiles to multi-volume comprehensive sets. *The Writings of Charles Darwin on the Web*, a website maintained by John van Wyhe, presently offers the most authoritative and scholarly online editions. A CD-ROM from Lightbinders, Goldie and Ghiselin 1997, is especially good value. There are several useful anthologies, notably Ridley 1994 and Glick and Kohn 1996. For bibliographic details of books written by Darwin and published either in his lifetime or since, see Freeman 1977. Of the multi-volume editions, only one, in 29 volumes, approaches completeness: Barrett and Freeman 1986. Almost all of the papers published by Darwin in his lifetime are in Barrett 1977. Of posthumously published books that have appeared more recently, the most important is C. Darwin 1975. Changes in the text of the *Origin of Species* through its several editions can be studied in C. Darwin 1959. The searching out of particular words and phrases is easily accomplished with the online texts, of course; but traditional concordances also exist, in online and published formats. The latter include Barrett, Weinshank *et al.* 1981, 1986 and 1987.

DARWIN'S NOTEBOOKS AND MARGINALIA

A great deal of notebook material has been published in recent years. The most significant edition is that of the 1836–44 notebooks: Barrett *et al.* 1987. Also important is Keynes 2000, comprising Darwin's zoology notes and specimen lists from the *Beagle* voyage. The introductions to these volumes contain much useful information about the editing in recent decades of other manuscript materials. Weinshank *et al.* 1990 is a concordance to the 1987 notebook edition.

For Darwin's annotations on the books in his personal library, see Di Gregorio 1990. A second volume, of Darwin's annotations on his large collection of offprints of articles, is in preparation. By far the most extensive body of manuscript material is in the Cambridge University Library. For the history and current locations of Darwin's manuscripts, a natural starting point is F. Burkhardt 1998.

CORRESPONDENCE

F. Burkhardt 1996 offers an inexpensive sampling of Darwin's correspondence up to 1859. For Darwin's later years, two sets of older volumes remain indispensable: F. Darwin [1888] 1969 and F. Darwin and Seward 1903. These are in the process of being superseded by the superbly scholarly volumes of the Darwin Correspondence Project: F. Burkhardt *et al.* 1985–2001. Apart from letters to and from Darwin, these volumes include other significant manuscripts and invaluable appendices on particular aspects of Darwin's life and work. The most up-to-date guide to the whole of Darwin's correspondence is the calendar in Burkhardt and Smith 1994 – now available online from the Darwin Correspondence Project website.

SECONDARY WORKS

Two recent biographies surpass all earlier ones, especially in their use of the best specialist studies: Desmond and Moore 1991 and Browne 1995, 2002. A useful compendium of information about Darwin is Freeman 1978. A major collaborative volume on Darwin and his legacies is Kohn 1985a. Its bibliography, though now somewhat dated, is excellent, as is the bibliography in Oldroyd 1984. For the wider story of Darwinism's place in history, several recent books can be recommended, not least for their bibliographic guidance: E. Mayr 1982; Keller and Lloyd 1992; Depew and Weber 1995; Bowler 1989 (a new edition is imminent); Gayon 1998; Jardine, Secord and Spary 1996; and Ruse 1996, 1999a and 2000b.

For historians of all things Darwinian, old and current, as for historians of science generally, the main resource is the History of Science, Technology and Medicine bibliographic database, available online through many institutions. For historical scholarship in this area, the leading journals are the *Journal of the History of Biology* and, increasingly, *Studies in History and Philosophy of Biological and Biomedical Sciences*. A still-helpful guide to historiographic trends is Olby, Cantor, Christie and Hodge 1990. A remarkably generous encyclopaedia of Darwinism and evolution has been published in French: Tort 1996.

DARWINISM AND NATURALISM IN PHILOSOPHY

Here one volume provides an especially lively introduction: Callebaut 1993. It features extensive interviews with nearly two dozen leading figures in naturalist philosophy of science, including philosophy of biology. See also several of the books published in the Cambridge Studies in Philosophy and Biology series, from Cambridge University Press, notably Rosenberg 2000. This series is uniquely useful for tracking developments in its interdisciplinary area. Two anthologies of recent articles are Sober 1994a and Hull and Ruse 1998. This last appears in the Oxford Readings in Philosophy series, and so marks a milestone in the progress of philosophy of biology towards professional acceptance. Of journals, *Biology and Philosophy* and *Studies in History and Philosophy of Biological and Biomedical Sciences* are the most important. Beyond that, the standard bibliographic resources for philosophy and the biological sciences serve well, especially *The Philosopher's Index*, now available online through many institutions.

REFERENCES

Achinstein, P. 1993. 'Waves and Scientific Method.' *PSA 1992*, vol. 2, pp. 193–204. East Lansing, Mich.: Philosophy of Science Association.

Adams, Mark B., ed. 1994. *The Evolution of Theodosius Dobzhansky: Essays on his Life and Thought in Russia and America*. Princeton: Princeton University Press.

Allan, Mea. 1977. *Darwin and his Flowers: The Key to Natural Selection*. London: Faber and Faber.

Allen, David Elliston. 1994. *The Naturalist in Britain: A Social History*. Princeton: Princeton University Press.

Alter, Stephen. 1999. *Darwinism and the Linguistic Image*. Baltimore: Johns Hopkins University Press.

Amigoni, David and Wallace, Jeff, eds. 1995. *Charles Darwin's The Origin of Species: New Interdisciplinary Essays*. Manchester: Manchester University Press.

Amundson, Ron. 1996. 'Historical Development of the Concept of Adaptation.' In Michael R. Rose and George V. Lauder, eds., *Adaptation*, pp. 11–53. London: Academic Press.

Anderson, Perry. 1992. *English Questions*. London: Verso.

Anon. 1836. *Laws and List of Members of the Cambridge Philosophical Society*. Cambridge: Pitt.

Appel, Toby A. 1987. *The Cuvier–Geoffroy Debate: French Biology in the Decades Before Darwin*. Oxford: Oxford University Press.

Aquinas, T. 1970. *Summa Theologiae: 11, Man (1a. 75–83)*. London: Eyre and Spottiswoode.

Aristotle. 1985. *Nicomachean Ethics*. Trans. T. Irwin. Indianapolis: Hackett.

Armstrong, D. M. 1968. *A Materialist Theory of Mind*. London: Routledge & Kegan Paul.

Axelrod, Robert. 1984. *The Evolution of Cooperation*. New York: Basic Books.

Ayala, F. J. 1967. 'Man in Evolution : A Scientific Statement and some Theological and Ethical Implications.' *The Thomist* 31: 1–20.

1998. 'Human Nature: One Evolutionist's View.' In W. S. Brown, N. Murphy and H. N. Malony, eds., *Whatever Happened to the Soul? Scientific and Theological Portraits of Human Nature*, pp. 31–48. Minneapolis: Fortress Press.

Ayer, A. J. 1936. *Language, Truth and Logic*. London, Gollancz.

1954. 'Freedom and Necessity.' *Philosophical Essays*, pp. 271–84. London: Macmillan.

Babbage, C. 1837. *The Ninth Bridgewater Treatise*. London: Murray.

Bacon, F. [1620] 1960. *The New Organon and Related Writings*. Ed. F. H. Anderson. Indianapolis: Bobbs-Merrill.

Bagehot, Walter. [1872] 1974. *Physics and Politics: Or Thoughts on the Application of the Principles of 'Natural Selection' and 'Inheritance' to Political Society*. Reprinted in N. St John-Stevas, ed., *The Collected Works of Walter Bagehot*, vol. VII, pp. 65–78. London: The Economist, 1974.

Bannister, Robert C. 1979. *Social Darwinism: Science and Myth in Anglo-American Social Thought*. Philadelphia: Temple University Press.

Barbour, I. 1988. 'Ways of Relating Science and Theology.' In R. J. Russell, W. R. Stoeger and G. V. Coyne, eds., *Physics, Philosophy, and Theology: A Common Quest for Understanding*, pp. 21–48. Vatican City: Vatican Observatory.

Barkow, J., Cosmides, L. and Tooby, J., eds. 1992. *The Adapted Mind*. New York: Oxford University Press.

Baron-Cohen, S. 1995. *Mindblindness: An Essay on Autism and the Theory of Mind*. Cambridge, Mass.: MIT Press.

Barrett, P. H., ed. 1977. *The Collected Papers of Charles Darwin*. 2 vols. Chicago: University of Chicago Press.

Barrett, P. H. and Freeman, R. B., eds. 1986. *The Works of Charles Darwin*. 29 vols. London: Pickering.

Barrett, P. H., Gautrey, P. J., Herbert, S., Kohn, D. and Smith, S., eds. 1987. *Charles Darwin's Notebooks, 1836–1844: Geology, Transmutation of Species, Metaphysical Enquiries*. London: British Museum (Natural History) and Cambridge University Press.

Barrett, Paul H., Weinshank, Donald J. *et al.* 1981. *A Concordance to Darwin's Origin of Species*. London: Cornell University Press.

1986. *A Concordance to Darwin 's The Expression of the Emotions in Man and Animals*. Ithaca, N.Y.: Cornell University Press.

1987. *A Concordance to Darwin 's The Descent of Man, and Selection in Relation to Sex*. Ithaca, N.Y.: Cornell University Press.

Barrow, J. D. and Tipler, F. J. 1986. *The Anthropic Cosmological Principle.* Oxford: Clarendon.

Bartholomew, Michael. 1979. 'The Singularity of Lyell.' *History of Science* 27: 276–93.

Bartley, Mary M. 1992. 'Darwin and Domestication: Studies on Inheritance.' *Journal of the History of Biology* 25: 307–33.

Barton, Ruth. 2000. 'Haast and the Moa: Reversing the Tyranny of Distance.' *Pacific Science* 54: 251–63.

Beatty, John. 1985. 'Speaking of Species: Darwin's Strategy.' In Kohn 1985a, 265–81.

1987. 'On Behalf of the Semantic View.' *Biology and Philosophy* 2: 17–23.

Beddall, Barbara G. 1968. 'Wallace, Darwin, and the Theory of Natural Selection: A Study in the Development of Ideas and Attitudes.' *Journal of the History of Biology* 1: 261–323.

1988. 'Darwin and Divergence: The Wallace Connection.' *Journal of the History of Biology* 21: 1–68.

Beer, Gillian. 1983. *Darwin's Plots: Evolutionary Narrative in Darwin, George Eliot and Nineteenth-Century Fiction.* London: Routledge & Kegan Paul.

Behe, M. 1996. *Darwin's Black Box: The Biochemical Challenge to Evolution.* New York: Free Press.

Bell, Charles. [1844] 1873. *Expression: Its Anatomy and Philosophy*, 3rd edn. New York: Wells. This edition was first published in 1844 as *The Anatomy and Philosophy of Expression as Connected with the Fine Arts.* London: George Bell.

Bellamy, Edward. 1888. *Looking Backward.* New York: New American Library.

Bellomy, Donald C. 1984. '"Social Darwinism" Revisited.' *Perspectives in American History*, New Series, 1: 1–129.

Benton, Ted. 1982. 'Social Darwinism and Socialist Darwinism in Germany: 1860 to 1900.' *Rivista di Filosofia* 73: 79–121.

1995. 'Science, Ideology and Culture: Malthus and *The Origin of Species.*' In Amigoni and Wallace 1995, pp. 68–94.

Berry, Andrew, ed. 2002. *Infinite Tropics: An Alfred Russel Wallace Anthology.* London: Verso.

Bezirgan, Najm A. 1974. 'The Islamic World.' In Thomas F. Glick, ed., *The Comparative Reception of Darwinism*, pp. 375–87. Austin: University of Texas Press.

Bickerton, D. 1990. *Language and Species.* Chicago: University of Chicago Press.

1995. *Language and Human Behavior.* Seattle: University of Washington Press.

Blackburn, S. 1998. *Ruling Passions*. Oxford: Clarendon.

Borges, J. L. 1962. *Labyrinths: Selected Stories and Other Writings*. New York: New Directions.

Bowlby, John. 1990. *Charles Darwin: A New Life*. New York: Norton.

Bowler, Peter J. 1983. *The Eclipse of Darwinism: Anti-Darwinian Evolution Theories in the Decades around 1900*. Baltimore: Johns Hopkins University Press.

1989. *Evolution: The History of an Idea*. 2nd edn. Berkeley: University of California Press.

1990. *Charles Darwin: The Man and His Influence*. Oxford: Blackwell.

1996. *Life's Splendid Drama: Evolutionary Biology and the Reconstruction of Life's Ancestry, 1860–1940*. Chicago: University of Chicago Press.

Boyd, R. and Richerson, P. 1985. *Culture and the Evolutionary Process*. Chicago: University of Chicago Press.

Boyle, Robert. 1688. *A Disquisition about the Final Causes of Natural Things: Wherein it is Inquir'd, Whether, And (if at all) With What Cautions, a Naturalist Should Admit Them?* London: John Taylor.

Braddon-Mitchell, D. and Jackson, F. 1996. *The Philosophy of Mind and Cognition*. Cambridge, Mass.: Blackwell.

Brandon, R. 1990. *Adaptation and Environment*. Princeton: Princeton University Press.

Brandon, R. and Carson, S. 1996. 'The Indeterministic Character of Evolutionary Theory – No "No Hidden Variable Proof" but No Room for Determinism Either.' *Philosophy of Science* 63: 15–37.

Brent, Peter. 1981. *Charles Darwin: A Man of Enlarged Curiosity*. New York: Harper and Row.

Brooke, John H. 1974. *Natural Theology in Britain from Boyle to Paley*. Units 9–10 in *Science and Belief: From Copernicus to Darwin*. Milton Keynes: Open University Press.

1985. 'The Relations between Darwin's Science and his Religion.' In J. Durant, ed., *Darwinism and Divinity*, pp. 40–75. Oxford: Blackwell.

1990. '"A Sower Went Forth": Joseph Priestley and the Ministry of Reform.' In A. Truman Schwarz and J. McEvoy, eds., *Motion Toward Perfection*, pp. 21–56. Boston: Skinner.

1991. *Science and Religion: Some Historical Perspectives*. Cambridge: Cambridge University Press.

Brooke, John H. and Cantor, Geoffrey. 1998. *Reconstructing Nature: The Engagement of Science and Religion*. Edinburgh: T. & T. Clark.

Brooks, John Langdon. 1984. *Just Before the Origin: Alfred Russel Wallace's Theory of Evolution*. New York: Columbia University Press.

Brougham, Henry. 1839. *Dissertations on Subjects of Science concerned with Natural Theology: Being the Concluding Volumes of the New Edition of Paley's Work*. London: Knight.

Browne, Janet. 1989. 'Botany for Gentlemen: Erasmus Darwin and *The Loves of the Plants*.' *Isis* 80: 593–621.

1995. *Charles Darwin: Voyaging*. New York: Knopf.

2002. *Charles Darwin: The Power of Place*. New York: Knopf.

Bryan, William Jennings. [1924] 1967. 'Bryan's Last Speech.' Reprinted in L. H. Allen, ed., *Bryan and Darrow at Dayton; The Record and Documents of the 'Bible-Evolution Trial'*, pp. 529–55. New York: Russell and Russell.

Buchwald, J. Z. 1993. 'Waves, Philosophers and Historians.' *PSA 1992*, vol. 2, pp. 205–11. East Lansing, Mich.: Philosophy of Science Association.

Bukharin, Nicholai *et al.* [1931] 1971. *Science at the Cross Roads*. 2nd edn. London: Frank Cass.

Burch Brown, Frank. 1986. 'The Evolution of Darwin's Theism.' *Journal of the History of Biology* 19: 1–45.

Burchfield, Joe D. 1975. *Lord Kelvin and the Age of the Earth*. New York: Science History Publications.

Burkert, W. 1996. *Creation of the Sacred: Tracks of Biology in Early Religions*. Cambridge, Mass.: Harvard University Press.

Burkhardt, Frederick, ed. 1996. *Charles Darwin's Letters: A Selection 1825–1859*. Cambridge: Canto/Cambridge University Press.

1998 'The Darwin Papers.' In Peter Fox, ed., *Cambridge University Library: The Great Collections*, pp. 118–35. Cambridge: Cambridge University Press.

Burkhardt, Frederick and Smith, Sydney, eds. 1994. *A Calendar of the Correspondence of Charles Darwin, 1821–82: with Supplement*. 2nd edn. Cambridge: Cambridge University Press.

Burkhardt, Frederick *et al.*, eds. 1985–2001. *The Correspondence of Charles Darwin*, 12 vols. Cambridge: Cambridge University Press.

Burkhardt, Richard W. 1977. *The Spirit of System: Lamarck and Evolutionary Biology*. Cambridge, Mass.: Harvard University Press.

1979. 'Closing the Door on Lord Morton's Mare: The Rise and Fall of Telegony.' *Studies in the History of Biology* 3: 1–21.

Burleigh, Michael. 1994. *Death and Deliverance: 'Euthanasia' in Germany 1900–1945*. Cambridge: Cambridge University Press.

Burrow, John. 1966. *Evolution and Society: A Study in Victorian Social Theory*. Cambridge: Cambridge University Press.

Burt, A. 1989. 'Comparative Methods Using Phylogenetically Independent Contrasts.' *Oxford Surveys in Evolutionary Biology* 6: 33–54.

Bury, J. B. 1920. *The Idea of Progress; An Inquiry into its Origin and Growth*. London: Macmillan.

Buss, D. M. 1994. *The Evolution of Desire: Strategies of Human Mating*. New York: Basic Books.

Cabanne, Pierre. 1971. *Dialogues with Marcel Duchamp*. Trans. Ron Padgett. New York: Viking.

Cain, P. J. and Hopkins, A. G. 1993. *British Imperialism: Innovation and Expansion, 1688–1914*. London: Longman.

Callebaut, Werner, ed. 1993. *Taking the Naturalistic Turn, or How Real Philosophy of Science is Done*. Chicago: University of Chicago Press.

Camerini, Jane R., ed. 2001. *The Alfred Russel Wallace Reader: A Selection of Writings from the Field*. Baltimore: Johns Hopkins University Press.

Campbell, Donald. 1974. 'Evolutionary Epistemology.' In P. Schilpp, ed., *The Philosophy of Karl Popper*, pp. 413–63. La Salle: Open Court.

Campbell, John. 1974. 'Nature, Religion and Emotional Response: A Reconsideration of Darwin's Affective Decline.' *Victorian Studies* 18: 159–74.

Cannon, S. F. 1978. *Science in Culture: The Early Victorian Period*. New York: Science History Publications.

Cannon, W. 1961. 'The Bases of Darwin's Achievement: A Revaluation.' *Victorian Studies* 5: 109–34.

Cantor, Geoffrey. 2001. 'Quaker Responses to Darwin.' *Osiris* 16: 321–42.

Carus, Carl Gustav. 1837. 'The Kingdoms of Nature, their Life and Affinity.' *Scientific Memoirs* 1: 223–54.

Chalmers, D. J. 1996. *The Conscious Mind: In Search of a Fundamental Theory*. Oxford: Oxford University Press.

[Chambers, Robert.] [1844] 1994. *Vestiges of the Natural History of Creation*. London: Churchill. Reprinted in facsimile with an introduction by James A. Secord, Chicago: University of Chicago Press.

Chandrasekhar S. 1990. *Truth and Beauty: Aesthetics and Motivations in Science*. Chicago: University of Chicago Press.

Churchland, Patricia. 1986. *Neurophilosophy: Towards a Unified Science of Mind-Brain*. Cambridge, Mass.: MIT Press.

Churchland, Paul M. 1981. 'Eliminative Materialism and the Propositional Attitudes.' *Journal of Philosophy* 78: 67–90.

1996. *The Engine of Reason, The Seat of the Soul: A Philosophical Journey into the Brain*. Cambridge, Mass.: MIT Press.

Clark, A. 1997. *Being There: Putting Brain, Body, and World Together Again*. Cambridge, Mass.: MIT Press.

Clark, J. C. D. 2000. *English Society, 1660–1832: Religion, Ideology and Politics During the Ancient Regime*. 2nd edn. Cambridge: Cambridge University Press.

Cohen, G. A. 1978. *Karl Marx's Theory of History: A Defence*. Oxford: Clarendon.

Coleman, William. 2001. 'The Strange "Laissez-Faire" of Alfred Russel Wallace: The Connection Between Natural Selection and Political

Economy Reconsidered.' In J. Laurent and J. Nightingale, eds., *Darwinism and Evolutionary Economics*, pp. 36–48. Cheltenham: Edward Elgar.

Conway Morris, Simon. 1998. *The Crucible of Creation: The Burgess Shale and the Rise of Animals*. Oxford: Oxford University Press.

Cope, D. and Hofstadter, D. 2001. *Virtual Music: Computer Synthesis of Musical Style*. Cambridge, Mass.: MIT Press.

Corballis, M. 1991. *The Lopsided Ape: Evolution of the Generative Mind*. Oxford: Oxford University Press.

Corsi, Pietro. 1988. *Science and Religion: Baden Powell and the Anglican Debate, 1800–1860*. Cambridge: Cambridge University Press.

1998. 'Darwin: Roundtable.' *Journal of Victorian Culture* 3: 129–37.

Cosmides, L. and Tooby, J. 1989. 'Evolutionary Theory and the Generation of Culture, part II. Case Study: A Computational Theory of Social Exchange.' *Ethology and Sociobiology* 10: 51–97.

1992. 'Cognitive Adaptations for Social Exchange.' In Barkow, Cosmides and Tooby 1992, 163–227.

1994. 'Beyond Intuition and Instinct Blindness: Towards an Evolutionarily Rigorous Cognitive Science.' *Cognition* 50: 41–77.

1995. 'Origins of Domain Specificity: The Evolution of Functional Organization.' In L. A. Hirschfeld and S. A. Gelman, eds., *Mapping the Mind: Domain Specificity in Cognition and Culture*. Cambridge: Cambridge University Press.

Covington, Syms. 1995. *The Journal of Syms Covington, Assistant to Charles Darwin Esq. on the Second Voyage of the HMS Beagle*. Ed. Vern Weitzel. Australian Science Archives Project, University of Melbourne. On the web.

Creath, Richard and Maienschein, Jane, eds. 2000. *Biology and Epistemology*. Cambridge: Cambridge University Press.

Crick, F. 1968. 'The Origin of the Genetic Code.' *Journal of Molecular Biology* 38: 367–79.

Cronin, Helena. 1991. *The Ant and the Peacock: Altruism and Sexual Selection from Darwin to Today*. Cambridge: Cambridge University Press.

Crook, Paul. 1994. *Darwinism, War and History: The Debate Over the Biology of War from the 'Origin of Species' to the First World War*. Cambridge: Cambridge University Press.

1998. 'Social Darwinismism and British "New Imperialism": Second Thoughts.' *European Legacy* 3: 1–16.

Currie, G. and Sterelny, K. 2000. 'How to Think about the Modularity of Mind Reading.' *The Philosophical Quarterly* 50: 145–60.

Curtis, R. C. 1987. 'Darwin as an Epistemologist.' *Annals of Science* 44: 379–408.

Darwin, Charles. [1839] 1986. *Journal of Researches into the Geology and Natural History of the Various Countries Visited by H.M.S. Beagle.* London: Colburn. Reprinted in Barrett and Freeman 1986, II.

[1859] 1964. *On the Origin of Species by Means of Natural Selection, or the Preservation of Favoured Races in the Struggle for Life.* London: John Murray. Reprinted in facsimile with an introduction by Ernst Mayr, Cambridge, Mass.: Harvard University Press.

[1860] 1962. *The Voyage of the Beagle.* Ed. Leonard Engel. Garden City, N.Y.: Doubleday. Reprints *Journal of Researches*, 2nd edn of 1845.

1862. *On the Various Contrivances by which British and Foreign Orchids are Fertilised by Insects, and on the Good Effects of Intercrossing.* London: John Murray.

1868. *The Variation of Animals and Plants Under Domestication.* 2 vols. London, John Murray.

[1871] 1981. *The Descent of Man, and Selection in Relation to Sex.* 2 vols. London: John Murray. Reprinted in facsimile with an introduction by J. T. Bonner and R. M. May, Princeton: Princeton University Press.

[1872] 1998. *The Expression of the Emotions in Man and Animals.* London: John Murray. Reprinted with additional photographs, notes from Francis Darwin's 1890 edition and an introduction, afterword and commentaries by Paul Ekman, London: HarperCollins.

[1875] 1998. *The Variation of Animals and Plants under Domestication.* 2 vols. London: John Murray. American issue of 1883 reprinted in facsimile with an introduction by Harriet Ritvo, 2 vols., Baltimore: Johns Hopkins University Press.

1877. *The Different Forms of Flowers on Plants of the Same Species.* London: John Murray.

1909. *The Foundations of the Origin of Species: Two Essays Written in 1842 and 1844 by Charles Darwin.* Ed. Francis Darwin. Cambridge: Cambridge University Press.

1958. *The Autobiography of Charles Darwin, 1809–1882.* Ed. Nora Barlow. London: Collins.

1959. *The Origin of Species by Charles Darwin: A Variorum Text.* Ed. Morse Peckham. Philadelphia: University of Pennsylvania Press.

1975. *Charles Darwin's Natural Selection: Being the Second Part of His Big Species Book written from 1856 to 1858.* Ed. R. C. Stauffer. Cambridge: Cambridge University Press.

Darwin, Charles and Wallace, Alfred Russel. 1859. 'On the Tendency of Species to Form Varieties, and on the Perpetuation of Varieties and Species by Natural Means of Selection.' Read 1 July 1858. *Journal of the Proceedings of the Linnean Society of London, Zoology* 3: 45–62.

1958. *Evolution by Natural Selection*. Ed. Gavin de Beer. Cambridge: Cambridge University Press. Includes Darwin and Wallace 1859 and a revised edition of C. Darwin 1909.

Darwin, Francis, ed. [1888] 1969. *The Life and Letters of Charles Darwin*. 3 vols. London: John Murray. American issue in 2 vols. Reprinted in facsimile, New York: Johnson Reprint.

Darwin, Francis and Seward, A. C., eds. 1903. *More Letters of Charles Darwin*. 2 vols. London: John Murray.

Daunton, M. J. 1995. *Progress and Poverty: An Economic and Social History of Britain 1700–1850*. Oxford: Oxford University Press.

Dawkins, Richard. 1976. *The Selfish Gene*. Oxford: Oxford University Press.

1982. *The Extended Phenotype: The Gene as the Unit of Selection*. Oxford: Freeman.

1983. 'Universal Darwinism.' In D. S. Bendall, ed., *Evolution from Molecules to Men*, pp. 403–25. Cambridge: Cambridge University Press. Reprinted in Hull and Ruse 1998, pp. 15–37.

1986. *The Blind Watchmaker*. Harmondsworth: Penguin.

1995. *A River Out of Eden*. New York: Basic Books.

1997a. 'Human Chauvinism [Review of Gould 1996].' *Evolution* 51: 1015–20.

1997b. 'Obscurantism to the Rescue.' *Quarterly Review of Biology* 72: 397–9.

Dawkins, R. and Krebs, J. R. 1979. 'Arms Races Between and Within Species.' *Proceedings of the Royal Society of London, B* 205: 489–511.

de Rooy, Piet. 1990. 'Of Monkeys, Blacks, and Proles: Ernst Haeckel's Theory of Recapitulation.' In Jan Breman, ed., *Imperial Monkey Business: Racial Supremacy in Social Darwinist Theory and Colonial Practice*, pp. 7–34. Amsterdam: VU Amsterdam Press.

Deacon, T. W. 1997. *The Symbolic Species: The Co-evolution of Language and the Brain*. New York: W. W. Norton.

Degler, Carl N. 1991. *In Search of Human Nature: The Decline and Revival of Darwinism in American Social Thought*. New York: Oxford University Press.

Dembski, W. 1998a. *The Design Inference: Eliminating Chance through Small Probabilities*. Cambridge: Cambridge University Press.

(Ed.) 1998b. *Mere Creation: Science, Faith and Intelligent Design*. Downers Grove, Ill.: Intervarsity Press.

Dennett, D. C. 1984. *Elbow Room*. Cambridge, Mass.: MIT Press.

1987. *The Intentional Stance*. Cambridge, Mass.: MIT Press.

1991. *Consciousness Explained*. Boston: Little Brown.

1993. Review of Searle 1994. *Journal of Philosophy* 60: 193–205.

1995. *Darwin's Dangerous Idea: Evolution and the Meanings of Life*. New York: Simon and Schuster.

1996. 'Granny versus Mother Nature – No Contest.' *Mind and Language* 11: 263–9.

1998. 'Do-It-Yourself Understanding.' In *Brainchildren*, pp. 59–80. Cambridge, Mass.: MIT Press.

Forthcoming. 'From Typo to Thinko: When Evolution Graduated to Semantic Norms.' In Pierre Jaisson and Stephen Levinson, eds., *Evolution and Culture*. Cambridge, Mass.: MIT Press.

Denton, Michael. 1985. *Evolution: A Theory in Crisis*. London: Burnett Books.

Dépéret, C. 1907. *Les transformations du monde animal*. Paris: Flammarion.

Depew, David J. and Weber, Bruce H. 1995. *Darwinism Evolving: Systems Dynamics and the Genealogy of Natural Selection*. Cambridge, Mass.: MIT Press.

Desmond, Adrian. 1982. *Archetypes and Ancestors*. London: Blond and Briggs.

1989. *The Politics of Evolution: Morphology, Medicine, and Reform in Radical London*. Chicago: University of Chicago Press.

2001. 'Redefining the X Axis: "Professionals," "Amateurs" and the Making of Mid-Victorian Biology – A Progress Report.' *Journal of the History of Biology* 34 : 3–50.

Desmond, Adrian and Moore, James. 1991. *Darwin*. London: Michael Joseph.

1998. 'Roundtable: Darwin.' *Journal of Victorian Culture* 3: 147–68.

Dettelbach, Michael. 1996. 'Global Physics and Aesthetic Empire: Humboldt's Physical Portrait of the Tropics.' In D. P. Miller and P. H. Reill, eds., *Visions of Empire: Voyages, Botany, and Representations of Nature*, pp. 258–92. Cambridge: Cambridge University Press.

De Waal, Frans. 1984. *Chimpanzee Politics*. Baltimore: Johns Hopkins University Press.

1989. *Peacemaking Among Primates*. Cambridge, Mass.: Harvard University Press.

Dickens, Peter. 2000. *Social Darwinism: Linking Evolutionary Thought to Social Theory*. Buckingham: Open University Press.

Dickinson, A. and Balleine, B. W. 2000. 'Causal Cognition and Goal Directed Action.' In C. Heyes and L. Huber, eds., *The Evolution of Cognition*, pp. 185–204. Cambridge, Mass.: MIT Press.

Di Gregorio, Mario. 1990. *Charles Darwin's Marginalia*. Vol. 1. New York: Garland.

Dixon, Thomas. 1999. 'Theology, Anti-Theology and Atheology.' *Modern Theology* 15: 287–330.

Dobzhansky, Theodosius. 1937. *Genetics and the Origin of Species*. New York: Columbia University Press.

Doolittle, F. 1997. 'A Delicate Balance.' *Boston Review* 22: 28–9.

Doskow, Minna. 1997. 'Charlotte Perkins Gilman: The Female Face of Social Darwinism.' *Weber Studies* 14: 9–22.

Dretske, F. 1981. *Knowledge and the Flow of Information*. Oxford: Blackwell.

Dupré, John. 1981 'Natural Kinds and Biological Taxa.' *Philosophical Review* 90: 66–90.

Durant, John R. 1985. 'The Ascent of Nature in Darwin's *Descent of Man*.' In Kohn 1985a, pp. 283–306.

Eigen, Manfred. 1992. *Steps Towards Life*. Oxford: Oxford University Press.

Ekman, P. 1972. *Emotions in the Human Face*. New York: Pergamon.

1992. 'Are There Basic Emotions?' *Psychological Review* 99: 550–3.

1998. 'Introduction,' 'Afterword' and commentaries to Darwin [1872] 1998.

Elder, Gregory P. 1996. *Chronic Vigour: Darwin, Anglicans, Catholics, and the Development of a Doctrine of Providential Evolution*. Lanham: University Press of America.

Eldredge, Niles. 1989. *Macro-Evolutionary Dynamics: Species, Niches and Adaptive Peaks*. New York: McGraw-Hill.

Eldredge, Niles and Cracraft, J., eds. 1980. *Phylogenetic Pattern and the Evolutionary Process*. New York: Columbia University Press.

Eldredge, Niles and Gould, Stephen Jay. 1972. 'Punctuated Equilibria: An Alternative to Phyletic Gradualism.' In T. J. M. Schopf, ed., *Models in Paleobiology*, pp. 82–115. San Francisco: Freeman.

Ellegård, Alvar. [1958] 1990. *Darwin and the General Reader: The Reception of Darwin's Theory of Evolution in the British Periodical Press, 1859–1972*. Göteborg: Göteborgs Universitets Årsskrift, vol. 64. Reprinted. Chicago: University of Chicago Press.

Enç, B. 1986. 'Essentialism without Individual Essences.' *Midwest Studies in Philosophy* 11: 403–26.

Endler, J. 1986. *Natural Selection in the Wild*. Princeton: Princeton University Press.

Engels, Friedrich. [1845] 1987. *The Condition of the Working Class in England*. Harmondsworth: Penguin.

Ereshefsky, M. 1991. 'Species, Higher Taxa, and the Units of Evolution.' *Philosophy of Science* 58: 84–101.

(Ed.) 1992. *The Units of Evolution: Essays on the Nature of Species*. Cambridge, Mass.: MIT Press.

Erskine, Fiona. 1987. 'Darwin in Context: The London Years'. Unpublished PhD dissertation. Open University.

1995. '*The Origin of Species* and the Science of Female Inferiority.' In Amigoni and Wallace 1995, pp. 95–121.

Evans, L. T. 1984. 'Darwin's Use of the Analogy between Artificial and Natural Selection.' *Journal of the History of Biology* 17: 113–40.

Evans, Richard J. 1997. 'In Search of German Social Darwinism: The History and Historiography of a Concept.' In Manfred Berg and Geoffrey Cocks, eds., *Medicine and Modernity: Public Health and Medical Care in 19th- and 20th-Century Germany*, pp. 55–79. Cambridge: Cambridge University Press.

Farley, John. 1982. *Gametes and Spores: Ideas about Sexual Reproduction, 1750–1914*. Baltimore: Johns Hopkins University Press.

Felsenstein, J. 1978. 'Cases in which Parsimony and Compatibility Methods can be Positively Misleading.' *Systematic Zoology* 27: 401–10.

Fisch, Menachem and Schaffer, Simon, eds. 1991. *William Whewell: A Composite Portrait*. Oxford: Clarendon.

Fisher, Ronald A. 1930. *The Genetical Theory of Natural Selection*. Oxford: Clarendon.

1947. 'The Renaissance of Darwinism.' *Listener* 37: 1001. Reprinted in J. H. Bennett, ed., *Collected Papers of R. A. Fisher*, 5 vols., vol. IV, pp. 616–20. Adelaide: University of Adelaide Press, 1971–4.

Flanagan, O. 1996. 'Ethics Naturalized: Ethics as Human Ecology.' In L. May, M. Friedman and A. Clark, eds., *Mind and Morals: Essays on Ethics and Cognitive Science*, pp. 19–44. Cambridge, Mass.: MIT Press.

2000a. *Dreaming Souls: Sleep, Dreams, and the Evolution of the Conscious Mind*. New York: Oxford.

2000b. 'Destructive Emotions.' *Consciousness and Emotion* 1: 67–88.

2002. *The Problem of the Soul: Two Visions of Mind and How to Reconcile Them*. New York: Basic Books.

Flanagan, O., Hardcastle, V. G. and Nahmias, E. 2001. 'Is Human Intelligence an Adaptation? Cautionary Observations from Philosophy of Biology.' In R. Sternberg, ed., *The Evolution of Intelligence*, pp. 199–222. New York: Oxford University Press.

Fleming, John, 1822. *The Philosophy of Zoology*. 2 vols. Edinburgh: Constable.

Fodor, J. A. 1975. *The Language of Thought*. New York: Thomas Y. Crowell.

1983. *The Modularity of Mind*. Cambridge, Mass.: MIT Press.

1987. *Psychosemantics: The Problem of Meaning in the Philosophy of Mind*. Cambridge, Mass.: MIT Press.

1990. *A Theory of Content and Other Essays*. Cambridge, Mass.: MIT Press.

2000. *The Mind Doesn't Work That Way*. Cambridge, Mass.: MIT Press.

Frank, P. 1988. *Passion Within Reason: The Strategic Role of the Emotions*. New York: W. W. Norton.

Frede, M. 1992. 'On Aristotle's Conception of the Soul.' In M. C. Nussbaum and A. O. Rorty, eds., *Essays on Aristotle's* De Anima, pp. 93–107. Oxford: Clarendon.

Freeland, S., Knight R., Landweber, L. and Hurst L. 2000. 'Early Fixation of an Optimal Genetic Code.' *Molecular Biology and Evolution* 17: 511–18.

Freeman, R. B. 1977. *The Works of Charles Darwin: An Annotated Bibliographical Handlist*. 2nd edn. Folkestone, Kent: Dawson.

1978. *Charles Darwin: A Companion*. Folkestone, Kent: Dawson.

Fyfe, Aileen. 1997. 'The Reception of William Paley's *Natural Theology* in the University of Cambridge.' *British Journal for the History of Science* 30: 321–35.

2000. 'Industrialised Conversion: The Religious Tract Society and Popular Science Publishing in Victorian Britain'. Unpublished PhD dissertation. University of Cambridge.

Galton, Francis. 1865. 'Hereditary Talent and Character.' *Macmillan's Magazine* 12: 157–66, 318–27.

Gasman, Daniel. 1971. *The Scientific Origins of National Socialism: Social Darwinism in Ernst Haeckel and the German Monist League*. London: Macdonald.

Gaudry, A. 1866. *Considérations générales sur les animaux fossiles de Pikermi*. Paris: Savy.

Gayon, Jean. 1997. 'The Paramount Power of Selection: From Darwin to Kauffman.' In M. L. Dalla Chiara, K. Doets, D. Mundici and J. van Benthem, eds., *Structures and Norms in Science*, pp. 265–82. Dordrecht: Kluwer.

1998. *Darwinism's Struggle for Survival: Heredity and the Hypothesis of Natural Selection*. Rev. of 1992 French original. Trans. Matthew Cobb. Cambridge: Cambridge University Press.

Geison, Gerald L. 1969. 'Darwin and Heredity: The Evolution of His Hypothesis of Pangenesis.' *Journal of the History of Medicine and Allied Sciences* 24: 375–411.

Ghiselin, Michael T. 1969. *The Triumph of the Darwinian Method*. Berkeley: University of California Press.

1973. 'Darwin and Evolutionary Psychology.' *Science* 179: 964–8.

1974. 'A Radical Solution to the Species Problem.' *Systematic Zoology* 23: 536–44.

Gibbard, A. 1990. *Wise Choices, Apt Feelings: A Theory of Normative Judgment*. Cambridge, Mass.: Harvard University Press.

Gillespie, Neal C. 1979. *Charles Darwin and the Problem of Creation*. Chicago: University of Chicago Press.

1987. 'Natural History, Natural Theology, and Social Order: John Ray and the "Newtonian Ideology".' *Journal of the History of Biology* 20: 1–49.

1990. 'Divine Design and the Industrial Revolution: William Paley's Abortive Reform of Natural Theology.' *Isis* 81: 214–29.

Gillispie, C. C. [1951] 1996. *Genesis and Geology: A Study in the Relations of Scientific Thought, Natural Theology, and Social Opinion in Great Britain, 1790–1850*. Cambridge, Mass.: Harvard University Press.

Glick, Thomas F. and Kohn, David, eds. 1996. *Darwin on Evolution: The Development of the Theory of Natural Selection*. Indianapolis: Hackett.

Godfrey-Smith, P. 1991. 'Signal, Decision, Action.' *Journal of Philosophy* 88: 709–22.

1992. 'Indication and Adaptation.' *Synthese* 92: 283–312.

1994a. 'A Continuum of Semantic Optimism.' In S. P. Stich and T. A. Warfield, eds., *Mental Representation*, pp. 259–77. Oxford: Blackwell.

1994b. 'A Modern History Theory of Functions.' *Noûs* 28: 344–62.

1996. *Complexity and the Function of Mind in Nature*. Cambridge: Cambridge University Press.

Goldie, Peter and Ghiselin, Michael, eds. 1997. *Darwin Multimedia CD-ROM: The Collective Works of Charles Darwin on CD-ROM*. 2nd edn. San Francisco: Lightbinders.

Golinski, Jan. 1998. *Making Natural Knowledge: Constructivism and the History of Science*. Cambridge: Cambridge University Press.

Gordon, Scott. 1989. 'Darwin and Political Economy: The Connection Reconsidered.' *Journal of the History of Biology* 22: 437–59.

Gould, Stephen Jay. 1980. 'The Panda's Thumb.' In *The Panda's Thumb: More Reflections in Natural History*, pp. 19–26. London: Norton.

1989. *Wonderful Life: The Burgess Shale and the Nature of History*. London: Hutchinson Radius.

1996. *Life's Grandeur: The Spread of Excellence from Plato to Darwin*. London: Jonathan Cape. Published in the USA as *Full House: The Spread of Excellence from Plato to Darwin*. New York: Harmony Books.

1998. 'On Transmuting Boyle's Law to Darwin's Revolution.' In A. C. Fabian, ed., *Evolution: Society, Science and the Universe*, pp. 4–27. Cambridge: Cambridge University Press.

1999. *Rocks of Ages: Science and Religion in the Fullness of Life*. New York: Ballantine.

2000. 'A Sly Dullard Named Darwin: Recognizing the Multiple Facets of Genius.' In *The Lying Stones of Marrakech: Penultimate Reflections in Natural History*, pp. 169–81. London: Jonathan Cape.

2002. *The Structure of Evolutionary Theory*. Cambridge, Mass.: Harvard University Press.

Gould, Stephen Jay and Lewontin, Richard C. 1979. 'The Spandrels of San Marco and the Panglossian Paradigm: A Critique of the Adaptationist

Programme.' *Proceedings of the Royal Society of London, B* 205: 581–98. Reprinted in Sober 1994a, pp. 73–90.

Greene, John. 1981. 'Darwin as a Social Evolutionist.' In *Science, Ideology, and World View: Essays in the History of Evolutionary Ideas*, pp. 95–127. Berkeley: University of California Press.

Greg, William R. 1868. 'On the Failure of "Natural Selection" in the Case of Man.' *Fraser's Magazine* 68: 353–62.

Gregory, Frederick. 1986. 'The Impact of Darwinian Evolution on Protestant Theology in the Nineteenth Century.' In D. Lindberg and R. Numbers, eds., *God and Nature: Historical Essays on the Encounter between Christianity and Science*, pp. 369–90. Berkeley: University of California Press.

Griffiths, Paul E. 1996. 'The Historical Turn in the Study of Adaptation.' *British Journal for the Philosophy of Science* 47: 511–32.

1997. *What Emotions Really Are: The Problems of Psychological Categories.* Chicago: University of Chicago Press.

Gruber, Howard E. 1981. *Darwin on Man: A Psychological Study of Scientific Creativity.* 2nd edn. Chicago: University of Chicago Press.

Gruner, Rolf. 1975. 'Science, Nature and Christianity.' *Journal of Theological Studies* 26: 55–81.

Hacking, Ian. 1990. *The Taming of Chance.* Cambridge: Cambridge University Press.

1991. 'A Tradition of Natural Kinds.' *Philosophical Studies* 61: 109–26.

1992. '"Style" for Historians and Philosophers.' *Studies in History and Philosophy of Science* 23: 1–20. Reprinted in *Historical Ontology*, pp. 178–99. Cambridge, Mass.: Harvard University Press, 2002.

1999. *The Social Construction of What?* Cambridge, Mass.: Harvard University Press.

2000. 'How Inevitable are the Results of Successful Science?' *Philosophy of Science* 67 (Supp.): S58–71.

Haeckel, Ernst. 1866. *Generelle Morphologie der Organismen.* 2 vols. Berlin: G. Reimer.

1868. *Natürliche Schöpfungsgeschichte.* Berlin: Reimer. Published in English as *The History of Creation*, trans. E. Ray Lankester, 2 vols. London: Henry King, 1876.

1879. *Freedom in Science and Teaching.* New York: Appleton.

Hagen, Joel B. 1999. 'Retelling Experiments: H. B. D. Kettlewell's Studies of Industrial Melanism in Peppered Moths.' *Biology and Philosophy* 14: 39–54.

Haldane, J. B. S. 1927. *Possible Worlds, and Other Papers.* London: Chatto and Windus.

Hall, A. Rupert. 1969. *The Cambridge Philosophical Society: A History, 1819–1969*. Cambridge: Cambridge Philosophical Society.

Hamilton, W. D. 1995. *Narrow Roads of Gene Land*. San Francisco: Freeman.

Harvey, P. and Pagel, M. 1991. *The Comparative Method in Evolutionary Biology*. Oxford: Oxford University Press.

Haught, J. F. 1995. *Science and Religion: From Conflict to Conversation*. New York: Paulist Press.

Hawking, Stephen. 1988. *A Brief History of Time*. New York: Bantam.

Hawkins, Mike. 1997. *Social Darwinism in European and American Thought, 1860–1945: Nature as Model and Nature as Threat*. Cambridge: Cambridge University Press.

Hayek, F. 1982. *Law, Legislation and Liberty: A New Statement of the Liberal Principles of Justice and Political Economy*. London: Routledge & Kegan Paul.

Henslow, John S. 1828. *Syllabus of a Course of Botanical Lectures*. Cambridge: Hodson.

1833. *Sketch of a Course of Lectures on Botany for 1833*. Cambridge: Privately printed.

Herbert, Sandra. 1985. 'Darwin the Young Geologist.' In Kohn 1985a, pp. 483–510.

1995. 'From Charles Darwin's Portfolio: An Early Essay on South American Geology and Species.' *Earth Sciences History* 14: 23–36.

Herrnstein, Richard and Murray, Charles. 1994. *The Bell Curve: Intelligence and Class Structure in American Life*. New York: Free Press.

Herschel, J. F. W. [1830] 1987. *A Preliminary Discourse on the Study of Natural Philosophy*. Longman: London, 1830. Reprinted. Chicago: University of Chicago Press.

1841. 'Review of *History of the Inductive Sciences from the Earliest to the Present Times* by William Whewell (1837) and *The Philosophy of the Inductive Sciences, Founded upon their History* by William Whewell (1840).' *Quarterly Review* 68: 177–238.

1861. *Physical Geography of the Globe*. Edinburgh: Adam and Charles Black.

Hick, J. 1978. *Evil and the God of Love*. New York: Harper and Row.

Hodge, M. J. [Jonathan] S. 1977. 'The Structure and Strategy of Darwin's "Long Argument".' *British Journal for the History of Science* 10: 237–46.

1982. 'Darwin and the Laws of the Animate Part of the Terrestrial System (1835–1837): On the Lyellian Origins of His Zoonomical Explanatory Program.' *Studies in the History of Biology* 7: 1–106.

1983. 'The Development of Darwin's General Biological Theorizing.' In D. S. Bendall, ed., *Evolution from Molecules to Men*, pp. 43–62. Cambridge: Cambridge University Press.

1985. 'Darwin as a Lifelong Generation Theorist.' In Kohn 1985a, pp. 207–43.

1986 'Darwin, Species and the Theory of Natural Selection.' In S. Atran *et al.*, *Histoire du concept d'espèce dans les sciences de la vie*, pp. 227–52. Paris: Fondation Singer-Polignac.

1989. 'Darwin's Theory and Darwin's Argument.' In Michael Ruse, ed., *What the Philosophy of Biology Is: Essays Dedicated to David Hull*, pp. 163–82. Dordrecht: Kluwer.

1990. 'Darwin Studies at Work: A Re-examination of Three Decisive Years (1835–37).' In T. H. Levere and W. R. Shea, eds., *Nature, Experiment and the Sciences: Essays on Galileo and the History of Science in Honor of Stillman Drake*, pp. 249–73. Dordrecht: Kluwer.

1991a. 'The History of the Earth, Life and Man: Whewell and Palaetiological Science.' In Fisch and Schaffer 1991, pp. 255–89.

1991b. *Origins and Species: A Study of the Historical Sources of Darwinism and the Contexts of Some Other Accounts of Organic Diversity from Plato and Aristotle On*. New York: Garland.

1992a. 'Biology and Philosophy (Including Ideology): A Study of Fisher and Wright.' In Sarkar 1992, pp. 231–93.

1992b. 'Discussion: Darwin's Argument in the *Origin*.' *Philosophy of Science* 59: 461–4.

1994. 'Natural History, Physiology, Biology and the Peculiarities of English Capitalism.' Unpublished paper. Read at the conference *Science and British Culture in the 1830s*, Trinity College, University of Cambridge, 6–8 July.

2000. 'Knowing about Evolution: Darwin and His Theory of Natural Selection.' In Creath and Maienschein 2000, pp. 27–47.

Hodge, M. J. S. and Kohn, D. 1985. 'The Immediate Origins of Natural Selection.' In Kohn 1985a, pp. 185–206.

Hofstadter, Douglas and Dennett, Daniel C., eds. 1981. *The Mind's I: Fantasies and Reflections on Self and Soul*. New York: Basic Books.

Hofstadter, Richard. 1944. *Social Darwinism in American Thought*. Philadelphia: University of Pennsylvania Press.

Holden, C. 2000. 'Oklahoma Lawmakers Take a Shot at Darwin.' *Science* 288: 431.

Hooper, Judith. 2002. *Of Moths and Men: Intrigue, Tragedy and the Peppered Moth*. London: Fourth Estate.

Hrdy, S. B. 1999. *Mother Nature: A History of Mothers, Infants, and Natural Selection*. New York: Pantheon Books.

Hudson, Pat. 1992. *The Industrial Revolution*. London: Arnold.

Hull, David L. 1964. 'Consistency and Monophyly.' *Systematic Zoology* 13: 1–11.

1965. 'The Effect of Essentialism on Taxonomy – 2000 Years of Stasis.' *British Journal for the Philosophy of Science* 15: 314–26 and 16: 1–18.

1973. *Darwin and his Critics: The Reception of Darwin's Theory of Evolution by the Scientific Community*. Cambridge, Mass.: Harvard University Press.

1978. 'A Matter of Individuality.' *Philosophy of Science* 45: 335–60.

1979. 'The Limits of Cladism.' *Systematic Zoology* 28: 416–40.

1986. 'On Human Nature.' *PSA 1986*, vol. 2, pp. 3–13. East Lansing, Mich.: Philosophy of Science Association. Reprinted in Hull and Ruse 1998, pp. 383–97.

1987. *Science as a Process: An Evolutionary Account of the Social and Conceptual Development of Science*. Chicago: University of Chicago Press.

1995. 'Die Rezeption von Darwins Evolutionstheorie bei britischen Wissenschaftsphilosophen des 19. Jarhunderts.' In E-M. Engels, ed., *Die Rezeption von Evolutionstheorien im 19. Jahrhundert*, pp. 67–105. Frankfurt: Suhrkamp.

2000. 'Why Did Darwin Fail? The Role of John Stuart Mill.' In Creath and Maienschein 2000, pp. 48–88.

2001. *Science and Selection: Essays in Biological Evolution and the Philosophy of Science*. Cambridge: Cambridge University Press.

Hull, David L. and Ruse, Michael, eds. 1998. *The Philosophy of Biology*. Oxford: Oxford University Press.

Humboldt, Alexander von. [1814–29] 1966. *Personal Narrative of Travels to the Equinoctial Regions of the New Continent During the Years 1799–1804*. Trans. Helen Williams. 7 vols. London: Longman, Hurst, Rees, Orme, and Brown. Reprinted in facsimile in 6 vols., New York: Ams Press.

1845–62. *Kosmos. Entwurf einer physichen Weltbeschreibung*. 5 vols. Stuttgart: J. G. Gotta'scher Verlag.

Hume, David [1739] 1888. *Treatise of Human Nature*. Ed. L. A. Selby-Bigge. Oxford: Clarendon.

Hurka, Thomas. 1993. *Perfectionism*. New York: Oxford University Press.

Huxley, Julian. 1942. *Evolution: The Modern Synthesis*. London: Allen and Unwin.

Huxley, Thomas H. 1896. *Darwiniana*. New York: Appleton.

Jaki, Stanley L. 1978. *The Road of Science and the Ways to God*. Chicago: University of Chicago Press.

Jann, Rosemary. 1994. 'Darwin and the Anthropologists: Sexual Selection and its Discontents.' *Victorian Studies* 37: 287–306.

Jardine, Nicholas, Secord, James A. and Spary, Emma C., eds. 1996. *Cultures of Natural History*. Cambridge: Cambridge University Press.

Jenkin, F. [1867] 1973. 'The Origin of Species.' *The North British Review* 44: 277–318. Reprinted in Hull 1973, pp. 302–50.

Jevons, W. S. 1869. *The Substitution of Similars*. London: Macmillan.

1874 *The Principles of Science, a Treatise on Logic and Scientific Method*. London: John Murray.

John Paul II. 1997. 'The Pope's Message on Evolution.' *Quarterly Review of Biology* 72: 377–83.

Jones, Greta. 1980. *Social Darwinism in English Thought: The Interaction Between Biological and Social Theory*. Sussex: Harvester Press.

1998. 'Theoretical Foundations of Eugenics.' In Robert A. Peel, ed., *Essays in the History of Eugenics*, pp. 1–19. London: The Galton Institute.

Jordanova, Ludmilla J. 1984. *Lamarck*. Oxford: Oxford University Press.

Kauffman, Stuart A. 1993. *The Origins of Order: Self-Organization and Selection*. Oxford: Oxford University Press.

Kavaloski, Vincent Carl. 1974. 'The Vera Causa Principle: An Historico-Philosophical Study of a Metatheoretical Concept from Newton through Darwin'. Unpublished PhD dissertation. University of Chicago.

Kaye, Howard L. 1997. *The Social Meaning of Modern Biology: From Social Darwinism to Sociobiology*. New Brunswick, N.J.: Transaction Publishers.

Keller, Evelyn Fox and Lloyd, Elisabeth A., eds. 1992. *Keywords in Evolutionary Biology*. Cambridge, Mass.: Harvard University Press.

Kellogg, Vernon. 1917. *Headquarters Nights*. Boston: Atlantic Monthly Press.

Kelly, Alfred. 1981. *The Descent of Darwin: The Popularization of Darwinism in Germany, 1860–1914*. Chapel Hill: University of North Carolina Press.

Kettlewell, H. B. D. 1955. 'Selection Experiments on Industrial Melanism in the Lepidoptera.' *Heredity* 9: 323–42.

Keynes, R. D., ed. 1988. *Charles Darwin's Beagle Diary*. Cambridge: Cambridge University Press.

2000. *Charles Darwin's Zoology Notes and Specimen Lists from H.M.S. Beagle*. Cambridge: Cambridge University Press.

Killingley, Dermot. 1995. 'Hinduism, Darwinism and Evolution in Late-Nineteenth-Century India.' In Amigoni and Wallace 1995, 174–202.

Kimura, M. 1968. 'Evolutionary Rate at the Molecular Level.' *Nature* 217: 624–6.

1983. *The Neutral Theory of Molecular Evolution*. Cambridge: Cambridge University Press.

King, J. L. and Jukes, T. H. 1969. 'Non-Darwinian Evolution: Random Fixation of Selectively Neutral Mutations.' *Science* 164: 788–98.

Kingsley, F. E., ed. 1883. *Charles Kingsley: His Letters and Memories of his Life*. London: Kegan Paul.

Kitcher, Patricia. 1992. *Freud's Dream*. Cambridge, Mass.: MIT Press.

Kitcher, Philip. 1983. *The Nature of Mathematical Knowledge*. New York: Oxford University Press.

1985a. *Vaulting Ambition: Sociobiology and the Quest for Human Nature*. Cambridge, Mass.: MIT Press.

1985b. 'Darwin's Achievement.' In Nicholas Rescher, ed., *Reason and Rationality in Science*, pp. 123–85. Washington, D.C.: University Press of America.

1990. 'Developmental Decomposition and the Future of Human Behavioral Ecology.' *Philosophy of Science* 57: 96–117.

1993a. *The Advancement of Science: Science without Legend, Objectivity without Illusions*. New York: Oxford University Press.

1993b. 'Function and Design.' *Midwest Studies in Philosophy* 18, 379–97. Reprinted in Hull and Ruse 1998, pp. 258–79.

1993c. 'Knowledge, Society, and History.' *Canadian Journal of Philosophy* 23, 155–78.

1993d. 'The Evolution of Human Altruism.' *Journal of Philosophy* 90: 497–516.

1994. 'Four Ways of "Biologicizing" Ethics.' In Sober 1994a, pp. 439–50.

1996. *The Lives To Come: The Genetic Revolution and Human Possibilities*. New York: Simon and Schuster.

1998. 'Psychological Altruism, Evolutionary Origins, and Moral Rules.' *Philosophical Studies* 89: 283–316.

1999. 'Essence and Perfection.' *Ethics* 110: 59–83.

2000. 'A Priori Knowledge Revisited.' In Paul Boghossian and Christopher Peacocke, eds., *New Essays on the A Priori*, pp. 65–91. Oxford: Oxford University Press.

2001. 'Infectious Ideas.' *The Monist* 84: 363–91.

Klaaren, Eugene M. 1977. *The Religious Origins of Modern Science*. Grand Rapids: Eerdmans.

Knoll, Elizabeth. 1997. 'Dogs, Darwinism, and English Sensibilities.' In Robert W. Mitchell, Nicholas S. Thompson and H. Lyn Miles, eds., *Anthropomorphism, Anecdotes, and Animals*, pp. 12–21. Albany, N.Y.: State University of New York Press.

Koerner, K., ed. 1983. *Linguistics and Evolutionary Theory: Three Essays by August Scheicher, Ernst Haeckel, and Wilhelm Bleek*. Amsterdam: John Benjamins.

Koerner, Lisbet. 1996. 'Carl Linnaeus in His Time and Place.' In Jardine, Secord and Spary 1996, pp. 145–62.

1999. *Linnaeus: Nature and Nation*. Cambridge, Mass.: Harvard University Press.

Kohn, David. 1981. 'On the Origin of the Principle of Diversity.' *Science* 213: 1105–8.

(Ed.) 1985a. *The Darwinian Heritage*. Princeton: Princeton University Press.

1985b. 'Darwin's Principle of Divergence as Internal Dialogue.' In Kohn 1985a, 245–57.

1989. 'Darwin's Ambiguity: The Secularization of Biological Meaning.' *British Journal for the History of Science* 22: 215–239.

1996. 'The Aesthetic Construction of Darwin's Theory.' In A. I. Tauber, ed., *The Elusive Synthesis: Aesthetics and Science*, pp. 13–48. Dordrecht: Kluwer.

Kottler, M. J. 1974. 'Alfred Russel Wallace, the Origin of Man, and Spiritualism.' *Isis* 65: 145–92.

1985. 'Charles Darwin and Alfred Russel Wallace: Two Decades of Debate over Natural Selection.' In Kohn 1985a, 367–432.

Kripke, Saul. 1980. *Naming and Necessity*. Cambridge Mass.: Harvard University Press.

1992. *Wittgenstein on Rules and Private Language: An Elementary Exposition*. Cambridge, Mass.: Harvard University Press.

Kuhn, Thomas S. 1970. *The Structure of Scientific Revolutions*. 2nd edn. Chicago: University of Chicago Press.

La Vergata, Antonello. 1985. 'Images of Darwin: A Historiographic Overview.' In Kohn 1985a, 901–72.

Lakatos, Imre. 1970. 'Falsification and the Methodology of Scientific Research Programmes.' In I. Lakatos and A. Musgrave, eds., *Criticism and the Growth of Knowledge*, pp. 91–196. Cambridge: Cambridge University Press.

Landes, David S. 1983. *Revolution in Time: Clocks and the Making of the Modern World*. Cambridge, Mass.: Harvard University Press.

Larson, Edward J. 1998. *Summer for the Gods: The Scopes Trial and America's Continuing Debate over Science and Religion*. Cambridge, Mass.: Harvard University Press.

Laudan, L. 1977. *Progress and its Problems*. Berkeley: University of California Press.

1981. *Science and Hypothesis: Historical Essays in Scientific Methodology*. London: D. Reidel.

1993. 'Waves, Particles, Independent Tests and the Limits of Induction.' *PSA 1992*, vol. 2, pp. 212–23. East Lansing, Mich.: Philosophy of Science Association.

Laudan, R. 1982. 'The Role of Methodology in Lyell's Science.' *Studies in History and Philosophy of Science* 13: 215–49.

Lewis, P. 1998. 'Maximum Likelihood as an Alternative to Parsimony for Inferring Phylogeny using Nucleotide Sequence Data.' In D. Soltis, P. Soltis and J. Doyle, eds., *Molecular Systematics of Plants II*. Boston: Kluwer.

Lewontin, Richard C. 1970. 'The Units of Selection.' *Annual Review of Ecology and Systematics* 1: 1–18.

1974. *The Genetic Basis of Evolutionary Change*. New York: Columbia University Press.

1993. *The Doctrine of DNA: Biology as Ideology*. Harmondsworth: Penguin.

Lewontin, R. C., Rose, S. and Kamin, L. 1984. *Not In Our Genes: Biology, Ideology, and Human Nature*. New York: Pantheon.

Lieberman, P. 1998. *Eve Spoke: Human Language and Human Evolution*. New York: Norton.

Liebknecht, William. 1901. *Karl Marx: Biographical Memoirs*. Trans. Ernest Untermann. Chicago: C. H. Kerr.

Lightman, Bernard, ed. 1997. *Victorian Science in Context*. Chicago: University of Chicago Press.

Limoges, Camille. 1994. 'Milne-Edwards, Darwin, Durkheim and the Division of Labour: A Case Study in Reciprocal Conceptual Exchanges between the Social and the Natural Sciences.' In I. B. Cohen, ed., *The Natural Sciences and the Social Sciences*, pp. 317–43. Dordrecht: Kluwer.

Livingstone, David N. 1992. 'Darwinism and Calvinism: The Belfast–Princeton Connection.' *Isis* 83: 408–28.

Lloyd, Elisabeth. 1983. 'The Nature of Darwin's Support for the Theory of Natural Selection.' *Philosophy of Science* 50: 112–29.

1988. *The Structure and Confirmation of Evolutionary Theory*. New York: Greenwood Press.

1999. 'Evolutionary Psychology: The Burdens of Proof.' *Biology and Philosophy* 14: 211–33.

Love, Alan C. 2002 'Darwin and *Cirripedia* Prior to 1846: Exploring the Origins of the Barnacle Research.' *Journal of the History of Biology* 35: 251–89.

Lovejoy, A. O. 1936. *The Great Chain of Being: The History of An Idea*. Cambridge, Mass.: Harvard University Press.

Lyell, Charles. [1830–3] 1990. *Principles of Geology*. 3 vols. London: John Murray. Reprinted in facsimile with an introduction by M. J. S. Rudwick, Chicago: University of Chicago Press.

1863. *The Geological Evidences of the Antiquity of Man*. London: John Murray.

McCord, Norman. 1991. *British History, 1815–1906*. Oxford: Oxford University Press.

McDonald, Roger. 1998. *Mr Darwin's Shooter*. London: Anchor.

[MacKenzie, Robert Beverley.] 1868. *The Darwinian Theory of the Transmutation of Species Examined*. London: Nisbet & Co. Quoted in a review, *Athenaeum* no. 2102, 8 February: 217.

McMullin, E. 1991. 'Plantinga's Defense of Special Creation.' *Christian Scholar's Review* 21: 55–79.
1993. 'Evolution and Special Creation.' *Zygon* 28: 299–335. Reprinted in Hull and Ruse 1998, pp. 698–733.
1996. 'Evolutionary Contingency and Cosmic Purpose.' In M. Himes and S. Pope, eds., *Finding God in All Things*, pp. 140–61. New York: Crossroad.
McOuat, Gordon. 2001. 'Cataloguing Power: Delineating "Competent Naturalists" and the Meaning of Species in the British Museum.' *British Journal for the History of Science* 34: 1–28.
Madden, E. H. 1963. *Chauncey Wright and the Foundations of Pragmatism*. Seattle: University of Seattle Press.
Malthus, Thomas Robert. 1826. *An Essay on the Principle of Population; Or, A View of its Past and Present Effects on Human Happiness, with an Inquiry into Our Prospects Respecting the Future Removal or Mitigation of the Evils which it Occasions*. 6th edn. 2 vols. London: John Murray.
Mandelbaum, Maurice. 1958. 'Darwin's Religious Views.' *Journal of the History of Ideas* 19: 363–78.
Manier, Edward. 1978. *The Young Darwin and His Cultural Circle: A Study of Influences which Helped Shape the Language and Logic of the First Drafts of the Theory of Natural Selection*. Dordrecht: Reidel.
Marchant, James, ed. 1916. *Alfred Russel Wallace: Letters and Reminiscences*. 2 vols. London: Cassell.
Margulis, Lynn. 1981. *Cell Evolution*. San Francisco: Freeman.
Marx, Karl. [1859] 1959. Preface to *A Contribution to the Critique of Political Economy*. Reprinted in L. S. Feuer, ed., *Marx and Engels: Basic Writings on Politics and Philosophy*, pp. 83–7. London: Collins.
Maryanski, A. and Turner, J. 1992. *The Social Cage*. Palo Alto: Stanford University Press.
Maynard Smith, John. 1974. 'The Theory of Games and the Evolution of Animal Conflicts.' *Journal of Theoretical Biology* 47: 209–21.
1978. 'Optimization Theory in Evolution.' *Annual Review of Ecology and Systematics* 8: 31–56.
Maynard Smith, John and Szathmary, Eörs. 1995. *The Major Transitions in Evolution*. Oxford: Freeman.
Mayr, E. 1963. *Animal Species and Evolution*. Cambridge, Mass.: Harvard University Press.
1970. *Populations, Species, and Evolution*. Cambridge, Mass.: Harvard University Press.
1976. 'Typological versus Population Thinking.' In *Evolution and the Diversity of Life*, pp. 26–30. Cambridge, Mass.: Harvard University Press.

1982 *The Growth of Biological Thought: Diversity, Evolution, and Inheritance.* Cambridge, Mass.: Harvard University Press.

1991. *One Long Argument: Charles Darwin and the Genesis of Modern Evolutionary Thought.* Cambridge, Mass.: Harvard University Press.

Mayr, Ernst and Provine, William B., eds. 1980. *The Evolutionary Synthesis: Perspectives on the Unification of Biology.* Cambridge, Mass.: Harvard University Press.

Mayr, Otto. 1986. *Authority, Liberty and Automatic Machinery in Early Modern Europe.* Baltimore: Johns Hopkins University Press.

Medawar, P. 1967. Review of English translation of Teilhard de Chardin 1955. In *The Art of the Soluble*, pp. 71–84. London: Methuen. First published in *Mind* 70 (1961): 99–106.

Mill, J. S. [1843] 1973. *A System of Logic, Ratiocinative and Inductive, Being a Connected View of the Principles of Evidence, and the Methods of Scientific Investigation.* London: Longman. Reprinted in J. M. Robson, ed., *The Collected Works of John Stuart Mill*, 33 vols. Toronto: University of Toronto Press, 1963–91, vols. VII and VIII (1973).

1872. *A System of Logic, Ratiocinative and Inductive, Being a Connected View of the Principles of Evidence, and the Methods of Scientific Investigation.* 8th edn. London: Longman.

1874. *Three Essays on Religion: Nature, the Utility of Religion, and Theism.* London: Longman.

Miller, Geoffrey. 2000. *The Mating Mind: How Sexual Choice Shaped the Evolution of Human Nature.* London: Heinemann.

Miller, K. 1999. *Finding Darwin's God.* New York: Harper and Row.

Millikan, Ruth. 1984. *Language, Thought and Other Biological Categories.* Cambridge, Mass.: MIT Press.

1989. 'In Defense of Proper Functions.' *Philosophy of Science* 56: 288–302.

1993. *White Queen Psychology and Other Essays for Alice.* Cambridge, Mass.: MIT Press.

Mills, S. and Beatty, J. 1978. 'The Propensity Interpretation of Fitness.' *Philosophy of Science* 46: 263–88.

Milton, John R. 1981. 'The Origin and Development of the Concept of the "Laws of Nature".' *European Journal of Sociology* 22: 173–95.

Mineka, F. E. and Lindley, D. N., eds. 1972. *The Later Letters of John Stuart Mill.* London: Routledge & Kegan Paul. Vols. XIV–XVII of *The Collected Works of John Stuart Mill.*

Mitman, Gregg. 1997. 'The Biology of Peace.' *Biology and Philosophy* 12: 259–64.

Mivart, St George Jackson. 1871. *On the Genesis of Species.* London: Macmillan.

Moore, G. E. [1903] 1988. *Principia Ethica.* New York: Prometheus Books.

Moore, James R. 1979. *The Post-Darwinian Controversies*. Cambridge: Cambridge University Press.

1985. 'Herbert Spencer's Henchmen: The Evolution of Protestant Liberals in Late Nineteenth-Century America.' In John Durant, ed., *Darwinism and Divinity: Essays on Evolution and Religious Belief*, pp. 76–100. Oxford: Blackwell.

1986. 'Socializing Darwinism: Historiography and the Fortunes of a Phrase.' In Les Levidow, ed., *Science as Politics*, pp. 38–80. London: Free Association Books.

1991. 'Deconstructing Darwinism: The Politics of Evolution in the 1860s.' *Journal of the History of Biology* 24: 353–408.

1997. 'Wallace's Malthusian Moment: The Common Context Revisited.' In Lightman 1997, pp. 290–311.

2001. *Good Breeding: Science and Society in a Darwinian Age: Study Guide*. A426 Study Guide, sections 1–2. Milton Keynes: Open University Press.

In press. 'Revolution of the Space-Invaders: Darwin and Wallace on the Geography of Life.' In David N. Livingstone and Charles W. J. Withers, eds., *Geography and Revolution*. Chicago: University of Chicago Press.

Morrell, J. B. 1990. 'Professionalisation.' In Olby *et al.* 1990, pp. 980–9.

1997. *Science at Oxford, 1914–1939: Transforming an Arts University*. Oxford: Clarendon.

Morrell, J. B. and Thackray, A. 1981. *Gentlemen of Science: Early Years of the British Association for the Advancement of Science*. Oxford: Oxford University Press.

Muñoz-Rubio, Julio. 1999. 'On Darwinian Discourse, Part I: Political Economy Naturalized; Part II: Re-anthropologizing Nature by Naturalizing Competitive Man.' *Science as Culture* 8: 47–74, 171–87.

Murphy, J. 1982. *Evolution, Morality, and the Meaning of Life*. Totowa, N.J.: Rowman and Littlefield.

Nicolson, Malcolm. 1987. 'Alexander von Humboldt, Humboldtian Science and the Origins of the Study of Vegetation.' *History of Science* 25: 167–94.

1990. 'Alexander von Humboldt and the Geography of Vegetation.' In A. Cunningham and N. Jardine, eds., *Romanticism and the Sciences*, pp. 169–85. Cambridge: Cambridge University Press.

Numbers, Ronald L. 1992. *The Creationists: The Evolution of Scientific Creationism*. Berkeley: University of California Press.

Nyhart, Lynn K. 1996. 'Natural History and the "New" Biology.' In Jardine, Secord and Spary 1996, pp. 426–43.

Olby, Robert. 1966. *Origins of Mendelism*. London: Constable.

1979. 'Mendel no Mendelian?' *History of Science* 17: 53–72.

Olby, Robert C., Cantor, Geoffrey N., Christie, John R. R. and Hodge, M. J. S., eds. 1990. *Companion to the History of Modern Science*. London: Routledge.

Oldroyd, David R. 1980. *Darwinian Impacts: An Introduction to the Darwinian Revolution*. Kensington, NSW: University of New South Wales Press.

1984. 'How Did Darwin Arrive at His Theory? The Secondary Literature to 1982.' *History of Science* 22: 325–74.

1986. *The Arch of Knowledge: An Introductory Study of the History of the Philosophy and Methodology of Science*. London: Methuen.

Orzack, S. and Sober, E. 1994. 'Optimality Models and the Test of Adaptationism.' *American Naturalist* 143: 361–80.

2001. 'Adaptationism, Phylogenetic Inertia, and the Method of Controlled Comparisons.' In S. Orzack and E. Sober, eds., *Adaptationism and Optimality*, pp. 45–63. Cambridge: Cambridge University Press.

Ospovat, Dov. 1980. 'God and Natural Selection: The Darwinian Idea of Design.' *Journal of the History of Biology* 13: 169–94.

1981. *The Development of Darwin's Theory: Natural History, Natural Theology, and Natural Selection, 1838–1859*. Cambridge: Cambridge University Press.

Paley, William. [1785] 1806. *The Principles of Moral and Political Philosophy*. 2 vols. 16th edn. London: R. Faulder. 1st edn published in 1785.

1819. *Natural Theology; Or, Evidences of the Existence and Attributes of the Deity Collected from the Appearances of Nature*. 19th edn. Vol. v in *The Miscellaneous Works of William Paley, D.D.*, 5 vols, 1820. London: Baldwyn. 1st edn published in 1802.

Papineau, D. 1984. 'Representation and Explanation.' *Philosophy of Science* 51: 550–72.

1987. *Reality and Representation*. Oxford: Blackwell.

Passmore, John. 1970. *The Perfectibility of Man*. London: Duckworth.

Paul, Diane B. 1995. *Controlling Human Heredity: 1865 to the Present*. Amherst, N.Y.: Humanity Books.

Peacocke, Arthur. 1985. 'Biological Evolution and Christian Theology – Yesterday and Today.' In J. Durant, ed., *Darwinism and Divinity: Essays on Evolution and Religious Belief*, pp. 101–30. Oxford: Blackwell.

Pennock, R. 1998. *Tower of Babel: Scientific Evidence and the New Creationism*. Cambridge, Mass.: MIT Press.

Penny, D., Foulds, L. and Hendy, M. 1982. 'Testing the Theory of Evolution by Comparing Phylogenetic Trees Constructed from Five Different Protein Sequences.' *Nature* 297: 197–200.

Pessoa, Osvaldo. 2001. 'Counterfactual Histories: The Beginning of Quantum Physics.' *Philosophy of Science* 68 (Supp.): S519–30.

Pinker, Steven. 1994. *The Language Instinct: How the Mind Creates Language.* New York: Morrow.

1997. *How The Mind Works.* New York: Norton.

Pittinger, Mark. 1993. *American Socialists and Evolutionary Thought, 1870–1920.* Madison: University of Wisconsin Press.

Plantinga, A. 1997. 'Methodological Naturalism.' *Perspectives on Science and Christian Faith* 49: 143–54.

Poundstone, William. 1985. *The Recursive Universe: Cosmic Complexity and the Limits of Scientific Knowledge.* New York: Morrow.

Powell, Baden. 1861. 'On the Study of the Evidences of Christianity.' In the multi-authored volume *Essays and Reviews*, pp. 94–144. London: Longman.

Price, Richard. 1999. *British Society, 1680–1880: Dynamism, Containment and Change.* Cambridge: Cambridge University Press.

Provine, W. B. 1971. *The Origins of Theoretical Population Genetics.* Chicago: University of Chicago Press.

Putnam, H. 1975. 'The Meaning of Meaning.' In K. Gunderson, ed., *Language, Mind, and Knowledge*, pp. 131–93. Minnesota Studies in the Philosophy of Science, VII. Minneapolis: University of Minnesota Press. Reprinted in H. Putnam, *Philosophical Papers*, 2 vols., vol. II: *Mind, Language and Reality*, pp. 215–71. Cambridge: Cambridge University Press, 1975.

Pyenson, Lewis and Sheets-Pyenson, Susan. 1999. *Servants of Nature: A History of Scientific Institutions, Enterprises and Sensibilities.* London: HarperCollins.

Quine, W. 1987. *Quiddities: An Intermittently Philosophical Dictionary.* Cambridge, Mass.: Harvard University Press.

Raby, Peter. 2001. *Alfred Russel Wallace: A Life.* London: Chatto and Windus.

Radick, Gregory. 1998. 'The *Origin* Unbound.' *Studies in History and Philosophy of Biological and Biomedical Sciences* 29: 349–57.

2000. 'Two Explanations of Evolutionary Progress.' *Biology and Philosophy* 15: 475–91.

2002. Review of Hacking 1999. *British Journal for the History of Science* 35: 97–9.

(In press.) 'Cultures of Evolutionary Biology.' *Studies in History and Philosophy of Biological and Biomedical Sciences.*

Railton, Peter. 1986. 'Moral Realism.' *Philosophical Review* 95: 163–207.

Raup, D. 1991. *Extinction: Bad Genes or Bad Luck?* New York: Norton.

Ray, John. 1692. *The Wisdom of God Manifested in the Works of the Creation, in Two Parts.* 2nd edn. London: Samuel Smith. First published in 1691.

Recker, D. 1987. 'Causal Efficacy: The Structure of Darwin's Argument Strategy in the *Origin of Species.' Philosophy of Science* 54: 147–75.

Rehbock, Philip. 1983. *The Philosophical Naturalists: Themes in Early Nineteenth-Century Philosophical Biology.* Madison: University of Wisconsin Press.

Reichenbach, B. R. 1976. 'Natural Evils and Natural Laws: A Theodicy for Natural Evil.' *International Philosophical Quarterly* 16: 179–96.

Richards, Evelleen. 1983. 'Darwin and the Descent of Women.' In David Oldroyd and Ian Langham, eds., *The Wider Domain of Evolutionary Thought*, pp. 57–111. Dordrecht: Reidel.

1994. 'A Political Anatomy of Monsters, Hopeful and Otherwise: Teratogeny, Transcendentalism, and Evolutionary Theorizing.' *Isis* 85: 377–411.

1997. 'Redrawing the Boundaries: Darwinian Science and Victorian Women Intellectuals.' In Lightman 1997, pp. 119–42.

Richards, Richard A. 1997. 'Darwin and the Inefficiency of Artificial Selection.' *Studies in History and Philosophy of Science* 28: 75–97.

Richards, Robert J. 1987. *Darwin and the Emergence of Evolutionary Theories of Mind and Behavior.* Chicago: University of Chicago Press.

1992. *The Meaning of Evolution: The Morphological Construction and Ideological Reconstruction of Darwin's Theory.* Chicago: University of Chicago Press.

1999. 'Darwin's Romantic Biology: The Foundation of His Evolutionary Ethics.' In J. Maienschein and M. Ruse, eds., *Biology and the Foundation of Ethics*, pp. 113–53. Cambridge: Cambridge University Press.

2002a. 'The Linguistic Creation of Man: Charles Darwin, August Schleicher, Ernst Haeckel, and the Missing Link in Nineteenth-Century Evolutionary Theory.' In Matthias Dörries, ed., *Experimenting in Tongues: Studies in Science and Language*, pp. 21–48 Stanford: Stanford University Press.

2002b. *The Romantic Conception of Life: Science and Philosophy in the Age of Goethe.* Chicago: University of Chicago Press.

Ridley, Mark, ed. 1994. *A Darwin Selection.* 2nd edn. London: Fontana Press.

Ritvo, Harriet. 1987. *The Animal Estate: The English and Other Creatures in the Victorian Age.* Cambridge, Mass.: Harvard University Press.

Rose, Hilary. 2000. 'Colonising the Social Sciences?' In Hilary and Steven Rose, eds., *Alas, Poor Darwin: Arguments Against Evolutionary Psychology*, pp. 106–28. London: Jonathan Cape.

Rose, Jonathan. 2001. *The Intellectual Life of The British Working Classes.* New Haven: Yale University Press.

Rosen, Michael. 1996. *On Voluntary Servitude: False Consciousness and the Theory of Ideology.* Cambridge: Polity Press.

Rosenberg, Alexander. 1990. 'The Biological Justification of Ethics: A Best Case Scenario.' *Social Policy and Philosophy* 8: 86–101. Reprinted in Rosenberg 2000, pp. 118–36.

1995. *Philosophy of Social Science*. 2nd edn. Oxford: Westview Press.

2000. *Darwinism in Philosophy, Social Science and Policy*. Cambridge: Cambridge University Press.

Rudge, David W. 1999. 'Taking the Peppered Moth with a Grain of Salt.' *Biology and Philosophy* 14: 9–37.

Rudwick, M. J. S. 1982. 'Charles Darwin in London: The Integration of Public and Private Science.' *Isis* 73: 186–206.

1986. 'The Shape and Meaning of Earth History.' In D. Lindberg and R. Numbers, eds., *God and Nature: Historical Essays on the Encounter between Christianity and Science*, pp. 296–321. Berkeley: University of California Press.

Rupke, Nicolaas A. 1983. *The Great Chain of History*. Oxford: Oxford University Press.

1994. *Richard Owen: Victorian Naturalist*. New Haven: Yale University Press.

1996. 'Foreword.' In Gillispie [1951] 1996.

Ruse, Michael. 1975. 'Darwin's Debt to Philosophy: An Examination of the Influence of the Philosophical Ideas of John F. W. Herschel and William Whewell on the Development of Charles Darwin's Theory of Evolution.' *Studies in History and Philosophy of Science* 6: 159–81.

1985. *Sociobiology: Sense or Nonsense?* 2nd edn. Dordrecht: Reidel.

1987. 'Darwin and Determinism.' *Zygon* 22: 419–42.

1992. 'Darwinism.' In Keller and Lloyd 1992, pp. 74–80.

1993a. 'Evolution and Progress.' *Trends in Ecology and Evolution* 8: 55–9.

1993b. *The Darwinian Paradigm: Essays on its History, Philosophy, and Religious Implications*. London: Routledge.

1994. *Evolutionary Naturalism: Selected Essays*. London: Routledge.

1996. *Monad to Man: The Concept of Progress in Evolutionary Biology*. Cambridge, Mass.: Harvard University Press.

1999a. *The Darwinian Revolution: Science Red in Tooth and Claw*. 2nd edn. Chicago: University of Chicago Press.

1999b. *Mystery of Mysteries: Is Evolution a Social Construction?* Cambridge, Mass.: Harvard University Press.

2000a. *Can a Darwinian be a Christian? The Relationship between Science and Religion*. Cambridge: Cambridge University Press.

2000b. *The Evolution Wars: A Guide to the Debates*. Santa Barbara: ABC-CLIO.

2000c. 'Darwin and the Philosophers: Epistemological Factors in the Development and Reception of the Theory of the *Origin of Species*.' In Creath and Maienschein 2000, pp. 3–26.

Ruse, M. and Wilson, E. O. 1985. 'The Evolution of Morality.' *New Scientist* 1478: 108–28.

1986. 'Moral Philosophy as Applied Science.' *Philosophy* 61: 173–92. Reprinted in Sober 1994a, pp. 421–38.

Russett, Cynthia. 1989. *Sexual Science*. Cambridge, Mass.: Harvard University Press.

Sahlins, Marshall. 1976. *The Use and Abuse of Biology: An Anthropological Critique of Sociobiology*. Ann Arbor: University of Michigan Press.

Samuels, R. 1998. 'Evolutionary Psychology and the Massive Modularity Thesis.' *British Journal for The Philosophy of Science* 49: 575–92.

Sandow, Alexander. 1938. 'Social Factors in the Origin of Darwinism.' *Quarterly Review of Biology* 13: 315–26.

Sapp, Jan. 1994. *Evolution by Association: A History of Symbiosis*. Oxford: Oxford University Press.

Sarkar, Sahotra, ed. 1992. *The Founders of Evolutionary Genetics*. Dordrecht: Kluwer.

Scarre, Geoffrey. 1998. 'Mill on Induction and Scientific Method.' In John Skorupski, ed., *The Cambridge Companion to John Stuart Mill*, pp. 112–38. Cambridge: Cambridge University Press.

Schaffer, Simon. 1990. 'Genius in Romantic Natural Philosophy.' In A. Cunningham and N. Jardine, eds., *Romanticism and the Sciences*, pp. 82–98. Cambridge: Cambridge University Press.

1996. 'Our Trusty Friend the Watch.' *London Review of Books* 31 October: 11–12.

Schiebinger, Londa. 1996. 'Gender and Natural History.' In Jardine, Secord and Spary 1996, pp. 163–77.

Schindewolf, O. H. 1936. *Paläontologie, Entwicklungslehre und Genetik: Kritik und Synthese*. Berlin: Bornträger.

Schleicher, August, 1863. *Die Darwinsche Theorie und die Sprachwissenschaft*. Weimar: Böhlau. English translation in K. Koerner 1983.

1865. *Über die Bedeutung der Sprache für die Naturgeschichte des Menschen*. Weimar: Böhlau. English translation in K. Koerner 1983.

Schmidt, Alfred. 1971. *The Concept of Nature in Marx*. Trans. Ben Fowkes, from the 1962 German edition. London: NLB.

Schuster, John A. and Yeo, Richard R. 1986. *The Politics and Rhetoric of Scientific Method: Historical Studies*. Dordrecht: Reidel.

Schwartz, Jeffrey H. 1999. *Sudden Origins: Fossils, Genes, and the Emergence of Species*. New York: John Wiley and Sons.

Schweber, S. S. 1977. 'The Origin of the *Origin* Revisited.' *Journal of the History of Biology* 10: 229–316.

1980. 'Darwin and the Political Economists: Divergence of Character.' *Journal of the History of Biology* 13: 195–289.

1983. 'Demons, Angels, and Probability : Some Aspects of British Science in the Nineteenth Century.' In A. Shimony and H. Feshbach, eds., *Physics as Natural Philosophy*, pp. 319–63. Cambridge, Mass.: MIT Press.

Searle, John. 1980. 'Minds, Brains and Programs.' *Behavioral and Brain Sciences* 3: 417–58.

1994. *The Rediscovery of the Mind*. Cambridge, Mass.: MIT Press.

Secord, James A. 1981. 'Nature's Fancy: Charles Darwin and the Breeding of Pigeons.' *Isis* 72: 163–86.

1985. 'Darwin and the Breeders: A Social History.' In Kohn 1985a, 519–42.

1991. 'The Discovery of a Vocation: Darwin's Early Geology.' *British Journal for the History of Science* 24: 133–57.

1997. 'Introduction.' To Charles Lyell, *Principles of Geology*, 1830–3, single-volume abridgement. Harmondsworth: Penguin.

2000. *Victorian Sensation: The Extraordinary Publication, Reception, and Secret Authorship of Vestiges of the Natural History of Creation*. Chicago: University of Chicago Press.

Sedgwick, A. [1860] 1973. 'Objections to Mr. Darwin's Theory of the Origin of Species.' In Hull 1973, pp. 159–70. First published in 1860 in the *Spectator* 24 March, pp. 285–6 and 7 April, pp. 334–5.

Sellars, Wilfrid. 1963. 'Philosophy and the Scientific Image of Man.' In *Science, Perception and Reality*, pp. 1–40. London: Routledge & Kegan Paul.

Semmel, B. 1970. *The Rise of Free Trade Imperialism: Classical Political Economy, the Empire of Free Trade and Imperialism, 1750–1850*. Cambridge: Cambridge University Press.

Shapin, Steven. 1982. 'History of Science and its Sociological Reconstructions.' *History of Science* 20: 157–211.

1996. *The Scientific Revolution*. Chicago: University of Chicago Press.

Shapin, Steven and Barnes, Barry. 1979. 'Darwin and Social Darwinism: Purity and History.' In Barry Barnes and Steven Shapin, eds., *Natural Order: Historical Studies of Scientific Culture*, pp. 125–42. London: Sage.

Simpson, G. G. 1944. *Tempo and Mode in Evolution*. New York: Columbia University Press.

1967. *The Meaning of Evolution*. Rev. edn. New Haven: Yale University Press.

Singer, Peter. 1999. *A Darwinian Left: Politics, Evolution and Cooperation*. London: Weidenfeld and Nicolson.

Skinner, B. F. 1966. 'Selection by Consequences.' *Science* 153: 652–4.
Skyrms, B. 1996. *The Evolution of the Social Contract*. Cambridge: Cambridge University Press.
Sloan, Phillip R. 1985. 'Darwin's Invertebrate Program, 1826–1836: Preconditions for Transformism.' In Kohn 1985a, 71–120.
1986. 'Darwin, Vital Matter, and the Transformism of Species.' *Journal of the History of Biology* 19: 369–445.
2001. ' "The Sense of Sublimity": Darwin on Nature and Divinity.' *Osiris* 16: 251–69.
Smart, J. J. C. 1959. 'Sensations and Brain Processes.' *Philosophical Review* 88: 141–56.
Smith, Charles H., ed. 1991. *Alfred Russel Wallace: An Anthology of His Shorter Writings*. New York: Oxford University Press.
Smith, Crosbie. 1998. *The Science of Energy: A Cultural History of Energy Physics in Victorian Britain*. London: Athlone Press.
Smocovitis, V. B. 1999. 'The 1959 Darwin Centennial Celebration in America.' *Osiris* 14: 274–323.
Sober, Elliott. 1984. *The Nature of Selection: Evolutionary Theory in Philosophical Focus*. Cambridge, Mass.: MIT Press.
1988. *Reconstructing the Past: Parsimony, Evolution and Inference*. Cambridge, Mass.: MIT Press.
1993. *Philosophy of Biology*. Boulder: Westview Press.
1994a. *Conceptual Issues in Evolutionary Biology*. 2nd edn. Cambridge, Mass.: MIT Press.
1994b. 'Evolution, Population Thinking, and Essentialism.' In Sober 1994a, pp. 161–90. First published in *Philosophy of Science* 47 (1980): 350–83.
1994c. 'Did Evolution Make Us Psychological Egoists?' In *From A Biological Point of View*, pp. 8–27. Cambridge: Cambridge University Press.
1999. 'Physicalism from a Probabilistic Point of View.' *Philosophical Studies* 95: 135–74.
2002. 'Philosophy of Biology.' In Nicholas Bunnin and Eric Tsui-James, eds., *The Blackwell Companion to Philosophy*, 2nd edn, pp. 317–44. Oxford: Blackwell.
Sober, Elliott and Wilson, David Sloan. 1998. *Unto Others. The Evolution and Psychology of Unselfish Behavior*. Cambridge, Mass.: Harvard University Press.
Spencer, Herbert. [1851] 1970. *Social Statics: Or, the Conditions Essential to Human Happiness Specified and the First of Them Developed*. London: Chapman. Reprinted in facsimile, Farnborough: Gregg.
[1864–7] 1884. *The Principles of Biology*. 2 vols. London: William and Norgate. Reprinted New York: D. Appleton.

Sperber, D. 1996. *Explaining Culture: A Naturalistic Approach*. Oxford: Blackwell.

Stamos, David N. 1996. 'Was Darwin Really a Species Nominalist?' *Journal of the History of Biology* 29: 127–44.

1999. 'Darwin's Species Category Realism.' *History and Philosophy of the Life Sciences* 21: 137–86.

Stark, Rodney. 1996. *The Rise of Christianity*. San Francisco: HarperCollins.

Stepan, Nancy L. 1987. 'Nature's "Pruning Hook": War, Race and Evolution, 1914–18.' In J. M. W. Bean, ed., *Political Culture of Modern Britain: Studies in Memory of Stephen Koss*, pp. 129–48. London: Hamilton.

Sterelny, Kim. 1990. *The Representational Theory of Mind: An Introduction*. Oxford: Blackwell.

2000. *The Evolution of Agency and Other Essays*. Cambridge: Cambridge University Press.

Sterelny, Kim and Griffiths, Paul E. 1999. *Sex and Death: An Introduction to Philosophy of Biology*. Chicago: University of Chicago Press.

Sterrett, Susan G. 2002. 'Darwin's Analogy Between Artificial and Natural Selection: How Does it Go?' *Studies in History and Philosophy of Biological and Biomedical Sciences* 33C: 151–68.

Stevenson, C. L. 1944. *Ethics and Language*. New Haven: Yale University Press.

Stoddart, D. R., ed. 1962. 'Coral Islands, by Charles Darwin.' *Atoll Research Bulletin* 88: 1–20.

Strawson P. F. 1962, 'Freedom and Resentment.' *Proceedings of the British Academy* 48: 1–25.

Strick, James E. 2000. *Sparks of Life: Darwinism and the Victorian Debates over Spontaneous Generation*. Cambridge, Mass.: Harvard University Press.

Sulloway, Frank. J. 1982a. 'Darwin and His Finches: The Evolution of a Legend.' *Journal of the History of Biology* 15: 1–53.

1982b. 'Darwin's Conversion: The *Beagle* Voyage and its Aftermath.' *Journal of the History of Biology* 15: 327–98.

Swetlitz, Marc. 1999. 'American Jewish Reponses to Darwin and Evolutionary Theory, 1860–1890.' In R. L. Numbers and J. Stenhouse, eds., *Disseminating Darwinism: The Role of Place, Race, Religion, and Gender*, pp. 209–45. Cambridge: Cambridge University Press.

Symons, D. 1979. *The Evolution of Human Sexuality*. Oxford: Oxford University Press.

Tammone, William. 1995. 'Competition, the Division of Labor, and Darwin's Principle of Divergence.' *Journal of the History of Biology* 28: 109–31.

Taub, Liba. 1993. 'Evolutionary Ideas and "Empirical" Methods: The Analogy between Language and Species in Works by Lyell and Schleicher.' *British Journal for the History of Science* 26: 171–93.

Tax, Sol, ed. 1960. *Evolution After Darwin*. 3 vols. Chicago: University of Chicago Press.

Teilhard de Chardin, P. 1955. *Le phénomène humaine*. Paris: Editions de Seuil. Published in English as *The Phenomenon of Man*, London: Collins, 1959.

Thagard, Paul. 1978. 'The Best Explanation: Criteria for Theory Choice.' *Journal of Philosophy* 75: 78–92.

Thompson, Paul. 1988. *The Structure of Biological Theories*. New York: SUNY Press.

Todes, Daniel P. 1989. *Darwin without Malthus: The Struggle for Existence in Russian Evolutionary Thought*. Oxford: Oxford University Press.

Todhunter, I. 1876. *William Whewell, D.D.: An Account of His Writings with Selections from his Literary and Scientific Correspondence*. 2 vols. New York: Macmillan.

Tooby, J. and Cosmides, L. 1992. 'The Psychological Foundations of Culture.' In Barkow, Cosmides and Tooby 1992, pp. 19–136.

Tort, Patrick, ed. 1996. *Dictionnaire du darwinisme et de l'évolution*. 3 vols. Paris: Presses Universitaires de France.

Turner, Frank M. 1978. 'The Victorian Conflict between Science and Religion: A Professional Dimension.' *Isis* 69: 356–76. Reprinted in Turner 1993, pp. 171–200.

1993. *Contesting Cultural Authority: Essays in Victorian Cultural Life*. Cambridge: Cambridge University Press.

Tyndall, John. [1874] 1970. 'Presidential Address' to the Belfast meeting of the British Association for the Advancement of Science. In G. Basalla, W. Coleman and R. Kargon, eds., *Victorian Science*, pp. 436–78. New York: Anchor.

Valéry, Paul. 1973–4. *Cahiers*. Ed. Judith Robinson. 2 vols. Paris: Edition de la Pléiade.

Vermeij, G. J. 1987. *Evolution and Escalation: An Ecological History of Life*. Princeton: Princeton University Press.

Vialleton, L. 1929. *L'origine des êtres vivants: L'illusion transformiste*. Paris: Plon.

Wagar, W. 1972. *Good Tidings: The Belief in Progress from Darwin to Marcuse*. Bloomington: Indiana University Press.

Wallace, Alfred Russel. [1864] 1991. 'The Origin of Human Races and the Antiquity of Man Deduced from the Theory of "Natural Selection."' *Anthropological Review* 2: clviii–clxxxvii. Reprinted in Smith 1991, pp. 14–26.

1870. 'The Limits of Natural Selection as Applied to Man.' In *Contributions to the Theory of Natural Selection: A Series of Essays*, pp. 332–71. London: Macmillan.

1905. *My Life: A Record of Events and Opinions*. London: Chapman and Hall.

Wallwork, E. 1982. 'Thou Shalt Love Thy Neighbour as Thyself: The Freudian Critique.' *Journal of Religious Ethics* 10: 264–319.

Walters, Max and Stow, E. A. 2001. *Darwin's Mentor: John Stevens Henslow, 1796–1861*. Cambridge: Cambridge University Press.

Ward, K. 1996. *God, Chance and Necessity*. Oxford: Oneworld.

Waters, C. Kenneth. 1986. 'Taking Analogical Inference Seriously: Darwin's Argument from Artificial Selection.' *PSA 1986*, vol. 1, pp. 502–13. East Lansing, Mich.: Philosophy of Science Association.

Wedgwood, Hensleigh. 1866. *On the Origin of Language*. London: Trübner.

Weikart, Richard. 1993. 'The Origins of Social Darwinism in Germany, 1859–1895.' *Journal of the History of Ideas* 54: 469–88.

1995. 'A Recently Discovered Darwin Letter on Social Darwinism.' *Isis* 86: 609–11.

1998a. 'Laissez-Faire Social Darwinism and Individualist Competition in Darwin and Huxley.' *The European Legacy* 3: 17–30.

1998b. *Socialist Darwinism: Evolution in German Socialist Thought from Marx to Bernstein*. San Francisco: International Scholars.

Weinberg, Steven. 2001. 'The Future of Science, and the Universe.' *New York Review of Books* 15 November: 58–63.

Weindling, Paul J. 1991. *Darwinism and Social Darwinism in Imperial Germany: The Contribution of the Cell Biologist Oscar Hertwig (1849–1922)*. Stuttgart: Gustav Fischer Verlag.

1998. 'Dissecting German Social Darwinism: Historicizing the Biology of the Organic State.' *Science in Context* 11: 619–37.

Weinshank, Donald J. *et al.*, eds. 1990. *A Concordance to Charles Darwin's Notebooks*, 1836–1844. Ithaca, N.Y.: Cornell University Press.

Weiss, Sheila F. 1987. *Race Hygiene and National Efficiency: The Eugenics of Wilhelm Schallmayer*. Berkeley: University of California Press.

Wells, Algernon. 1834. *On Animal Instinct*. Colchester: Longman, Rees, Orme, Brown, Green and Longman.

[Whewell, William.] 1831. Review of Herschel 1830. *Quarterly Review* 45: 374–407.

1835. Review of 3rd (1835) edn of Lyell 1830–33. *Quarterly Review* 53: 406–48.

1840. *The Philosophy of the Inductive Sciences, Founded upon Their History*. 2 vols. London: John W. Parker.

1849. *Of Induction, with Especial Reference to Mr. J. Stuart Mill's System of Logic*. London: John W. Parker.
1853. *The Plurality of Worlds*. London: John W. Parker.
1864. *Astronomy and General Physics Considered with Reference to Natural Theology*. London: Pickering. 7th edn 1st edn published in 1833.
Whiten, A. and Byrne, R., eds. 1997. *Machiavellian Intelligence II: Extensions and Evaluations*. Cambridge: Cambridge University Press.
Wiley, E. 1981. *Phylogenetics: The Theory and Practice of Phylogenetic Systematics*. New York: John Wiley.
Williams, G. C. 1966. *Adaptation and Natural Selection*. Princeton: Princeton University Press.
Wilson, David B. 1984. 'A Physicist's Alternative to Materialism: the Religious Thought of George Gabriel Stokes.' *Victorian Studies* 28: 69–96.
Wilson, E. O. 1975. *Sociobiology: The New Synthesis*. Cambridge, Mass.: Harvard University Press.
1978. *On Human Nature*. Cambridge, Mass.: Harvard University Press.
1992. *The Diversity of Life*. Cambridge, Mass.: Harvard University Press.
Wilson, J. Dover. 1951. *What Happens in Hamlet*. Cambridge: Cambridge University Press.
Winch, Donald. 1987. *Malthus*. Oxford: Oxford University Press.
Wittgenstein, Ludwig. [1922] 1961. *Tractatus Logico-Philosophicus*. London: Routledge & Kegan Paul.
Wood, Ellen M. 1991.*The Pristine Culture of Capitalism: A Historical Essay on Old Regimes and Modern States*. London: Verso.
Woese, C. R. 1998. 'Default Taxonomy: Ernst Mayr's View of the Microbial World.' *Proceedings of the National Academy of Sciences of the United States of America* 95: 11043–6.
Woese, C. R., Kandler, O. and Wheelis, M. L. 1990. 'Towards a Natural System of Organisms: Proposal for the Domains Archaea, Bacteria, and Eucarya.' *Proceedings of the National Academy of Sciences of the United States of America* 87: 4576–9.
Wooldridge, D. 1963. *The Machinery of the Brain*. New York: McGraw-Hill.
Wright, Chauncey. 1865. 'The Philosophy of Herbert Spencer.' *North American Review* 100: 423–76.
1871. 'The Genesis of Species.' *The North American Review* 113: 63–103. Reprinted in abridged form in Hull 1973, pp. 384–408.
2000. *The Evolutionary Philosophy of Chauncey Wright*. 3 vols. Eds. Frank X. Ryan and Edward H. Madden. Bristol: Thoemmes Press.
Wright, Larry. 1976. *Teleological Explanations: An Etiological Analysis of Goals and Functions*. Berkeley: University of California Press.
Wright, Robert. 1994. *The Moral Animal*. New York: Pantheon.

Wynne-Edwards, V. C. 1962. *Animal Dispersion in Relation to Social Behaviour*. Edinburgh: Oliver and Boyd.

Yeo, Richard R. 1979. 'William Whewell, Natural Theology and the Philosophy of Science in Mid-Nineteenth Century Britain.' *Annals of Science* 36: 493–516.

1993. *Defining Science: William Whewell, Natural Knowledge and Public Debate in Early Victorian Britain*. Cambridge: Cambridge University Press.

Young, Robert M. 1985a. *Darwin's Metaphor: Nature's Place in Victorian Culture*. Cambridge: Cambridge University Press.

1985b. 'Darwinism *Is* Social.' In Kohn 1985a, 609–38.

Zirkle, Conway. 1946. 'The Early History of the Idea of the Inheritance of Acquired Characteristics and of Pangenesis.' *Transactions of the American Philosophical Society* 35: 91–150.

Zittel, Karl von. 1895. 'Paleontology and the Biogenetic Law.' *Natural Science* 6: 305–12.

INDEX

Note: unless otherwise indicated, 'Darwin' refers to Charles Darwin.